AZTEC ANTICHRIST

PUBLICATION NO. 1
*Archaeology and Ethnohistory of the
Central Quiche*, edited by Dwight T.
Wallace and Robert M. Carmack

PUBLICATION NO. 2
Basic Quiche Grammar, by
James L. Mondloch

PUBLICATION NO. 3
*Bibliography of Mayan Languages
and Linguistics*, by Lyle Campbell
with Pierre Ventur, Russell
Stewart, and Brant Gardner

PUBLICATION NO. 4
*Codex Vindobonensis Mexicanus 1:
A Commentary*, by Jill Leslie Furst, with
a preface by Mary Elizabeth Smith

PUBLICATION NO. 5
*Migration Across Frontiers:
Mexico and the United States*,
Vol. 3, edited by Fernando Camara
and Robert Van Kemper

PUBLICATION NO. 6
*The Historical Demography of Highland
Guatemala*, edited by Robert Carmack,
John Early, and Christopher Lutz

PUBLICATION NO. 7
*Aztec Sorcerers in Seventeenth Century
Mexico: The Treatise on Superstitions*,
by Hernando Ruiz de Alarcón,
edited and translated by Michael
D. Coe and Gordon Whittaker

PUBLICATION NO. 8
Maya Hieroglyphic Codices, by Yuri
Knorosov, translated by Sophie Coe

PUBLICATION NO. 9
*Phoneticism in Mayan Hieroglyphic
Writing*, edited by John Justeson
and Lyle Campbell

PUBLICATION NO. 10
*A Consideration of the Early Classic
Period in the Maya Lowlands*, edited by
Gordon R. Willey and Peter Mathews

PUBLICATION NO. 11
*Hach Winik: The Lacandon
Maya of Chiapas, Southern
Mexico*, by Didier Boremanse

PUBLICATION NO. 12
*Classic Period Mixtequilla,
Veracruz, Mexico: Diachronic
Inferences from Residential
Investigations*, by Barbara Stark

PUBLICATION NO. 13
*Before Guadalupe: The Virgin
Mary in Early Colonial Nahuatl
Literature*, by Louise Burkhart

PUBLICATION NO. 14
*Postclassic Soconusco Society: The Late
Prehistory of Chiapas, Mexico*, edited
by Barbara Voorhies and Janine Gasco

PUBLICATION NO. 15
*Utatlán: The Constituted Community
of the K'iche' Maya of Q'umarkaj*,
by Thomas F. Babcock

PUBLICATION NO. 16
*Aztec Antichrist: Performing
the Apocalypse in Early Colonial
Mexico*, by Ben Leeming

AZTEC ANTICHRIST

Performing the Apocalypse
in Early Colonial Mexico

BEN LEEMING

UNIVERSITY PRESS OF COLORADO
Louisville, Colorado

INSTITUTE FOR MESOAMERICAN STUDIES
Albany, New York

University Press of Colorado
245 Century Circle, Suite 202
Louisville, Colorado 80027

Institute for Mesoamerican Studies
Arts and Sciences, SUNY
233 University at Albany
1400 Washington Avenue
Albany, New York 12222

 The University Press of Colorado is a proud member of
Association of University Presses.

The University Press of Colorado is a cooperative publishing enterprise supported, in part, by Adams State University, Colorado State University, Fort Lewis College, Metropolitan State University of Denver, University of Alaska Fairbanks, University of Colorado, University of Denver, University of Northern Colorado, University of Wyoming, Utah State University, and Western Colorado University.

∞ This paper meets the requirements of the ANSI/NISO Z39.48-1992 (Permanence of Paper)

ISBN: 978-1-64642-298-2 (hardcover)
ISBN: 978-1-64642-299-9 (paperbook)
ISBN: 978-1-64642-300-2 (ebook)
https://doi.org/10.5876/9781646423002

Library of Congress Cataloging-in-Publication Data

Names: Leeming, Ben, author.
Title: Aztec antichrist : performing the apocalypse in early colonial Mexico / Ben Leeming.
Other titles: IMS monograph ; 16.
Description: Louisville : University Press of Colorado ; Albany, New York : Institute for Mesoamerican Studies, [2022] | Series: IMS monograph series; publication no. 16 | Includes bibliographical references and index. | Text in English, Nahuatl and Spanish.
Identifiers: LCCN 2022019652 (print) | LCCN 2022019653 (ebook) | ISBN 9781646422982 (hardcover) | ISBN 9781646422999 (paperback) | ISBN 9781646423002 (ebook)
Subjects: LCSH: Nahuatl drama—16th century—History and criticism. | Nahuatl drama—16th century—Translations into English. | Antichrist—Drama. | Indigenous peoples—Religious life—Mexico. | Indians of Mexico—Religion. | Syncretism (Religion)
Classification: LCC PM4068.75.E5 L44 2022 (print) | LCC PM4068.75.E5 (ebook) | DDC 897/.4522—dc23/eng/20220511
LC record available at https://lccn.loc.gov/2022019652
LC ebook record available at https://lccn.loc.gov/2022019653

Credits: Digital Archive of the Collections of the National Museum of Anthropology. Ministry of Culture-INAH-Canon (*front, back*); Diego Muñoz Camargo, *Historia de Tlaxcala*. Used by permission of University of Glasgow Library, Archives & Special Collections, MS Hunter 242, f. 239v (*background*).

CONTENTS

FIGURES

TABLES

FOREWORD

MARK CHRISTENSEN

RELIGION in its many forms is a constant in every society. And how humankind develops, interprets, and conveys religion remains a topic of endless study. Indeed, Christianity and its global spread certainly has occupied its share of conversations. Did people convert, resist, a little of both? What did they make of Christ and Mary, heaven and hell, and how did it sit with preexisting beliefs? How was Christianity conveyed, and who did the teaching? Over the years, Ben Leeming and I have spent many hours discussing such questions often extending them to modern-day circumstances, and his knowledge of Nahuatl, colonial religion, and Catholicism in general always ensured a great chat.

Of course, we are not the only nor the first to have such conversations. Over the decades, scholarship examining the spread of Catholicism in central Mexico among its Indigenous inhabitants offered various conclusions from capitulation to resistance, European dominance to Indigenous survival, syncretism, and *nepantlism*. Amidst the dialogue, Indigenous voices have become clearer, sharper, and their participation in evangelization more recognized to reveal how they made sense of Christianity and their role in its colonial formation.

In the scholarly discussion of colonial Christianity, it should come as no surprise that religious drama showed up to contribute more than a few words. Like a colonial version of the currently popular television series *The Chosen*, the theatrical reenactments of important Christian events in early modern Europe and Mexico found an eager audience. After all, watching a play with its costumed actors, music, and props must have been better than listening to a sermon. Early scholars noted as much, and Fernando Horcasitas's *El teatro náhuatl* (1974) proved a seminal work. Later, Barry Sell and Louise Burkhart's *Nahuatl Theater* project (2004–2009) produced four volumes that provided English readers unprecedented access to the religious plays that Nahuas helped create in their own language and, certainly, perform. Indeed, the plays revealed in new ways how Nahuas could promulgate Christian themes and stories in familiar ways.

Moreover, Indigenous people could take a lead role in preserving and shaping these plays along with other religious texts—something colonial officials largely tried to prevent. As a result, the conversation about what colonial Christianity looked like expanded beyond something Indigenous people simply tolerated to include something they actively adopted and constantly refashioned as a part of their everyday lives. Leeming's *Aztec Antichrist* and its examination and translation of two previously unknown Nahuatl Antichrist plays carries on this conversation while contributing important words of its own to the understanding of colonial religion.

The plays derive from a sixteenth-century notebook attributed to the Nahua author Fabián de Aquino and discovered by Leeming. All indications suggest that Aquino composed his notebook and its various religious texts outside the direct supervision of ecclesiastics. This is significant as it shows what Aquino decided to record regarding Christianity and how he interpreted and familiarized himself with its teachings. The plays provide uncommon examples of how Indigenous culture made its way into Christian doctrine to form various understandings and interpretations of the faith. Philological analysis and cultural background play an important role in revealing such examples. Yet they can threaten to steal the show. Here, however, Leeming welcomes into the discussion European antecedents and influences and effectively moderates the voices of both sides of the Atlantic, allowing Aquino's notebook to be a product of Indigenous and European cultures. This allows for a clearer understanding of the many parallels and differences between the two, while also recognizing the impact of Indigenous worldviews, the colonial context, and Franciscan mission and religious discourse in giving birth to the Aztec Antichrist. And all presented by Leeming in a friendly yet astute prose that beckons the reader to continue turning the pages.

The plays and their creative, sometimes unorthodox depiction of Christianity speak loudly of the contributions figures like Aquino could make to the Christianities circulating in the Americas. Moreover, viewing Aquino as a "cultural broker" and placing his work in the colonial and religious context of the early to mid-sixteenth century allows Leeming to view Aquino's Aztec Antichrist and apocalypticism in general as a possible response to the cultural and physical trauma experienced in the wake of Spanish colonization. This, then, adds another important perspective when considering why Indigenous people adopted Christianity. After all, perhaps the greatest role of religion is to bring order and meaning to the seemingly chaotic and unexplainable aspects of life. And, perhaps, for Aquino, what was needed to fill such a bill was an Aztec Antichrist.

Future research will continue to add additional voices and perspectives into the conversation discussing colonial religion. But this book has something to say now that is well worth our attention. So let us sit back and listen to Leeming and Aquino tell the story of Aztecs and Antichrists.

ACKNOWLEDGMENTS

THIS BOOK owes much to a small cohort of mentors and advisors who have devoted the most time to reading and commenting on the first incarnation of *Aztec Antichrist*. Initially this was limited to Louise Burkhart, Davíd Carrasco, and Walter Little; later on, William B. Taylor graciously accepted an invitation to read it and offer critical feedback. To these four must be added two anonymous readers who reviewed the manuscript for the University Press of Colorado, offering both positive feedback and extremely helpful guidance on further improving the work. To these individuals I express my profound gratitude and admiration. From among the above, it was the encouragement of Carrasco and Taylor in particular that inspired me to rewrite major portions of the original work; what you will read here is less a revision than a new attempt on my part to tell the story of Fabián de Aquino and the Nahuatl Antichrist plays he copied into his notebook some four and a half centuries ago.

I also wish to express my gratitude to my early collaborators and teachers of Nahuatl, beginning with Galen Brokaw and Pablo García, then, fortunately for me, including Joe Campbell and eventually John Sullivan. *Huei tlamachtiani* Joe Campbell is the silver bullet for any *nahuatlahto* lucky enough to be on the receiving end of his generous helpings of advice; I am doubly lucky for being able to call him friend as well. It was with John Sullivan that I had my first intensive classroom instruction in Colonial and Modern Nahuatl at the Instituto de Docencia e Investigación Etnológica de Zacatecas in Zacatecas, Mexico, in the summer of 2009. John played a pivotal role in my decision to begin PhD studies upon my return to the United States. Others who I have encountered along the way have aided me with their wisdom, insight, and encouragement. Principle among these are Mark Christensen, valued colleague and friend, as well as Fritz Schwaller, Frances Karttunen, Barbara Mundy, Camilla Townsend, Kelly McDonough, Lori Diel, Allison Caplan, Justyna Olko, Nathaniel Tarn, David Tavárez, Magnus Hansen, Julia Madajczak, Gordon Whittaker, Berenice Alcántara Rojas, Mario Sánchez Aguilera, Bérénice Gailleman, Agnieszka Brylak, Molly Bassett, Magnus Pharao Hansen, and many other generous colleagues at the annual meetings of the Association of Nahuatl Scholars. Many of these offered helpful suggestions regarding how to translate difficult passages from Aquino's plays. Working with this group over the past decade has been both an honor and a whole lot of fun. Despite all the help these individuals have offered, any errors in this book, be they in translation or analysis, are my own.

Thanks also to John O'Neill and Vanessa Pintado at the Hispanic Society of America in New York who aided me in accessing the archives that yielded Fabián de Aquino's devotional notebook back in 2014. I am also deeply grateful to the administration of The Rivers School, where I have been on the faculty for twenty-five years, for their unflagging moral and financial support. Special thanks are due to former Head of School Tom Olverson, Patti Carbery, Joan Walter, current Head of School Ned Parsons, and Dean of Faculty Leslie Fraser who have been important supporters of my work since the late 1990s when I first arrived at Rivers. Among the faculty, my friends and colleagues David Burzillo, Amy Enright, and Meghan Regan-Loomis have been treasured sources of encouragement and willing listeners for years; Darren Sullivan has offered the frequent wisecracks that have kept me humble (and laughing); for all of this I am very grateful.

Finally, to my family, *notlazohpiltzitzinhuan ihuan notlazohnamictzin*, I offer and dedicate this book. It bears your presence in every page and between every line since it was your support, patience, and love that formed a steady foundation enabling me to think and write (and rewrite) over the past ten years.

ca cenca namechnotlazohtilia amehuantin annocozqui annoquetzal

A NOTE ABOUT TRANSLATIONS

UNLESS otherwise indicated, all translations from Nahuatl or Spanish to English are my own. The Nahuatl orthography of the primary texts reproduced in this book has not been altered or standardized according to modern conventions but appears here as it does either in the unpublished manuscripts or in the modern editions from which they are taken. However, when Nahuatl words appear outside of the primary texts as part of the book's narrative, the standardized ACK orthography (Andrews, Campbell, Karttunen) proposed by John Sullivan and Justyna Olko is employed. A more detailed discussion of my approach to translating the two Nahuatl Antichrist plays precedes their presentation in the appendix of this book.

PROLOGUE

Discovery

Toptli, Petlacalli

Injn tlatolli itech mjtoaia: in aqujn vel quipia in jchtacatlatolli, piallatolli:
anoço in jtla aqualli ijxpan muchioaia: aiac vel qujnextiliaia, vel toptli, vel
petlacalli: mjtoaia. Vel qujpia in tlatolli, anoço tenemjliz.
—"THE DEEP BASKET, THE CHEST OF REEDS"

This proverb used to be said about the one who carefully harbored words that
were whispered in secret, words that were entrusted to them, or something
bad that happened in their presence; this person would not reveal it to anyone; they used to call this person "a deep basket, a chest of reeds"; they closely
guard what is said or how people behave around them.
—FLORENTINE CODEX, BOOK 6[1]

MANHATTAN is an unlikely place to encounter an Aztec Antichrist—or any kind
of Aztec for that matter (Antichrists are perhaps more readily found).[2] The fact that
the Aztec Antichrist in question lived four and a half centuries ago and has lain forgotten since then only adds to the oddity. This book is my attempt to unravel this
mystery and to explain how it was that in the decades following the Spanish Invasion
of the Americas a native speaker of Nahuatl (the language of the Nahuas) came to
write the first American translation of the medieval legend of the Antichrist.

On the morning of July 15, 2014, I stood outside of the Hispanic Society of
America, waiting for the building to open. The air's heaviness augured another
hot New York City summer day. While waiting, I took a picture or two, eager to
document this next stop on my pilgrimage to a number of important archives and
libraries. My area of research is the encounter of religions in early colonial Mexico;
on that morning I was hunting for primary source material for my next research
project. The Hispanic Society's collection of colonial Latin American books and

https://doi.org/10.5876/9781646423002.c000c

manuscripts held a number of items written in my research language, Nahuatl, a language I had struggled for over a decade to learn. Finally in possession of the linguistic "key," I was looking for historical "chests" to open. As the sun crested over the apartment blocks of the Upper West Side, the door swung open, and I stepped into the museum's cool, marble interior.

Precontact Nahuas used the expression *in toptli, in petlacalli* (the deep basket, the chest of reeds) to describe a person who carefully guarded secrets entrusted to her. Linguists refer to expressions like these as *difrasismos*, or semantic couplets, sayings where a pair of words render a third, figurative meaning. In addition to describing a trustworthy person, *in toptli, in petlacalli* is suggestive of something hidden, mysterious, or valuable. In precontact times, Nahuas carefully wrapped sacred deity effigies or ritual objects in cloth bundles called toptli and stored their most valuable possessions—delicate quetzal plumes or finely woven cloth mantles—in deep reed baskets called petlacalli. As a researcher interested in the Nahuas before and after contact, I have come to view early colonial Nahuatl manuscripts as kinds of toptli or petlacalli. Many remain "bundled" in their original leather covers, their "secret words" hidden not just behind the sealed doors of the archive but also behind the veil of language. Seen in this light, translation becomes the act of opening these textual reed chests, revealing the fine quetzal plumes of Nahuatl writing.

Once inside the building, I performed the necessary ritual preparations common to visiting archives and special collections: deposit belongings in locker, remove laptop and pencil, show ID, sign in, fill out call slip, settle at table. While waiting, I took in my surroundings. The Hispanic Society's reading room shared certain features with all such spaces: long oaken tables for researchers, walls lined with shelved volumes behind glass, and staid portraits gazing down from above. Here, the entire ceiling was an expansive skylight, which obviated the need for lamps on the tables and filled the room with bright, filtered light. Large standing fans cycled back and forth lackadaisically, slowly stirring the thick, warm air. The room was heavy with that unmistakable smell of the archive: a faint mustiness that is the product of dust, leather, and paper. This smell always triggers in me a sort of Pavlovian response, an intellectual salivation that precedes the arrival of the materials I have requested from the vault.

According to the catalog, the item I had requested that morning bore the title *Sermones y miscelánea de devoción*, "sermons and miscellany of devotion[al works]." Although the title was given in Spanish, the manuscript was written almost entirely in Nahuatl, the lingua franca of the Mexica Empire at the time of first contact. In the years immediately following the Spanish-Mexica War of 1519–1521, Franciscan, Dominican, and Augustinian friars had collaborated with native speakers to produce written materials in Indigenous languages as part of their effort to indoctrinate the Indigenous population. These included *doctrinas* (catechisms), *sermonarios* (collections of sermons), *confessionarios* (manuals for the administration of confession), as well as other works of a devotional nature: miracle stories, lives of the saints, prayers and songs, and even works of religious theater. The vast majority of these were written in Nahuatl; those that survive to this day constitute a corpus that numbers in the thousands of pages.

Initially, I had been drawn to the study of colonial Nahuatl upon discovering the existence of this corpus and realizing that there were few scholars equipped to read and interpret such a massive trove of documentation. Over time, my growing facility with Nahuatl eventually led to graduate studies in historical anthropology. I had grown increasingly fascinated by the way early colonial translations of Christianity had resulted in the proliferation of a diverse array of Indigenous "Christianities," hyper-local manifestations of the colonizers' religion.[3] Up until relatively recently, Nahuatl sermonarios and doctrinas had been ignored by scholars in favor of the more visually appealing colonial painted codices, whose brightly colored glyphs and gods made for irresistible publishing. However, in the 1980s, some scholars had begun to pay more attention to the corpus of colonial Nahuatl religious writing, breaking open an invaluable new vein of data relevant to the religious experiences of colonial Indigenous peoples. Since this turn was still relatively new—and since friars and their Nahua colleagues had been so prolific in their literary production— there was still much uncharted territory in the field. My pilgrimage that summer was an attempt to find materials that had been overlooked, in hopes that I might discover a text suitable for translation and analysis.

After a short wait, a librarian approached my table holding the *Sermones y miscelánea de devoción* in her hands. I was immediately struck by the size of the item. It was a tiny, bound manuscript measuring roughly 4 inches by 5 1/2 inches. Though diminutive in size, it was of considerable length, reaching three hundred folios, or six hundred pages if each side of the leaf is counted. A modern binding, probably added by a collector in the nineteenth century, replaced the original leather one, now long lost. Gingerly opening its cover, I was treated again to the smell of paper and must. Wormholes and tidelines (signs of water damage) marred many pages. I noticed the characteristic stains caused by the oils from human fingers that darkened the most well-worn of its folios. These telltale signs not only hinted at the antiquity of the manuscript, they spoke of the many generations of Nahuas who had turned its pages, read its contents, and uttered its prayers. At what point the notebook had left Indigenous hands I did not know. I wondered how many people had turned its pages in the years since the manuscript first showed up in the historical record (in 1869) and was then acquired by the Hispanic Society (in 1914). In all likelihood the number was small. As to how many of those few could read and comprehend Nahuatl, surely the number was smaller still. Outside of a couple of references I would eventually dig up in nineteenth-century auction catalogs, neither the manuscript nor its contents had ever been mentioned in the time between its acquisition and the moment I called it from storage on that hot summer day precisely one hundred years later.

On the inside of the front cover of the manuscript a short description of its contents was pasted (see figure P.1). I later traced its authorship to noted German bookseller Karl Wilhelm Hiersemann (1854–1928). The description he wrote was included in the catalog for the auction at which the Hispanic Society purchased the manuscript in 1914. Evidently someone had simply cut out the relevant material from the auction catalog and pasted it onto the manuscript's front endpaper. Written in Spanish it read,

> Aquino, Fabián de, order of Saint Francis, sermons and miscellany of devotion[al] and moral [works] in the Mexican language, Nahuatl. Manuscript from the end of the sixteenth century, with the signature of the author repeated various times.[4]

Taken at face value, this seemed to suggest that the author of this devotional notebook was a Spaniard and a member of the Franciscan order. However, this picture was immediately clouded by Hiersemann's next statement. He went on to observe that this Aquino's handwriting was *más india que española*, "more Indian than Spanish," and certain of the texts he redacted contained *titulos en un latin muy bárbaro, y castellano no menos corrumpido*, "titles in a barbaric Latin and no less-corrupt Spanish." Further complicating the picture, Hiersemann concluded with these words,

> Friar Fabián was probably one of the Indians who related the ancient histories of the Mexicans to Father Bernardino de Sahagún, and in this sense we could have here a kind of supplement to the immortal work of that wise Franciscan. It would merit, in any case, being examined and published by a courageous Americanist.

Here was an arresting statement. The name Bernardino de Sahagún looms large over both Nahua history and the history of early colonial Mexico. Sahagún was the famed Franciscan who, from the 1540s through the 1570s, worked with a team of Nahua scholars and scribes to interview surviving members of the nobility in an effort to record the history and culture of the Nahua people before it was lost. His *Historia universal* [or *general*] *de las cosas de Nueva España* has been called history's first ethnography, an encyclopedic work in twelve books that is more commonly known as the Florentine Codex after the library where it currently resides. Simply put, there are few works as consequential to our understanding of Nahua culture as the work Sahagún oversaw. That the manuscript I held in my hands may have

1 **Aquino,** Fabian de, o. S. Franc., sermones y miscelánea de devoción y moral en lengua mexicana (nahuatl). Manuscrito de fines del siglo XVI., con la firma autógrafa del autor varias veces repetida. En-8 menor (13,5×9,5 cm.). Encuad. moderna de m. piel. 300 hh. fols.

Manuscrito de letra mas india que española, y de puño muy menudo, bastante legible, con algunos títulos encarnados.

El Conde de la Viñaza describe el presente manuscrito (pág. 261, núm. 846): „Sermones en mexicano. M. S. en-8, de muy mala letra, al parecer del siglo XVII. — Falta el principio, y la foliatura es moderna. — Contiene 300 hojas. — Hasta la hoja 55 llega la primera parte, que parece sea un tratado de moral. — Siguen después otras muchas piezas, entre las cuales se ven unos diálogos ó coloquios. — Es una verdadera miscelánea y no un Sermonario. — (Colección del P. Fischer.) — Icazbalceta, Apuntes, adiciones manuscritas, número 181.“

Es, en verdad, una colección de textos homiléticos, devotos y morales, en lengua mexicana, con títulos en un latin muy bárbaro y castellano no menos corrompido. Basten como muestras: Sto. Anprossio, in tomum tuam, ad temprum, sacripicium, benetictos, saceltotes etc. El libro entero es de puño y letra de un fraile franciscano, indio converso, que á repetidas veces firma con su nombre en religión, Fabian de Aquino (hh. 55, 66 etc.) Una firma en la última página dice Fabian de ....; el resto es ilegible.

Citamos aquí algunos tratados con sus títulos originales:

De terrebilitate judicii finali et penie iuterni. h. 37—55.

Nican mitohua yntlahtla colpollolliztli ynitoca ynidulgencias y huan perdones (sobre las indulgencias obtenidas en 1560 por) totlaçotatzin fray Francisco de Zamora, ministro general de la órden. h. 67—70.

Las hh. 71—115 parecen contener miráculos de la Virgen (estos sen miraglos acadus del maria de rosario yntonic del discipulo). Sin duda composición original.

En las hh. 131—150 hay profecías de las Sibilas, Elias, Enoc etc. Al mismo tema se refiere un tratado que empieza en la h. 155 y termina en la h. 187. Parece que un hermitano habla de los demonios y especialmente de los antiguos dioses mexicanos: Dlaloc (sic), Dezcatlipoca (sic), Vitzilopochtli, Quetzalcovatl, Otontecuhtli, Civacovatl etc. y de las costumbres de los Mexicanos, mercaderos, alcahuetes, hipócritos etc.

H. 188—212: Historia de Adam.

Siguen pláticas de la Virgen María, pasos sacados de los Evangelios y otras historias del Nuevo Testamento. La ultima pieza (h. 297—300) es la historia de un cierto Martin: Cetlacatl nemiya ytoca mardin....

Sin duda este libro muy curioso incluye aun muchas particularidades relativas á los Mexicanos antiguos, á fuera de aquellas pocas que hemos podido comprender nosotros con nuestras escasas luces acerca de la lengua. Probablemente fr. Fabian fué uno de los Indios que contaron al P. Bernardino de Sahagun las historias antiguas de los Mexicanos, y de esta manera tendriamos aquí una especie de suplemento á la obra inmortal del sabio Franciscano. Merecería, en todo caso, ser examinado y publicado por un americanista valiente.

Aunque la letra sea mala, el texto resulta bastante bien legible é inteligible para quien entiende la lengua mexicana. El papel está poco apolillado, sin que por eso el texto hubiese sufrido daño perceptible.

FIGURE P.I. Catalog description of the contents of Fabián de Aquino, *Sermones y miscelánea de devoción y moral en lengua mexicana.* Hispanic Society of America MS NS 3/1, ca. 1550–1600. Courtesy of the Hispanic Society of America, New York City.

been written by one of Sahagún's Indigenous informants was a graduate student's dream come true. If Hiersemann were correct, I had stumbled upon a text of singular importance, a potential trove of information. Even though he was probably incorrect about Aquino being a Franciscan—Indigenous people were almost never admitted to the order in those early years—these few scraps of information left behind by Hiersemann were tantalizing. Time would tell whether or not I would be the "courageous Americanist" he called for. Nevertheless, I eagerly began to explore the contents of Aquino's devotional notebook.

Roughly halfway through my survey I came upon something that caused me to stop short. At the top of the verso of folio 169 was a word written out in letters larger than all the others, the writer's equivalent of using bold font. The word was "Tezcatlipoca" (see figure P.2). Tezcatlipoca, whose name means "Smoking Mirror" in Nahuatl, was an important deity, or *teotl*, of the Nahuas prior to contact with the Spanish. The quintessential trickster, he was the deity the Spanish most closely associated with the devil. It is common knowledge that in the sixteenth century Catholic friars had carried out aggressive campaigns of extirpation, seeking to expunge the Nahuas' gods from the collective memories of their newly converted subjects. What was Tezcatlipoca doing in this notebook filled with Christian devotional texts?

On the next page, another caption read "Huitzilopochtli," the patron deity of the Mexica, god of the sun and of war. It was Huitzilopochtli who had guided the ancestors of the Mexica from their mythical place of origin in Aztlan to the lacustrine site of their future capital, Tenochtitlan. With growing curiosity, I continued turning pages and found the names of four more Mexica *teteoh* (plural of teotl, "deities"): Tlaloc (god of rain and lightning), Quetzalcoatl (Feathered Serpent), Cihuacoatl (Serpent Woman), and Otontecuhtli (Otomí Lord) (see figure P.3). The colonial Nahuatl religious literature I have worked with often makes general references to these deities, but almost never by name, as if merely writing them would somehow ensure a dangerous perpetuation of their presence in the lives of Christianized Nahuas. Instead, the friars consigned these figures to hell, declaring them to be demons or perhaps *mictlan tecuanimeh*, "wild beasts of Mictlan [among the dead]." In the preaching and teaching of the friars, deities like Tezcatlipoca and Huitzilopochtli had been banished from the vocabularies and memories of Christianized Nahuas. Or so was the friars' intention. The presence of these six teteoh here in the pages of a Nahuatl-Christian miscellany was a true oddity.

Backtracking in search of the beginning of this text and some kind of explanation, I came upon another heading that I had missed the first time through: *Qu[i]toz antexp̄o* (see figure P.4). Right away I recognized the cluster of letters "x̄p̄o" as an abbreviation for *Cristo* (Christ), one that was commonly used by Franciscan writers

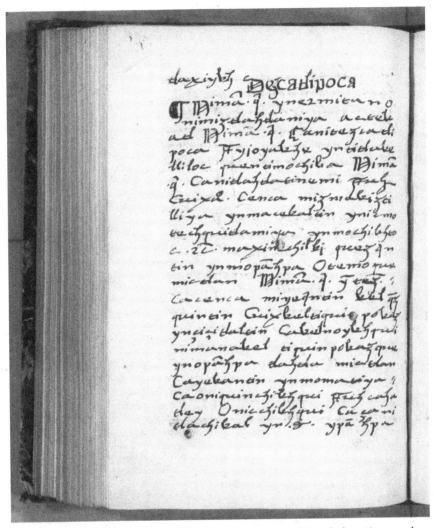

FIGURE P.2. Tezcatlipoca. Fabián de Aquino, *Sermones y miscelánea de devoción y moral en lengua mexicana*. Hispanic Society of America MS NS 3/1, ca. 1550–1600, f. 169v–170r. Courtesy of the Hispanic Society of America, New York City.

and the Nahuas trained by them. But the addition of *ante-* here resulted in something entirely different: "Anti-Christ." This, too, took me by surprise. Although the Antichrist was a prominent figure in medieval Europe, I could not recall a single instance in colonial Nahuatl religious literature where this harbinger of the Apocalypse was mentioned. The word preceding "Antichrist" was the Nahuatl verb

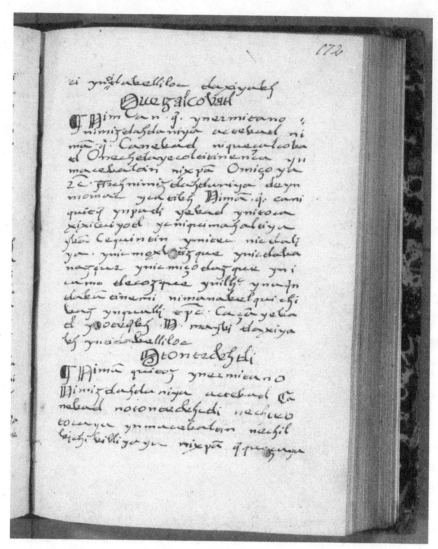

FIGURE P.3. Quetzalcoatl and Otontecuhtli. Fabián de Aquino, *Sermones y miscelánea de devoción y moral en lengua mexicana.* Hispanic Society of America MS NS 3/1, ca. 1550–1600, f. 171v–172r. Courtesy of the Hispanic Society of America, New York City.

quitoz, "he/she will say it." It appeared that this Antichrist was saying something. After some time, I was able to decode his speech. Over four centuries ago, a Nahua writer, perhaps the person named Fabián de Aquino, penned the following words for this mysterious, Nahuatl-speaking Antichrist:

FIGURE P.4. *Quitoz antecristo*, "Antichrist will say." Fabián de Aquino, *Sermones y miscelánea de devoción y moral en lengua mexicana.* Hispanic Society of America MS NS 3/1, ca. 1550–1600, f. 155v–156r. Courtesy of the Hispanic Society of America, New York City.

Come, all of you. What are you doing? Do you want to die by my hand? Right now I will spill your blood if you do not believe in me. Have you not seen that those living with me are rich? Did I not say to you that I alone am all powerful, that I made all that lies growing? Do not behave foolishly! Why did you dismantle my home? In times past you served me well when you slashed open the chests of your captives and when you bled yourselves. And you, O rulers, why do you diminish your way of living?

Why do you abandon your women? You used to have many mistresses! Now, devote yourselves to all the women, however many you want. This will really satisfy me. And also you women, I really wonder at you. You do not paint your faces anymore, you do not cover yourselves with feathers. And now, what has happened to you? Who has confused you? Devote yourselves to everything that you used to devote yourselves to! O my children, didn't you used to honor my words? I am your deity, your ruler! I am Christ! (f. 156r–157r)

The Antichrist that I began to glimpse in the pages of the Hispanic Society manuscript bore many of the recognizable traits of his European cousin. He was a powerful and frightening figure who spouted threats of violence, sought to deceive Christians into worshipping him as the Christ, and exercised evil powers granted to him by Satan to work false miracles. However, the author of this American incarnation had given him a decidedly Indigenous hue. His lament "Why did you dismantle my home?" suggested the author may have identified him as one of the Nahua teteoh (deities) targeted by the friars for erasure. Shortly after the military conquest, the Spanish authorities attempted to end the state religion of the Mexica, razing temples to the ground, burning deity images and sacred books, and most significantly, putting an end to the public performance of ritual sacrifices that were central to the maintenance of the cosmic and political order of the Mexica imperial state.

The ease with which Aquino's Antichrist slipped into this new Indigenous role was due in part to the plasticity of the legend itself. In Europe, much of its popularity was due to the ease with which it could be molded to fit whatever frightening or threatening circumstances captivated the public's interest at any given moment. At times the Antichrist was associated with the Jews, the Turks, despotic rulers, or even epidemics like the Black Death. Whoever had conceived of this Nahuatl adaptation seemed to have grasped the malleability of the Antichrist legend and deftly molded it to fit the local conditions of early postcontact Mexico. This figure was a powerful Indigenous being, an "Aztec Antichrist," who violently opposed the evangelizing efforts of the friars and sought to draw converted Nahuas back to the religious practices of their ancestors. He urged men to reject the friars' insistence on monogamy and to return to the traditional practice of polygyny, and he pleaded with women to once more don paint and feathers as traditional adornments. Demanding a complete rejection of the new regime and its state religion, he cried, "Devote yourselves to everything that you used to devote yourselves to!" and proclaimed, "I am your deity [teotl]!"

The questions raised by this Aztec Antichrist soon began to fill my head and spill over into the pages of my own notebook. If the Antichrist was virtually absent from the official discourses of the friars, how had an Indigenous person like Aquino learned of the legend? Was Aquino even the author, or was it instead some friar? What significance might this legend have had for Indigenous people living in the midst of what surely qualified as apocalyptic times? And, most tantalizing of all, in light of the friars' relative silence on the subject, how should one interpret a Nahuatl-speaking Antichrist? Should it be seen as a sign of submission to the dominant regime, an act of resistance, or something in between? Much scholarly ink has been spilled on the matter of Indigenous appropriations of the colonizers' discourses, of the many creative ways that colonized subjects undermined, critiqued, countered, and reinterpreted the very narratives that were used to disenfranchise and dominate them. "Hidden transcripts," counter-narratives, and subtexts abound in the Indigenous-language documentation that has been the subject of much revisionist historiography since the 80s.[5] Assuming that Aquino was the author, the text I was holding was clearly the product of the process of transculturation, whereby cultural material from a dominant culture is appropriated and invested with new meaning by members of a subordinate culture. This could explain the seemingly incongruous blending of Christian legend with references to pre-Christian deities like Tezcatlipoca, Huitzilopochtli, and Quetzalcoatl, not to mention polygyny, face painting, and heart sacrifice.

Returning to the six Nahua deities, I could now see that they, too, were speaking. So were other people that I had not noticed before: a pagan oracle known as a sibyl, the Old Testament prophets Elijah and Enoch, one group of converts and another of martyrs, and a person simply called *ermitano* [*sic*] (hermit). Reading further, I observed that the six deities' speeches were followed by additional individuals who also seemed to be speaking. However, these were human beings drawn from the ranks of Indigenous society: a group of six *tletlenamacaqueh* (Indigenous priests), a *tonalpouhqui* (ritual specialist), a *ticitl* (Indigenous healer), a *pochtecatl* (merchant), and a *tlahtoani* (Indigenous ruler). Every time one of these people spoke, their words were preceded by statements like *niman quitozque*, "then they will say," or *niman valquiçazque*, "then they will enter." With this it became clear that what I was looking at was the script of a play, that statements like *niman valquiçazque* were stage directions, and Tezcatlipoca, Tlaloc, the merchant and the healer, were characters in a lengthy production that seemed to center around the Antichrist, the Final Judgment, and a character called "Hermit."

I was very familiar with Nahuatl religious theater. My mentor, Louise Burkhart, was (and remains) one of the leading authorities of colonial Nahuatl theater. Just a few years prior to my discovery, she and her colleague Barry Sell completed a decade-long project that published nearly all of the known, surviving examples of what they termed "America's First Theater."[6] I knew that soon after the military conquest, Spanish friars had worked with their Nahua colleagues to compose

religious plays in Nahuatl for the purposes of engaging Nahua audiences and inculcating them in the basics of Christian doctrine. Thanks to Sell and Burkhart's work,
I also knew that literate Nahuas soon appropriated this genre and began writing
their own religious plays and that these Indigenous productions made ecclesiastical
authorities nervous, eventually leading the church to ban them outright in the early
eighteenth century.[7]

In the hands of Indigenous writers, Nahuatl religious theater—like all writing by
Indigenous people—could quickly become the vehicle for the transmission of unofficial religious discourses. While these discourses rarely contradicted Christian doctrine overtly, they often altered and undermined the official message in more subtle
ways. Just the act of casting Indigenous actors in the roles of Christ, Mary, and the
saints and giving them lines that conform to Indigenous manners of speaking "indigenized" the message. These weren't merely Christian performances by Indigenes
but performances of Indigenous Christianity (or *Christianities*). This was a dangerous reality that the church struggled to control throughout the entire colonial
period. Unauthorized religious writing by Indigenous people was officially banned
as early as 1555, and additional restrictions continued throughout the colonial
period. All of these were largely unsuccessful. Wielding their literacy, Indigenous
writers inverted the claim of Spanish humanist Antonio de Nebrija that "language
is the instrument of empire." Rather, once it had broken free from the control of
colonial authorities, Indigenous writing demonstrated how language could also be
the perfect instrument for pushing back against empire's hegemonic claims.

Although there was no signature at the end of the play, it was easy to see that it
was written in the very same hand as texts Fabián de Aquino had himself signed.
Many questions remain about the identity of this person and the precise nature of
his role in composing what turned out to be not one but two Nahuatl Antichrist
plays. After months of research, I came to conclude that not only were these plays
likely the earliest surviving presentations of the Antichrist legend in the Americas
but also that they could very well be the earliest surviving play scripts in the whole
of the Americas in any language—Nahuatl, Spanish, or otherwise.

It strikes me as fitting to use the Nahuas' expression *in toptli, in petlacalli*
to describe this mysterious Fabián de Aquino. As an educated member of the
Indigenous noble class who copied, translated, and composed religious texts for
the spiritual nourishment of his people, he was indeed someone who "carefully
harbored" words that were "entrusted to him." And his notebook, too, was *in toptli, in petlacalli*, since its covers guarded those "secret, entrusted" words. During
Aquino's day, only those with the kind of education attained at one of the friars'
schools could access the meaning of words written with the Roman alphabet.
These words remained safely hidden deep within their Nahuatl "chests of reeds,"

unintelligible to those who ultimately snatched the notebook from Nahua hands, secreted it out of Mexico, and auctioned it off to the highest bidder. The discovery of Fabián de Aquino's devotional notebook enables me to present my unbundling of Aquino's "secret words" for the first time since his notebook left the possession of its Indigenous protectors.

AZTEC ANTICHRIST

Introduction

FABIÁN'S NOTEBOOK

IF SIXTEENTH-CENTURY manuscripts can be likened to baskets that guard precious things, then translation might be seen as their unwrapping or opening. Translation is an effortful labor that recalls another Nahuatl proverb reported by Sahagún's Indigenous informants, *cuicuitlahuilli in tlalticpac*, "chipping away on earth."[1] The Nahua elders explained that this expression was uttered when "we apply ourselves to something, we give it great care; we get really absorbed in it even when it's very difficult, such as with carving wood or sculpting stone . . . or some field of knowledge, song, grammar, etc." Beyond hard work, "chipping away on earth" suggests digging and excavation, which in turn suggests archaeology. Just as the archaeologist excavates artifacts from the ground, so too does the translator "excavate" knowledge from the archival record. We're told that Howard Carter, upon opening the coffin of King Tutankhamun, detected faint wafts of cedarwood and embalming oils emanating from the pharaoh's innermost coffin. This, too, is analogous to the translator's work. Translation opens what has been closed for ages. In place of entombed sarcophagi, the translator opens manuscripts whose words have been shut up for long stretches of time, closed off from comprehension and perhaps forgotten all together. With each phrase parsed, thoughts and ideas that have lain dormant waft upward and are comprehended, often for the first time in centuries.

Unwrapping and opening also calls to mind the Nahua practice of creating sacred bundles they called *tlaquimilolli*.[2] These were very special kinds of bundles that contained objects associated with important *teteoh* and were revered as precious

https://doi.org/10.5876/9781646423002.c000d

and powerful manifestations of the divine. The objects bundled into tlaquimilolli could include fragments of bone or ashes, flints, mirrors, or precious stones. Once priests wrapped up these precious objects into a bundle, they became an embodiment of the deity (*teotl*) and were revered above all other images and effigies of the gods. This alludes to a very Indigenous American way of conceiving of divinity: as an assemblage of constituent parts. When the parts are properly collected together under the right ritual conditions, the teotl is assembled, its sacred presence infiltrating and pervading the physical components that have been gathered.

Proceeding throughout the winter of 2014–2015, the process of translation "unbundled" Fabián de Aquino's notebook of miscellaneous Christian texts. What was found within? What were its constituent parts? I have chosen three as subjects of this chapter, each one acting as a point of departure for an introduction to the plays that are presented at the end this volume. The first constituent part is the language that encodes the knowledge Aquino set down in writing. The second is the signature that Aquino left on folio 55 recto of the manuscript, which I will analyze as a kind of artifact of self. And the third is the miscellaneous texts Fabián's notebook holds. European and Christian in origin but Indigenous in presentation, they are cultural hybrids whose interpretation requires care and some special conceptual and methodological tools. Each of these three elements—the constituent parts Aquino bound within the leather covers of his tlaquimilolli notebook—will be used to open a discussion into essential matters of context and interpretation relevant to the plays themselves. The language in which he encoded knowledge, Nahuatl, will be used to explore the historical and religious context in which Aquino wrote. The signatures will serve as points of entry into discussions about the identity of the person whose hand recorded the plays. And the hybrid texts that fill the pages of Aquino's notebook will be used to frame a discussion of the core analytical frameworks and methodologies that will be employed to interpret the plays.

NAHUATLAHTOLLI, "ONE'S NATIVE LANGUAGE, NAHUATL"

The vast majority of Fabián de Aquino's small notebook of Christian texts is written in his native language, Nahuatl. Often referred to in the sixteenth-century sources as *la lengua mexicana*, "the Mexican language," Nahuatl is a member of the Uto-Aztecan family of Indigenous American languages. As this label suggests, Uto-Aztecan encompasses a geographically wide swathe of the Americas that stretches from the territory of the Utes of present-day Utah south to California, the Great Basin, and the Southwest, and down into central Mexico to the region inhabited by the Nahuas. The southernmost Uto-Aztecan language is Pipil, which is still spoken today in parts of El Salvador.[3] Currently there are approximately 1.5 million native speakers of Nahuatl, most of whom live in the states of central Mexico. Like all Indigenous languages in Mexico today, Nahuatl is under threat of extinction, as various social and political pressures cause many young Nahuas to lose touch with their mother tongue. However, in certain quarters, Nahuatl is in the midst of something of a renaissance, with language instruction growing increasingly common both inside and outside of Mexico. Mexican primary school curricula, intensive summer language programs, and the publishing of literature and instructional materials in modern variants of Nahuatl make it clear that *mexicano* is far from a dead language.[4]

At the time of first contact in the early sixteenth century, Nahuatl was the lingua franca of the Mexica Empire.[5] Spread widely through conquest and trade, it was spoken by many non-Nahuatl-speaking Indigenous communities as a necessary means of communication with their Mexica overlords. After the Spanish-Mexica War and the toppling of Mexica imperial rule, the new rulers of the land made the pragmatic decision to adopt Nahuatl as the unofficial second language of the colony of New Spain. Since the Mexica had built administrative and economic networks all across their empire, simple pragmatism dictated that as much of that structure be left in place as possible. Indigenous scribes, called *tlahcuilohqueh* (those who paint/write things), quickly mastered the technology of alphabetic writing, which they used to write both in Spanish and in their own native tongues. Together with their own unique, hieroglyphic writing system, their work produced a corpus of early colonial hybrid texts called pictorial manuscripts that documents this fertile period of cultural cross-fertilization.

Alphabetic writing was first introduced in the years following the Spanish-Mexica War as a part of the Catholic Church's efforts to indoctrinate Spain's Indigenous subjects. Arriving members of the mendicant orders—the Franciscans in 1524, the Dominicans in 1526, and the Augustinians in 1533—quickly set about learning Indigenous languages so that the gospel could be communicated, and souls could be saved (see figure 0.1). These barefoot and roughly dressed friars, each in their own way determined to imitate Christ's humility and poverty, set about their task with an urgency driven by their understanding of Christ's call to convert the "gentile" races before the end of time. The task was a daunting one. At the time of contact it has been estimated that the Basin of Mexico alone was home to upwards of 1.5 million people.[6] The handful of friars who had arrived on its shores were vastly outnumbered. In light of this, it was deemed expedient for the friars to learn Indigenous languages rather than teach millions of Indigenous people to comprehend theirs. Thus, the lingua franca of the Mexica Empire became the lingua franca of the Christian kingdom the friars hoped to build in the Americas.

From this critical early decision flowed a series of others. These included the founding of schools, such as the Colegio de Santa Cruz in the neighborhood of

FIGURE 0.1. The *Twelve Apostles of Mexico*, a sixteenth-century mural at the Convento de San Miguel Arcángel in Huejotzingo, Puebla. Photograph by Alejandro Linares García, CC BY-SA 4.0

Santiago Tlatelolco in Mexico City. Founded in 1536, Santa Cruz was the first college established in the Americas. It was in schools like this that the friars gathered young boys drawn from the ranks of the Indigenous nobility and taught them to read and write Latin, Spanish, and Nahuatl using the Roman alphabet. In turn, these students taught the friars their *nahuatlahtolli*, the language that would come to define Indigenous Christian expression in New Spain. From the very earliest moments, then, we find an inseparable intertwining of writing and religion, words and ideas, orthography and theology.

The friars' emphasis on education was part of a broader plan aimed at the wholesale transformation of Indigenous society into a model Christian society, what William Hanks has referred to as the "total project" of *reducción*.[7] In its colonial usage, the verb *reducir*—from which reducción is derived—did not mean "to reduce or shrink" but instead "to persuade or attract someone with reasons and arguments"[8] and also "to put in better order."[9] The friars' mission, then, involved the "persuading" of Indigenous hearts and minds and the "ordering" of Indigenous society. The project had two main objectives. One targeted the diffuse distribution of Indigenous communities across the landscape and the necessity of resettling them into more condensed Spanish-style towns called *pueblos reducidos*, "ordered towns." This eased the monumental task being shouldered by the friars by making it possible for a small number of missionaries to indoctrinate and monitor large Indigenous populations. This policy, called *congregación*, exacted a heavy toll on Indigenous communities, who complained bitterly to authorities about the hardships of relocation.

However, by far the more ambitious of the two objects of *reducción* was the aspect that involved the "persuasion" of Indigenous hearts and minds. This process went far beyond the mere physical relocation of Indigenous bodies and communities. It aimed at transforming Indigenous behavior and, Hanks argues, language as well, resulting in both *indios reducidos* and *lenguas reducidas*. The friars' efforts to order Indigenous conduct are vividly recorded in a colonial source known as the Códice Franciscano, a collection of correspondence by New Spain's Franciscans that dates to the late 1560s and early 1570s. In it we read the following description of how Christian doctrine was taught on Sundays and church feast days:

> At dawn the Indians gather in the patio of the church where they are distributed like squadrons by their tribunes and centurions who are responsible for collecting each one from their neighborhood. There they count them, and to those who fail in coming when they are obliged they give half a dozen lashes over the clothing.[10]

The account goes on to note that this was how discipline had always been done among them in precontact times, and those who would suggest that the practice of corporal punishment be ended threatened to take away from them "their very being and the means of governing them," since, "they are like children and in order to control them properly it must be with them just as school teachers are with children." The anonymous author of this account then returns to the subject of the teaching of doctrine:

> Upon finishing the counting, they make them sit in order where they are to be preached to, and before the sermon they recite the entire doctrine two or three times in a loud voice, and then a religious [a friar] preaches to them in their own language. Upon finishing the sermon, mass is sung, and mass having been said, they will finish at more or less nine o'clock, then they go to their homes.[11]

These excerpts remind us of the asymmetrical nature of power between friars and Indigenous people in the colonial context. It is the friars who wield the whip, the ones who dictate when to assemble, where to sit, and what will be taken as "true" and "proper." The paternalism of the friars is nakedly evident in the way they consign Indigenous people—regardless of age—to the category of perpetual children. The "indios" were the clay, the friars the potters, molding their conduct in hopes of shaping them into indios reducidos, compliant subjects who conform to an ordered

FIGURE 0.2. Fray Pedro de Gante teaching Indigenous children. Author's line drawing based on the original in Diego de Valadés, *Rhetorica Christiana* (1579).

manner of Christian living. This is the process one scholar has referred to as "spiritual colonization"; others refer to it as "cultural trauma" (see figure 0.2).[12]

Indigenous spaces and bodies were not the only targets of reducción. According to Hanks, so too were Indigenous languages. In short, he argues that through the process of creating *artes* (grammars) and dictionaries of Indigenous languages, the friars subjected the language itself to the ordering process of reducción. Words were defined, foreign grammatical principles applied, and language itself came to receive the imprint of colonial domination. These lenguas reducidas were then employed in the creating of doctrinal literature such as catechisms, sermons, confession manuals, and devotional works. As we saw above, Indigenous people were required to listen to and repeat, recite and memorize Christian doctrine, doctrine that was communicated in lenguas reducidas.

Despite the oppressive nature of Spanish colonial domination, learning and literature flourished in the Indigenous educational centers of New Spain. Santa Cruz's most illustrious students achieved a level of mastery over Latin that matched or surpassed that of many educated Europeans. One Nahua Latinist worth mentioning by name was don Antonio Valeriano, a native of Azcapotzalco who would go on to be the governor of Mexico City for twenty-three years.[13] He was a close colleague of both Bernardino de Sahagún and his fellow Franciscan of the next generation, Juan Bautista. In the introduction to Bautista's collection of sermons, published in 1606, he wrote of that Valeriano was "one of the best Latinists and rhetoricians that came out of [Santa Cruz]. . . . He was such a great Latinist that he used to speak ex tempore . . . with such propriety and elegance that he seemed a Cicero or Quintilian."[14] Scholars like Valeriano played a central role in bringing to pass what has been dubbed the Golden Age of Nahuatl literary production, a period of time lasting from the 1540s through the 1640s.[15]

Nahuas in mendicant schools didn't spend their entire time learning Latin and studying theology. A significant portion of their energies were devoted to assisting the friars in the creation of grammars and dictionaries as well as in the translation and composition of doctrinal materials in Nahuatl and also Zapotec, Mixtec, Otomí, and other Mesoamerican languages. Sahagún himself testified to their essential role when he made the following statement:

> they have helped and still help in many things in the implanting and maintaining of our Holy Catholic faith, for if sermons, apostilles [commentaries] and catechisms have been produced in the Indian language, which can appear and may be free of all heresy, they are those which were written with them. And they, being knowledgeable in the Latin language, inform us to the properties of words, the properties of their manner of speech. And they correct for us the incongruities we express in the sermons we write or in the catechisms. And whatever is to be rendered in their language, if it is not examined by them, if it is not written congruently in the Latin language, in Spanish, and in their languages, cannot be free of defect.[16]

For years, the labors of Nahuas such as these have been obscured behind the friars whose names appear on the title pages of the works for which they only partly deserve credit. At the time of their composition, this was deemed a necessity. In order to successfully shepherd a text through the publishing process, numerous licenses and official approvals had to be procured from the ecclesiastical authorities. It is highly unlikely that projects like those referenced by Sahagún would have been approved if the role of Indigenous collaborators had been highlighted. Even though friars like Sahagún and Bautista took pains to credit the Nahuas who assisted them, historians in subsequent centuries have tended to ignore the essential role played by Indigenous writers and translators. For years they were sidelined in the historiography, referred to as "assistants," "amanuenses," and "students." What more recent scholarship has begun to highlight is the inadequacy of these terms in conveying both the centrality of their role as well as the degree and stature of their position in the missionary project. Terms like "Indigenous scholar" or "Nahua intellectual" ring much truer, at least in the case of ones such as Valeriano and others.[17] Rather than thinking of these scholars as assistants to the friars, it strikes me as far more appropriate to refer to them as the friars' colleagues, and to their work as a collaboration.

The literary fruits of this collaboration can scarcely be contained in a single paragraph. Between the years of 1539, when the first book in the Americas was printed in Mexico City, to Mexican Independence in 1821, approximately 196 different works written in Indigenous languages left the printing presses.[18] It must be remembered that each individual printing would have resulted in many dozens or hundreds of individual copies; the largest print runs of colonial texts may have reached up to a thousand copies. These 196 works constituted 60 percent of all Indigenous-language imprints in the Spanish Indies, which includes Spanish territories in the Philippines and South America, during this time period. Of these, Nahuatl was by far the most commonly printed Indigenous language, with 112 of the 196 different imprints.[19]

As a way of parsing the intertwined roles of friars and Nahuas in the production of native-language religious texts, Mark Christensen has devised three broad categories.[20] The imprints discussed above are what he refers to as "Category One" texts (see figure 0.3). This first category was the result of the collaboration between friars and Nahuas previously discussed. Destined for the printing press, they were subjected to the most extensive process of review, editing, and censorship by ecclesiastical authorities. As such, Category One texts capture the church's official discourses on religion in Indigenous languages. Their intended audience was primarily the clergy responsible for the indoctrination of the Indigenous population, but they were also targeted at the upper echelon of literate Indigenous society, who were interested in collecting and reading such texts.

No accurate count of unpublished colonial Nahuatl religious manuscripts is possible, but they surely number in the hundreds if not thousands. In any case, they were certainly far more numerous than the relatively few texts that made it all the way to the printing press. Christensen refers to these as "Category Two" texts. These handwritten documents either weren't intended for the press or never made it there. They, too, were the product of collaboration between friars and Indigenous scholars. However, since they never passed through the licensing and review process they were not censored. Therefore, Category Two texts sometimes manifest a greater diversity in the way Christianity was presented and in certain cases may contain material that can be considered nonstandard or even heterodox.

Manuscripts like Fabián de Aquino's Christian miscellany fall into the third category proposed by Christensen. These religious texts were authored by Indigenous writers exclusively for Indigenous use. Like Category Two texts, they were also handwritten and never passed through the church's censoring process. Importantly, "Category Three" texts were created with much less supervision by the friars than those of the first two categories. Some may never have passed through a friars' hands. As a result, they tend to convey the most diverse and least-orthodox interpretations of Christianity of all the categories. When they came to the attention of ecclesiastical authorities, many of these texts were confiscated. That manuscripts like

¶ Confessionario ma

yor, Instruction y Doctrina, para el que
se quiere bien confessar: compuesto por el reuerendo pa
dre fray Alóso de Molina de la orden de señor sant
Francisco: traduzido y buelto en la lengua de
los nauas, por el mismo autor

Ica ynitocatzin sanctissi
ma trinidad, tetatzin, te-
piltzi, yua espiritu sancto. Mi-
can ompeua yn neyolmelaua-
loni, yn oquimotlalili yn oqui-
motecpamili padre fray Alon
so de Molina, sant Francisco reopixqui: ynipan oquimo-
cuepili yn nauatlatolly.

En el nombre de la sanctis-
sima trinidad, padre, hi-
jo, y espiritu sancto. Aqui comiença vn confessionario, que
compuso y ordeno el R. padre
fray Alonso de Molina, de la
ordé de señor sant frácisco: tra
duzido en légua de los nauas
por el mismo autor.

¶ Tlatolpeuhcayotl.

¶ Prologo.

Nolla
çopiltze.
¶ in çaço
acteuatl}
tymoma-
quitizneq,
in vel tiqc
nopilhuiz
neq cemi-
cac yuiliz
tli, cenca
motech
moneci in
tinechma-

Amado hijo.
¶ qualqe-
ra q tu se-
as, q pre-
tédes sal-
uarte}pa
ra que pu
edas al-
cançar la
vida eter
na, tc es
muy ne-
cessario,

ti3

a iij que

FIGURE 0.3. An example of a Category One Nahuatl religious text. Fray Alonso
de Molina's *Confessionario mayor en lengua mexicana y castellana* (1565: f. 3r). Courtesy of
the John Carter Brown Library.

Fabián's notebook survived at all is due to the fact that they were carefully guarded by trusted members of the communities that held them. Various additions to their contents over the years, including signatures, baptismal records, and other miscellaneous annotations, tell us that these important communal records were passed down from generation to generation.

The Nahuatl language—and the Nahuas who taught it and wrote in it—was the Catholic Church's most essential tool for communicating its message to Indigenous people in the early period stretching from the 1520s through the middle of the seventeenth century. And yet, as the ecclesiastical authorities of New Spain well knew, teaching Indigenous subjects to read and write in their native tongue was a double-edged sword. On the one hand, Nahuatl-language texts were indispensable aids in communicating Christian doctrine to and inculcating Christian morals in Indigenous communities. On the other hand, once Nahuas had mastered alphabetic writing, it proved to be enormously difficult to control what they wrote. Here we have one of the great ironies of the colonial encounter: language was intended as a tool of reducción as a way to "order" Indigenous behaviors and "persuade" Indigenous minds and bodies to conform. However, as Kelly McDonough has rightly pointed out, alphabetic writing also "provided Indigenous people with a practice and a tool with which to act, to negotiate, and to contest within the framework of colonialism."[21] Recent studies are replete with examples demonstrating how Indigenous people seized upon alphabetic writing to tell their own versions of history, argue for better treatment by colonial authorities, explain their defeat by the Spanish, and control how their land and possessions are distributed after death.[22] Studies of religious writing by Nahuas, not to mention Zapotecs, Mixtecs, and Mayas, have also shown how Indigenous writers used the pen to subtly alter and shape the Christian message in ways that made it more comprehensible to Indigenous people.[23] The result of such (re)writings of Christianity by Nahuas (and Mixtecs and Zapotecs) was not the proliferation of a monolithic Indigenous Christianity but of innumerable Indigenous Christianities all across Mesoamerica.

FABIAN DEAQUINO YTLATEPANOL, "THE WORK OF FABIÁN DE AQUINO"

Fabián de Aquino's notebook was the product of the historical forces summarized above, as was Aquino himself. Educated in a Franciscan colegio, he was likely born within one or two generations of the fall of the Mexica Empire and the arrival of the first wave of mendicant missionaries. It was in a Franciscan school that he learned to write in his native language using the Roman alphabet. Aquino's carefully drawn picture of the Franciscan knotted cord belt (see figure 0.4) is one of the many subtle

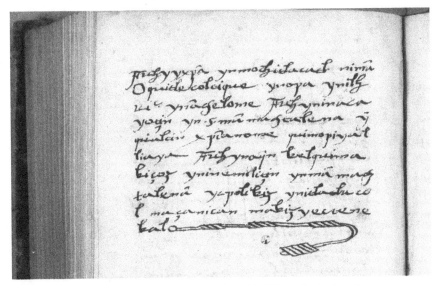

FIGURE 0.4. Drawing of a Franciscan knotted cord by Fabián de Aquino, *Sermones y miscelánea de devoción y moral en lengua mexicana*. Hispanic Society of America MS NS 3/1, ca. 1550–1600, f. 230v. Courtesy of the Hispanic Society of America, New York City.

clues that bears quiet testimony to this. Whether or not he participated with the friars in the kinds of collaborative projects mentioned above we may never know. However, what we do know is that at some point he acquired a tiny blank notebook and began to fill it with Christian texts that he deemed useful, important, and meaningful. Some of these he probably copied or translated—as he had been trained to do in the convent school—but others it seems he composed himself. Aquino's signature on folio 55 recto is evidence of this.

A signature is a claim of ownership, a statement of identity that distinguishes an individual from the larger group to which he belongs. In Aquino's time, the signing of names by Indigenous writers was still a relatively new practice that had been introduced along with alphabetic writing in the convent schools of the mendicants. While Indigenous signatures are common in the notarial genres, its presence here in the context of religious writing is exceptionally rare. In fact, Aquino's signature appears not once but four times in the notebook's three hundred folios. The first instance comes at the end of the first text, one that appears to be some kind of manual for the moral education of Christian youth (see figure 0.5). He initiates his signature with a fancy capital letter "F," a practiced flourish that he used each time he signed his name. Employing the abbreviation strategies he learned under

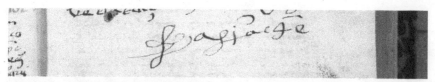

FIGURE 0.5. Signature of Fabián de Aquino on f. 37r of *Sermones y miscelánea de devoción y moral en lengua mexicana*. Hispanic Society of America MS NS 3/1, ca. 1550–1600. Courtesy of the Hispanic Society of America, New York City.

FIGURE 0.6. Signature of Fabián de Aquino on f. 66v of *Sermones y miscelánea de devoción y moral en lengua mexicana*. Hispanic Society of America MS NS 3/1, ca. 1550–1600. Courtesy of the Hispanic Society of America, New York City.

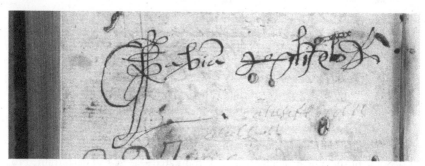

FIGURE 0.7. Signature of Fabián de Aquino on f. 300r of *Sermones y miscelánea de devoción y moral en lengua mexicana*. Hispanic Society of America MS NS 3/1, ca. 1550–1600. Courtesy of the Hispanic Society of America, New York City.

the Franciscans, he abbreviated his name using a macron over the "a" of "Fabián"; he extended the macron's abbreviatory power by condensing "de Aquino" to merely *dē*. On folio 66 verso (see figure 0.6) Aquino's elaborate "F" appears again but this time he writes out his entire name without abbreviation. His handwriting has changed somewhat since the earlier text; note the difference in the way he writes the "b" of "Fabian." The last signature in the notebook appears on folio 300 recto (see figure 0.7). Here Aquino's signature has evolved even more, with a highly ornate capital letter "F" and a return to the abbreviated final letters of "Fabian."

The second of Aquino's four signatures, the one that appears on folio 55 recto, is notably different (see figure 0.8). This signature comes at the end of the second text

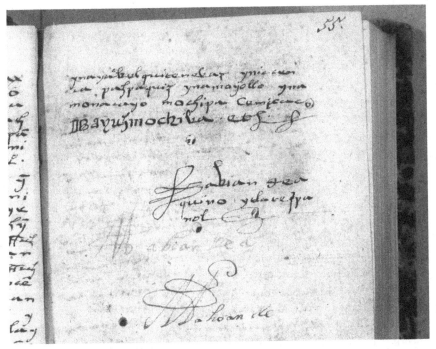

FIGURE 0.8. Signature of Fabián de Aquino on f. 55r of *Sermones y miscelánea de devoción y moral en lengua mexicana.* Hispanic Society of America MS NS 3/1, ca. 1550–1600. Courtesy of the Hispanic Society of America, New York City.

in the notebook, one that Aquino titled *De terrebilitate judicii finali et penie iuterni* [*sic*], "On the Terrible Final Judgment and Eternal Punishment." This text is essentially a narrative of what is known in Catholic theology as the Four Last Things: Death (including the resurrection of the dead at the end of time), Final Judgment, Hell, and Heaven. After completing his discussion of the glorious happiness of the souls in heaven, Aquino concluded with the words, *Ma iuh mochiva*, "May it thus be done," the formula devised by friars and their Nahua colleagues as an equivalent for "Amen." Then he left some space and added his signature. Here, too, we see Aquino's characteristic "F" and the separation of "de Aquino" into "dea" and "quino." Then, following his name he added the Nahuatl phrase, *ytlateqpanol*, "his work." What sort of datum is this? Can anything meaningful be extracted from so few strokes of the pen? Looking closer at his choice of words, we catch a glimpse of something meaningful about Aquino himself.

First of all, it should be noted that there were other words he might have chosen for "work," such as *tequitl* or *tlachihualli.* In his 1571 *Vocabulario*, Fray Alonso de Molina defines the first term, tequitl, in such a way that implies the kind of work one does as an obligation or duty; one's chores are tequitl, as is one's tributary requirement.[24] Nahuas of Aquino's day would have likely associated the choice of tequitl with a very specific kind of work, one Aquino deemed unfitting in this case. The second, tlachihualli, refers to something one has made or done, a creation or accomplishment of some sort; one's offspring could be their tlachihualli, for example.[25] However, Aquino chose not to use either of these two, instead selecting a third option, *tlatequipanolli*. Molina defines tlatequipanolli this way: *cosa obrada, o que se trabajo en ella quando se hizo*, "something labored upon; or having toiled on something when it was made."[26] When Aquino signed his name on folio 55 recto he added an inflected form of tlatequipanolli. In Nahuatl, nouns can be either possessed or unpossessed. When a noun is possessed, it gains a possessive prefix (in this case i- for "his, hers, its") and it drops its absolutive suffix (in this case -*li*). The resulting item *itlatequipanol* yields a statement that sounds stilted to English speakers: "Fabián de Aquino, his work." Rendered in a more familiar fashion, his statement was the equivalent of writing "The work of Fabián de Aquino."

Aquino's particular choice in this instance can be interpreted as a statement of authorship of the text he had just finished writing in his notebook. His choice of tlatequipanolli instead of tequitl or tlachihualli suggests that his composition was a work of intellectual labor, the kind of labor recalled in the Nahua proverb that opened this chapter, cuicuitlahuilli in tlalticpac, "chipping away on earth." As that ancient saying implied, he had applied himself to his work, had given it his care, and as a result had gained ability. His work had not been dissimilar to that of the woodcarvers, stone sculptors, or composers of songs and grammars cited as examples of "chipping away on earth." Is this reading too much into such a brief statement? Would it be pushing this vein of interpretation too far to identify a note of pride in his claim of authorship? Although he redacted dozens of texts into his notebook over the years, signing four in total, this was the only one that he claimed as his work.

Apart from a statement of authorship, what might this mean? For one, it's significant in that it's rare. At least in the official collaborations between friars and Nahuas that were destined for the printing press, collaborations that fall into Christensen's first and second categories, examples of Nahuas signing their names to texts of an overtly religious nature are exceedingly rare.[27] We do have the aforementioned statements by the likes of Sahagún and Bautista who credited their Nahua colleagues by name. There are also some historical sources that name specific Nahuas as coauthors of religious texts. But this is not the same as individual Nahuas signing their names and claiming authorship. Just to be clear, the phenomenon of Nahuas identifying themselves by name was ubiquitous in the notarial genres like cabildo records, land deeds, and testaments, etc. But in terms of *religious* texts, it was exceedingly rare for Nahua authors to assert authorship in this way.

This was partly due to the fact that starting in the middle years of the sixteenth century, support for the composition of religious texts in Indigenous languages had fallen under increasing scrutiny. From the 1520s through the end of Franciscan fray Juan de Zumárraga's term as the first archbishop of Mexico (1548), the Franciscans had enjoyed uncommon freedom in the creation of Indigenous language doctrinal materials. Their approach to Indigenous people and culture as well as the project of indoctrination was notably humanist in character. As we've seen, they were supportive of Indigenous higher education and they favored the translation of a diverse range of religious literature into Indigenous languages, even parts of the Bible. Most importantly of all, the pope had granted them a striking degree of independence from civil and ecclesiastical authorities, a freedom that emboldened them to carry out the mission in the manner they saw fit. This all began to change with the ascendency of Dominican episcopal leadership at mid-century, beginning with the election of Fray Alonso de Montúfar in 1551. One scholar has used the term "hyperorthodox" to characterize the reign of this Dominican bishop.[28] He made an impact on the matter of Indigenous-language religious writing almost immediately. In 1555, Montúfar oversaw the gathering of the first colony-wide church council. Among the many official pronouncements of the conciliar assembly, we find the following statement:

> [We order] that no sermons be given to the Indians in their language and no doctrine be translated into Indian languages without being examined by a cleric or friar who knows the language in question. We have discovered great mistakes that continue to be preached in Indian languages, either from not understanding or not having translated things well; we require and state by law that from now on no sermon be given to Indians to translate or keep in their power; and if any Indian has any it must be confiscated.[29]

The statements of the First Mexican Church Council of 1555 must be seen within the context of the Catholic Church's response to the Protestant Reformation in Europe. This response is known as the Counter Reformation because of its efforts to "counter" what was seen as an assault on Catholic orthodoxy by the movements of Luther, Calvin, and humanists like Desiderius Erasmus. In the Council of Trent (1545–1563) the church redoubled its efforts to ensure that Christian doctrine was presented in a clear and uniform manner so that orthodoxy could be promoted and heterodoxy rooted out. One result was the creation and propagation of official guides to doctrine and practice, like the *Catechismus Romanus* of 1566 and the *Missale Romanum* of 1570.[30] In addition to standardizing doctrine, the church took a tougher stance on the translation of the Bible, seeking to retain its exclusive power to interpret the word of God. In 1559, the infamous Index of Prohibited Books banned all vernacular translations of scripture, a move which would make waves on the far side of the Atlantic.

In New Spain, Archbishop Montúfar and his successor Fray Pedro Moya de Contreras (1573–1591), also a Dominican, were the official arms of Counter Reformation orthodoxy in the Americas. Under Moya de Contreras the Inquisition was officially established in 1571, and with it, religious writing in Indigenous languages came under intense scrutiny. Not all friars agreed on the matter; opinions can't even be neatly separated by order either. In general, the Dominicans were less supportive of creating doctrinal materials in Indigenous languages and not in favor of giving them the kind of advanced education favored by the Franciscans. They tended to be much stricter in their adherence to the letter of the Council of Trent's law, and some were bitterly critical of the Franciscans' humanism and independent-mindedness.[31] But debates over the wisdom of Indigenous language writing and publication were ongoing throughout the rest of the century. Many friars, especially Franciscans, argued passionately that their mission simply couldn't continue without adequate doctrinal materials—including translations of the scriptures themselves—in Indigenous languages. Detractors feared that if the Franciscans were permitted to move forward with their efforts to make the scriptures available in translation along with major works of devotional literature—works like the best-selling *The Imitation of Christ* by Thomas à Kempis—the church risked the spread of humanism and heretical Protestantism in the Americas.

There would be no clear resolution to the matter in the sixteenth century: Franciscans kept on with their Indigenous language writing and Dominican ecclesiastical authorities kept pushing back. In fact, the period from c. 1550 through the first quarter of the seventeenth century saw the greatest flowering of Nahuatl religious writing in the three hundred years leading up to Independence. It was during this period that nearly all of the monumental works of colonial Nahuatl literature were produced. Works like the early collection of sermons (1540–1563) composed under Sahagún's direction, Molina and his colleagues' translation of Denys the Carthusian's *De regimine politiae* (c. 1565), Molina and Ribas's translation of the *Imitation of Christ* (see figure 0.9), and Bautista, Ribas, and Baptista Contreras's translation of Fray Diego Estella's *Libro de las vanidades del mundo* (c. 1606) are just a few of the major translation projects undertaken by Nahuas and Franciscans centered at the Colegio de Santa Cruz at this time.[32]

For their part, detractors sought to stem the tide of Nahuatl-language writing and translation. Not even Sahagún's magnum opus, the *Historia general*, was spared; it was officially banned in 1577, and all copies were ordered confiscated

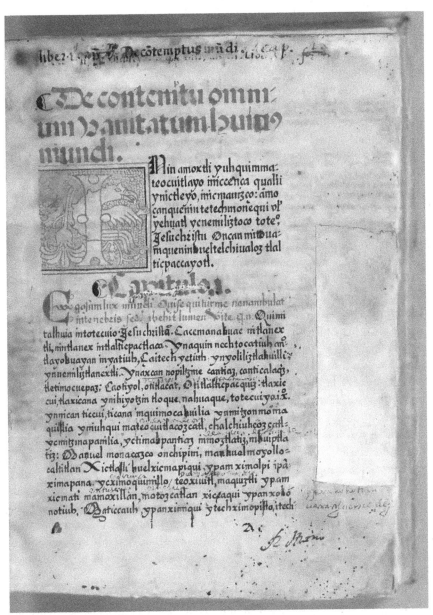

FIGURE 0.9. *De contempu[s] omnium vanitatum huius mundi*, Codex Indianorum 23, f. 1r. Courtesy of the John Carter Brown Library, Brown University.

and sent to the royal court in Spain. At issue in this case wasn't so much the presentation of Christian doctrine but the fact that the *Historia general* threatened to perpetuate knowledge about pagan religious beliefs and practices. These were the very elements of Indigenous culture that were the target of the church's efforts of eradication. A similar fate befell a Nahuatl translation of the Proverbs of Solomon. Generally considered to be the first translation of extensive portions of a book of the Bible into an Indigenous American language, it was likely produced prior to 1562 by Franciscan fray Luis Rodríguez and various Nahua scholars.[33] It too was banned in 1577. Miraculously, one of at least two copies has recently resurfaced at (of all places) the Hispanic Society of America in New York, the very same collection which holds Aquino's devotional notebook.[34]

Despite the debates over Indigenous language religious writing, debates that were carried out largely by and among friars and church officials, literate Nahuas like Aquino continued the work of copying, translating, composing, and circulating religious materials, often out of sight of the friars. By the second half of the sixteenth century the production of Category Three religious texts had created something of a clandestine subculture of Indigenous language textual production. These unofficial, unapproved texts, authored by Nahuas exclusively for Nahua consumption, were copied and circulated in and among the Indigenous communities of New Spain. This was a reality of which the friars were well aware and that made them profoundly uneasy. Sahagún alludes to this in a short note he penned at the end of a set of Nahuatl spiritual exercises he edited in 1574. He wrote, "I found this book of spiritual exercises among the Indians. I don't know who composed it, or who gave it to them. It had many mistakes and inconsistencies. But it can truly be said that it was rewritten rather than corrected."[35] In 1577 Augustinian friar Juan de la Anunciación commented sourly that the plethora of unofficial notebooks of sermons in circulation resulted in doctrine "so varied, so indigestible, so confusing" that the entire project of evangelization was at risk.[36] It is within this specific context that Fabián de Aquino's notebook, and his signature along with it, must be placed. In light of the fierce debates over the permissibility of Indigenous language religious writing, Aquino's signature and his claim of authorship are not just rare as statements of individuality. They also situate him at the fringes of what was deemed licit activity for Nahuas in the latter half of the sixteenth century.

The signature on folio 55 recto has allowed the emergence of the rough outlines of the historical figure of Fabián de Aquino: a Franciscan-educated Nahua intellectual who redacted numerous religious texts in a historical context that wasn't entirely supportive of the work he was doing. Beyond his signature, what else can we glean about the identity of Aquino? To date, all efforts to locate Aquino in the historical record have failed. Therefore, we must instead look to the physical artifact he left.

Just limiting ourselves to the evidence it contains, we can say something about the region he may have come from, his likely status and role in society, and the degree to which he had adopted aspects of Spanish language and culture.

Based on linguistic clues gleaned from the various texts he redacted, it can be safely posited that Aquino spoke an eastern variant of Nahuatl. More specifically, he may have hailed from the important *altepetl* (Indigenous polity, ethnic state) of Tlaxcala.[37] Tlaxcala was a powerful Indigenous state that had resisted conquest by the Mexica Empire in the years leading up to the arrival of the Spanish. On Cortés's trek from the coast to Tenochtitlan in the spring and summer of 1519, he first attacked Tlaxcala, and then, once he learned that they were enemies of the Mexica, succeeded in convincing them to join forces against the Mexica. For their part, the Tlaxcaltecah identified the Spanish as an avenue for freeing themselves once and for all from the threat of the Mexica, and they became participants in the military conquest of Tenochtitlan. After the war, Tlaxcala skillfully negotiated with the Spanish Crown for an extensive set of privileges, such as an exemption from being given in encomienda (a system of forced labor and tribute) to various conquistadors and eventually being granted a royal coat of arms by the king of Spain. In their own telling of their history, Tlaxcala's historians touted their early and enthusiastic conversion to Christianity and fidelity to the new regime.

Locating Aquino in time is similarly difficult to do with any great precision. However, establishing general chronological "bookends" can be achieved with some certainty through an analysis of Aquino's writing. In James Lockhart's seminal publication, *The Nahuas After the Conquest*, he described three broad stages of Nahuatl linguistic development as Nahuatl speakers came into increasingly regular contact with speakers of Spanish.[38] In his analysis, Stage One was a very brief period immediately following contact in which Nahuatl showed little or no Spanish influence. Stage Two began around the 1540s and lasted approximately a century. In this stage, Nahuatl began to borrow from Spanish, but mainly nouns. Finally, in "Stage Three" (c. 1640 onward), the floodgates opened as bilingualism among Nahuas mushroomed. During this stage, Nahuatl incorporated a vast amount of Spanish material, including Spanish verbs, idioms, and even certain Spanish sounds that were missing in Nahuatl.[39] The language used by Aquino in his notebook is, without a doubt, Stage Two Nahuatl. The non-linguist will be spared the details by relegating them to the notes, but the evidence is hard to dispute.[40]

This permits us to situate Aquino and his oeuvre between the historical bookends of c. 1540 and c. 1640. Efforts to get more precise than this lead us down increasingly speculative paths. However, he has left us with one important datum that must be mentioned. On folio 67, Aquino began a text about indulgences with the words *Nican mitohua yn tlahtlacolpollolliztli yn itoca ynidulsencias* (Here the destruction of sin, what is called "indulgences," is spoken of). This important text provides the names of not one but two historical personalities, Fray Francisco de Zamora, minister general of the Franciscan order from 1559–1565, and *yn cenca vey teopixqui pahpa parilo 4* (the very great priest pope *parilo* the fourth), presumably Pope Pius IV, who also ruled from 1559–1565. More importantly, the author recorded the date that the pope granted a special plenary indulgence to Zamora and the Franciscan Order. The date is written first using the traditional Nahuatl count of "twelve hundred and three hundred and also sixty years" and then in the Spanish fashion, *mil e quinientos e sesenta anos* (1560). This critical datum constitutes a *terminus post quem*, the earliest possible date of that this specific text could have been redacted. Since there are a number of texts that precede the indulgence text, it is possible to imagine that the terminus post quem of the entire manuscript might possibly predate 1560. However, playing it safe we can state that this information, when considered along with Lockhart's dates for Stage Two Nahuatl we arrive at narrower range of c. 1560–1640.

One final compression of this window occurs under the influence of an even more highly specialized set of data, that which relates to Aquino's orthography. Here, again, the interested reader can look to the notes for the specific details.[41] Briefly, the alphabetic rendering of Nahuatl sounds in the early colonial period varied widely until the mid- to late-sixteenth century at which point they became standardized in most instances. Since Aquino's spellings of certain phonemes, such as Nahuatl's ubiquitous [w] and [tˢ] phonemes, are *not* standardized and in fact follow demonstrably early patterns, it is reasonable to argue that c. 1600 represents the manuscript's *terminus ante quem*. Putting all of this evidence together, the evidence leaves us with the approximate window of c. 1560–1600 as the most likely period during which Aquino filled his notebook with miscellaneous Christian texts, including the two Antichrist plays.[42]

As to the social status of Fabián de Aquino, we are on similarly speculative ground here as well. That he was literate suggests a noble heritage. However, certain clues cast doubt about this hypothesis. Most notably, he never signed his name with the honorific "don." Early in the contact period the Spaniards assigned this title to most of the highest echelon of Indigenous nobles at the time of their baptism. However, management of its application was quickly appropriated by Nahuas themselves and by the late sixteenth century had come to be associated much more broadly with the higher-ranking members of Indigenous society.[43] Even so, the lack of "don" before each of the three instances where Aquino signed his name in his devotional notebook neither indicates nor counter-indicates noble status, at least not definitively. Lockhart's study of colonial naming patterns among Nahuas demonstrates that the use of "don" varied depending on which time period the writer lived. If

Aquino indeed wrote during the latter part of the sixteenth century, his omission of "don" suggests a greater likelihood that he wasn't a member of the Indigenous nobility. However, as Lockhart points out, the use of "don" among Nahuas was much more fluid than among Spaniards and tended to be acquired and lost depending on the gaining or losing of prominent positions in Indigenous society, such as high municipal office.[44]

Other clues in his writing point toward a middling status, perhaps a lower-ranking member of the nobility or an upper-level member of the *macehualtin* (commoner class). His name itself, the very Spanish-sounding Fabián de Aquino, would have been highly unlikely for a commoner. From contact through the middle of the sixteenth century most commoners bore combined Spanish baptismal names and Indigenous surnames such as Diego Maçaihuitl, Pedro Coçamalocatl, or Juana Xoxopanxoco. By Aquino's time, however, it was increasingly more the norm among ordinary Nahuas to adopt two Spanish first names, such as Juan Martín and Barbara Agustina. More complex appellations such as Antonio de San Juan or Juan de la Cruz bespoke higher status, as did the wholesale adoption by Nahuas of surnames of the Spaniards who served as godparents, mentors, or baptismal sponsors. This may very well have been the case with Fabián de Aquino. Based on the evidence of his literacy, education, his name, and the fact that he had access to a wide array of Christian literature, the most likely hypothesis is that Aquino was a member of the Indigenous nobility who, whether due to change in rank or occupation, did not use the honorific "don" at the time of his notebook's composition.[45]

There will probably always be mystery surrounding the identity of this Nahua writer and the exact circumstances under which he came to adapt the Antichrist legend for the Nahuatl stage. In the next chapter, analysis of the subject matter and contents of the two Antichrist dramas redacted by Aquino will add some more information relevant to the question of authorship. The remaining pages of this chapter will "unbundle" the final artifact from Aquino's textual *in toptli, in petlacalli* in order to lay out some of the methodological and analytical tools useful in the interpretation of Aquino's Aztec Antichrist.

YN TLOQUE YN NAVAQUE YN CEMANAVAC TLATOVNI JESU CRISTO, "LORD OF THE NEAR, LORD OF THE NIGH, TLAHTOANI OF THE WORLD, JESUS CHRIST"

The phrase above appears in one of the thirty-three short miracle stories of the Virgin Mary that Aquino added between folios 71 recto and 114 verso of his notebook. Its compositional elements highlight something essential about colonial Nahuatl religious writing (hybridity), the complex processes that produced it (cultural contact), as well as the frameworks adopted in this study to make sense out of both (philological analysis and transculturation).

In the phrase above we see that the author of the text has described the Christian deity using language deeply rooted in Indigenous Mesoamerican culture. To the Nahuatl-speaking peoples of precontact central Mexico, the *tlahtoani* (lit. "one who says things, speaker") was the title held by the altepetl's dynastic ruler. The couplet *in tloqueh, in nahuaqueh* was one of the epithets of the god Tezcatlipoca, "Smoking Mirror," whom Sahagún's sources also referred to as *iuhquin ioalli i ehecatl,* "like the night, the wind."[46] On the surface, the author's choice seems straightforward enough: a tlahtoani was a powerful ruler, *in tloqueh, in nahuaqueh* evoked the ineffability of the divine; on the surface both appear suitable descriptors of Spanish deity, Christ.

But translation between cultures, especially those as different as European and Nahua, is never a straightforward matter. This is because language doesn't merely communicate a single meaning but is laden with a host of secondary meanings, associations, and assumptions that are particular to the culture of origin. The friars seem not to have understood this aspect of language and the inevitability that translation would subtly alter the meaning of the source word. Hence tlahtoani didn't simply mean "ruler" and *in tloqueh, in nahuaqueh* didn't simply mean "God." These terms were embedded within a constellation of assumptions about leadership and divinity that were culturally specific and not so easily divested of their cultural baggage. Therefore, the description of Christ as "Lord of the Near, Lord of the Nigh, Tlahtoani of the World" is necessarily a cultural hybrid with a meaning that incorporates elements from two worlds and results in something that is simultaneously foreign to both.

Evidence of the hybrid nature of Fabián's notebook abounds. As a physical object, it is a book in the European sense of the word: sheets of European paper are folded, bound at the spine, cut into pages, and encased in a leather cover. Alphabetic writing, still a relatively new technology in Aquino's day, fills the book's pages in horizontal lines reading from left to right and top to bottom. Yet despite its European appearance, Fabián's notebook must also be seen as the product of an Indigenous culture of writing and books that stretched back centuries before contact. As a member of the nobility, Aquino likely had ancestors who were tlahcuilohqueh, ones who grasped the brush and applied *in tlilli, in tlapalli,* "the black [ink], the red [ink]," (i.e., "writing") to pages of bark paper. These books, called *amoxtli,* recorded information using a complex graphic system of communication involving logograms and phonograms that required expert knowledge to read, or "perform," since most served as mnemonic aids for oral recitations before an audience.[47] As such, Fabián's notebook sits at the confluence of two ancient traditions of writing and books, a hybrid Nahua-Christian *amoxtli* preserving texts of European origin in the language of the *tlahcuilohqueh* of ancient Mexico.

The individual texts copied by Aquino also betray the notebook's bicultural roots. On the surface they appear thoroughly European. An abbreviated survey of the notebook's contents includes miracle stories centering on the Virgin Mary and the Eucharist, the aforementioned tract on the "Terrible Final Judgment and Eternal Punishment," the text on indulgences, a set of confraternity ordinances, and numerous sermons, prayers, and citations from the Bible. Despite the overwhelmingly Christian and European nature of these texts, we must remember that each one has gone through the process of being rendered in Nahuatl by a Nahua writer, a process that necessarily pulled European material into an Indigenous sphere where Indigenous words, concepts, sensibilities, and intentions colored how those texts would be read.

As an example, consider how the practice of describing the Christian God as Tloqueh Nahuaqueh may have allowed the transfer of Indigenous concepts and understandings into Christianity. Until the arrival of the first friars and their *icel teotl dios*, "Only Deity, God," Tloqueh Nahuaqueh was a title borne by Tezcatlipoca (see figure 0.10). This ambivalent deity, whose nature was symbolically captured in the dim reflection of his totemic obsidian mirror, was a capricious sower of discord, both a creator and a bringer of destruction. Of him, Sahagún's informants recalled "he stirred up trouble between people; because of this he was called 'enemy on both sides.'"[48] They also called him *nahualli*, a form-shifting shaman that the friars labeled "sorcerer" and also *tlacatecolotl*, "human horned owl" or "were-owl," another enigmatic shaman figure diabolized by the Spanish.[49] It was this last one whose name the early friars and their Nahua assistants borrowed as the equivalent for "devil" and "demon" in their doctrinal writing. It was to Tezcatlipoca that the ancestors of Aquino had called out, saying, *Tloquee naoaqueie, ipalnemoanie, titlacaoane; xinechtlaocolili*, "O Lord of the Near, Lord of the Nigh! O Giver of Life! O Titlacahuan! Have mercy on me!"[50]

In light of this reading, consider the following passage, taken from the aforementioned set of Christian spiritual exercises edited by Sahagún in 1574. It comes from a discussion of the Trinity, a complex theological concept that Christian missionaries throughout the ages have struggled to explain. Writing as one speaking directly to God, the author declares, "You are not three deities (*teteoh*), you are not three rulers (*tlahtohqueh*); you are three people (*tlacah*). Your divinity is just one: just one God, just one deity, *tloque nahuaque ipalnemohuani* (Lord of the Near, Lord of the Nigh; Giver of Life)."[51] Read against the backdrop of the statement in the previous paragraph, the one directed at Tezcatlipoca, this statement seems far from the unambiguous declaration of God's triune unity that the author intended.

FIGURE 0.10. Tezcatlipoca. Author's line drawing based on the original in the Codex Borgia, central Mexico, late fifteenth or early sixteenth century, p. 17.

How are we to understand this collision of ideas? What sort of religiosity did it yield? Making sense out of cultural contact and the changes it produces has been the work of scholars for over a century. Historians of the past tended to cast the clash of cultures in the starkly binary terms of conquest and defeat, leaving no middle ground for hybridity. The classic example is Robert Ricard's *La conquête spirituelle du Mexique* from 1933, which was published in translation as *The Spiritual Conquest of Mexico* in 1966. Ricard, like generations of writers before him, deemed the efforts of the Catholic Church to convert the Nahuas as having been largely successful: sacrifices were ended, temples torn down, and people converted to Christianity en masse. Even though some resisted conversion and clung to their "paganism," in the final accounting Indigenous religion was gradually replaced by Christianity. Interpretations such as these imply a specific view of cultural contact and change that tends to emphasize a unidirectional flow from the dominant to the subordinate culture. Subordinate cultures capitulate and gradually become more and more like the dominant culture, eventually losing all connection to the former. This process has gone by many names, such as assimilation and acculturation.

However, as with many historical trends, the interpretive pendulum eventually swung in the opposite direction. Starting in the 1940s and 1950s, there emerged in Mexico a generation of scholars—Angel María Garibay and Miguel León-Portilla principal among them—whose work rejected the implication that Nahua culture had been inferior to Western culture and had been displaced by conquests spiritual and otherwise. Works such as Garibay's *Historia de la literatura náhuatl* (1953) and León-Portilla's *La filosofía náhuatl estudiada en sus fuentes* (1956) forced the conversation about the impacts of colonization to reconsider earlier narratives of conquest and the disappearance of Indigenous culture. Mexican historian Alfredo López Austin proposed the existence of what he called the *núcleo duro*, the "hard nucleus," of Mesoamerican culture, a core of essential cultural traits that he deemed "quite resistant to historical change."[52] Seen from this perspective, it was tempting to view Indigenous engagement with Christianity as a superficial layering of certain elements of European religion over a largely unchanged Indigenous cultural core (or nucleus). This is sometimes referred to as syncretism. However, this emphasis on the "hardness" of Indigenous culture and its "survival" into modern times has contributed to some degree of glossing over of the significant ways Indigenous culture was impacted by contact with the European other.

With the rise of postcolonial interpretations in the 1970s and 1980s, scholars focused increasingly on the ways Indigenous people engaged with European culture and adapted to it through various strategies aimed at cultural preservation. Romanticized notions of resistance and survival were largely jettisoned in favor of more complex narratives that emphasized the appropriation of Hispano-Catholicism by Indigenous colonial subjects. In 1979 Jorge Klor de Alva announced the failure of the assimilationist "spiritual conquest" view and instead proposed a middle state he called *nepantlism*, a term he borrowed from León-Portilla.[53] Derived from the Nahuatl *nepantla*, "in the middle of something," he argued that rather than acceding to Christianization or rejecting it outright, early colonial Nahuas existed in a kind of "neither/nor" limbo.

Starting in the late 1970s and picking up steam in the 1980s, scholars increasingly began to turn to Indigenous-language documents in an effort to recover Indigenous voices from beneath a dominant Eurocentric narrative that had been built on Spanish-language sources. León-Portilla's hugely influential *Visión de los vencidos* (1959), published in the United States as *The Broken Spears* (1962), was an early and important contribution to this turn. Charles E. Dibble and Arthur J. O. Anderson's decades-long translation of the Nahuatl text of the Florentine Codex (1950–1982) also generated interest in and access to one of the largest and most important corpuses of Nahuatl-language writing. Other scholars delved into the diverse and rich landscape of so-called "mundane" Nahuatl texts (wills and testaments, land sales, petitions, etc.), a turn that shifted attention from the precontact to the colonial, from pictorial codices to alphabetic texts, and from the urban center to a broader social field.[54] James Lockhart and a generation of scholars who trained under him broadened this philological approach to the sources. Some of these turned the "New Philology" toward other Indigenous people groups, opening new paths into the colonial experiences of Mixtec, Zapotec, and Yucatec Maya communities through the translation and analysis of writing in their own languages.

As understanding of the religious experiences of these communities deepened, scholars rejected the limbo-like status suggested by the concept of *nepantlism* and instead emphasized Indigenous agency and a more active engagement with Christianity. Louise Burkhart's work carefully charted how Nahuas appropriated European religious narratives and moralizing discourses to shape an indigenized Christianity that more comfortably matched their ways of thinking and being in the world.[55] Thinking about cultural change from the perspective of the indigenization of Christianity furthered the reversing of historical narratives that have tended to assume the process always worked in the opposite direction. In place of the binaries of "resistance" and "assimilation," new scholarship continues to shed light on a vastly more complex flow of ideas that were shaped by a variety of interconnected processes. For example, many scholars have adopted the framework of negotiation, where cultural intermediaries or "brokers" leverage their bicultural fluency to navigate between the demands of the colonizer and their local constituents.[56] This is an approach well-suited to the New Philology school, since most of the texts that constitute the documentary corpus were produced by members of the Indigenous elite, whose literacy, education, and cross-cultural competency made them the essential intermediaries of their communities.

Efforts to understand Nahuas' engagement with Christianity can be further enriched by adopting the framework of "transculturation" as articulated by Mary Louise Pratt. She writes, "ethnographers have used the term *transculturation* to describe processes whereby members of subordinated or marginal groups select and invent from materials transmitted by dominant or metropolitan culture."[57] She notes that while subordinate peoples cannot control what the dominant culture forces upon them, "they do determine to varying extents what they absorb into their own, how they use it, and what they make it mean." This take on cultural contact is preferable to the frameworks of "encounter" and "dialogue." Critics of these models charge that they obscure the brutality of colonialism and suggest instead a degree of intercultural harmony that doesn't adequately expose the realities of systematic repression, and as some have argued, genocide.[58] Transculturation acknowledges the asymmetrical nature of power in the colonial contact zone and that Indigenous choices are constrained by the reality of their subordination. However, it also denies the assertion still held by some that Indigenous people "disappeared" in the face of the European invasion by helping us to see how they "selected and invented" in an effort to negotiate a place in the new order.

We see this tension between agency and domination in the notebook kept by Fabián de Aquino. All of the texts he recorded were Christian texts that, at least on the surface, aligned with approved topics and discourses. However, it was Aquino who selected *which* texts to copy down and, as the following chapters aim to show, *how* to render their contents in his native language. The results of transculturation are by their very nature ambivalent, a word whose roots in Latin consist of *ambi*, "in two ways," and *valere*, "to be strong." As a member of the Nahua nobility and a literate cultural intermediary, Aquino's fortunes were linked to both the Spanish and his own community. He had to "be strong" in "two ways," accommodating the Spanish just enough to keep them from intruding too deeply into Indigenous affairs while simultaneously advocating for the needs of his people.

His tactics involved, among other things, using his literacy to fill a notebook with nahuatlahtolli, Nahuatl words. These words recorded a wide variety of texts he culled from the books in the library of his local Franciscan convent. His access to that repository of knowledge, with its faint mustiness of dust, leather, and paper, was itself a sign of his status. It was likely in that darkened sanctum that he thumbed through the sermons of St. Vincent Ferrer, the fifteenth-century Valencian preacher known as the "Angel of the Apocalypse," as well as collections of miracle stories and hagiographies like the *Flos Sanctorum*, and perhaps the script of doomsday plays where demons and one called Antichrist strode onto the stage.[59] Those texts he chose to copy down he may have hoped would nurture the Christian religion among those of his altepetl. This was the tactic taken by many Nahua leaders of his day; by promoting a close affiliation with the Franciscans and their "Only Deity," he stood the best chance to preserve his position in the new social order as well as the favor of his people. On a broader level, this too was *Fabian deaquino ytlatequipanol*, "the work of Fabián de Aquino."

Each of the chapters that follow reveal the ambivalent nature of Aquino's role as a cultural broker and the hybrid nature of the Antichrist plays he wrote or copied. Chapter 1 seeks to locate these two newly discovered works within a series of temporally and geographically overlapping contexts. First, they are situated in the context of colonial Nahuatl religious drama, an important subgenre of early colonial literature has been called the "first truly American theater."[60] Arriving with the friars as part of their evangelizing mission, European-style religious plays written in Indigenous languages were enthusiastically embraced by both Nahuas and friars, but for different reasons. Friars saw in them an engaging medium for inculcating the population in the fundamental tenets of Hispano-Catholicism, and Nahuas found in them a useful vehicle for the expression of community religiosity, solidarity, and in some cases autonomy, as Indigenous playwrights quickly began copying, modifying, and circulating their own versions of Passion and Epiphany plays. This chapter also contextualizes the plays in relation to the European genre of religious theater and shows that they are part of a long tradition of plays dramatizing the Final Judgment and the career of the Antichrist. Although the chapter identifies no definitive source, a number of European Antichrist and Final Judgment plays are considered, and close parallels with their Nahuatl cousins are established. Continuing in this comparative vein, chapter 1 then compares the Antichrist plays to seven extant plays from the colonial Nahuatl corpus that are their closest analogs. This analysis reveals that while the new plays are clearly related to previously studied Nahuatl morality plays, they are different in two significant ways. First, they are unique in being the only surviving treatments of the legend of the Antichrist in early colonial Nahuatl literature. Second, for religious texts at least superficially associated with the friars' campaigns against idolatry, they contain a surprising amount of detailed information about the precontact religious practices of the Nahuas. These features make the Antichrist dramas collected by Fabián de Aquino two of the most riveting and intriguing texts from the early contact period.

Chapter 2 inquires whether there were specific events or conditions in the early history of the colony that served to inspire the composer of the plays to presage the coming of the Antichrist in the Americas. It argues that the proper contextualization of the plays situates their inspiration in the tumultuous years of the late 1520s through the 1540s. It was during this time that the Franciscan mission confronted a series of challenges that together amounted to an existential crisis that would have been understood as constituting the apocalyptic conditions thought necessary to trigger the advent of the Antichrist and the beginning of the End of Days. These apocalyptic conditions included acts of violence against newly converted Christians, such as those that took place in Tlaxcala in the late 1520s; pressure from the Dominican order on the Franciscans to reform their methods of evangelization and cede their unchecked powers; and mounting evidence that the Franciscans' early efforts had resulted in shallow conversions, as numerous stories emerged detailing Indigenous refusal to completely abandon their precontact religious practices. However, this chapter argues that the chief threat to the Franciscans at this tenuous moment were certain members of the Indigenous nobility (tlahtohqueh) and itinerant ritual specialists (*nanahualtin*) who either covertly or overtly resisted Christian indoctrination and sought to return the commoner class (macehualtin) to traditional forms of religiosity and cultural practices. The thesis advanced here claims that these resistant rulers and ritual specialists were the collective inspiration for the Aztec Antichrist, a tough-talking, Nahuatl-speaking tlahtoani and archenemy of the Franciscan mission in New Spain. Although it seems unlikely that Aquino copied the plays into his notebook prior to the year 1560, evidence strongly suggests they were either composed in the period of the 1530s–1540s or were written after 1560 by someone who had lived through these early, apocalyptic years.

This someone, whether it were Fabián de Aquino or a predecessor, was closely aligned with the Franciscans' ideology and approach to combating the threats posed by those who resisted fully embracing the Christian religion. That this someone was an Indigenous writer who trained in the Franciscans' schools and participated in the linguistic work of the friars is beyond reasonable doubt. However, it would be a mistake to see the plays he adapted as mere translations or impersonations of the friars' dogmas and discourses. The third chapter of this study employs the concept of autoethnography as an analytical lens through which to better understand the complex and at times contradictory ways in which the Indigenous author engages with these dogmas and discourses. Mary Louise Pratt, whose understanding of the concept is used here, defines autoethnography as writing authored by the subjects of European ethnographers' analytical gaze (i.e., Indigenous people). If that gaze sought to control the Indigenous other by presenting authoritative descriptions, autoethnographic writing appropriates the idiom of the colonizer to formulate representations of the Indigenous self that interrupt and counter that controlling gaze. This chapter argues that the Nahuatl Antichrist plays engage in precisely this sort of dialogical intervention. It argues that that while the plays' author adopts central features of Nahuatl-Christian rhetoric, he simultaneously pushes back against aspects of the friars' discourses targeting Indigenous Christians and Indigenous Christianity. Specifically, it is the friars' negative judgments of Indigenous Christians—judgments that viewed their culture as irrevocably diabolical and their Christianity as perpetually immature—that are contested. The counter-narrative he weaves presents a thoroughly Indigenous perspective of Indigenous Christianity, one that is rarely encountered in the colonial sources.

Finally, this study's conclusion seeks a firmer understanding of Fabián de Aquino and the Antichrist dramas by identifying him as an Indigenous apocalypticist and situating the works he collected in his notebook within the framework of apocalyptic thought. Apocalypticism hasn't often been used as a framework for understanding how Nahuas experienced or made sense out of the massive changes brought about by the Spanish invasion.[61] Even less studied are the connections between apocalyptic thought among Nahuas and the phenomenon of cultural trauma. Trauma studies has had a significant impact on efforts to address the legacy of colonialism on North America's Indigenous peoples, and yet few scholars have attempted to apply its theories and methods in the case of early colonial Mexico. This book's conclusion is no place to attempt to address this omission. Instead, it joins the voices of scholars like Justyna Olko and Agnieszka Brylak in suggesting that others explore this potentially fruitful vein of inquiry as a way of shedding new light on the experiences of Nahuas like Fabián de Aquino and the audiences he imagined for his Nahuatl Antichrist dramas.

As an Indigenous person, Aquino chose to affiliate himself closely with the Franciscans, the very people who actively sought to eradicate certain core elements of his culture and who deemed Indigenous people like him to be of inferior quality. But his affiliation came with certain conditions, principally, the right to present Christianity on his own terms and in his own language. And he did it in such a way that would afford his people a measure of autonomy and continuity with the past. Such is the complex nature of colonial Nahuatl religious writing, two examples of which are presented in translation at the end of this volume. They are *in toptli, in petlacalli*, deep reed baskets filled with precious quetzal feathers of colonial Nahuatl literature. As with Aquino's work, their debut in English is the product of years of "chipping away on earth." This book represents the unbundling of his efforts and mine, and I hope that they will bring you as much pleasure as they have brought me.

FIRST THEATER OF THE AMERICAS

ON JANUARY 6, 1587, Epiphany Sunday, Franciscan *visitador* (inspector) Fray Alonso Ponce witnessed the performance of an open-air Nativity play in the Nahua *altepetl* of Tlaxomulco, near the present-day city of Guadalajara, Jalisco (see figure 1.1).[1] In those days, Tlaxomulco was a small, dusty, Indigenous community far from the urban sprawl of Mexico City. Nevertheless, the account written by Fray Antonio de Ciudad Real reports that a crowd of Nahuas estimated to be five thousand strong had gathered to watch the event. Although European-style religious theater had been introduced to Nahuas in urban centers like Mexico-Tenochtitlan, it had very quickly spread to the peripheries of colonial and ecclesiastical power. There, in towns like Tlaxomulco it was enthusiastically embraced by Indigenous communities who adopted it, adapted it according to local preferences, and codified it as a treasured practice integral to communal identity. Such was the case with Tlaxomulco's Nativity play. This chapter argues that the Antichrist plays collected by Fabián de Aquino were also the product of these complex processes. By locating the plays within the contexts of both medieval European and colonial Nahuatl theater and comparing and contrasting them to their closest analogues, important questions about the plays' origins, authorship, and significance will be laid out.

Fray Antonio de Ciudad Real tells us that for that special day the residents of Tlaxomulco had constructed an elaborate Nativity scene in their church's courtyard. To one side of the church door stood the stable where the Christ child's birth would

FIGURE 1.1. Church of Santiago Tlaxomulco, late-seventeenth century, Hidalgo, Mexico. From Stephanie Wood, ed., "Mapa Techialoyan de Tolcayuca," Mapas Project, University of Oregon, 2000–2008. Courtesy of the Arthur Dunkelman/Kislak Foundation.

be performed, and to the other an enclosure for King Herod and his retinue. As the moment drew closer, a hush spread across the thousands of amassed spectators as all eyes turned toward the town's sacred *tepetl*, a sage green mountain with gentle sloping flanks that rose above and framed their church. Many of the *abuelos* in that crowd had participated in the construction of the Franciscan's imposing stone pile, which they referred to as the *teohcalli* (*teotl*-house). However, in their childhood days there had loomed in its place a stepped pyramid (which they also referred to as a *teohcalli*) dedicated to their patron deity. So much had changed since the arrival of the *Caxtiltecah* (Castilians), but some things must have felt as ancient and untouched as ever.

For weeks leading up to Epiphany, the Nahuas who were to play the roles of Mary, Joseph, Herod, angels, and shepherds met to rehearse their lines. Tlaxomulco had been in possession of a handwritten script of their Epiphany play for decades, perhaps since the 1550s, and it was reverently guarded by members of town's nobility, or *pipiltin*. Since there was only one copy, and due to the fact that most of the players could not read its words, the play's organizer, perhaps the church sacristan, or *fiscal*, would read the lines out loud and each player would repeat and memorize them. While they rehearsed, an army of their neighbors had sewn costumes, constructed the *Belén*, and prepared food and drink. Others worked out the kinks from the show's special effects masterpiece: a tinsel-covered star that would descend majestically from the summit of the mountain, running along an impossibly long rope guideline.

At the appointed time, Nahua players impersonating the Three Kings began to wend their way down the scrabbly trail from the mountain's peak with the star leading the way. Fray Antonio remarks that the journey took nearly two hours, due as much to the solemnity of the occasion as to the steep grade of the path. Behind the Kings trailed an eighty-year-old Nahua man bearing a heavy pack that held the Kings' gifts for the Christ Child. Before them walked another man bearing aloft the script itself—as a treasured community possession, it occupied a place of honor in the performance. And above the heads of these bobbed the star, its maguey-twine guideline physically linking *tepetl* and *teohcalli*, hill and church. This connection must have borne deep meaning for the residents of Tlaxomulco. Like Nahuas from communities all across New Spain, they had long envisioned their pyramid temples as manmade mountains mirroring the sacred hills that gave their *altepemeh* (sing. altepetl) their names and from which flowed the essential forces that animated the world around them. After the arrival of the Caxtiltecah and the order to raze their temple, the Nahuas of Tlaxomulco had set about constructing a new teohcalli on the same foundation as its predecessor, using many of the same stones.

While the Kings made their solemn procession down to the church-side stable, Fray Antonio described what the crowd of spectators did to pass the time. He wrote, "In the interim, a group of dancing angels came out and danced and whirled in front of the stable, singing some songs in the Mexican language [i.e., Nahuatl], with many mortifications and genuflections to the Child."[2] Next, out came the shepherds, dressed in rough pastoral clothing and bearing their crooks. To these an angel proclaimed *Gloria in excelsis deo* from high up in a wooden tower that had been erected for the purpose. We are told that since the shepherds could not understand the Latin words, the angel "consol[ed] them in the Mexican language, and g[ave] them the news of the birth of the Child." With this they raced to the stable and presented their humble gifts, a lamb, a loaf of bread (or perhaps tortillas), and a handwoven veil. Thereupon they commenced to dance and leap and sing joyful songs of praise. This soon turned to rough play, as the shepherds tussled and wrestled with each other, laughing and shouting, "hugging and rolling" on the ground. Fray Antonio writes with amazement that this was *muy de ver*, "a sight to see."

When at last the Three Kings, the two Nahua attendants, and the star entered the atrium of the church, an aura of dignity returned to the scene. Following the gospel story, they proceeded first to King Herod to inquire where they might find the one born King of the Jews. Herod called to his advisors who came bearing a large book and demanded that they find the prophecy spoken of by the Kings. One at a time, they related their prophecies to Herod who, growing more and more upset, threw each one aside and demanded the next to read. Finally accepting that the prophecy must be true, he erupted with fury, "at times scolding them and at times throwing the book on the table and on the floor, showing much anger and rage, arrogance and presumption, as much in his face as in his thrashing, his actions, and his words, as if he were actually angry and were the real King Herod."[3]

After this vivid performance, which surely must have left the audience rapt, the star began the final leg of its journey, bouncing and hovering about the heads of the assembly, at last coming to rest over the stable and the Holy Family. There the Kings prostrated themselves, offering their gifts, and each one uttering "a short prayer in the Mexican language." What words they spoke there have not survived, but we can get a feel for their poetry and cadence in lines drawn from another Nahuatl Epiphany play that has survived. In a script that makes no mention of the date of its creation nor the altepetl that once possessed it, King Balthasar utters these lines of elegant Nahuatl, "O personage, O ruler, you have in your keeping the sky and the earth, nobility and rulership. And it is indeed true that you are God, O Lord of the Near, O Lord of the Nigh, O He by Whom All Live. And I believe in you utterly, with all my spirit, my soul, and my life."[4]

Fray Antonio closes his account of this marvel by relating how *el indio viejo*, "the old Indian," who bore the Kings' gifts down from the mountain assured Fray Ponce that he "had done that for more than thirty years every year on such a day." Apparently, this elaborate Epiphany performance had been carried out annually since the 1550s, a mere three decades after the fall of Tenochtitlan and the Mexica Empire. After that, the "old Indian" put his pack back on and, turning to face the Nahua actors playing Mary, Joseph, and the Christ child, "stood speaking to [the Child] in the same Mexican language, saying that he had nothing else to offer him but the burden he bore." With that, the angel once again appeared in his tower and begged the Kings to return to their homes by another route, "and thus they left the courtyard and the feast was concluded."

By the late sixteenth century, performances such as these were happening all across New Spain. Many communities also staged elaborate Passion plays at Easter and still others at the feast of Corpus Christi. While there are other accounts of colonial performances that could be cited, this one in particular has been chosen because it raises a number of questions that are pertinent to the contextualization and analysis of the Nahuatl Antichrist dramas bound with the pages of Fabián's notebook. First of all, it is clear from the description captured by Ciudad Real that the Tlaxomulco Epiphany play bore an obvious resemblance to theatrical forms and religious narratives that have their origin in Christian Europe. However, what are we to make of the elements that appear to be more homegrown? How are we to understand, for example, the spatial and geographic dimensions of this performance? Surely, the linking of tepetl and teohcalli was an innovation that reflects an Indigenous sensibility. More than that, it reflects an active manipulation of the European tradition by Indigenous minds, an appropriation that more firmly roots the performance in local soil. What kind of performances resulted from these appropriations? Are they European? Indigenous? Something else? These questions will be explored in the first part of the chapter that follows.

Ciudad Real's mention that the script of the Epiphany play was carried down the mountain by a man preceding the Three Kings is a captivating detail. What does this minute historical datum suggest about the role played by this handwritten artifact in the drama of Indigenous colonial life? What are we to conclude from the obvious reverence with which it was treated? In turn, it raises the question of the existence of other scripts. How many are known to exist, and how many more may still be carefully secreted away by their communal guardians? Sadly, we know of very few scripts that have survived. Nevertheless, the thirty or so that are known today constitute a small but important genre of Indigenous language literature that has been the focus of numerous critical studies over the past century or more. Most recently, Barry Sell and Louise Burkhart's *Nahuatl Theater* has made twenty-two of these available in translation. In the final volume of the series the authors conclude by stating, "Undoubtedly, more plays lie in archives, awaiting recovery and publication. Most of these will correspond to the general types represented in the *Nahuatl Theater* set, such as morality plays, Passion plays, and dramatizations of other Christian narratives, but there may also be surprises."[5] The two Antichrist plays that came to light in the summer of 2014 confirm Sell and Burkhart's suspicion. The second part of this chapter seeks to contextualize these new additions to the corpus by comparing and contrasting them to the plays that were published in *Nahuatl Theater*.

Lastly, in lieu of more well-known colonial descriptions of Nahuatl theater—such as Motolinía's famous narrative of Tlaxcala's performances in 1538 and

1539—the case of Tlaxomulco is pertinent because it highlights the dynamics of center and periphery that relate directly to this study's interpretation of the plays Aquino copied into his notebook. Like many other cultural phenomena in colonial Mexico, native-language theater originated in mendicant cloisters located in urban centers like Tlatelolco, Tenochtitlan, and Tlaxcala. It was there that missionary friars first introduced what scholars have referred to as "the edifying play" as an instrument of *reducción*, the "ordering" of Indigenous spaces, bodies, and language.[6] However, as we witness in the case of Tlaxomulco's Nativity play, these phenomena had the tendency to migrate outward, away from urban centers and ecclesiastical control and into the periphery and the hands of Indigenous writers, like the anonymous Nahua who penned the Tlaxomulco script. Like Tlaxomulco's, the two Antichrist plays fall into Christensen's third category of religious texts: those written exclusively by Nahuas for Nahuas and likely with little or no priestly supervision. The final section of this chapter will argue that the unsupervised conditions in which the author of the plays worked explains their unconventional subject matter and content. Specifically, these conditions enabled him to choose a subject for his plays—the medieval legend of the Antichrist— that was almost entirely absent from the corpus of Nahuatl-language religious writing that flourished in the period of 1540–1640. Again, we are confronted by the question of the identity of Fabián de Aquino and whether he was the author of the Antichrist plays or simply copied them into his notebook. Although his identity ultimately will remain a mystery, in this chapter we take a few steps closer to understanding this enigmatic figure who wrote at the peripheries of power in early colonial Mexico.

THE COLONIAL *NEIXCUITILLI*: THE AMERICAS' FIRST THEATER

Fifty-four years before the performance of the Nativity play recorded by Ciudad Real, the sources provide us with the earliest mention of a European-style play being performed in the Americas. The year was 1533, just twelve years after the fall of Tenochtitlan and a decade following the arrival of the first Franciscan missionaries. In light of theories about the millenarian mindset of these friars, it is unsurprising that the subject of this early spectacle was Christ's return at the end of the world and the Final Judgment. This performance made a deep impression on those that were there to observe it, Spaniard and Nahua alike. Not long afterward, Sahagún would include a mention of it in the *Historia general*, writing "In Tlatelolco a great marvel, a great *neixcuitilli* about the end of the world was performed."[7]

In contrast to the Tlaxomulco play of 1587, the Tlatelolco *Final Judgment* was a product of the urban center, where the newly established Franciscan mission oversaw the introduction of European religious theater as a tool for indoctrinating Spain's new subjects. The play's message was clear: convert or face a terrible judge who will cast the soul into hell. From the urban center, reports of this performance would have radiated outwards, bringing its troubling message to the various altepemeh that ringed the central valley of Mexico. So great was its impact that in the first decades of the next century the famous Nahua annalist don Domingo de San Antón Muñón Chimalpahin Cuauhtlehuanitzin would include it in his record for the year 2 Reed, 1533: "And it was then that a neixcuitilli was performed there in Santiago Tlatelolco, Mexico about how the world will end. The Mexica greatly marveled at it and were frightened."[8]

Since Chimalpahin, numerous chroniclers, historians, and scholars have shown an intense interest in the phenomenon of Indigenous performances of European religious plays. This genre of theater has been referred to using a variety of descriptors, including "missionary theater," "el teatro catequístico" (catechistic theater), and "el teatro de evangelización" (theater of evangelization).[9] However, in the two Nahuatl accounts cited above, Sahagún and Chimalpahin both use the term neixcuitilli to name this particular kind of play. Precisely what sort of performance was the colonial neixcuitilli? Was it simply a European genre transferred to the Americas? A tool of indoctrination? Before we can adequately interpret the two Antichrist plays—which the author also referred to as neixcuitilli—we need to understand how this performance genre came about and what distinguished it from its European and Indigenous antecedents. Since many in-depth studies of this phenomenon have already been written, nothing but a brief summary of its salient features will be offered here.

The emergence of what Sell and Burkhart call the "first truly American theater," like the emergence of alphabetic writing in Indigenous languages previously discussed, must be approached with an eye to two worlds and their fateful collision in the early decades of the sixteenth century.[10] As with Nahuas' ready adoption of alphabetic writing, the existence of certain cultural characteristics prior to contact may have smoothed the way for their adoption of other European cultural forms. Observers from the sixteenth century to the twentieth have similarly turned to precontact Mexica ritual for signs of a nascent "Indigenous theater" that would explain why Indigenous communities adopted the friars' theater of evangelization so swiftly. The sources left to us by the early friar-ethnographers are filled with vivid descriptions of the kind of large-scale state rituals that marked the Mexica calendar prior to contact. Any one of these makes it apparent why comparisons between Mexica ritual and European theater are made. Picking one out of many, Dominican fray Diego Durán's description of the festival known as Atamalcualiztli, "[the time of] the eating of water tamales," will suffice as an illustration:

Regarding the dance in the main *momoztli* of the temple of their great god Huitzilopochtli, they made a house of roses and they made some trees by hand, very full of fragrant flowers, where they seated the goddess Xochiquetzal. While they danced, some boys descended, dressed all like birds, and others, like butterflies, very well adorned with rich feathers, green and blue and red and yellow. They climbed these trees and walked from branch to branch sucking the dew from those roses. Then the gods came out, dressed each with their adornments, just as they were on their altars, the Indians were dressed in the same way and, with their blowguns in hand, they went shooting at the pretend birds that walked through the trees.[11]

A number of salient harmonies between Mexica and European performances can be noted from this description. Like theater in the European tradition, Mexica ritual performances involved costumed actors impersonating sacred beings and enacting sacred narratives before crowds of people. These performances followed established scenarios and patterns of speech and action that echo the scripted performances of Western theater. Similarly, both modes of performance were enacted in public spaces specially dedicated to the event. The account above references something called a momoztli, a type of elevated platform on which sacrifices and ritual displays were performed. In precontact times these were located in the large open plazas in front of pyramids. Other locations included within temples themselves or at the summit of pyramids. This is not unlike the setting of early medieval theater, which was staged first inside the church, then later moved just outside the building. In addition to these "stages," we read that elaborate "sets" were erected that provided a backdrop against (or in) which the action took place. The link between the religious calendar and the Atamalcualiztli performance is also worth noting, since European theater arose in the Middle Ages as a way of celebrating the high feasts of Christmas, Easter, and Corpus Christi. Finally, although it is not mentioned in Durán's description, these ritual performances were important social events that drew communities together and strengthened shared identities through participation in the singing of songs, the enjoyment of the music, and through dancing, feasting, and drinking.

However, despite these similarities, we should be cautious about proclaiming the existence of an "Aztec theater" prior to contact.[12] This is due to the existence of certain fundamental differences between Western notions of theater and Indigenous ritual performances (not the least of which being that many Mexica performances ended with the sacrifice of one or more of their performers!) Indigenous deity impersonators were not "actors" quite in the same way Westerners understand the term and calling their performances "acting" doesn't neatly fit either. While it is tempting to interpret what seem to be stages, props, scenery, costumes, and audience in the Western mode, this is misleading. In referring to cultural phenomena such as the Atamalcualiztli performance as "theater" we open the door to mapping non-Indigenous concepts back onto Indigenous ones. For example, when in the description above we read that "the gods came out, dressed each with their adornments, just as they were on their altars," how are we to understand the nature of this performance? More to the point, how did the Nahua people understand this performance?

Burkhart comments that all performance requires that the performer enter into a kind of "liminal space" where they are "no longer quite themselves, nor are they the character represented."[13] However, in the Western tradition there remains an unspoken but clear distinction between performance and reality. Even in premodern Europe, audiences were well aware of the essential difference between the performance of Christ's death in a Passion play, for example, and the actual Crucifixion of the Savior. Due to critical differences in how Mesoamerican people understood divinity and its embodiment through ritual, and in part due to a metaphysics that was utterly foreign to Europe's, Nahuas simply did not make the same clear distinction between "representer" and "represented." Suffice it to say that understanding the cultural factors that may have conditioned the Antichrist plays and their reception by the imagined audience is fundamental for adequately coming to terms with the plays and their surprising subject matter. This is a theme that will resurface in the final chapter of this study.

James Lockhart explained the adoption of foreign cultural forms by colonial Nahuas by stating "whenever the two cultures ran parallel, the Nahuas would soon adopt the relevant Spanish form without abandoning the essence of their own form."[14] This basic principle has been shown to be true over and over again by ethnohistorians working with colonial documents written by Indigenous people in Indigenous languages. It was certainly true in the case of the friars' introduction of European religious theater. Lockhart and others have also demonstrated that what resulted from these appropriations was much more than a "mixture" or a "blending" of two cultures. Instead, the result was the emergence of wholly new forms in which Nahuas reformulated the European and the Indigenous in ways that made sense in the context of the realities of their existence. Such is the case with the colonial performance genre called the neixcuitilli.

Burkhart posits that the term neixcuitilli was probably chosen by early friars and their Nahua colleagues to translate the Spanish word *ejemplo* or the Latin *exemplum*, meaning "example."[15] In both the classical and medieval traditions, an exemplum was a story that presented an "example" intended to teach an audience a moral lesson. Aesop's Fables are a recognizable illustration from Greek times.[16] In the Middle Ages, printed collections of *exempla* circulated widely, and priests drew from them when composing sermons. Medieval morality plays were essentially performed exempla, where characters representing humankind were tempted by good or evil, and audiences watched as they were made to suffer the consequences of their choices.[17] This connection between the sermon and morality play is relevant since the primary purpose of the New Spanish neixcuitilli—at least in the minds of the friars—was didactic and moralistic. They were intended to teach the basic doctrinal tenets of the Catholic religion and inculcate Christian morality in Indigenous audiences.

As we saw in the Tlaxomulco Nativity, colonial neixcuitilli were performed by casts made up entirely of Indigenous players. Even in instances more closely tied to urban centers and the Franciscans who resided there, these were Indigenous productions through and through. Performances were mostly staged outdoors, taking advantage of the large, walled-in spaces called atria that were built in front of all early colonial churches. This was also necessary to accommodate the large crowds that invariably turned out to witness productions. Nevertheless, colonial Nahuatl theater retained a strong connection to the liturgy: plays were typically performed on Sundays, and mass was celebrated either before or after the performance. When plays were performed during Lent, audiences were urged to participate in the sacrament of confession immediately afterward; in performances that took place during the feast of Corpus Christi, the consecrated Host was often displayed. There are some accounts of plays even being performed inside churches. For example, the *Adoración de los reyes* published by Paso y Troncoso in 1900 indicates that the crèche was located at the altar and that the kings processed down the center aisle bearing their gifts while the mass was in progress.[18] However, ecclesiastical authorities made an effort to ban this practice as early as 1555.[19]

In the early period, all characters were played by men, even female roles, but we know from the sources that eventually women were cast for female roles like the Virgin Mary. Motolinía's report of the Tlaxcala performances of 1538 and 1539 show that neixcuitilli were sometimes staged in elaborate, built environments, with sets that replicated in vivid detail locales like the Garden of Eden and Jerusalem. Many of the scripts that survive contain stage directions that offer further clues about the scenic arts employed by the producers of neixcuitilli. We know, for example, that in some plays heaven was located on a raised platform above the stage and could be accessed by ladders, and hell was located underneath the stage and was accessed through trap doors. From these trap doors demons emerged to snatch sinners and take them off to hell, a scene made all the more visually arresting by the sight of sinners clawing at the edges of the trap door as they were dragged from sight. Actors wore costumes and carried props, performances were accompanied by music, and fireworks were even employed for dramatic effect when demons prowled the stage.

Script production, like so much of religious writing in Indigenous languages, was often, but not exclusively, a collaborative affair between Spanish friars and their Indigenous colleagues. While the genesis of the project, the characters and major plot forms are likely attributable to a friar, most scripts bear the unmistakable marks of Indigenous involvement. These range from characteristically Indigenous spellings of words to the presence of errors in doctrinal or biblical information. The Antichrist scripts contain such errors, which will be discussed later, but what they reveal is that some scripts, even though initially supervised by a friar, at some point left the friar's hands and became Indigenous possessions. Some surviving scripts contain prefatory information that refers to the widespread practice among Indigenous communities of the copying and circulation of neixcuitilli scripts. The important role played by Tlaxomulco's script underscores the importance of scripts that escaped the hands of friars and became the treasured possessions of the Indigenous communities that protected them from generation to generation.

Today, approximately thirty-four complete or fragmentary scripts of colonial neixcuitilli have been identified and are located in archives and libraries in Mexico and the United States.[20] Nearly all of these date to the seventeenth and eighteenth centuries, although is it quite likely that a number of them are copies of scripts that date to earlier times, possibly even the sixteenth century.[21] Up until 2014, there was only one script in the corpus that could be convincingly dated to the sixteenth century, the play that goes by the title *Miercoles santo*, "Holy Wednesday," which dramatizes an exchange between the Virgin Mary and Christ prior to the Crucifixion. Burkhart assigns the date of c. 1591 to this script.[22] I have proposed that Aquino redacted the two Antichrist dramas into his notebook sometime during the period of 1560–1600, which brings the tally of extant sixteenth-century Nahuatl scripts up to at least three. Whereas scripts dating to the later colonial period are valuable means of tracking linguistic and cultural change over time, these sixteenth century scripts allow us to assess colonial Nahuatl writing (and colonial Nahua Christianities) in a much earlier stage of development.

THE ANTICHRIST PLAYS IN CONTEXT

In a general sense all of the surviving colonial neixcuitilli center around religious themes, as would be expected. However, it is possible to group the plays into a number of subgenres. These include biblical plays (such as Tlaxomulco's Epiphany play), saints plays (including a number portraying the legend of the Virgin of Guadalupe), what Sell and Burkhart call the "historical play"[23] (such as one depicting the destruction of Jerusalem by the Romans in 70 CE), and morality plays. Of these, the Antichrist plays are most closely related to the morality plays, as the survey below will demonstrate. However, properly speaking they are mystery plays, a medieval tradition with close ties to the feast of Corpus Christi and medieval Europe.

Theater as we know it in the West developed as an extension of the Christian liturgy. In the year 1264, Pope Urban IV promulgated Corpus Christi, a new feast in the Roman Catholic calendar celebrating the doctrine of the "real presence" of Jesus Christ in the consecrated Eucharistic Host, known as transubstantiation. In 1317, a papal decree required that on the feast of Corpus Christi, the host be brought out of the church and processed through the streets where it could be seen and adored by the faithful. In parts of Europe, Spain in particular, these processions soon evolved into elaborate events of great pageantry that came to include the staging of *tableaux vivants* that recreated important events in the Christian salvation narrative. By the end of the thirteenth century in England, local guilds were sponsoring short, one-act plays where actors portrayed these events for their audiences. This soon grew into lengthy "cycles" of plays performed during Corpus Christi that dramatized the great "mysteries" of God's creation from the Fall to the End of Time (see figure 1.2). Although these "mystery cycles" were also performed in France and Spain, the only surviving complete examples come from England. There, cycles such as the one associated with the town of York, could contain upwards of three dozen individual plays that were enacted over days during Corpus celebrations. Since they covered Christian history from beginning to end, most mystery cycles concluded with dramatizations of the Final Judgment. Tellingly, the mystery cycle from the town of Chester also includes two plays dealing with the legend of the Antichrist.

Although it wasn't a large genre, Antichrist dramas were fairly common in medieval Europe. Klaus Aichele's *Antichristdrama*, the most comprehensive catalog of medieval Antichrist plays to date, identifies seventeen from the medieval period, twelve dating to the Reformation, and fourteen to the Counter-Reformation period.[24] Although the figure of the Antichrist would make appearances in other play genres, most notably certain Final Judgment plays, true Antichrist dramas focused exclusively on the life and career of the Son of Perdition. Some, like the extensive Middle French *Jour du jugement*, narrated the entire life of the Antichrist from prophecies of his advent to his conception, birth, education, career, and death.[25] Others focused primarily on his career, the most famously example being the twelfth-century German play *Ludus de Antechristo*. Frequently these plays narrated the efforts the Antichrist makes to deceive the faithful, relying on the legend's standard set of three methods: enticement with gifts, threats of violence, and the performance of false miracles. Antichrist dramas also introduced characters representing the Jews who, according to the legend, would be the first to fall prey to the Antichrist's lies. The Old Testament prophets Elijah and Enoch are universally present in the plays examined for this study. They preach against the Antichrist, urging

FIGURE 1.2. Representation of a fifteenth-century Passion play, Coventry, England. Frontispiece in Thomas Sharp, *A Dissertation on the Pageants Or Dramatic Mysteries Anciently Performed at Coventry, by the Trading Companies of that City* (Coventry: Merridew and Son, 1825).

those who have been deceived to return to the faith and, having some effect, are in the end killed by the Antichrist or his servants. Some plays, particularly the German ones, incorporated the legend of the Last World Emperor, a powerful Christian ruler who opposes the Antichrist in accordance with the prophecies of the Tiburtine Sibyl and an ancient apocalyptic text known as the Pseudo-Methodius. Demons are frequent members of the cast. In the *Jour du jugement* they convene in a "parliament of hell" to plan for the coming of the Antichrist.[26] In the Chester play "The Coming of Antichrist" they bear off the slain body of the Antichrist to hell.[27]

In the German *Churer weltgerichtsspiel* demons appear to be associated with the seven deadly sins.[28]

Notably absent from Aichele's list are any Antichrist dramas that originate in Spain. Research for this study included extensive efforts to identify a Spanish example that predates Juan Ruiz de Alarcón's Golden Age play *El anticristo*, an important Antichrist drama but one that is too late to be considered the source of the Nahuatl *neixcuitilli* discussed here. None of the four volumes of Léo Rouanet's extensive catalog *Autos, farsas y coloquios del siglo XVI* contains an Antichrist drama.[29] Hilaire Kellendorf, who consulted over eight hundred Spanish plays for her book *Sins of the Fathers*, reported that she has not encountered a single Antichrist drama predating the seventeenth century.[30] Richard K. Emmerson, author of numerous studies of the medieval Antichrist legend, similarly came up empty-handed when asked this question.[31] This quest resulted in only a single reference to a Spanish Antichrist play, one titled *Auto de la venida del ante Christo* which seems to have dated to 1585.[32] Although efforts to locate a copy of this play have been fruitless, this reference offers some meager evidence that pre-Alarconian Spanish Antichrist dramas existed at one time. However, the profusion of Antichrist literature in Spain during the fourteenth through the sixteenth centuries, together with the demonstrable popularity of the theme in religious theater outside of Spain, strongly suggests that such plays did exist, even if surviving evidence is scant.

From this examination of extant Antichrist play scripts, it is clear that they shared certain common features with morality plays. Rather than narrating aspects of Christian history or legend, medieval moralities centered around a character or characters who represented humanity and the struggle to choose good from evil. In a famous English morality of the late-fifteenth century, this character simply bears the name Everyman. Other cast members often took the form of allegorical figures such as *Everyman*'s "Death," "Good Deeds," "Knowledge," and "Confession." Whereas the medieval mystery play brought biblical narratives to life, the purpose of moralities was to impress the Roman Catholic Church's moral code upon the population. Morality plays depicted their central characters as being caught in a supernatural battle for the souls of humans in which demons did the bidding of Satan and angels that of God. We see characters pulled this way and that, placed into situations where they are tempted to break God's commands. This they often do, and must therefore face a terrifying judgment before Christ that inevitably ended with their being condemned to hell for all eternity. The obvious intent was to present audiences with a frightening vision of their own future and so inspire them to amend their ways in the present. Performed during Lent, the season of penance and preparation before Easter, morality plays were written inducements to participate in the sacrament of confession.

The two plays presented at the end of this study, *Antichrist and the Final Judgment* (hereafter referred to as Aquino's *Final Judgment* to avoid confusing it with other plays of this variety) and *Antichrist and the Hermit* (hereafter *Hermit*),[33] bear close resemblance to both medieval mystery plays and moralities. In some respects, Aquino's *Final Judgment* most closely aligns with the depictions of doomsday often associated with mystery plays. It is a straightforward narrative of the Antichrist legend, which is then followed by the standard representation of the Final Judgment. The combination of both narratives into a single play was relatively rare in the medieval tradition, but there are surviving examples.[34] *Hermit*, on the other hand, is something of a hybrid whose complex intertextuality with Aquino's *Final Judgment* will be discussed below. It begins in the vein of a mystery play, with a second presentation of the life and career of the Antichrist. However, midway through, it pivots in the direction of the moralities for the extended scene where seven demons and the souls of eighteen sinners are paraded on stage to confess their sinful behavior to the audience. Here the emphasis is clearly on confession, and each condemned soul bemoans not having availed themselves of this life-saving sacrament before death shut the door of opportunity. In light of these peculiarities, it is therefore not a simple matter associating the Antichrist plays with the rest of the corpus of surviving neixcuitilli.[35]

However, if we extend our field of view beyond the matter of subject alone, the connection becomes clearer. Both of the Nahuatl Antichrist plays share the same "bleak moral vision" of "human frailty, demonic temptation, angelic despair, and sudden death" that is associated with those Nahuatl plays that belong to the morality genre.[36] Additionally, they operate in a common didactic mode where elements of doctrine are woven into the narrative through speeches or "sermonettes" addressed directly to the audience. Like their European counterparts, the Nahuatl morality plays wield a blunt rhetorical instrument in order to persuade their audiences. That instrument is terror, most commonly inspired by visions of hell and punishment. Finally, in employing terror, the Antichrist plays and their seven cousins share a common telos: the confession of sin. Therefore, in light of these similarities, what follows is a comparative analysis of Aquino's *Final Judgment* and *Hermit* and the seven extant Nahuatl morality plays. These seven bear the following titles in the *Nahuatl Theater* set: *Souls and Testamentary Executors* (hereafter *Souls*), *Final Judgment* (*Judgment*), *How to Live on Earth* (*How to Live*), *The Merchant* (*Merchant*), *The Life of Don Sebastián* (*Don Sebastián*), *The Nobleman and his Barren Wife* (*Nobleman*), and *Don Rafael* (*Don Rafael*).

As a way of illustrating the characteristics outlined above and the degree to which the Antichrist dramas align with the other seven Nahuatl moralities, consider the following two extended quotes. Both are drawn from the very first lines of two plays, the anonymous *Judgment* (*not* the one redacted by Aquino) and the second of Aquino's Antichrist plays, *Hermit*. These two speeches encapsulate the "bleak moral vision" characteristic of the genre as well as their didacticism, the rhetoric of fear, and the desired outcome of confession. At the beginning of *Judgment*, a Nahua actor playing the archangel Michael steps onto the stage and addresses the audience with these words:

> O creations of God! Know, and indeed you already know, for it is in the sacred commands of our Lord God he will destroy, he will finish off all that he made, the various birds, the various living creatures, along with you. He will destroy you, you people of the world. But be certain that the dead will revive. The good and proper ones who served the just judge, the sentencer, God, he will take his royal home, the place of eternal and utter bliss, glory, the place of utter bliss of all the male and female saints. But the bad ones who did not serve our Lord God, may they be certain that they will merit suffering in the place of the dead. So then, weep, remember it. Fear it, be scared to death, for the day of judgment will happen to you. It is very frightening, it is very shocking, it scares people to death, it makes people faint with fright. So then, emend your lives. The day of judgment is about to happen to you. It is the time, it is the moment, now.[37]

In Aquino's *Hermit*, the first character on stage is an actor portraying a sibyl, a pagan oracle that medieval tradition imagined as having predicted the return of Christ at the end of time. Also addressing herself to the audience, she begins:

> O my children, please look here! . . . You will know that by his command Only Deity, God, has sent me to say to you that the whole world will end. There will be dying everywhere, nothing will be left behind for it will all be burned. But before the world ends, first a wicked person will come, will be born whose name will be Antichrist. But in order to thoroughly deceive you he will call himself Christ. However, he is really just a were-owl [demon].[38] He will come to give you gold and cloaks, etc. So that you will go with him, he will say to you, "I am Christ," and with this he will deceive you. He will cause those who obey him to marvel. The bad ones will believe in him alone, and the good Christians will die for God in order to go to the heavens. Today, O my children, take strength! Do not accept anything he gives you so that you will not go suffering forever with him in Mictlan [hell]. Strengthen yourselves so that you will die for God (f. 155r–156r).

The medieval morality play has been referred to by more than a few scholars as an example of the *sermo corporeus*, "embodied sermon."[39] Indeed, it is not difficult to hear the words of a preacher in the speeches uttered by St. Michael and Sibyl, quoted above. If on one level these plays are operating in the realm of homiletics, what then is the sermon's argument, and how has that argument been structured? Recalling that morality plays were proper to the Lenten season and were employed as instruments to persuade Christians to confess their sins gets us close to an answer. The "sermon" that was "embodied" by the plot and characters of a morality play centered around sin, its consequences on the lives of the faithful, and the means by which it may be removed. The way that morality plays deliver this message is through bringing to the stage a variety of characters who serve as individual exempla, their words and actions embodying the church's teaching on the kind of virtuous moral behavior to be imitated and wicked behavior to be eschewed.

Judging by the Nahuatl-language sermons and catechisms the friars left behind, sixteenth-century Nahuas would have heard a great deal about sin and its consequences. In particular, the seven deadly sins, or *in temictiani tlahtlacolli* (sins that kill people) featured prominently in the corpus of ecclesiastical Nahuatl materials. Franciscan friar Alonso de Molina and his Nahua colleagues, whose 1546 catechism was the first one printed in Nahuatl, summarized the church's theology of sin and punishment as well as the "remedy" by which the faithful could be saved. They begin a short sermon on the seven deadly sins by writing, "Deadly sins [in temictiani tlahtlacolli] are those by means of which we break God's commands."[40] They continue, "They are called deadly sins because they kill the body and the soul, and because of this he will suffer forever in Mictlan." In the church's theology of salvation, sin represents the ultimate impediment to redemption and is the cause of eternal damnation. There simply can be no salvation unless the problem of sin is dealt with. Regarding the remedy for sin, Molina and his Nahua colleagues explain, "But if the sinner is very sorry for all of his sins, and if he firmly determines never again to commit them, and if he determines to confess when commanded by the Holy Church," then they will enjoy all the happiness of those who merit God's mercy.[41] In a sense, the church's teaching on the capital sins establishes the entire rationale for the morality play, essentially providing a plot structure that was replicated in both medieval and Nahuatl moralities: sinners break God's commands, they are given the opportunity to avail themselves of the church's remedy, they refuse due to their moral weakness, and when they must ultimately stand before Christ, they are judged unworthy and cast into hell's eternal flame.

The modeling of virtuous behavior is common to the Antichrist plays as well as the other moralities in the Nahuatl corpus. In *How to Live*, a Nahua named Lorenzo properly models the desire to go to mass, saying "Let us enter [God's] home every day," and the necessity of praying to the Virgin Mary, "Let us pray to God's beloved mother that for our sake she pray to her beloved child"; in *Souls*, don Pedro laments the fate of the departed and correctly suggests the church's prescribed response, declaring "Let us go make a prayer for the dead for the sake of the souls who are suffering in purgatory so that God will have pity on them where they lie fallen"; and in *Merchant*, Priest advises the dying Sick Man with the words, "Go to the home of

God, confess, prepare yourself, receive the precious honored body of your beloved savior, Jesus Christ."[42] In a similar way, virtuous behavior is modeled by characters representing the victims of Antichrist's[43] campaign of deception in Aquino's *Hermit*: one named Martyr rebuffs Antichrist's enticements with the words, "I absolutely do not want your bribes! I want to live suffering for the true God so that he will have mercy on me, so that I will merit the joy of the heavens"; a group of converts correctly recognizes his evil lies, declaring, "You are not the deity, you are just a coyote!"; some of these even model their righteousness by accepting death at the hand of Antichrist, crying "O our Lord! O God! O Jesus Christ! Receive us into your home."[44]

However, it is the characters who model the vices who are the true stars of both medieval and Nahuatl morality plays. Playwrights spared no detail in highlighting the behavior of sinful characters who served as exempla of moral corruption for their assembled audiences. The character Merchant demonstrates both greed and cruelty by charging excessive interest and reneging on his contracts, don Sebastián plots to murder his wife, Nobleman's Wife scoffs at the idea of bearing children ("they are really disgraceful, annoying, dirtying, and corrupting the way they cry and the way they pee in front of people!"[45]), and Lucía indulges her lust by fornicating with multiple partners and rejecting Christian marriage. In *Hermit*, the author picks up and runs with this theme, envisioning a parade of twenty-five characters, each of which is associated with a specific category of sin. These characters bear the titles of a wide variety of social types common in colonial Nahua society, each one displaying their own vices. Types include Day Keeper (Tonalpouhqui), who sins by performing false divinations to deceive people, Ruler (Tlahtoani), whose vices include pride and abusing his subjects, and Merchant (Pochtecatl), who steals people's property and charges them excessive interest. In representing universal human and social types, Aquino's Antichrist plays and the other Nahuatl moralities are following a well-established pattern in medieval morality and doomsday plays.[46] Characters like Nobleman, Young Man, and Merchant—not to mention Day Keeper and Healer—were not intended to portray specific individuals as much as types that could be found in any altepetl across New Spain. David Leigh points out that this practice allowed the audience to "find itself on stage" and thereby more closely identify those characters' sins with their own.[47]

In all the Nahuatl moralities, including those presented here, these flawed human characters are goaded on by demons who tempt and torment their human victims, often providing some comic relief to the dour business at hand. In the medieval tradition, these demons could be accompanied by personifications of the seven deadly sins. Characters bearing the names Pride, Avarice, Envy, Wrath, Lust, Gluttony, and Sloth can be found in a fifteenth-century French play titled *Lo jutgamen general* and in an early sixteenth-century doomsday play from the German town of Chur. In a French morality play from the fifteenth century, titled *La moralité des sept péchés mortels et des sept vertus*, characters representing the seven deadly sins clash with characters representing the corresponding seven virtues.[48] In certain instances, demons themselves were associated with specific deadly sins. Emmerson and Hult report that in the French *Jutgamen general*, each of the deadly sins' personifications are accompanied by "a corresponding devil" (see figure 1.3).[49] While demons are common to all seven of the Nahuatl moralities published in the *Nahuatl Theater* set, none of those plays contain personifications of the deadly sins nor are their demons associated with specific deadly sins. However, this is precisely the tradition drawn upon in the composition of Aquino's *Hermit*, where the author brings to the stage seven demons representing the seven deadly sins. In a twist that constitutes one of the play's most original local adaptations, the author identifies six of these demons as precontact Nahua *teteoh* like the two mentioned in the prologue, Tezcatlipoca and Huitzilopochtli.

Finding oneself on stage was made all the more frightening by the way that the Nahuatl moralities detailed the punishments inflicted on wicked characters due to their sins. These descriptions served to drive home the church's theology of sin by displaying in graphic detail the pain and suffering that would result from the failure to confess and receive absolution. José Guadalajara Medina refers to this strategy as "didactic terror": the use of terrifying imagery with the intent to teach tenets of Christian doctrine and produce the desired outcomes of repentance and conversion.[50] This approach was near universal in the preaching and teaching of the missionary friars, especially the Franciscans. From sermons to catechisms, from devotional texts to songs, and from mural paintings in open-air chapels to sculpted friezes, terror was the dominant modality of the indoctrination of New Spain's Indigenous people.

One of the best examples of didactic terror from the Nahuatl moralities is the shocking depiction of the fate suffered by Barren One in *The Nobleman and His Barren Wife*. Due to her vanity and worldliness, this unfortunate soul has been condemned to hell. In order to make a proper exemplum out of her, demons have brought her out of hell (probably up through a trap door in the stage), to stand before the audience. In order to make the scene more terrifying, the stage directions indicate that "a snake is lying on her head, fire lizards are sucking on her [breasts], fire dogs are biting her feet, and she has fire butterflies on her blouse. And fire arrows are coming out of her ears."[51] At this sight, Priest is so frightened that he cries out, "Jesus! Jesus! Jesus!" and demands that she explain the meaning of her torment. Barren One explains that the creature on her head is punishment for having spent so much time on her hair, the fire lizards emerging from her ears torment

FIGURE 1.3. Demons representing the seven deadly sins by Hans Baldung-Grien. From Johannes Geiler von Kaysersberg, *Das Buch Granatapfel* (1511).

her because she adorned herself vainly with earrings, and the fire butterflies that "suck my breasts stand for how I never suckled anyone here on earth," meaning she never bore any children. She concludes her speech with a final admonition to the audience that lays bare the exemplary didacticism of the genre, "O beloved of God [referring to the character Priest], teach this to others so that no one does the same thing. Let my neighbors learn a lesson from me, the wicked women who are here, so that they do not do the same thing."[52]

This short, embodied sermon, this live-action exemplum, is precisely the format that the author of *Antichrist and the Hermit* replicated in the speeches of the eighteen condemned souls that dominate the final two-thirds of the play. Only the briefest comparison will be necessary to make this clear. At one point in the final scene, the author imagined an interaction between Hermit and a soul named Martín who has been brought back from hell for his moment in the spotlight. Acting as inquisitor, Hermit demands to know why Martín went to hell. Martín responds, "Because I slept with a woman who was my relative. As a result I deeply offended God, as a result he cast me into Mictlan because I did not confess. And my relative also went to Mictlan because of me. Even though I forced her, I just did not confess [and therefore] both of us are continually burning. Likewise, some others who are there go along whipping me. There are many [there] who had sex with their relatives. This is my very great sin" (f. 185r). With that, Hermit sends him back to hell crying, "Please go, you wicked one!" As in a number of other instances, before moving on to the next sinner, Hermit concludes by addressing the audience saying, *Auh ynin macayac yvhqui q[ui]chivaz.* "Furthermore, don't anyone do this!"

The comparisons cited above clearly establish the links between the Antichrist dramas and the seven surviving morality plays of the corpus. However, as similar as they are, they also introduce something new into this history of Nahuatl theater: the Nahuatl mystery play, and more precisely, the Nahuatl Antichrist drama. This unique choice of subject matter—a subject that was almost universally avoided by the friars—raises a number of questions. For that matter, so do the author's decisions to imagine demons in the form of Nahua teteoh and to include so much detailed information about Indigenous religious practices in plays whose overt goal seems to have been aligned with the systematic program to eradicate them. Questions are also raised about what specific role Aquino played in the creation of the plays. Did he generate these ideas on his own or was he working with a friar? If he was working alone, did he have a source text, either a play script or other sources of information about the legend of Antichrist? These questions allow us now to pivot to an examination of the significant ways the Nahuatl Antichrist dramas secreted within Aquino's devotional notebook differ from the other surviving scripts in the corpus of colonial Nahuatl theater.

FABIÁN DE AQUINO'S IDIOSYNCRATIC NEIXCUITILLI

One of the most striking differences between the two neixcuitilli Aquino included in his notebook and the other thirty-odd scripts in the corpus of colonial Nahuatl theater is the subject matter: the medieval legend of the Antichrist. At the outset of research for this study, I fully expected to encounter the Antichrist in Nahuatl doctrinal and homiletic writing, especially in texts authored or supervised by Franciscans. There were plenty of reasons for such an expectation, not the least of which was the supposed millenarianism of the Franciscans who were New Spain's earliest and most fervent missionaries. This narrative has been a standard feature of the historiography since at least 1970 when John Leddy Phelan published *The Millennial Kingdom of the Franciscans in the New World*. While his interpretation has been updated since then, it is difficult to challenge the thesis that the Franciscan mission in the Americas was by nature fundamentally eschatological in the sense that they viewed their work as a necessary, final step preceding the second coming of Christ and the end of the world. There are excellent treatments of this narrative to which one can turn.[53] Other studies have also established strong connections between medieval Antichrist treatises and the vein of Joachimite apocalypticism that played such a profound role in shaping the Spiritual and Observant branches of the Franciscan order from the late twelfth through the early sixteenth centuries.[54] Taken together, the links between New Spain's Franciscans, Joachimite apocalypticism, and Antichrist narratives should predict an active presence of the Antichrist in the doctrinal writings of early colonial Mexico's mendicant missionaries. However, my survey of this body of literature showed that the two neixcuitilli collected by Aquino are the only known treatments of the legend of the Antichrist in the Nahuatl language from the period when Nahuatl literary production peaked, c. 1540–1640. In fact, since this body of literature represents some of the earliest writing in all the Americas, it is quite possible that these plays are the earliest extant manifestations of the Antichrist legend in the Western Hemisphere.

To be fair, the Antichrist is not entirely absent from the writings of New Spain's Franciscans, Dominicans, Augustinians, and their Nahua colleagues. To date, I have located six brief mentions of the Antichrist in the literature, one of these being the Antichrist character in the well-known neixcuitilli referred to as *Final Judgment* in the Sell and Burkhart collection.[55] However, these six tend to be relatively brief appearances, and none of them engage in a full narration of the rich and multi-faceted legend that was so much a part of the medieval apocalyptic mindset. One example will suffice to illustrate. In Fray Juan Bautista's devotional work titled *Libro de la miseria y breuedad de la vida del hombre*, published in 1604, in Book 3, chapter 2, he addresses the signs that will appear before Judgment Day.[56] One of the signs he discusses is the coming of the Antichrist, who he refers to as the *itetótocacauh in itecocolicauh . . . iteyaochiuhcauh*, "the persecutor, tormenter [and] attacker" of the church.[57] He mentions that the Antichrist will work many *tetzauhtlamahuiçolli*, "ominous marvels," and will persecute the one called Martyr to the point of death.

However, this passage amounts to no more than about 120 words, or half a folio, of Bautista's text. And this is the longest and most detailed Antichrist passage I have identified to date. Absent from Bautista's account are any of the signs that are supposed to predict his coming, any mention of the interventions of Elijah and Enoch, any details about the kinds of false miracles he will work, or how he will meet his end at the tip of St. Michael's sword. So, while it would be technically inaccurate to say that the Antichrist played no role whatsoever in the Nahuatl-Christian literature, it seems that in traversing the Atlantic, the Antichrist went from holding center stage to being relegated to the wings of Nahuatl-Christian discourse in sixteenth-century New Spain. This makes the author's decision to compose not one but two full-length neixcuitilli starring the Antichrist all the more surprising and noteworthy. That this popular legend should make its American debut on the Nahuatl stage and from the pen of an Indigenous author only compounds the significance of these pieces coming to light after so many years of silence.

The second glaring difference between the two Antichrist dramas and the other scripts in the Nahuatl theater corpus has to do with what can be referred to as the plays' ethnographic content. Along with the decision to dramatize the Antichrist legend, the inclusion of detailed information about Indigenous religious practices constitutes one of the plays' greatest surprises. Although both Aquino's *Final Judgment* and *Hermit* contain such content, it is *Hermit* that holds the most. We are made aware of these cultural details by means of *Hermit*'s interrogation of the seven demons associated with the seven deadly sins and the eighteen condemned souls he calls forth from hell to serve as living exempla. Over the course of these twenty-five interactions, the characters questioned by Hermit mention numerous elements of Indigenous religion, presented in table 1.1.

This list is all the more remarkable when contrasted with the other plays in the Nahuatl theater corpus. When those plays' characters divulge their sins, they invariably focus on transgressions of specific church teachings, teachings intended to replace precontact beliefs and practices. But they are careful not to mention any illicit pagan beliefs and practices by name. For example, in *Judgment* Lucía confesses "I used to scoff at the holy sacrament [and] marrying in a sacred way [i.e., monogamous Christian marriage]"; in *Nobleman* Barren One laments "I used to receive [communion] while I was concealing a sin from my confessors because of shame"; and in *Don Raphael* Condemned Man admits "I always used to see the exemplary models [neixcuitilli] our mother holy church would show to people, but I used to laugh at them, I used to say that maybe they weren't true."[58] In contrast, when the star of Aquino's *Hermit* asks Fire Priests why they ended up in hell, they state "we used to cut open people's chests with flint knives and kill people in front of our teteoh"; Otonteuctli confesses to Hermit that "the common people

TABLE 1.1. Elements of Indigenous religion mentioned in *Antichrist and the Hermit*

Character	Elements of Indigenous religion
Huitzilopochtli	» important calendrical ritual mentioned but not by name (perhaps Toxcatl or Panquetzaliztli?) » deity's impersonator (*teixiptla*) also mentioned
Quetzalcoatl·	» ritual bloodletting (auto-sacrifice)
Otontecuhtli	» important calendrical ritual mentioned but not by name (most likely Xocotl huetzi) » erecting the sacred Xocotl tree » ritual dancing
Cihuacoatl	» ritual cannibalism? or human sacrifice » priestly auto-sacrifice
Year Keepers (Indigenous priests)	» ritual offerings » deity impersonators (*teixiptlahuan*) » heart sacrifice with flint knives » blowing of conch-shell trumpets » auto-sacrifice » ritual use of blood of sacrificial victims » ritual sweeping of temples
Unbelievers (Nahuas who refused to convert)	» practice of keeping effigies of *teteoh* » auto-sacrifice » ritual burning of paper » offering of incense
Day Keeper (Tonalpouhqui)	» use of divinatory codex (*tonalamatl*) » divination (ritual naming of newborns)
Healer (Ticitl)	» ritual healing » divination by casting maize kernels » preparation of medicinal infusions (e.g., abortifacients)
One Who Sterilizes Herself	» procurement of the services of a traditional healer

(macehualtin) used to take me for a deity, they used to celebrate a feast in my honor. They used to raise a tree called the guava tree before me. Then the young men and women danced before me"; and two "unbelievers" explain their lack of faith by blaming "the serpent that we used to follow as a deity, he before whom we bled ourselves and before whom we burned papers and before whom we offered incense" (ff. 175r, 172r–v, 177r).

None of the other surviving scripts come anywhere near this degree of specificity when discussing precontact religion and culture. The reason why is simple: information like that which is presented above was exactly the kind of Indigenous knowledge the church was actively seeking to suppress at the time. In fact, the very existence of Indigenous-language theater was considered highly suspect by ecclesiastical authorities due to fears that unless they were closely supervised, neixcuitilli might result in heterodox performances. At a time when the church was growing increasingly anxious about the persistence of Indigenous religious practices, content of the sort included in Aquino's plays was deemed dangerous and could potentially expose the author and his text to censure or worse. During the second half of the sixteenth century, precisely the period during which this study argues Aquino copied the plays into his notebook, there were numerous ecclesiastical pronouncements banning Indigenous-language writing under certain circumstances, as well as confiscations of manuscripts due to content deemed at risk of perpetuating Indigenous "superstitions." Perhaps the most famous example was the aforementioned confiscation of Fray Bernardino de Sahagún's *Historia general* in 1577. In the royal decree mandating the confiscation of the friar's cultural encyclopedia, the Crown issued the following directive to colonial authorities: "You are warned not to consent in any way to any person writing things that touch on the superstitions and the ways of living that these Indians had, in any language."[59] In this context, both the subject matter and the contents of Aquino's neixcuitilli would have been deemed unconventional at best, and at worst, could be considered running counter to the express command of church and Crown.

The striking choice of subject matter and the inclusion of highly suspect content return us once again to the question of authorship and to the related question of source texts. What is the correct way of understanding how these plays came into existence? Starting with the latter, two basic options become clear: either there was a source text, perhaps a Spanish Antichrist and Final Judgment play provided by the friars, or there wasn't. If there wasn't, then someone with knowledge of medieval theater and the relevant Antichrist literature had to have compose the plays from scratch. If there was a source text, then the question becomes not one of authorship but of translation, and we ought to speak of their originator as the translator of the plays rather than their author. However, every translator exerts a different degree of influence over their source in the process of translation. We have to imagine a spectrum of intervention in the source text, beginning with a very minimal intervention on the one hand and progressing to a more robust intervention. At the robust end of the spectrum, it seems to me to be more appropriate to refer to the plays as adaptations rather than mere translations. If we rule out a source text and argue that the plays were composed from scratch, then we are talking about authorship of the scripts. Finally, whether we are talking about identifying a translator, an adaptor, or an author of the two Nahuatl Antichrist plays, we ought to ask whether the person in question was a Spaniard or a Nahua.

This chapter concludes by offering the best answer to these thorny questions that can be given at this point. In doing so, it is important to note that there will likely be readers who challenge these hypotheses and propose alternative scenarios that could prove more convincing. The truth is that we may never truly know the precise details surrounding who wrote these marvelous works of literature. What is presented here is the result of years of thinking, researching, and talking with colleagues in an effort to draw closer to knowing Fabián de Aquino and the circumstances under which he came to redact these two Nahuatl Antichrist dramas.

Regarding the question of whether there was a source text or not, it most likely that the originator of the plays had access to a script of a Spanish play that dramatized the career of the Antichrist and the Final Judgment. This he creatively adapted (rather than translated or composed) for the Nahuatl stage to produce the first play in Aquino's notebook, referred to here as *Antichrist and the Final Judgment*. This play probably represents his first attempt to create a Nahuatl version of his source text. In this version he hued more closely to his source, retaining the same general plot structure and characters. The introduction to the play that precedes the opening scene (ff. 131r–133r) represents his highly ambitious plan for his adaptation. In it he lists all the characters that will be required, adapting his source text's cast of demons representing the seven deadly sins so that they now become Nahua deities and expanding and adapting the cast of condemned souls to include members of Nahua society. One possible scenario imagines that sometime during the writing process he decided to compress the scenes involving Hermit and the demons and remove the interrogation of the damned souls so as to proceed directly to the Final Judgment (ff. 143r–144v). Perhaps he did this because he sensed the play was growing too long. Whatever the case may be, this may have left him desirous of realizing his creative vision for these excised parts, and so he set about writing a second play upon completion of the first. In order to ensure that he had space for the material passed over in the first play, he shortened the Antichrist narrative in the second. However, by the time he approached the end of the long sequence involving the damned souls, he may have realized that this play, too, had grown too long and decided to end it before introducing the Final Judgment sequence. In sum, this proposed scenario would classify *Final Judgment* as a more faithful adaptation of the hypothesized source text and *Hermit* as a highly original adaptation based on the first.

Moving on to the question of the identity of the plays' adaptor, I can be stated with confidence that both plays were adapted by an Indigenous person and not a Spanish friar. (There is absolutely no doubt that the plays were redacted by an Indigenous *writer*, who may or may not have also been the composer.) The evidence that most strongly supports this assessment is the presence of such a great deal of detailed information about precontact religious practices like human sacrifice, bloodletting, and ritual divination. These were practices that the entire weight of the Catholic mission was bent on eradicating, inclusion of this content in other writings got those texts banned and confiscated, and detailed mention of these practices was largely expunged from the official writings of the church. Outside of the ethnographic sources produced under the direction of friars like Olmos and Sahagún, content such as we have in *Hermit* is exceptionally rare in religious writings overseen by Spaniards. Therefore, it is very difficult to imagine that scripts such as these could have been written by a friar or to imagine that if the scripts had ever come to the attention of a friar that they wouldn't immediately have been seized.

The same holds true for the highly unusual—indeed, one of a kind—decision to bring characters to the Nahuatl stage representing the Nahua teteoh Tlaloc, Tezcatlipoca, Huitzilopochtli, Quetzalcoatl, Otontecuhtli, and Cihuacoatl. Again, outside of the ethnographic sources even the mention of these entities by name was largely taboo in the Nahuatl religious literature.[60] Instead, friars employed the rhetorical strategy of diabolization, transforming deities into devils, and only referring to them as generically as *demonios, diablos*, and their preferred Nahuatl equivalent, *tlatlacatecoloh* (were-owls). Even in the ethnographic writing, when Nahua deities are mentioned, the authors make sure to clarify their "true" identities. In the Codex Magliabechiano for example, each of the beautifully drawn teteoh is glossed with a statement that begins with the words *Este demonio se llamaba*, "This demon was called" (see figure 1.4).[61] The unique way theater brought Christian doctrine to life, embodying teachings in the form of living, breathing actors, presented a risk of which ecclesiastical authorities were well aware. If even performances of Nativities and Passions could fall under suspicion, how what do we imagine the response would have been to performances involving Huitzilopochtli or Tezcatlipoca? The fact that the author condemned these characters to hell and used them as exempla of immoral behavior would not have mattered in the eyes of ecclesiastics sensitive to the way Indigenous people tended to blur the lines between "representer" and "represented." Indigenous authorship seems to me the most logical way to explain the decision to bring these six characters to the colonial Nahuatl stage.

The presence of biblical and doctrinal incongruities is another marker of Indigenous authorship. In the scene where Hermit interrogates Cuiloni (roughly, "homosexual"),[62] the author confuses the story of the Flood with the destruction of Sodom and Gomorrah, eliding the two. He explains that God hates this particular sin above all others, stating "this was the reason that long ago the flood spread over the world. Everyone was carried away by the water, they died by the water because they went around doing *cuiloni*. By God's command only eight were saved in the boat. And one person, God's beloved, was saved along with his two children. His name was Lot" (f. 185v–186r). The church has always taught that the sin of sodomy was what was behind God's decision to destroy Sodom, hence the origin of that

FIGURE 1.4. "Este demonio se llamaba." Author's line drawing based on the original in Codex Magliabechiano, central Mexico, ca. 1529–1553, f. 55v–56r.

particular act's name. But here the author seems to believe that either sodomy was the sin responsible for the Flood or that Lot and his children were on the ark with Noah and his family. Either way, it is both highly unlikely that a friar would have made this mistake and that if the script had ever been reviewed that this mistake would have been caught and corrected.

However, that does not mean that no friar had any hand whatsoever in the plays' genesis. Friars routinely devised translation projects that were then handed off to a Nahua colleague or colleagues for execution. Of course, we should also assume that some Nahuas conceived of their own projects or collaborated with friars to jointly brainstorm new projects. Lockhart envisions a scenario that attempts to explain how the *Miercoles santo* play in particular came about. He begins with the assumption that the friars were ultimately the ones responsible for the selecting subject matter for Nahuatl plays and dictating key aspects of their plots and characters. He ponders the question of whether the friars would have written this information down on paper and passed it along to Nahua writers or just communicated it orally in a mixture of Spanish and Nahuatl. However, he also notes that none of the text's many spelling mistakes or "theological irregularities" were ever corrected, which suggests that after handing off the project to Nahuas, the friar left it to them to decide how to translate the text. He concludes by writing, "In a word, the *Holy Wednesday* script confirms ultimate Spanish authorship and sponsorship as well as a large field of Nahua discretion and independence in translation, extending to numerous adaptations and additions."[63]

This scenario could quite possibly be the one that explains the genesis of the two Nahuatl Antichrist plays. The next chapter will argue that the inspiration for the plays came from a series of dramatic and disturbing events early in the history of the Mexican church. It would have been just as likely that a Franciscan would have imagined the Antichrist's coming in these events as a Nahua, perhaps more so. Coupled with the theory that the Nahua adapter was working from a source text—a text he would only have gained access to with the approval of the friars—also tilts us in the direction of the scenario outlined by Lockhart. However, regardless of whether it was an apocalyptic-minded friar or a like-minded Nahua who had the first inspiration to create a neixcuitilli about the Antichrist, once the project was in the Nahua's hands it took off in directions that would have troubled its Franciscan originator.

If this chapter has succeeded in making the case that the one who adapted the plays was a Nahua, this still leaves the question of whether or not that Nahua was Fabián de Aquino. Regrettably, at this point it is impossible to say for certain whether or not it was Aquino who adapted the plays himself, or some anonymous Nahua who preceded him. There is some evidence that can be cited which, at a minimum, makes Aquino seem like a likely candidate. For one, the plays are written in his own hand. This is made evident by a comparison between the hand that redacted the two scripts and that of any one of the four other texts that bear his signature. Next, the previous chapter argued that Aquino composed (not adapted or translated) at least one other text in the notebook, which suggests he possessed the degree of creativity and originality that we would expect as well as the inclination to do so. And finally, there is his predilection for eschatological and apocalyptic themes, which is manifest in other texts scattered throughout the three hundred folios of his notebook. However, none of this comes anywhere near constituting definitive proof, so we must entertain the possibility that Aquino merely collected the scripts, copying them into his notebook. This in turn this opens up the tantalizing possibility that the original adaptations were produced during the decades leading up to the *terminus post quem* of 1560. This would move the scripts back into the formative decades of alphabetic writing in Nahuatl, a period from which precious few Nahuatl texts have come to light.

The identity of the Nahua who adapted a Spanish Antichrist and Final Judgment play for a Nahua audience—be it Aquino or some unknown predecessor—may forever remain a mystery. However, in his preference for eschatological themes he reveals his spiritual kinship with the Franciscans, and that, at a certain level, he aligned himself with their mission goals, too. Perhaps he was an alumnus of one of their schools. Perhaps it was this connection that gained him access to the library that held the proposed source script. There, he would have put the powerful tool of alphabetic literacy to use, combing through volumes of bound books and manuscripts in search of material to add to his growing notebook of Christian texts. He seems to have been drawn to the friars' sermons about the end times, the return of Christ, the Final Judgment, and the *tetzauhmachiyotl*, "ominous signs" that would accompany the end. He discovered an affinity for the sermons of St. Vincent Ferrer that fired his imagination and inspired him to explore European demonology in greater detail than what he had been exposed to in the friars' preaching or catechism class. He learned how this "Anti-Christ" would appear when evil powers threatened the moral and social order and when great crises and calamities rocked the world. He also learned that the Antichrist would persecute the faithful, murdering them for proclaiming the message of Christ before ultimately being defeated. Christ would then return to judge the living and the dead, and the faithful ones would be called to an eternity of happiness and prosperity in heaven. And so, when his hands fell upon the script of a play dramatizing these frightening events, perhaps it was then that he had the inspiration. Perhaps he would do what none of his friar-teachers had yet done: he would bring this Antichrist to life on the Nahuatl stage in the form of a neixcuitilli about the end of the world.

2

AMERICAN APOCALYPSE

PREDICTING the precise moment of Antichrist's advent has been something of civilizational pastime since the time of Christ. Perhaps due to an innate human tendency to see portents of doom in world events, preachers and prophets have announced the End more times than the proverbial boy cried wolf. Human nature aside, the Antichrist legend contains elements that account for its unique elasticity and render it adaptable to any age. Throughout the Middle Ages, the expectation that frightening signs would precede his coming was fulfilled by wars and epidemics. Similarly, ominous political threats (in the form of Ottoman sultans and wicked kings) and the destabilization of the status quo (by Jews, Protestants, and popes) were interpreted as augurs of the Antichrist's pending appearance on the world stage. The common denominators of these elements are, first, that they are nonspecific enough so as to permit observers from any age to identify their existence in any given time. Second, they are predicted to appear precisely when the established order feels under the greatest threat, when dark forces gather on the horizon and threaten to upend everything held dear. In light of this, the existence of two *neixcuitilli* dramatizing the career of the Antichrist demands that we ask the following two questions. First: were there specific events or conditions in the early history of the colony that served to inspire someone to declare his arrival? And second, who did that someone imagine this Antichrist to be?

In what follows, I will endeavor to show that the Nahuatl Antichrist plays are cultural products of a religiopolitical conflict that threatened the existence of the

https://doi.org/10.5876/9781646423002.c002

Franciscan mission in its earliest years. During the first wave of Christianization, a period that stretched from roughly 1525 to 1545, the Franciscans faced existential challenges to their missionary activities in New Spain. On the political front, Dominican critics threatened to undermine the legal basis for the extensive powers granted to the Franciscans by the pope and the emperor to conduct the evangelization as they deemed fit. Pointing to what was perceived to be the "shallowness" of Indigenous conversion, these critics blamed the Franciscans' practice of performing mass baptisms without first adequately educating neophytes in Christian doctrine. However, it was the spiritual battle for the "hearts and minds" of the Indigenous commoner class (*macehualtin*) at this time that threatened the Franciscans the most. This conflict pit the Franciscans and their Indigenous allies against some influential members of Indigenous society that resisted the imposition of Christian morals and the requirement to jettison all vestiges of their traditional religious practices. In particular, these were certain powerful native rulers (*tlahtohqueh*, pl. of *tlahtoani*) and itinerant ritual specialists (*nanahualtin*, pl. of *nahualli*) whose status, privilege, and wealth within Nahua society was threatened by the spiritual colonizers. In effect, these groups constituted an anti-Franciscan front that endangered the Franciscan conversion effort at precisely the time when they needed to demonstrate the effectiveness of their strategies. Taken all together, the political and spiritual challenges of this early period were interpreted by Franciscans like Fray Andrés de Olmos and Bishop Fray Juan de Zumárraga as apocalyptic signs and pushed them toward ever more extreme measures to contain the threat to the mission.

This apocalyptic fear reached a climax during the Inquisition trials of 1536–1543. It was then that rulers like Tetzcoca tlahtoani don Carlos Ometochtzin and nahualli Andrés Mixcoatl were brought to trial for "heretical dogmatizing" by bishop Zumárraga. In the aftermath of the dramatic burning at the stake of don Carlos in 1539, the Crown's disapproval of Zumárraga's zealous persecution turned the tide against further inquisitorial actions against Indigenous people. And yet, the threat of the tlahtohqueh and the nanahualtin continued unabated. After the failure of their legal strategy, Franciscan writers like Olmos poured all their creative energy into waging a rhetorical war against idolatry and idolaters, the central weapon of which involved associating the resistant rulers, ritual specialists, and all the "idolatrous" practices that they advocated with the devil and his demon army. This strategy of diabolization came to color the entire missionary enterprise of the Franciscans from the 1540s onward. It would be broadcast in sermons and in catechisms, in mural paintings and in sculptural friezes, in the confessional and on stage. This chapter will argue that the two neixcuitilli centering on the career of the Antichrist must be seen within the context of the apocalyptic conflict of the 1530s and 1540s and the emergence of the rhetorical campaign of diabolization devised to combat it. In this context, the character of the Antichrist can be seen as an embodiment of the central targets of that campaign, the tlahtohqueh and nanahualtin who clung to their "idolatry" and threatened friars' control over the hearts and minds of the macehualtin. In staging neixcuitilli dramatizing the defeat of the Antichrist, the two plays were, in a sense, intended as staged performances of the defeat of the Franciscans' enemies and the ultimate victory for which they so desperately hoped.

THE TLAHTOANI PROBLEM

On December 1, 1539, Tetzcoca tlahtoani don Carlos Ometochtzin, also called Chichimecatecuhtli (Chichimec Lord), ascended the scaffold in the great plaza in front of Mexico City's imposing cathedral. He was dressed in the clothing that marked him for condemnation as a heretic: on his head he wore the conical *coroza* and over his shoulders was draped the penitent's *sambenito*. The Inquisition record notes that before him stretched an assembled mass of thousands, both Spanish and Indigenous, who had come to witness this *auto da fé* on that winter morning. After the charges against him had been read, he begged permission to address his people, which he did in his native tongue, Nahuatl. According to the Inquisition's translator, he admonished his fellow Nahuas not to be blinded by the devil as he had been, to cast off idolatry, and to embrace the one true God. From there, the record states only that *fué entregado el dicho don Carlos á la justicia seglar desta dicha cibdad,* "The said don Carlos was handed over to the secular justice of said city,"[1] a bland phrase that nonetheless indicated the commencement of his execution. Having concluded his speech, the fire beneath don Carlos was lit, and his writhing body was consumed by flames.

How had it come to this? How was it that the one designated "Protector of the Indians," a title bestowed on Zumárraga by Charles V himself, could be capable of such violence against those he had sworn to defend?[2] The answer is, of course, complicated and lies in the nexus of political realities, human nature, and the power of ideology to shape the way people behave. Regarding the latter, it is likely that the apocalyptic mindset of the Franciscans predisposed them to take extreme actions in response to perceived threats. Scholars of apocalypticism have noted that apocalyptic thought is less about predicting the future than it is about making sense out of a present that has been disrupted by catastrophic events.[3] Moreover, apocalyptic interpretations can be seen as part of a powerful human instinct to rebuild following such disasters. Zumárraga's violent persecution of don Carlos can be seen within this context. He perceived the threats of the late 1530s as desperate enough, apocalyptic enough, as to warrant desperate measures. The stakes were high: if they failed to neutralize the threat of challengers like don Carlos and other resistant tlahtohqueh, the entire mission was in jeopardy.

In a sense, Franciscans like Zumárraga got what they came for. Their entire missionary ideology was eschatological; they arrived in the Americas believing that the conversion of "the infidel" would usher in the end times; they came ready for the apocalypse. This peculiar ideology emerged over the three centuries preceding the arrival of the Franciscans in 1524. It drew on multiple sources, from the apocalyptic visions of writers like Joachim of Fiore, from the *Rule of St. Francis*, and of course, from the words of Christ. It was in Christ's discourse known as the "Little Apocalypse,"[4] that Jesus delivered a preview of the end times that established the contours of how the Franciscans would conceptualize their work among the Indigenous peoples of New Spain. When asked by his disciples what signs would precede his return, Jesus predicted there would be "wars and rumors of wars," famines and earthquakes, and ominous celestial phenomena like the sun's darkening and stars falling from the sky (Matthew 24:6–7, 29). He also warned that they would experience painful trials, stating "you will be handed over to be persecuted and put to death, and you will be hated by all nations because of me" (verse 9). Jesus continued, "at that time many will turn away from the faith and will betray and hate each other, and many false prophets will appear and deceive many people" (verses 10–11), and concluded saying, "but the one who stands firm to the end will be saved. And this gospel of the kingdom will be preached in the whole world as a testimony to all nations, and then the end will come" (verses 14–15).

Fray Martín de Valencia, the leader of the first cohort of missionaries and one of the more apocalyptic Franciscans from this early period, manifests the eschatological tone of the mission in a vision he reportedly experienced while still in Spain. Franciscan chronicler Motolinía recalled that once when he was chanting matins, Fray Martín found himself contemplating the conversion of "the infidels" while reciting the Psalms. "When will this prophecy be fulfilled?" he thought to himself, noting that "We are already in the afternoon, at the end of our days, and in the world's final era."[5] So filled with zeal was he that he experienced a vision of a "vast multitude of infidels being converted, confessing the faith, and coming to receive Baptism." Unable to contain his joy he exclaimed "Praised be Jesus Christ!" three times in a loud voice, so upsetting his brothers that they had to restrain him in his cell for fear he had gone mad.

Once in the mission field, signs initially seemed to confirm the vision of Fray Martín. Motolinía left us one of the best accounts of Franciscan optimism regarding the apparent early and enthusiastic embrace of the conquerors' faith by the Indigenous population. He reported that almost right away crowds came seeking out the friars to teach them about Christianity, some even begging to be baptized.[6] Using language that echoes gospel accounts of Christ's initial reception by the Jews, he wrote, "When the friars set out on their visits to Indian towns, the Indians come to meet them on the road with children on their arms and the infirm on their backs."[7] The Franciscans were happy to oblige this apparent clamor for baptism and conversion. Motolinía reported that in some places "a single priest would baptize on one day four or five thousand Indians," so much so that they "were often unable to raise the pitcher with which they baptized because their arm was tired."[8] By 1536, Motolinía estimated upwards of five million souls had been baptized by his fellow friars.[9] Regarding the attitude of these eager converts toward their old religion, he declared:

> Although in some towns there may still be some idol, it is either decayed or so forgotten or hidden away that in a town of ten thousand souls not five souls know of its existence. The Indians know these idols for what they are. In other words, they consider them stones or pieces of wood. . . . [The Indians] have forgotten the idols as completely as if a hundred years had elapsed since they abandoned them.[10]

From the end of the Spanish-Mexica War until 1526, a period of five years, the Franciscans enjoyed a monopoly on the mission field. Cortés himself had written to the king and specifically requested that members of the Franciscan order be immediately sent over to begin the work of evangelization. Known for their austerity and piety—in contrast to the more worldly and less rigorous secular clergy—the mendicant orders were those chosen to lead the mission. The legal basis for their work was provided by the Vatican in a series of papal bulls known as the Omnimoda, promulgated by Adrian IV in 1522. The Omnimoda granted extensive and extraordinary privileges to the mendicants to carry out functions that were ordinarily the prerogative of bishops and diocesan officials.[11] In situations where the closest bishop was more than two days' journey away—which was virtually everywhere at that time—the friars were permitted to take any means they deemed necessary to do the work of evangelization. It was rationalized that given the vast scale of the American mission field and the massive task of converting millions of its Indigenous inhabitants, it would be far too costly and time consuming to first establish episcopal and diocesan institutions. The independence and power this granted to the mendicants would serve as the basis for increasingly contentious interactions between the Franciscans and other mendicant orders, and gradually, between the mendicants and episcopal authorities.

The arrival of the first contingent of Dominicans in 1526 and the Augustinians in 1533 would challenge the Franciscans' monopoly. The conflict that unfolded had both political and religious dimensions. Politically, the Dominicans and Augustinians complained that the Franciscans' head start had unfairly enabled them to establish themselves in all the choicest locations, which granted them easiest access to the most wealthy and densely populated Indigenous communities. Starting as they had in the more densely populated core of the former Mexica Empire, the Franciscans had quickly claimed territory all across the central valley of Mexico by building convents and churches in the major *altepemeh*. The first were in Mexico-Tenochtitlan, Tetzcoco, Tlaxcala, and Huexotzingo, four of the largest urban centers of precontact Mexico. Since labor and tribute had flowed to these urban centers for decades prior to their arrival, there was an economic benefit enjoyed by the Franciscans that rankled the other orders who were left to make do with the more far-flung and less-profitable regions surrounding the central zone. Finally, the Franciscans' head start had also enabled them to gain expertise in Indigenous languages, which made them all the more indispensable in the imperial designs of church and Crown.

However, the central religious conflict that roiled internecine relations between Franciscans and their brethren was over the baptismal practices of the former. From the outset, the Franciscans pursued mass baptisms with near-obsessive fervor, as demonstrated by the citations from Motolinía above. At the heart of the matter was criticism over the method the Franciscans used to administer the sacrament. In short, Indigenous initiates were given virtually no pre-baptismal instruction, and vast crowds were baptized en masse in ceremonies that left out certain elements that typically accompanied the ritual. The Franciscans justified the curtailed form of the rite due to the extreme urgency of converting millions of Indigenous souls and the paucity of ministers available to doing the work. Motolinía wrote, "Here in this newly converted land, how could one priest in the course of one day baptize two or three thousand Indians and observe in the case of each candidate individually the ceremony of salt, breathing, candle, white robe and all the other ceremonies?"[12] However, more conservative friars, principally the Dominicans, viewed such cornercutting as scandalous. Here, institutional culture came into play. The Dominicans were the Order of Preachers, after all. To them, doctrinal orthodoxy, careful instruction, and the letter of the law mattered deeply. The Franciscans tended to fall on the side of the spirit of the law, as can be seen in their approach to the administration of baptism. What mattered was saving souls, "snatching them from the maw of the dragon," to quote minister general Quiñones.[13] If the rules had to be bent in the process, this was more than justified by the urgency of the matter at hand.

In the contentious years of the 1520s and 1530s, when Dominicans and Augustinians were grasping for a secure foothold in the mission field, these issues quickly evolved into a dire crisis for the Franciscans that threatened their dominant position. Making matters worse, troubling signs began to appear that suggested their methods might not be producing the intended results, lending credence to their detractors' charges. Motolinía received word that some of the baptized had been placing images of the Virgin Mary and Christ right beside images of the *teteoh* in their household shrines. Other reports indicated that such "idols" were being hidden behind altars or in the bases of crosses so that they could continue to venerate them as they had before the friars came. The Franciscans' confidence that the Indigenous population had forgotten their former gods was starting to show cracks. By the early 1530s, the quiet persistence of traditional religious practices by masses of baptized Indigenous burst into a full-blown crisis for the Franciscan leadership. Motolinía admitted as much. Despite the fact that the Franciscans' campaigns had torn down many temples, disbanded the institutional priesthood, and ended public sacrifices, they discovered what he called "the most difficult thing of all, and the one that took the longest to be destroyed. This was that at night the Indians continued to meet and call upon the devil and celebrate his feasts with many and diverse ancient rights."[14] In an exasperated letter to the Council of the Indies written in 1536, Zumárraga agreed, confessing "the natives still practice their heathen rites, especially the superstitions and idolatry and sacrifices, though not publicly as they used to do. At night they go to their altars, pyramids, and temples."[15] Without immediate and drastic intervention, the Franciscans' entire mission stood on the brink of failure.

The widespread persistence of what was deemed idolatry pointed to the emergence of parallel spheres of religiosity among supposedly converted Indigenous Christians.[16] Publicly, they performed the requisite demonstrations of Catholicity: attending mass, listening to sermons, building churches, venerating saints. However, in private, Indigenous people tended to do what they had always done when dealing with the gods and rites of a conquering power: they simply absorbed them into their existing cosmology and continued on as before. Motolinía acknowledged as much when we complained, "It was as if those who had a hundred gods wished to have a hundred and one."[17] While some mendicants interpreted this as a sign of the limited capacity of the Indigenous to fully Christianize, we now know that the flexibility of the Indigenous approach to Christianity was due to essential differences between the religious worldviews of Mesoamericans and Europeans. The exclusive claims made by Christians about there being only one true God and one true faith were likely not well understood by Indigenous Christians. Their response to Christianity made sense in the context of their cultural understanding of divinity and religious practice, which is to say, they accepted Christianity on their own terms.

What made this a crisis for the Franciscans was that it served as political dynamite for their detractors. If the Franciscans' methods of baptism and indoctrination were shown to have produced insufficient results, if conversion were as shallow as reports were indicating, then the Franciscans' position of leadership in the mission, as well as their cozy relationship with the Crown and the pope, could be challenged. Lockhart calls the Dominicans "the greatest scourge of the Franciscans," and with good reason.[18] They pressed their advantage by complaining loudly to the ecclesiastical and secular authorities about the Franciscans' methods and the shallowness of Indigenous conversions. One avenue of attack was to undermine the Franciscans' faith in the premise that Indigenous converts could become full, mature Christians. This issue was part of the larger debate that raged in the decades following the European discovery of the Americas and its peoples of whether or not said peoples were fully human or instead merely a class of animals. Stakes for this debate were high, since if they were deemed less than human, then they could not be Christianized and were suitable for enslavement. The climactic moment of this debate famously occurred in 1550–1551 when Dominican fray Bartolomé de las Casas argued in favor of Indigenous humanity against the critic Juan Ginés de Sepúlveda. Although Las Casas has ever-after been remembered as the great defender of Indigenous rights, his views of Indigenous capacity for Christianity diverged from many of his brethren in New Spain. The head of the first Dominican province in New Spain, Fray Tomás de Ortiz, declared to the Council of the Indies that despite the great numbers of converts being reported by the Franciscans, "Indians are more stupid than asses and refuse to improve in anything."[19]

If Dominican detractors could sway the ecclesiastical authorities that Indigenous were only capable of limited, rudimentary conversion to Christianity, this too would undermine the Franciscan mission. Bishop Zumárraga lobbied the pope vigorously for an official pronouncement on the matter of Indigenous capacity for Christianization, and ultimately got what he wanted in 1537. In that year, Pope Paul III promulgated the bull *Sublimis Deus*, in which he stated, "We . . . consider . . . that the Indians are truly men and that they are not only capable of understanding Catholic faith but . . . they desire exceedingly to receive it."[20] Having gotten the validation he desired, however, Zumárraga was now obliged to hold Indigenous Christians to the same standard that a European Christian would be held.[21] This placed intense pressure on the Franciscan leadership of the 1530s to definitively end the practice of idolatry among the Indigenous population, to root out the idols behind altars, and to prove that Christian orthodoxy reigned in the Franciscans' "millennial kingdom." If they failed to do so, the Franciscans stood to lose their privileged status in the Americas. However, in light of the order's eschatological ideology, there was a great deal more at stake than the politics and economics of mendicant skirmishes. The defeat of Satan and the return of Christ depended on the successful conversion of the this newly discovered continent of people. By the mid-1530s, Zumárraga, Olmos, and their fellow friars faced a threat of existential proportions, a crisis that threatened impending doom.

Patricia Lopes Don has argued that in this moment of crisis Zumárraga and his confreres made a strategic decision in a desperate play to save themselves and their mission. Under intense pressure from the Dominicans and the royal authorities to account for the continuing existence of idolatry, they deflected the blame from themselves onto certain prominent members of Indigenous society.[22] These scapegoats included influential tlahtohqueh resisters like don Carlos of Tetzcoco and nanahualtin like Andrés Mixcoatl. Arguing that these individuals were responsible for poisoning the macehualtin and hampering widespread conversion, Franciscans launched a new campaign in what David Tavárez has referred to as the "invisible war" against idolatry.[23] This war was invisible because even though it targeted a broad range of Indigenous practices labelled idolatry, superstition, and sorcery, it was ultimately being waged against the devil and his army of demon helpers. Employing the privileges granted in the Omnimoda, Zumárraga assumed inquisitorial powers and subjected these individuals to "exemplary punishment" in an effort to have the widest possible impact on idolatry. Lopes Don argues that this strategy effectively defined the tlahtohqueh as a subversive class, an "Indian problem," that Zumárraga would attempt to solve using his powers as bishop, thus saving the mission and the Franciscans.[24]

A WINTER OF PUNISHMENT

Between 1536, when Zumárraga's Inquisition began, and 1541 when he was ultimately stripped of his powers, Zumárraga completed roughly 120 cases by Martin Nesvig's counting.[25] Nesvig, Tavárez, and Lopes Don all note the Inquisition's focus on Indigenous lords and the strategy of humiliating them by pursuing "exemplary punishment"—that is, the public display of punishment for the purpose of sending a message to the wider masses.[26] The records created by the Inquisition are, in Tavárez's words, "the most closely scrutinized records regarding Indigenous crimes of faith in New Spain."[27] Since publication in the early twentieth century, they have been extensively studied, and with good reason. In an era before widespread writing by Indigenous people in Indigenous languages, they offer invaluable—though not unproblematic—windows on the forces shaping the lives of Indigenous people during this early period. For our purposes here, these records help us gain a better understanding of the figures scapegoated by the Franciscans, the tlahtohqueh and nanahualtin, who posed an existential threat to the Franciscans. The argument put forth in this chapter is that these figures were collectively the inspiration for the Aztec Antichrist dramatized in the two neixcuitilli that are the focus of this study.

Events of the years immediately following the Spanish invasion had delivered a violent shock to the social institutions that had formerly supported and empowered central Mexico's tlahtohqueh. As rulers of their respective altepemeh, the tlahtohqueh were accustomed to enjoying broad privileges that accompanied their elite

FIGURE 2.1. A *tlahtoani* addresses assembled *teteuctin*. From Sahagún, Florentine Codex, 1575–1577, Book 4, f. 19v. Biblioteca Medicea Laurenziana, Florence, Med. Palat. 218–220. Courtesy of MiC. Any further reproduction by any means is prohibited.

status. They were members of ruling dynasties and ruled for life.[28] However, unlike European kings, the position of tlahtoani rotated among the heads of the *teccalli*, or "lord-house," that were the constituent parts of the precontact ethnic state, or altepetl.[29] Each tlahtoani was protector of a multitude of dependent members of the commoner class, the macehualtin, as well as lesser *teteuctin* (lords; see figure 2.1). From these dependents the tlahtoani received tribute in the form of labor and goods. Apart from the *huei tlahtoani*, "great speaker" or emperor, the tlahtohqueh were the most powerful and wealthy figures in precontact Nahua society.

The arrival of Spanish colonists, missionaries, and rulers disrupted these native institutions and ways of life. Following the collapse of Mexica rule, the tlahtohqueh were now colonial subjects, subservient to higher authorities, some of which lay hundreds or thousands of miles away. Flows of tribute were disrupted as the colonial government sought to extract the wealth that they deemed legitimate spoils of war, increasing the economic strain on tlahtohqueh and their many dependents. Add to all of this the ravages of epidemic disease, forced relocations of the population through the policy of *congregación*, and the rapacity of Spanish encomenderos, and the picture is clear: during the first two decades following the conquest, the tlahtohqueh were under assault.

Another vector of this threat to traditional powerholders was the missionary activity of the friars. Even before Zumárraga's Inquisition in the mid-1530s, the friars had pursued a strategy that identified Indigenous rulers as the first targets of conversion. Not converting was not an option; but acceding to the gods and rites of one's conquerors was not utterly unfamiliar to Indigenous Mesoamericans. However, conversion to Christianity came with strange and onerous requirements for the tlahtohqueh. Principal among these was the rigorous enforcement of Christian teaching on marriage and sexual mores. This meant the tlahtohqueh had to abandon all but one of the many wives they enjoyed as a royal prerogative. The friars seemed obsessed with what they perceived as the sexual immorality of the tlahtohqueh. In addition to their many wives, the tlahtohqueh were accused of keeping "concubines" from whom they sought companionship and sexual gratification. By demanding that they abandon all but one wife and completely disavow any sign of what the friars labelled adultery or fornication, the friars effectively "usurped the traditional authority of the tlahtohqueh, thus emasculating and insulting them."[30] By the time of Zumárraga's Inquisition, then, the traditional privileges, rights, and status of the tlahtohqueh were under attack from all directions, especially from the mendicant friars.

The nanahualtin were members of a broad group of traditional religious practitioners who were, like the tlahtohqueh in the 1520s and 1530s, living in a world turned upside down. In the Mesoamerican tradition, nahualli refers both to a shapeshifting shaman and the animal alter-ego that the shaman took on during rituals; the sense in which the term is used here is the former. However, according to Jorge Klor de Alva, who wrote about one of the most sensational cases to come out of the Inquisition records, that of Martín Ocelotl, the nanahualtin might also have been former members of the institutional Nahua priesthood, the *tlamacazqueh*.[31] This group may also have included *tonalpouhqueh* (day keepers, divination specialists) and *titicih* (traditional healers; see figure 2.2). For obvious reasons, all of these groups were instantly unemployed by the toppling of Indigenous polity and priesthood in 1521. Ocelotl and others like him adapted by parlaying their former skills and prestige into a new career as itinerant ritual specialists for hire, wandering the countryside offering their services to tlahtohqueh and macehualtin alike. They healed the sick, divined the fate of newborns, performed sacrifices in order to bring rain, prayed, chanted, sang, and otherwise filled the vacuum created by the "spiritual

FIGURE 2.2. Rituals specialists practicing divination. From Sahagún, Florentine
Codex, 1575–1577, Book 4, f. 3v, Biblioteca Medicea Laurenziana, Florence, Med. Palat.
218–220. Courtesy of MiC. Any further reproduction by any means is prohibited.

conquest." Some, like Ocelotl, accumulated great wealth and power as a result, collecting tribute, advising tlahtohqueh, and—most damning of all—in some cases
actively preaching against the friars and their gospel. In effect, these tlahtohqueh
and nanahualtin constituted a viable alternative to the friars and Christianity. They
offered to preserve continuity with the past and to breach the rupture opened by
the Spaniards. Their conservative message stood in stark counterpoint to the radi-
cal change demanded by the barefoot sons of Francis and Dominic. This inevitably brought them into conflict with the friars, since both contested for the hearts,
minds, and souls of the Indigenous population. There was no way both could win;
Zumárraga knew this and placed all of his authority behind his preferred solution
to the "Indian problem": the Inquisition.

The records of Zumárraga's trials from 1536–1540 were published in 1910 under
the title *Proceso inquisitorial del cacique de Tetzcoco* (Inquisition trial against the
ruler of Tetzcoco) and in 1912 as *Procesos de Indios idolatras y hechiceros* (Trials of
Indian idolaters and sorcerers). A brief summary of three of the trials provides a
general sense of the dynamics of the Franciscans' campaign to eliminate the threat
posed by the tlahtohqueh and nanahualtin:

On June 28, 1536 Spanish encomendero Lorenzo de Suárez accused two nanahualtin named Tacatetl and Tanixtetl of idolatry and making sacrifices to Tlaloc, the god of rain. Suárez reported that both men had been training youths for the Indigenous priesthood, led rituals involving bloodletting, and had hidden nine large idols in a cave. Tacatetl was said to have the power to transform himself into a jaguar and witnesses claimed to have been present when both men sacrificed ten individuals and presented their extracted hearts to the idols. When interrogated, Tacatetl confessed that he had been baptized, taken the Christian name Antonio, and understood Christian doctrine. Nevertheless, he claimed that he made sacrifices to Tlaloc in an effort to alleviate the effects of a devastating drought.[32]

On July 10, 1537 the tlahtoani of Xinantepec, don Juan, denounced a nahualli named Mixcoatl, thought to be the brother of Martín Ocelotl, mentioned above. Reports indicated that Mixcoatl was believed to be a god and frequently addressed his followers saying, "ídos conmigo" ("go with me"), a sly parody of Christ's command to his disciples to "Follow me, and I will make you fishers of men."[33] Mixcoatl was said to have performed miracles, such as making the rains come or cease, healing the sick, and setting parts of his body on fire without being burned. More explicitly anti-mendicant activities were alleged as well. In various altepemeh north and east of Mexico City he was said to have preached openly against the friars, urging the macehualtin to avoid being baptized and to reject learning the doctrine. He even warned ominously that the friars would one day be transformed into frightening stellar beings called *tzitzimimeh*, beings that threatened to devour humanity during the liminal period at the end of the 365-day *xiuhpohualli* cycle. All of this earned him the charge of "heretical dogmatism." When arrested and interrogated, he too declared his belief in Christianity and his desire to be a good Christian, confessing that his crimes were sinful and that the devil had deceived him.[34]

On June 22, 1539, the aforementioned Tetzcoca tlahtoani don Carlos Ometochtzin was denounced before the Inquisition by a young Nahua from Chiconautla named Francisco, who also happened to be his nephew. Based on his testimony and many others, don Carlos was charged with bigamy, idolatry, and heretical dogmatism, for which he was ultimately burned at the stake. Regarding the first charge, it was alleged that he had taken his niece, Inés, as a mistress, and had vigorously pursued other amorous relationships with women who weren't his one, lawful wife. As for idolatry, no definitive evidence was ever found. But regarding the charge of heretical dogmatism, that is to say the teaching of heresies, the court had more to go on. The most damning evidence against him was delivered by Francisco, who reported that at a meeting of Indigenous nobles in Chiconautla don Carlos had made a fiery speech that expressed vehemently anti-mendicant ideas. In it he railed against the intrusions of the Franciscans into the privileges and the honor of the tlahtohqueh, the way they had turned the macehualtin away from their obligatory responsibilities to their rulers, and the audacity of their insistence in celibacy and monogamy. Turning on Francisco, who was a young protégé of the Franciscans, he berated him saying, "Stop these things that are vanities . . . do not take care of these things and encourage the other people to believe what the friars say." To the assembled nobles he asked, "What are the things of God?," to which he replied "They are nothing."[35] Instead, he pleaded with them to "listen . . . to what our fathers and our grandfathers said when they died," insisting that they reject Christian teaching and return to their traditional religious beliefs and practices. All of this was corroborated by multiple witnesses, and Greenleaf speculates that it was this that convinced the authorities to order his "relaxation" for execution.[36] Here, again, it is important to note that don Carlos vehemently denied these charges, except perhaps for that of concubinage, and asserted his status as a faithful, baptized Christian. Nevertheless, as we have already heard, the sentence was carried out and don Carlos was burned at the stake on December 1, 1539.[37]

It doesn't take a legal expert or a professional historian to recognize the highly problematic nature of the trial records produced by Zumárraga's episcopal Inquisition from 1536 to 1543. As noted by Klor de Alva, witnesses routinely contradicted themselves while under oath, uttered declarations that were patently biased, and sought to extract personal benefit from the demise of others.[38] American and European Inquisition records alike are replete with examples of individuals using the Holy Office to settle scores and to undermine competitors. If one were determined to get to the "truth" behind accusations like those levelled at don Carlos, one would have to admit the ultimate futility of the task. However, in the context of the argument being developed in this chapter, assessing the innocence or guilt of the condemned is not the point. Instead, these records are useful for what they reveal about how Franciscans like Zumárraga conceptualized threats to their authority and their mission in the late 1530s. Regardless of whether the accused really said or did what was reported, the Franciscan authorities *believed* they did; the humiliating "exemplary punishments" meted out suggest as much. For example, Tacatetl and Tanixtetl were bound, mounted on burros, and paraded through the streets of Mexico and Tlatelolco. A crier preceded them, announcing loudly their crimes in Spanish and Otomí (apparently the native language of the convicted "sorcerers"). Periodically this train of humiliation would pause, and the two were flogged in various squares and marketplaces. Upon arrival at the great market in Tlatelolco, they were shorn of their hair and half of their idols were burned. Then they retraced their steps to the market in Mexico City and the other half was burned.[39] The ruthlessness with which Zumárraga pursued a solution to the threat posed by these individuals through inquisitorial means is evidence of the Franciscans' conviction that the very existence of the mission (and their central role in it) hung in the balance.

The central argument of this chapter is that the dynamics articulated in the Inquisition records summarized above were played out in the characters and dialogues of the Antichrist neixcuitilli preserved in Aquino's notebook. Links between Inquisition and stage are strongest in the second play, *Antichrist and the Hermit*, which on one level reads like a collection of condensed inquisitorial inquests. There are twenty-five such "inquests," seven directed at the demons representing the deadly sins and eighteen that interrogate condemned souls. Each one is structured in a similar fashion. Hermit, in the role of Inquisitor, asks each of the accused to state their name. He then asks them why they have been suffering in Mictlan (hell). This is followed by the accused's testimony, really more of a confession, in which they detail their crimes. Each inquest ends with pronouncing the guilt of the accused, who are sent off to serve their sentences in hell. The following example illustrates some of the ways these dramatized inquests parallel their legal sources of inspiration.

On folios 176r–177r, Hermit questions two characters who are referred to as *ahneltocani*, "unbeliever(s)." Hermit first demands to know their names. One of them responds, saying, "I am Tlacateuctli. My friend's name is Huitznahuatl" (f. 176r). Although it is not explicitly stated, it is clear that both men are unbaptized tlahtohqueh. Their names give their identity away. Tlacateuctli and Huitznahuatl were both proper names of powerful historical figures and official titles borne in precontact times by those in the very highest ranks of the Indigenous ruling class. Tlacateuctli, "ruler of people," was the title borne by Moteuczoma before he was chosen to be huei tlahtoani of the Mexica.[40] The same seems to have been true for Huitznahuatl, which Bierhorst identifies as "one of the high titles of Mexican officialdom" and/or "a close relative of Axayacatl 2, killed in the Michhuan War."[41] David Tavárez asserts that "Zumárraga and his associates frequently misread preconquest office titles as personal names during their trials."[42] He cites as an example the aforementioned Tacatetl, the spelling of which is also rendered "Tacatetle" and "Tactle" in the records. Tavárez claims this was a misreading of *tlacateccatl*, a "meritocratic title designating warriors who took captives in battle and exercised local political duties."[43] One wonders whether *Hermit*'s Tlacateuctli might have been the very same Tlacateccatl interviewed in Zumárraga's Inquisition. In either case, the two questioned by Hermit in this scene would have immediately been recognized by the audience as high-ranking Indigenous rulers.

Their confession reads as if it could have been copied out of the records of Zumárraga's Inquisition.[44] Speaking for both, Tlacateuctli explains that they are in hell because even though "the words of God reached us . . . we didn't take

believing seriously, we just made fun of it; we just looked down on it" (f. 176r).
He continues,

> So that the Christians wouldn't kill us, we broke down the houses of our *teteoh* [i.e.,
> temples]. But we didn't do it willingly. It was as if we erected their houses within us
> and carefully protected the images of our *teteoh* so that the Christians wouldn't burn
> them. But if in order to placate the Christians we did reveal them, the ones that we
> revealed were those that we didn't care about. Those that really are our *teteoh* we kept
> carefully hidden. What is more, we got baptized to satisfy the priests. (f. 176r–v)

This confession also reflects Zumárraga's obsession with locating hidden idols in
the 1530s. Throughout the Inquisition proceedings, he routinely questioned those
brought before the court regarding the whereabouts of such idols. Tacatetl and
Tanixtetl, mentioned above, were accused of hiding nine large idols in a secret cave.
When asked about the location of other idols in the region, Tacatetl's response was
that all the *indios señores* (i.e., the tlahtohqueh) had idols hidden away somewhere.[45]
He also stated that "the youths who are being indoctrinated in the monasteries
have looked for, found, and burned all [the idols]" (see figure 2.3).[46] In light of this,
there can be little doubt that the one who penned the words of Tlacateuctli and
Huitznahuatl in *Antichrist and the Hermit* had these specific historical events and
forces in mind.

However, for all his zeal, Zumárraga's strategy of applying exemplary discipline
to the "subversive class" of tlahtohqueh and nanahualtin backfired. Even before
1536, the question of whether or not Indigenous backsliders should be subjected to
physical discipline was a controversy. For many, Indigenous Christians were simply
too new to the faith to justify such extreme forms of motivation and discipline;
like tender young plants they required more gentle nurturing before they could
reasonably be held to the same standards as old-world Christians. This controversy
also brought Franciscans into confrontation with their detractors, especially the
Dominicans. The irony was that in this case, it was the humanistic Franciscans who
favored the practice of physical discipline and the Dominicans who challenged it.[47]
In April of 1539, the bishops and representatives of the three mendicant orders met
for a *junta eclesiástica* (church council). One of the official pronouncements this
meeting, Item Ten, forbade the imprisonment and whipping of Indigenous persons
as a means of forcing them to learn Christian doctrine.[48]

This apparently did not sit well with the Franciscans. Just two months later, on
June 10, Zumárraga promulgated a series of *Ordenanzas* that were to be read aloud
in Indigenous communities three times each year. These "decrees" explicitly enumerated practices that were forbidden. Among the items in the list, the following
were included: refusing to confess, "living in concubinage," multiple marriages

Incendio de todas las ropas y libros y ataudos de los guardotes y idolatrios
que se los quemaron los frayles

FIGURE 2.3. Franciscans burning deity images and *inamox in teteoh*, sacred books of the deities. From Diego Muñoz Camargo, *Historia de Tlaxcala*, MS Hunter 242, f. 242r. Used by permission of Archives and Special Collections, University of Glasgow Library.

(polygamy), consanguineal marriage, refusing to attend mass or come to hear the doctrine, "sorcery [and] casting lots," eating human flesh, taking potions (*pahtli*) to abort a fetus, dressing as a woman (for men), and having relations with another woman (for women).[49] The punishment for each offence was virtually the same: *que sean presos y luego azotados publicamente*, "let them be imprisoned and then publicly whipped."[50] With so much at stake, there would be no compromise in the methods deployed in eradicating the threat posed by idolaters and backsliders, whether they be tlahtohqueh like don Carlos or members of the macehualtin.

Fray Andrés de Olmos, one of Zumárraga's closest confidants and supporters, expressed his frustration at the situation in a letter written just days after don Carlos's execution. Speaking of stubborn elites who, though baptized, continued to resist full Christianization he wrote,

> It seems to me that they shower us with compliments, and yet I have not known three nobles who have voluntarily come to the religion and remain faithful to it. It is always May for them and there is no winter. The trees, however, will not turn by themselves, and if they do not experience the seasons, no fruit will be born. It is always May, and yet there has to be a winter and punishment for the things they have committed against their baptism, even if they have to be put into the fire, as Your Excellency is commencing to do.[51]

However, by 1540 putting people "into the fire" caused such an outcry that Zumárraga's days as self-styled inquisitor general were numbered. Reactions to his use of torture, imprisonment, and the public flogging of Indigenous Christians shocked observers in New and Old Spain. Coupled with his apparent disregard for the ecclesiastical consensus, this led to increasing pressure of Zumárraga to de-escalate the war on idolatry and idolaters. However, it was the execution of don Carlos that finally provoked the crown to action and caused them to intervene. In 1541 Zumárraga was rebuked for his "zealotry and violence" and stripped of his powers as inquisitor.[52] The Council of the Indies reviewed his trial and sentencing of don Carlos and made its recommendation to the Crown. In 1543 Charles V removed Zumárraga from his post as apostolic inquisitor. Those that followed him, like lawyer Tello de Sandoval in 1544 and Dominican bishop fray Alonso de Montúfar in 1554, attempted to reform the legal system by which heretics and dogmatizers were tried.[53] But few of these future inquisitions ever approached the violence of Zumárraga's.

While the extirpation campaigns raged, some Franciscans had simultaneously pursued other avenues for the eradication of idolatry. One of these involved extensive study of Indigenous culture in an effort to better identify practices to target for elimination. Between 1533 and 1539 Fray Andrés de Olmos conducted one of the earliest of these "ethnographic" research projects. Upon the completion of his investigations, he produced a voluminous report titled *Tratado de antiguedades mexicanas* (Treatise on Mexican antiquities), tragically now lost. What Olmos found only contributed to the Franciscans' assessment of the direness of the situation and stoked their obsession to combat idolatry, sorcery, and superstition. Sahagún, whose ethnographic research was even more extensive than Olmos's, wrote in the early 1540s:

> It is certainly a matter of great wonderment that, for so many centuries, our Lord God has concealed a forest of so many idolatrous peoples whose luxuriant fruits only the demon harvested and holds hoarded in the infernal fire. Nor can I believe that the Church of God would not be successful where the Synagogue of Satan has had so much success.[54]

In statements like these we can identify the mark of a strategy that emerged in the 1530s and was consolidated in the 1540s. Unlike the legal strategy pursued in the Inquisition of 1536–1543, this would be a rhetorical one, waged in the doctrinal and homiletic discourses that were just beginning to be composed in the 1540s. This strategy was to link the anti-mendicant tlahtohqueh and nanahualtin along with the clandestine paganism that lingered in caves, hills, and nighttime meetings with the devil. Armed with the rhetorical weapon of diabolization, the friars launched a new campaign in the 1540s targeting the existential threat posed by idolatry and idolaters.

THE WAR OF WORDS

The friars' turn from physical punishment to a war of words did not happen overnight. Instead, it coalesced in the context of the early extirpation campaigns of the 1530s and by the 1540s was an essential weapon in the invisible war. Fernando Cervantes writes about this transition in his study *The Devil in the New World*. He reminds us that from the very first moments of contact with Indigenous peoples, European explorers, conquistadors, and evangelizers saw evidence that the devil and his demons had arrived well before them and had been busily building corrupt kingdoms of cannibals and giants. The "devil in the New World" was a powerful and near-universal trope that colored European discourses from the late fifteenth century through the time of the Enlightenment. Running counter to this narrative was another trope that viewed the Americas as a kind of lost paradise in which noble savages lived in a state of "primeval innocence."[55] Although Indigenous people were seen as lacking certain hallmarks of civilization, like alphabetic writing and religion, they nevertheless occupied a verdant world that yielded bounties unimagined in late medieval Europe. However, eventually the tendency to see Indigenous people and cultures as demonic triumphed over this alternative. European chroniclers and friars alike believed that the devil had long ago claimed the Americas as his "fiefdom" and had ruled without challenge as a "tyrannical lord" over its native inhabitants.[56] Cervantes states that this transition was complete by the middle of the sixteenth century when this "negative, demonic view" triumphed, and its influence "was seen to descend like a dense fog upon every statement officially and unofficially made on the subject."[57]

Lopes Don argues for an even more precise window of time for this transition: the 1540s and the immediate aftermath of the failed legal strategy of Zumárraga. She writes,

> The rhetoric condemning diabolism—the practice of worshipping and advocating for the devil—had not yet been theologically linked to the practices of the *nanahualtin* or the native leaders. Zumárraga's native victims were only occasionally referred to as "brujos," and none of the Indigenous gods was consistently described as the devil.... In the decade following Zumárraga's Inquisition, Fray Andrés de Olmos began to make these theological linkages and equations.[58]

She goes on to argue that since the friars no longer had access to the legal means of the Inquisition in their pursuit of their enemies the tlahtohqueh and nanahualtin, they turned to a rhetorical campaign that diabolized these individuals and sought to turn the macehualtin against them.[59]

Sermons were the chief means by which the friars sought to convince them of the devil's evil presence in their lives. One of the earliest collections of sermons bears the name of none other than Sahagún, who writes that they were "composed in the year 1540."[60] He goes on to state that they were written "to the capacity of the Indians ... easy to understand for all who hear them, high [born] and low, lords and common folk (*macegoales*, or macehualtin)." Remarkably, even though the sermonary edited by Sahagún stands as one of the very earliest literary works in Nahuatl, it never saw the printing press in Sahagún's time and has only just recently been translated into Spanish.[61] References to the devil in this early sermonary weren't as frequent nor was the language of diabolism as terrifying as it would become in the hands of later writers. However, passages like the one below made clear to Nahua audiences the friars' stance on Indigenous authority figures and Indigenous religion. After the celebration of mass on the second Sunday of Advent, Nahuas could have heard the friars preach words such as these:

> The elders used to speak about how the world began and how the first person was made along with other laughable talk. This is just like the talk of jokers, the talk of drunks. In this way the were-owl [devil] lied to your grandfathers, your grandmothers [your ancestors] who lived long ago in order that they would follow things as gods [commit idolatry]. The wicked were-owl knew well how the world was made and who made it.... He knew it well for it happened in his presence. But he spoke to you with lying words so that you wouldn't recognize your creator, God. (p. 10)

Catechisms and doctrinal statements were another avenue through which the strategy of diabolism was used to undermine Nahuas' faith in traditional authorities and traditional beliefs and practices. Nahuas who lived in Dominican territory might have heard these words, read aloud from what is perhaps the second-oldest printed Nahuatl text, the 1548 *Doctrina christiana en lengua española y mexicana*:

> And these were-owls go around deceiving you all the time. They used to make you believe in them, saying that they were really deities. And also they used to make you serve them, and they made your fathers and your grandfathers serve them and build, construct for them what were their homes and their temples. . . . This is what those wicked devils did so that you would greatly offend God. Because of this you will suffer and be punished there in Mictlan, hell.[62]

Franciscan religious writing that specifically linked tlahtohqueh and the devil can be found in an important early manuscript dating to 1553 and authored by none other than Fray Olmos. The work is titled *Tratado de hechicerías y sortilegios* (Treatise on sorcery and spells) and is held in the Biblioteca Nacional de México and is cataloged as MS. 1488 *Sermones en mexicano*. It is a paraphrased translation of a Spanish text authored by Franciscan Martín de Castañega in 1527. Before traveling to New Spain, Olmos had collaborated with Castañega in the latter's efforts on behalf of the Holy Office of the Inquisition to combat witchcraft in the Basque region. Olmos's decision to produce a translation for the missionary work in New Spain reinforces the degree to which Olmos felt a similar "witch hunt" was necessary there, too. Unlike the *sermonario* and *doctrina* quoted above, which were aimed at the Nahua public, Olmos's *Tratado* was for use by fellow Franciscans as a manual for how to identify "sorcery and spells" among the Indigenous population of New Spain. Hence, it was another weapon in the invisible war.

Baudot, who has published a Spanish translation of Olmos's Nahuatl text, notes that there are very few substantive differences in content between the two works. However, one of the passages he points to as reflecting local conditions is in an anecdote Olmos relates from his own personal experience working in Cuernavaca. There he encountered a man who claimed that the devil had appeared to him. When Olmos asked the man to describe the devil's appearance and what he said, the man provided the following testimony:

> Very early in the morning, right before the dawn, out in a deserted place the devil revealed himself to me. He was arrayed like a *tlahtoani*, just as the *tlahtohqueh* of old arrayed themselves when they would dance. I was frightened. He said to me, "O won't you please come [over here to me]. Say to don Juan [a local lord] 'Why did you abandon me? Now go assemble the *macehualtin* so that there, at the edge of the forest,

they will come before me. Because it is not possible for me to enter Quaunahuac [Cuernavaca] on account of the cross they erected there and the *padres* [friars] that live there.' "[63]

In this telling, the devil manifests as a tlahtoani whose traditional dress suggests a rejection of Spanish clothing style, and perhaps by extension, of everything associated with the new regime.[64] The devil-tlahtoani tells the frightened man to go to don Juan, whose title indicates is also a member of the ruling class. Olmos's implication is that the earthly tlahtoani is in league with the devil, and both collude to target the macehualtin for enticing the man back to traditional forms of devotion. The devil-tlahtoani's aversion to the cross and the friars behind it betrays his anti-Christian, anti-mendicant stance. Baudot writes, "The devil represented, above all else, nostalgia for the pre-Columbian times."[65] In the estimation of Franciscans and the Nahuas allied with them, tlahtohqueh resisters like don Carlos Ometochtzin and don Juan in Olmos's *Tratado* were in league with the devil and competed with the friars for the souls of the macehualtin.

Through the efforts of friars like Olmos, over the course of the decade between the end of the Inquisition and the writing of Olmos's *Tratado*, the tlahtohqueh and nanahualtin were transformed into diabolical deceivers, wicked individuals who persecuted Christ's servants and vainly arrayed themselves in precontact finery. They represented the antithesis of everything the friars labored to teach. Their existence constituted an extreme crisis, one that threatened to upend all the friars' efforts, to turn the world upside down. In the mind of some apocalyptic thinker, perhaps Aquino or perhaps a friar, the existence of these malevolent enemies of the faith triggered an ominous realization: the Antichrist had come.

THE AZTEC ANTICHRIST

Might the inspiration to bring an Aztec Antichrist to the Nahuatl stage have come from Olmos or a member of his circle? It's a tempting thought, which will be addressed presently. Regardless of who it was, it seems most likely that the notion sprang into being in the context of the crisis of the late 1530s and the ensuing decade's "war of words" targeting the Franciscans' nemeses. As I have already written, this period witnessed a battle for the hearts, minds, and souls of the macehualtin, who represented the vast majority of the Indigenous population. On the one side were the traditionalist tlahtohqueh who relied on their subjects for tribute, labor, and prestige. On the other side were the mendicant orders, zealous for the harvest of souls.

The basic contours of this conflict are discernible throughout both plays, even before Antichrist opens his mouth. Over and over again, the author of the plays inserted not-so-subtle condemnations of the tlahtohqueh all the while extolling the macehualtin or depicting them as hapless victims. For example, during Sibyl's opening monologue in *Antichrist and the Final Judgment*, she makes it clear who the intended audience of the play is by declaring, "Here you are at last, you tail, you wing [i.e., you macehualtin]. Look here! Come to your senses, you neophyte! See the neixcuitilli so that you will know when God's heart will determine to end the world" (f. 133r–v). Later on in her monologue she explains how the Final Judgment will unfold. Her speech clearly illustrates the favorable light the plays cast on the macehualtin and the gloom that surrounds the ruling class: "[God] will favor all the good ones, he will really intercede for the common people [macehualtin], [but] those wicked ones will really burn forever. The nobles [*pipiltin*] will descend to Mictlan [where] their mistresses and a great many of their women are" (f. 137v).[66]

Over and over again the tlahtohqueh are denounced for their sexual immorality. Often, like the above, they are depicted as rapacious predators. This is precisely the charge levelled at the tlahtohqueh by the friars in their sermons and in the Inquisition trials, discussed above. The same theme crops up in Hermit's interrogation of the *teotl* Otonteuctli, depicted as a representation of the deadly sin of sloth. Hermit asks him why he has ended up in Mictlan, to which Otonteuctli responds, "All I do is go around placing laziness within the nobles [pipiltin] so that they will live slothfully, so that they will just do nothing but look for young women or perhaps some people's wives to have sex with" (f. 172v–173r). This pattern continues throughout.

One of the eighteen *condenados* (condemned souls) that Hermit interrogates is named Tontiyeyo, who introduces himself by stating tersely *nitlatovani*, "I am a tlahtoani." Tontiyeyo's unbaptized state is indicated by his lack of a Christian name. When Hermit demands of him "Why has God cast you into Mictlan?" he confesses, "because it was not possible for me to keep his commands, because I enriched myself [and] as a result I just lived haughtily. Likewise, I despised my subjects [macehualtin], causing them to suffer, imposing much work on them. . . . Also, I took their women as my property, I made them my mistresses" (f. 178r–v). Hermit sends the unrepentant tlahtoani back to hell by saying, "So be it! Please go, you wicked one!" However, before moving on, Hermit turns and directly addresses members of the ruling class who might be in attendance by saying, *av inin yc ximozcallicā tlatohe*, "In light of this, come to your senses, O rulers [tlahtohqueh]!" This is a remarkably transparent tell indicating the author's intended audience of the exchange between Hermit and a tlahtoani.

However, it is in the character of Antichrist that we find the clearest embodiment of the Franciscans' enemies, the resistant tlahtohqueh and the nanahualtin. Like the tlahtohqueh, Antichrist is a wealthy, powerful lord. In the opening scene of Aquino's

Final Judgment, Antichrist proclaims, "I am all powerful. There is absolutely no one like me on earth" (f. 138r). He threatens to kill anyone who refuses to believe in him and offers enticements that reveal his great wealth: delicious food, *pulque* (the preferred alcoholic beverage among Nahuas), great quantities of gold, and fine cotton cloaks. Antichrist also claims divine status, stating "I made the world" and "I am the deity [*teotl*], I am Christ" (f. 138r, 157v). With this, Antichrist also comes across an anti-mendicant nahualli along the lines of Martín Ocelotl and Andrés Mixcoatl. He urges the macehualtin to reject the teachings of the friars and return to the ways of their ancestors, and so avoid terrifying consequences. Early in *Hermit*, Antichrist gives an impassioned speech directed at the very same Nahua "hearts and minds" that were the object of the friars' preaching. It follows immediately upon Sibyl's opening monologue, one in which she warns the audience that the world will not end until "a wicked person will come, will be born, whose name will be Antichrist" (f. 155r). In his speech, Antichrist vacillates between tender entreaties to macehualtin converts and chilling threats in his effort to persuade them to reject Christianity.

As with resistant tlahtohqueh like don Carlos, he comes across as firmly anti-mendicant, opposing both the friars and their teachings about *icel teotl dios*, "Only Deity, God." He says as much when he states, "I really, really pity you because of all those who went around teaching you, those who went around deceiving you" (f. 157v). "Those who went around teaching you" is clearly a reference to the friars, the implication of his pity being that these disruptive preachers have caused turmoil and confusion among the *macehualtin*. He commands them, "Do not believe what they said to you!," an order that recalls don Carlos's mandate to his young nephew Francisco, "don't encourage the native people to believe what the friars say." The disruptive effects of the friars' preaching are lamented by Antichrist here and elsewhere in the two plays. Later on in *Hermit*, Antichrist confronts a group of Indigenous converts who have been returned to the faith through the preaching of Elijah and Enoch, spiritual authorities who act as stand-ins for the friars in both plays. Regarding the preaching of the two prophets (and by extension the friars), Antichrist complains, "Those two old men have blinded you" (f. 164r–v). It is against the friars that Antichrist rails and from them that he seeks to woo converted macehualtin.

Antichrist's anti-mendicant message parallels that of Ocelotl and Mixcoatl in his insistence that he is a teotl (deity). Echoing Mixcoatl's statement that "I became a god," Antichrist insists multiple times, "I am your deity [teotl], your ruler! I am Christ!" (f. 157r). Antichrist seizes on the friars' exclusive claims regarding the Christian God and rejects them by proclaiming himself to be a deity. Antichrist also embodies native resistance by urging the macehualtin to return to the ways of their ancestors. In his words we can sense the exasperation he feels at the new,

TABLE 2.1. The words of don Carlos and Antichrist compared

Don Carlos (Proceso inquisitorial, 54)	Antichrist (Sermones y miscelánea de devoción, f. 156v)
"If your husband desires to have other women, don't stop him or quarrel with the women that he takes or follow marriage under Christian law! I, too, am married, but, in spite of this, I do not refrain from having your niece as my mistress."	"And you, O rulers, why do you diminish your way of living? Why do you abandon your women? You used to have many mistresses! Now, devote yourselves to all the women, however many you want. This will really satisfy me."

Christian behavior of converts like don Carlos's nephew, Francisco. To the macehualtin he exclaims, "Why did you dismantle my home?" To the tlahtohqueh, "Why do you abandon your women?" And to women, "You do not paint your faces anymore!" (f. 156v). His exasperation echoes that of don Carlos, both in tone and in word. Don Carlos chided his fellow pipiltin for their abandonment of traditions and privileges that used to be accorded to the nobles and rulers. Especially vexing to him was the loss of sexual prerogatives of noblemen due to the friars' enforcing of Christian sexual norms. In order to make his point, he reportedly called his sister María into the room and told her in front of the assembled pipiltin that she and all women should follow "what our ancestors used to do" with regard to sexual privileges. In order to show how closely his message parallels that of the Aztec Antichrist, I presented their words side by side in table 2.1.

Both don Carlos and Antichrist make impassioned pleas to their fellow Nahuas to reject the teachings of the friars and return to their former ways. Antichrist cries, "Devote yourselves to everything that you used to devote yourselves to," (f. 156v) assuring the macehualtin that this is the way to return order to the world turned upside down by the friars and their strange prohibitions. When the macehualtin waver in their response to Antichrist, he resorts to direct threats, proclaiming, "if you do not obey me, then I will slay you with my own hands!" (f. 157v). Here, too, Antichrist sounds as if his words have been ripped right out of the Inquisition records from the 1530s. Compare Antichrist's words above with those one witness claimed were uttered by Andrés Mixcoatl in 1537: "Andrés said to the macehualtin, 'If you don't obey me, all of you will die.'" To this the witness added, "and in this way he frightened the macehualtin into believing he was a god."[67] Mixcoatl's threats seem to have been intended to increase his stature and amass wealth from offerings given to him by the frightened macehualtin as much as they were an effort to push back against the friars. In the neixcuitilli, Antichrist's menacing of Christian macehualtin is more squarely directed at countering Christianity and its mendicant ambassadors so as to reclaim for the devil the souls lost through their preaching.

CONCLUSION

In the period stretching from the mid-1520s through the middle of the century, Franciscan missionaries struggled to establish their dominion in New Spain. The monumental task of converting so many millions of people with so few ministers to do the work left them constantly under-resourced and over-stressed. Out of necessity—so they claimed—they adopted a controversial method of administering baptism before thoroughly indoctrinating the initiates. This led to two problems that seriously threatened their mission: fierce criticism from the Dominicans and their allies and masses of superficially indoctrinated new Christians. By the 1530s, evidence of persistent "idolatry" abounded, and many despaired that the total failure of the mission was inevitable. Particularly troubling was the emergence of prominent Indigenous personalities that constituted a countermovement of traditionalist resistance. Forcing a confrontation with what was deemed an existential threat, Zumárraga, Olmos, and others vigorously pursued Inquisitorial proceedings against tlahtohqueh like don Carlos of Tetzcoco and nanahualtin like Andrés Mixcoatl and Martín Ocelotl. When that tactic failed, they pursued a rhetorical war of words, demonizing the tlahtohqueh and traditional religious practices in their preaching.

This chapter has argued that the Aztec Antichrist was the inspiration of someone, perhaps a Franciscan or one of their Nahua associates, who considered the totality of these events and the threat they represented and, like so many before, saw in them the signs of the end times. The evidence considered above has again raised the question of who that someone was. In the course of research into this tumultuous early period of Mexican history, the name of Fray Andrés de Olmos has come up time and again. It is tempting to think that he might be the apocalyptic thinker who conceived of two neixcuitilli depicting the career of Antichrist. Although it is not possible to state it conclusively, there are a number of clues that suggest a connection between the plays and Fray Andrés, or his circle of Nahua colleagues and assistants.

For one, out of the scant references to the Antichrist that can be found in sixteenth-century sources, the two earliest ones are both associated with Olmos. The first one is found in the *Tratado de hechicerías y sortilegios*. In the relevant passage, Olmos writes that when "he whose name will be Antichrist" (*yehuatl yn itoca yez antecristo*) is born and lives on the earth, he will—just like the devil—deceive people into following him with bribes of gold. Drawing out further the comparison between the devil and the Antichrist, he concludes by stating that "the devil is very flattering, very cunning in how he promises, offers to give people many riches and afterward makes fun of people, slanders people."[68] The association between the devil and the tlahtohqueh in the *Tratado* is mirrored by the close association between the Antichrist and the tlahtohqueh in the plays. I argue that both the plays and the *Tratado* were written in the context of the Franciscans' invisible war against idolatry and its campaign against anti-mendicant Indigenous rulers, a connection that pulls Olmos and the author of the plays into each other's orbit.

The second early reference to the Antichrist is less-securely tied to Olmos. It is the much-discussed neixcuitilli depicting the Final Judgment, touted in many sources as the first play performed in the Americas.[69] As was discussed in the previous chapter, there exist a number of references to Final Judgment plays being performed in the 1530s in Mexico and in Tlatelolco. There are also a number of colonial sources that say Olmos himself wrote an "auto" about the Final Judgment.[70] We even have a script of a Nahuatl Final Judgment play that is preserved in the Library of Congress that, according to some, bears the marks of being a copy of an original dating to the sixteenth century.[71] What we *do not* have is any evidence that the script that survives is the Final Judgment play reported to have been written by Olmos and performed in the 1530s, although that hasn't stopped many scholars from connecting the dots. In any case, the script features a small part for an actor playing the Antichrist. Like all good Antichrists, he pretends to be the real Christ and tricks a Christian woman named Lucía into worshipping him, much to her detriment. Again, whether or not this Antichrist character was the literary creation of Olmos or not is impossible to say. However, it is worth noting the existence of an Antichrist character in a play that has long been associated with that venerable friar.

If one were to travel down this speculative path a bit farther, linking the plays with Olmos or his circle is made all the more tempting due to the amount of ethnographic material incorporated into the scripts. Olmos gained the reputation for being one of the friars most learned in the matters of Indigenous culture, due to his extensive research from 1533 to 1539. Much of the material incorporated into the plays is likely analogous to what Olmos recorded in his *Tratado de antiguedades*. This same ethnographic material is probably what led Karl Hiersemann to declare that Fabián de Aquino "was probably one of the Indians who related the ancient histories of the Mexicans to Father Bernardino de Sahagún." After reading this chapter, one may perhaps wonder whether Hiersemann had the wrong friar-ethnographer in mind. We will probably never be able to go any farther than these brief, tantalizing conjectures, but they are included here in hopes that someday someone will be able to add more to what we know about the author of these very early Nahuatl dramas.

The Aztec Antichrist preserved in the two Hispanic Society neixcuitilli is a pulque-swigging, *difrasismo*-uttering tlahtoani who sits on a reed throne (*icpalli*) and presides over the execution of those he calls *nomacehualhuan*, "my subjects, my macehualtin." A malevolent miracle-worker, he stood as a bulwark against the turning tide of his day. His impassioned pleas to his people to return to the traditions of their elders and reject the strange new morality of the friars established him as the nemesis of the Christians. Bringing this character to life on the stage, the Franciscan-affiliated Nahua who adapted the legend did so as a weapon in the invisible war against idolatry and idolaters. Performance was the chosen weapon. However, this weapon would prove to be a double-edged sword.

A NAHUA CHRISTIAN WRITES BACK

IF THE PERFORMANCE of an Antichrist play was intended as a weapon in the invisible war against idolatry, it is reasonable to ask what sort of work that weapon did, how effective it was, and whether it may have cut two ways. For while on one level the plays can be considered Christian performances, on another they were also Indigenous performances of Christianity, or better yet, performances of Indigenous Christianity. Although the original idea for a Nahuatl Antichrist play may have been that of a Franciscan friar, after handing off the project to an Indigenous colleague, this friar had little to do with the actual realization of either of the scripts. As a result, the performances imagined were unavoidably *both* Christian *and* Indigenous, or rather, Christian in a distinctly Indigenous way. This chapter argues that while the author of the plays was very much entrenched in the doctrines and doctrinal discourses of the friars, he deployed these in a thoroughly Indigenous manner that subtly pushed back against certain assumptions inherent in the friars' rhetoric. The author of the plays also reveals his familiarity with the cultural research of the friars and may even have had access to their ethnographic writings. However, here too, the way he deployed this ethnographic material reveals Indigenous concerns and may have undermined the friars' demonization of certain elements of Indigenous culture.

In this sense, both plays can be considered autoethnographic works of Indigenous American literature. Autoethnography here is understood as a form of subaltern writing that both engages with and challenges the ethnographic observations of the colonizer. Mary Louise Pratt articulates the concept this way:

https://doi.org/10.5876/9781646423002.c003

If ethnographic texts are those in which European metropolitan subjects represent to themselves their others (usually their conquered others), autoethnographic texts are representations that the so-defined others construct *in response to* or in dialogue with those texts. Autoethnographic texts . . . involve a selective collaboration with and appropriation of idioms of the metropolis or the conqueror. These are merged or infiltrated to varying degrees with indigenous idioms to create self-representations intended to intervene in metropolitan modes of understanding.[1]

Seen in this way, the Nahuatl Antichrist dramas can be read as performances or "self-representations" of Indigenous Christianity that engage with and intervene in the demonizing discourses of the friars and by so doing present an alternative mode of religiosity for Indigenous audiences. The deep intertextuality between the plays and the doctrinal and ethnographic work of the friars is one of the most pervasive features of these early colonial *neixcuitilli*. Its treatment here will be yet another "unbundling" of Fabián de Aquino's devotional notebook and the Nahuatl Antichrist plays it contains.

DOCTRINAL DISCOURSE

Central to the concept of autoethnography defined above is the role of the Indigenous interlocutor, an individual conversant in two cultures and able to deftly navigate the ambivalent space bridging them. The author of the Antichrist plays was one such as this. The scripts he adapted bear the marks of his indigeneity just as they are indelibly impressed with his Christian and Franciscan education. One of the most striking indicators of his education is his skillful appropriation of the doctrinal discourses that were constructed early in the mission by friars and Nahuas working in the major convent schools of New Spain. So thoroughly does he incorporate these discourses and so facilely are they deployed that it suggests he was no mere "amanuensis," or scribe, but may have been one of the Indigenous intellectuals who assisted the friars in developing such discourse and composing the doctrinal materials by which they were disseminated.

First, a word about the word *discourse*. As it is used here in the phrase "doctrinal discourse," discourse refers to language, both spoken and written, that was developed to communicate the dogmas of Hispano-Catholicism to the Indigenous people of New Spain. There is a sense in which discourse also indexes a much broader phenomenon than mere language. This view understands discourse as "language-in-action," a complex wielding of power and knowledge by dominant institutions that shapes the way people think and act. This secondary meaning is eminently relevant to our understanding of Nahuatl-Christian doctrinal discourse, as will be seen below.

Doctrinal discourse in Nahuatl, which is to say, the lexicon that was used to communicate Christianity to Nahuas, was a hybrid linguistic product of the early intercultural exchanges of the 1520s through the 1540s. Once friars and Nahuas had gained basic proficiency in each other's languages, the work of translating Christian doctrine into Nahuatl quickly ensued. The foundation of this process was the creation of a Nahuatl-Christian lexicon of terms and concepts central to Christianity. This was achieved using a variety of methods, but three are worth briefly mentioning.[2] The first was the construction of new words through lexical derivation (e.g., *cuaatequia*, "to throw water on the head," for "baptism").[3] A second method was semantic extension, where a word or concept that already existed in Nahuatl was repurposed and given a new, Christian meaning. The now-classic example of this method was the deriving of a word for "sin" (*tlahtlacolli*) from the common Nahuatl verb *ihtlacoa*, "to spoil or damage."[4] A final way of introducing new words into the Nahuatl lexicon was by loaning them from Latin or Spanish. In instances where the previous two methods were deemed inadequate or where the use of Nahuatl ran the risk of heterodox interpretations, the foreign word was simply substituted. Common examples of loans in Nahuatl-Christian texts include *Dios* (Span. "God"), *missa* (Span. "mass"), *cruz* (Span. "cross"), and *anima* (Lat. "soul"). Words fashioned according to these methods quickly became canonical forms that were a constant feature of Nahuatl-Christian discourse throughout the colonial period.

However, the development of doctrinal discourse involved more than merely finding equivalents for Christian terms in Nahuatl. In order for the new doctrine to be understood, the language used also needed to be persuasive. One means of doing this was to lend an air of authority to doctrinal discourse by adopting elements of Indigenous formal speech. Early on, the friars took an interest in speech genres like the *huehuetlahtolli*, "speech of the elders," with the likes of Olmos and Sahagún collecting examples of wise sayings and admonitions to serve as models for their writing of doctrine. What these early studies of language revealed were the rhetorical devices that structured Indigenous formal speech, the poetics of Nahuatl verbal art. This included the frequent use of complex parallel constructions, the repetition of words and phrases in twos, threes, and fours, the use of vocative expressions, and a reservoir of metaphorical language often involving symbolism of the sacred "flowery world" of Mesoamerican cosmology.[5] Incorporating parallel constructions, *difrasismos*, and metaphors into doctrinal discourse communicated to the audience (or reader) that the speaker (or writer) was an authority. Rooting Christian discourse in the traditional speech practices of the *huehuetqueh* (elders) and *tlahtohqueh* (rulers) lent it legitimacy and persuasive force. Indigenous poetics, together with the ample lexicon of Nahuatl-Christian terms, define the main contours of what is referred to here as doctrinal discourse. But they are not its only important features.

Before moving on, we must return to a broader understanding of the word *discourse*, the one that emphasizes "language in action."[6] Essentially, this view of discourse emphasizes the operation of language within a social field, the various tasks language carries out in society. Since discourse production is typically under the control of society's most influential institutions (like the media today, or church and state in sixteenth-century Mexico), discourse is fundamentally about power. By controlling discourse production and its deployment, these powerful institutions construct and maintain social order. Discourse is therefore closely related to ideology, since the institutions that give shape to discourse are themselves ideologically based and motivated. Discourse practices, then, can be seen as the deployment of dominant ideologies. Doctrinal discourse in early colonial Mexico met these criteria as well. Hanks's discussion of doctrinal discourse shows how it was deeply implicated in the processes of *reducción* and the creation of *policía cristiana*, the totalizing projects of ordering Indigenous spaces, bodies, and minds.[7] Inherently about power and control, colonial doctrinal discourse was shaped by the ideologies of the spiritual colonizer. One of the most ubiquitous of these viewed fundamental elements of Indigenous culture, principally religion, as diabolical. The diabolism of the early Franciscans, previously discussed in the context of a shift from legal to rhetorical strategies during the "invisible war" against idolatry, colored all of their writing and preaching. It viewed of the world as existing in a state of stark spiritual conflict, where the soldiers of Christ, Mary, and the saints did battle against the devil, his demons, and those under their sway. Elements of Indigenous culture that contradicted Christian doctrine or offended Christian sensibility were branded "works of the devil." Seen through this lens, Indigenous people were believed to be particularly susceptible to the devil's lies, with which he deceived them into worshipping demons as if they were gods and offering human beings as bloody sacrifices. Discourses of confusion, deception, perturbation, and mockery unfolded in numerous sermons and catechisms as friars sought to convince Nahuas to abandon their gods and embrace *icel teotl dios*, "Only Deity, God."

Diabolism gave birth to a number of important rhetorical offspring that were deployed in Nahuatl-Christian doctrinal writing and speaking aimed at Indigenous conversion. The first of these tactics is what Viviana Díaz Balsera refers to as "epistemic violence."[8] This phrase refers to rhetorical acts of domination within the realm of knowledge in which the capital-T "truth" the friars claimed to possess utterly negated Indigenous epistemologies. Díaz Balsera turns to the *Coloquios* of Sahagún for illustrations. In one exchange between the first friars and the Mexica *tlamatinimeh* ("knowers of things," or "wise men"), the friars declared, "All of these that you consider *teteoh*, absolutely no one is a *teotl*, ... all are devils."[9] A dozen more examples could be selected from this text alone. Statements like it are ubiquitous

FIGURE 3.1. Open-air chapel with sixteenth-century murals depicting demons tormenting souls in hell. San Nicolás de Tolentino, Actopan, Hidalgo. Wikimedia Commons image by RubeHM.

throughout the literature and reveal the lengths to which the friars went to exert the hegemonic claims of Christianity over Indigenous religion.

A second rhetorical strategy that served to drive home the ideology of diabolism was what José Guadalajara Medina has referred to as "didactic terror."[10] This tactic sought to induce a state of fear in Indigenous people that would compel them to abandon the teteoh and traditional religious practices and embrace the teachings of Christianity. If fear was the currency in the economy of salvation, the friars spent wildly, filling their books, sermons, murals, and plays with illustrations of hell and damnation that were shaped by what I have elsewhere called the "poetics of terror" (see figure 3.1).[11] Capitalizing on the rhetorical force of Nahuatl verbal art, certain writers—some of whom, it must be emphasized, were Indigenous—spun phantasmagoric nightmares of pain and suffering, elaborated in cascades of couplets, triplets, and longer strings of visually arresting words. The poetics of terror transformed devils into Indigenous monsters with "teeth like sacrificial stones" and warned audiences that on Judgment Day Christ "will strike you, will cut you in half, will split you, will cut you down the middle, will pulverize you, will break you into little pieces."[12] Fear as an educational tactic was not invented by New Spain's friars; indeed, medieval art and literature shows how central this approach was to the Catholic Church's ideological domination in Western history. However, in the American context, where it defined the first-ever presentations of Christianity to a wholly unfamiliar people, it was to have long-ranging effects, many of which are still visible in the various forms of Catholic religiosity in Mexico today.

Epistemic violence and didactic terror were two of the most ubiquitous rhetorical strategies deployed in support of the friars' ideology of diabolism, a cornerstone of Nahuatl-Christian doctrinal discourse. This discourse was constructed in the convent centers of New Spain, and it was disseminated throughout the colony via a multitude of media: it was proclaimed by friars in weekly sermons, it was recited by Nahuas in daily catechism class, and, as we have seen, it was performed and embodied in the neixcuitilli of early colonial Mexico. It's important to note that these strategies were developed very early in the mission, from the late 1520s through the 1540s. Hanks notes that the creation of Indigenous-language *doctrinas* canonized specific linguistic forms that were replicated with little variation across three centuries of colonial rule.[13] Mark Christensen's work with doctrinal materials from later in the colonial period supports this. He shows how the linguistic innovations of the sixteenth century formed reified speech patterns that later writers adhered to without alteration, suggesting that the authority of sacred speech (*teotlahtolli*) was inextricably linked to that early formative period.[14]

Whether we're talking about the 1540s or the 1740s, to speak or write according to these conventions, what we can call the performance of doctrinal discourse, telegraphed authority. This is precisely what the author of the Nahuatl Antichrist plays did when he composed lines for Sibyl, Enoch, Elijah, Hermit, and others. He did so in such a way that reveals his deep familiarity not only with the discursive strategies outlined above, but also with the various genres and situations in which they were performed. In his characters' words we hear the echoes of sermons and catechisms, texts that he himself may have had a hand in creating.

INDIGENOUS APPROPRIATION OF DOCTRINAL DISCOURSE

The Nahuatl Antichrist plays that Fabián de Aquino copied into his notebook are written in what Nancy Farriss calls the "doctrinal register," which is to say, they constitute examples of doctrinal discourse.[15] This is evidenced first of all by the way the author deftly employed the lexicon discussed above. Nahuatl-Christian neologisms like *cuaatequia* (baptism) and *tlahtlacolli* (sin), as well as others like *tlaneltoquiliztli* ("faith," lit. "the act of following something as true"), *tlateotoca* ("to idolize" lit. "to follow something as a teotl [deity]"), *tlamahcehualiztli* ("penance," from *mahcehua*, "to merit, deserve something"), *totemaquixticatzin* ("our Savior," from *maquixtia*, "to redeem, liberate"), and *totecuiyo* ("our Lord," referring to Jesus Christ) abound in both scripts. Additionally, many of the standard loan words—*Dios, ángel, cruz, cristiano, mártir, converso*, and even *auto*, "play"—are also peppered throughout.

None of this is especially surprising, since any Nahua trained in the friars' convent schools would have been introduced to this specialized lexicon from an early age. However, the presence of more complex linguistic formulae indicates a deeper level of familiarity with Nahuatl-Christian doctrinal discourse. For example, expressions like *icel teotl dios*, "the he-alone (i.e., "only") teotl, God," were devised to communicate the singular nature of the Christian deity. The author of the plays places this expression in the mouths of characters like Sibyl, who declares, "Only Deity, God [*yn icel teotl dios*], has sent me," and Hermit, who urges his audience to "Believe in Only Deity, Jesus Christ [*yn icel teotl Jesucristo*]" (f. 155r, 187r). Additionally, we find expert usage of what can be called Nahuatl-Christian difrasismos, couplets such as *cenca yectli, cenca qualli* ("very right, very good," for "virtuous"), *yn qualtin, yn aqualtin* ("the good ones, the bad ones," for "blessed and damned"), and *amoteovh, amotlatocavh* ("your teotl [deity], your ruler," for "the Christian God"). Like the lexicon of neologisms, these linguistic formulations of doctrine and discourse were second nature to our author.

Beyond these basic traits of his writing, a multitude of highly specific linguistic markers that indicate the author's familiarity with the different genres of doctrinal writing is discernible. Take, for example, his practice of composing speeches that co-opted the voice of the friar-preacher, so common in the Nahuatl sermons of the day. In sermons, friars addressed neophytes using stock expressions that communicated both authority and paternalism. Formulae like *In axcan tla xicmocaquiti notlazohpiltzine* (Today please listen, O my beloved child!), where the deictic marker *axcan* (today) precedes a command (often to "listen") that is followed by the ubiquitous expression of paternal affection in the vocative (O my beloved child). Many of the plays' characters address their audiences using this precise formula. These are the words of Sibyl: *Auh in axcan nopilhuane ma ximoyollapaltilican* (Today, O my children, take strength), and Enoch: *Nopilhuane tla xicmocaquitican* (O my children, won't you please listen), and St. Michael: *tla xicmocaquitican* ("Please won't you listen"; f. 155v, 161v, 165r).

Hermit's twenty-five interrogations of demons and condemned souls in *Antichrist and the Hermit* suggests familiarity with the specific kind of discourse that characterizes another genre of doctrinal writing, the confession manual. Confession manuals provided priests with lists of questions they might ask Nahua penitents so as to induce them to make a thorough confession of sin. Part of the function of confessional manuals such as the two written under the supervision of Fray Alonso de Molina was to introduce Nahuas to certain categories of acts that were deemed sinful. In order to do this, the questions were framed according to the Ten Commandments and the seven deadly sins. For example, the *Confessionario mayor* (1565, see figure 0.3) is broken into sections with headings like *Tetlatlaniliztli, ytechpa ynic centetl teonauatili*, "Questions regarding the first sacred command," *Tetlatlaniliztli, ytechpa yn teoyeuacatiliztli*, "Questions regarding greed," etc.[16] The seven demons interrogated by Hermit follow this model, each one representing one of the seven deadly sins.

The scene that follows this, in which Hermit interrogates eighteen condemned souls, merges the confession manual's obsessive documentation of specific sins with the genre of the medieval morality play. What results are what we might call "confessional dramas," in which each character confesses to specific sins that the ecclesiastical authorities of the day deemed to be in need of public condemnation. In *Antichrist and the Hermit*, some of the sins divulged by each character are of a generic nature that would also have been found in European moralities: adultery, theft, greed, etc. However, many of the sins confessed bear a striking resemblance to the sins listed in Nahuatl confession manuals like Molina's. These were "Indigenous sins" in the friars' estimation, particular areas of vice resulting from the devil's long history of "deceiving and confusing" Indigenous people. One of the most striking characteristics of the confession manuals is the highly specific nature of the sins enumerated and highly invasive nature of the questions priests were supposed to ask. The most economical way to illustrate the parallels between the confessional dramas of *Antichrist and the Hermit* and the Nahuatl confession manual is via a table (see table 3.1).

The side-by-side comparison of quotes from the main Nahuatl confession manual of the sixteenth century with quotes from *Antichrist and the Hermit* in table 3.1 offers further evidence that the author was well aware of the doctrinal writings like these. But unlike the discourses preserved in sermons, which were performed publicly and often, the discourses of the *confessionarios* were much more selectively available to Nahuas. They could have encountered them in the act of confession, but we know that the rates at which Indigenous people availed themselves of this sacrament were very low, which means that average Nahuas would have not been as familiar with this genre. However, Molina tells us that these manuals were intended not only for friars but also for members of the literate Nahua elite in order to assist them in preparing themselves to receive the sacrament.[17] It seems quite likely, then, that our author fell into this latter category.

The quotes above also reveal the extent to which the author of the plays was conversant with the friars' moral discourses, especially those focusing on sexual

TABLE 3.1. Confessional discourse in Molina and Aquino

Molina, *Confessionario mayor and breve*	Aquino, *Antichrist and the Hermit*
"Did you charge someone excessive interest (*tetech titlayxtlapan*)?" (*mayor*, f. 15r)	Merchant: "I charged people excessive interest (*tetech nitlaixtlapanaya*)" (f. 178v)
"Did you steal someone's property? Perhaps a cloak, precious metal, jade . . . ?" (*breve*, f.14r)	Thief: "I would steal like it was my job. I would take a person's cloak from him, a person's property" (f. 184v).
"Did you drink a deadly potion so that you aborted, so that you killed your child? (*breve*, f. 10v).	One Who Sterilizes Herself: "I asked the healer for a sterilizing potion and with it I sterilized myself" (f. 183v).
"Did you desire some woman in order to have sex with her? . . . Was she perhaps your relative? Was she perhaps your relation?" (*mayor*, f.32r)	This One Slept With His Relative: "I slept with a woman who was my relative and as a result I deeply offended God" (f. 185r).
Question for a *tlahtoani*: "Have you, at times, taken things from the *macehualtin* that you govern? . . . Did you augment, increase their tribute? (*breve*, f.15v–16r).	Ruler's Goods: "I despised my subjects (*macehualtin*), causing them to suffer, imposing much work on them. Many times I demanded their belongings from them." (f. 178r).
"Do you also keep an image of the were-owl, or do you know of anyone who keeps it [or] hides it?" (*mayor*, f. 20r).	Unbelievers (two *tlahtohqueh*): "We carefully protected the images of our deities (*toteovan*) so that the Christians wouldn't burn them" (f. 176v).
Question for a man: "Did you do *cuiloni* to someone or did someone do *cuiloni* to you?" (*breve*, f. 11v).	Cuiloni: "I am a *cuiloni*, I satisfied myself greatly when they did *cuiloni* to me" (185v).

sin. However, it is the discourse of diabolism that dominates the two Antichrist *neixcuitilli* and betrays just how deeply the author was engaged in the intellectual and spiritual labor of the friars. One of the easiest ways to identify the discourse of diabolism in colonial Nahuatl texts is to see where and when the label of "devil" is applied, and to whom. Searching for uses of the word *tlacatecolotl* and its plural form *tlatlacatecoloh* in the Antichrist plays reveals the contours of the author's diabolism of this medieval legend.

In short, it's utterly pervasive. We might start with the author's innovative decision to present six of the seven demons representing the seven deadly sins as precontact *teteoh*. The cast list at the beginning of *Antichrist and the Final Judgment* tells would-be organizers of the play "Then the *tlatlacatecoloh* will enter from Mictlan. . . . The first is named Lucifer, the second Tlaloc, the third Tezcatlipoca, the fourth," etc. (f. 132r). Hermit makes the association between precontact *teteoh* and the devil explicit with the terse accusation of the demon Tezcatlipoca, *ca titlacatecolotl*, "You are a/the *tlacatecolotl*!" (f. 170v). This statement echoes that of

Bernardino de Sahagún, who wrote in a sermon for the fourteenth Sunday after Pentecost, "the great *tlacatecolotl*, Lucifer, whom you used to call Tezcatlipoca, deceived you."[18] In the plays, the character Antichrist is universally identified using the word tlacatecolotl. The character of God himself denounces him as *yn vey tla-catecolotl*, "the great *tlacatecolotl*" (f. 142v), and Sibyl informs the audience, "in order to thoroughly deceive you he will call himself Christ. [However,] he is really just a/ the *tlacatecolotl*" (f. 155r).

Beyond unmasking the teteoh (and the Antichrist) as demons, the author gives other characters lines that portray the effects of diabolization. In his confession to Hermit, Huitzilopochtli admits, "I went around deceiving the people. They used to consider me a deity (*teotoca*), [but] I'm only God's creation" (f. 170v). Otontecuhtli makes a similar confession, "The people used to take me for a deity, they used to celebrate a feast in my honor. . . . With this I deceived them. I am not a deity, I am merely God's creation. Because of my sins he cast me into Mictlan where I live eternally burning" (172r–v). Indigenous "fire priests," members of the institutional priesthood responsible for offering human sacrifices before the conquest, admit to the audience, "We six are the were-owls' fire priests. Before us [people] spread out offerings. Those who we used to follow as deities are not true deities (*amo nelli teteo*), even though we earnestly served them. And now we suffer with them in Mictlan [hell] because we didn't acknowledge the true God (*yn nelli dios*)" (f. 174v).

Quotes like these also reveal the epistemic violence that was done through the diabolization of Indigenous people and practices. This violence is evident in the words of the character playing a *tonalpouhqui* (day-keeper, diviner). As interpreters of the pictorial divination manuals (*tonalamatl*), the *tonalpouhqueh* (pl. of tonalpouhqui) were essential guardians of traditional knowledge in Nahua society. Putting a tonalpouhqui on stage and scripting lines where he condemns himself and his ritual practices was akin to putting all of Indigenous epistemology on trial and condemning it worthless. He states,

> I used to read the book in order to deceive people. When someone was born the mother and father would bring him [or her] before me so that I would tell them under which day sign their child had been born, so that I would tell them what will happen to their child here on earth. *In this manner I used to deceive them. What I used to know is nothing.* (f. 177v; emphasis mine)

This short passage highlights (again) one of the plays' chief idiosyncrasies and is strongly suggestive of an Indigenous author working largely unsupervised: that is, the way it records in explicit detail elements of religious practice the friars had condemned as idolatrous. This necessitates addressing one final way in which the Nahua author reveals his close affiliation with the work of the Franciscans who were his teachers and, perhaps, colleagues: the ethnographic content of the two plays. Since this has been discussed in a previous chapter, only two examples are presented here.

However, it is first worth asking a critical question: Wouldn't *any* Indigenous writer have intimate knowledge of his people's traditional religious practices just by virtue of being Indigenous? Why should this indicate close affiliation with the ethnographic projects of the early friars? This is undoubtedly true, especially if the texts in question were written as early as I've argued they were. One *could* argue that as the colonial period progressed, detailed information about such matters may have faded somewhat from memory, but this was not the case here. The heart of the matter lies not so much in the *fact* of the plays' ethnographic content but in the *form* that it takes. It is the form, not the fact, that most strongly links the author and the friars, specifically the Franciscans in the orbit of Bernardino de Sahagún. In *Florentine Codex* Book 10, Sahagún and his Nahua collaborators condensed and categorized all the information they had gathered from their informants on the topic of numerous types of people and roles they played in Nahua society as well as the specific parts of the body and ailments that afflict it. Regarding people, the table of contents lists fathers and mothers, sons and daughters, nobles and commoners, "valiant men," gold casters and feather workers, carpenters, stone cutters, sorcerers, magicians, weavers, "bawds or pimps," merchants, and sellers of tamales.

However, unlike a modern ethnography where the observer refrains from introducing value judgments into their reporting, the "proto-ethnography" of Sahagún and his Nahua associates makes no such effort (hence "proto"). The opening words of Book 10 introduce its contents with the statement, "The Tenth Book . . . in which are told the different virtues and vices which were of the body and of the soul, whosoever practiced them."[19] Accordingly, when each category of person addressed, two sorts are described: the "good ruler" (for example) and the "bad ruler." The ensuing description takes the form of a catalog of traits, listed in Indigenous fashion, which is to say, their significance communicated through the accumulation of a long list of terms.[20] The description of the aforementioned "bad ruler" illustrates this "description through accumulation" as well as the value judgments inherent in early Franciscan proto-ethnography: "The bad ruler is a wild beast, a demon of the air (*tzitzimitl*), a demon (*coleletli*), an ocelot, a wolf—infamous, deserving of being left alone, avoided, detested as a respecter of nothing, savage, revolting."[21] The twenty-six chapters that constitute the first section of Book 10 offer a near-exhaustive list of people, each one extolled or excoriated for their virtues and vices and, in so doing, showing the friars' hand in steering this so-called ethnographic encyclopedia.

The interrogation and condemnation of the eighteen condemned souls in *Antichrist and the Hermit* reads like it was the product of the same school that produced Book 10's catalog of people types, except for the fact that only the "bad" types

TABLE 3.2. People types in *Antichrist and the Hermit* and Book 10 of the Florentine Codex

Antichrist and the Hermit	Book 10, The People[a]
Unbelievers (Atlaneltocani, both are rulers) and Ruler's Goods (Tlatovani Ytlatqui, another ruler; f. 176r–178r)	Ruler (Tlatoani; 10:15)
Day Keeper (Tonalpovhqui; f. 177r–v)	The Soothsayer, The Reader of Day Signs (Tlapouhqui, Tonalpouhqui; 10:31)
Merchant (Pochtecatl; f. 178v–179r)	The Merchant (Puchtecatl; 10:42, 59)
Young Man (Telpochtli; f. 179v–180r)	Youth (Telpuchtli; 10:12) and The Lewd Youth (Telpuchtlaueliloc; 10:37)
Procuress (Tetlanochilliyani; f. 180r-v)	The Procuress; [The Woman] Who Procures (Tetlanochili, Tetlanochiliani; 10:57)
One Who Indulges in Pleasure (Aviyani; f. 180v–181v)	The Harlot; The Carnal Woman (Ahuiani, Auilnenqui; 10:55–56)
Young Woman (Ychpochtli; f. 181v–182r)	The Maiden (Ichpuchtli; 10:12)
Healer (Ticitl; f. 182r–183r)	The Physician (Ticitl; 10:53)
Thief (Ychtequini; f. 184v–185r)	The Thief (Ichtecqui; 10:38–39)
Cuiloni (Cuiloni; f. 185v–186r)	The Sodomite (Cuiloni; 10:37–38)
Tepatlachviyani (Tepatlachhhuiani; f. 186v)	The Hermaphrodite (Patlache; 10:56)

[a] The data in this column preserves Dibble and Anderson's translations of these terms, some of which are out of date today.

are presented. Of the plays' eighteen sinners, twelve of them have their own, independent treatments in Book 10. These are listed in table 3.2.

There are six characters who don't receive direct treatment by way of having a category named for them in Book 10, but they are implicated in those that do. Take the character known only as One Who Sterilizes Herself (Motetzacatiliani). In her confession, she states, "I asked the healer for a sterilizing potion and with it I sterilized myself" (f. 183v). We find no category in Book 10 for a Motetzacatiliani; however, in the section for the Ticitl we read, "She makes one drink potions, kills people with medications, causes them to worsen, endangers them."[22] It's safe to say that, whether or not explicitly set apart as a "type" in Book 10, every one of the eighteen condemned souls finds its counterpart in the ethnographic catalog of diverse people-types. Both texts share the same cataloger's eye for types, and both condemn the same types for the same sorts of behaviors. The author of *Antichrist and the Hermit* does this with a more overt moral didacticism, but he seems to be working from the same template, the one established by friar-ethnographers in the 1540s through the 1570s.

One final linkage connects *Antichrist and the Hermit* with the ethnographic work of the friars, one that pertains more to the form in which the damning traits

FIGURE 3.2.
Ahuiani (Harlot).
From Sahagún,
Florentine Codex,
1575–1577, Book 10, f.
39v, Biblioteca Medicea
Laurenziana, Florence,
Med. Palat. 218–220.
Courtesy of MiC. Any
further reproduction
by any means is
prohibited.

are presented. In Hermit's Inquisition of the eighteen damned souls, when he arrives at the one called Ahuiani (lit. "One Who Indulges in Pleasure" but rendered as "Prostitute" in the friars' discourse),[23] he asks her, "Why did you go to Mictlan?" Her response bears a striking resemblance to the precise language and phrasing used in Book 10's description of The Harlot (see figure 3.2). I present them side-by-side in table 3.3 for closer comparison.

The author of the play has not *quoted* the text of Book 10. Instead, he has demonstrated his deep familiarity with the Indigenous modes of speech preserved in the ethnographic record. Moreover, he has demonstrated his familiarity with the

TABLE 3.3. One Who Indulges in Pleasure (Ahuiani) in *Antichrist and the Hermit* and Book 10 of the Florentine Codex

One Who Indulges in Pleasure (Aviyani); *Antichrist and the Hermit, f. 181r*	The Harlot (Ahuiani); Book 10:56
"I stuck out my tongue at people, I pointed my finger at people in the road, I laughed at people, I beckoned with my hand to people, I beckoned with my head to people . . ."	"[The *ahuiani*] waves her hand at one, gestures with her head, makes eyes at one, closes one eye at one, winks, beckons with her head, summons with the hand, turns her face . . ."

Indigenous manner of describing the physical behavior of the *ahuiani*, the way she entices and reels in her clients using gestures and glances. This captures a brief moment of alignment between the ethnographic project of Sahagún's circle, one Nahua playwright's riff off of the discourses that emanated from them. But this small detail is suggestive of a degree of familiarity with those critical texts and discourses.

This chapter has shown how thoroughly the author of two Nahuatl Antichrist plays adopted the ideologies and discourses of the friars. Perhaps the reader has been convinced that this alignment was *so* close that any possibility of a counter-vailing subtext is next to impossible. Pratt tells us autoethnography *should* involve "representations that the so-called others construct in response to or in dialogue with" the colonizers' texts. The evidence presented above may, at this point in the telling, seem utterly bereft of something as chary as "dialogue" between cultures. However, note the tension that exists between the author's embrace of diabolism and his cataloguing of detailed information about Indigenous religion and ritual. The former implies ideological proximity to the friars, the latter distance, since he includes what amounts to forbidden material. The next section will argue that the "self-representations" the author has constructed do, in fact, "intervene in" the colonizers' attempts at understanding the culture of the Nahuas and subjecting it to reducción.

WRITING BACK TO POWER

On one level, the adoption of the doctrinal and ethnographic discourses of the Franciscans aligns the author ideologically with their work. However, his skillful and innovative deployment of their discourses masks the existence of subtle counter-narratives detectable just beneath the textual surface of the two Antichrist neixcuitilli he composed. These counter-narratives disrupt two tropes common in European colonial writing about Indigenous people. The first portrayed Indigenous culture as diabolical and has already been thoroughly discussed above. The second demonizing trope viewed Indigenous Christians as perpetual neophytes.

By the third quarter of the sixteenth century, the approximate timeframe in which it is likely that Aquino added the plays to his notebook, the durability of Indigenous beliefs and ritual practices had become painfully apparent to the friars and the ecclesiastical authorities. Indigenous Christians seemed reluctant to completely abandon important elements of traditional religion and become compliant subjects in the Hispano-Catholic mode. In the friars' view, so strong was the devil's hold on them that many came to conclude Indigenous people would never attain the status of mature Christians. The First Mexican Provincial Council of 1555 cast Indigenous people as feeble and inconstant creatures who were naturally inclined to falling into sin.[24] The "Indian vices" of drunkenness and laziness were often cited as examples of this tendency. By the third quarter of the sixteenth century, Sahagún was so pessimistic about the prospects of a spiritually mature Indigenous Christianity that he lamented "we can be certain that, though preached to more than fifty years, if they were now left alone . . . I am certain that in less than fifty years there would be no trace of the preaching which has been done for them."[25] In 1585, the Third Mexican Provincial Council codified the widespread sentiment regarding Native Christianity by declaring that the "Indians" would likely remain perpetual neophytes, never rising above the level of spiritual children. It labeled them *rudes* in Latin and *de menor capacidad* in Spanish, and it repeatedly compared them to "new plants" that need tender care and nurturing.[26] By the end of the century, the dream of a native priesthood had been abandoned. Franciscan Gerónimo de Mendieta attributed this failure to Indigenous character, citing their persistent return to "the vomit of the rites and ceremonies of their gentility."[27] Thus, he concluded, "they are not good for leading and ruling but rather for being led and ruled."[28]

Certain characters realized by the Nahua author of the plays, most notably Converts, Martyrs, and Blessed, suggest a radically different view of Indigenous Christians and Indigenous Christianity than that of the ecclesiastical authorities of the day. For one, members of the Third Council would have been surprised to see how their "new plants" responded to Antichrist's reign of terror. Rather than "withering" or returning to the "vomit" of their former ways, a group of characters called Martyrs responds with vigorous denunciations of Antichrist. When presented with a mock cross as proof that he is Christ, they are not fooled. Instead, they correctly identify his ruse, proclaiming, "The cross on which *you* died is meaningless because what you're carrying there is meaningless. Therefore, you appear to be lying" (f. 157v). They also correctly recall what they learned from the friars, citing biblical and sibylline prophecies warning of the Antichrist's coming, as in their declaration, "it is written that a person will be born on earth who will be followed as a deity; because of this he will deceive many, because of this people won't believe" (f. 157v–158r). In one scene Antichrist promises a character named Martyr riches and a special place for him in his heavenly home if he will only believe in him. Martyr responds with a disparaging reference to Antichrist's "house" in an Indigenous mode, calling it "Urine Place, Excrement Place" (*axixtitlan, cuitlatitlan*; f. 160r).

Finally, a number of converts and martyrs make the ultimate sacrifice, choosing death at the hands of Antichrist rather than abandoning the faith. At the moment of their death, Martyrs fall to their knees and exclaim, "O our Lord! O our God! O Jesus Christ! Receive us into your home. Have mercy on them, pardon them of their sins" (f. 160v–161r). This statement closely echoes the words of Christ at his cruci-fixion, when he uttered the memorable words "Father, forgive them; for they know not what they do" (Luke 23:34). The author's move here is a daring one. By estab-lishing parallels between his Nahua Christian martyrs and Christ, the prototypical martyr, he pushed back against the negative assessments of Indigenous Christians promulgated by the ecclesiastical authorities. Had Aquino's work been brought to their attention, they would surely have been scandalized.

As the passages above illustrate, the plays repeatedly present Indigenous people as unwavering in their devotion to the faith and their allegiance to the friars. In envisioning Nahua Christians as fearless martyrs, the author may have had a specific historical model in mind, one that draws us back to the apocalyptic early decades discussed in chapter 2. In Motolinía's important chronicle of the early years of the mission, he records a number of incidents that took place in Tlaxcala in the late 1520s involving the activities of zealous young Nahua converts. He relates how a group of the friars' initiates were returning to the convent after a swim in the river when they observed someone "sauntering" through the marketplace "chewing or eating some sharp-edged stones (i.e., sacrificial blades)."[29] Seeing that a large crowd had gathered around to witness this spectacle, the boys asked the bystanders who this individual was. The bystanders responded, "Our god, Ometochtli." The boys' reply to this was, "That is not a god, but the devil who is lying and deceiving you." Motolinía continues his account:

> In the center of the marketplace was a cross where the boys, when out for a walk, would say a prayer. So these boys stopped here and waited until all the Indians were assembled; and these, being so many, were scattered about. When the boys got there, the wicked demon, that is, the minister who was wearing the demon's attire, approached and began to upbraid the boys in great anger, saying, "You are all going to die because you anger me, have deserted my house, and have gone to the house of Holy Mary." To this some of the older boys, being more courageous, replied, "You lie. We do not fear you, because you are not God; you are the devil and a wicked deceiver."

But the minister of the demon continued to assert that he was God and would have
to kill them all, at the same time pretending to be very angry in order to frighten the
boys. At this, one of the boys exclaimed, "Let us see now who is going to die, we or
this one." With this, he stooped to pick up a stone and said to the other boys: "Let us
drive this devil away from here; God will help us." Saying this, he hurled the stone at
the minister and immediately all the others did likewise. At first the demon put on a
bold front; but since so many boys attacked him he started to run. With a loud cry the
boys pursued him, hurling stones, so that the demon had to run fast. But God permitted, and the sins of the demon merited, that he should stumble and fall. He had hardly
fallen when the boys, thinking him dead, heaped stones on him and exclaimed with
great rejoicing: "We have killed the devil who wanted to kill us. Now the *macehuales*
(that is, the common people) can see that this person was not God but a liar; that God
and Holy Mary are good."[30]

A number of details from Motolinía's account bear striking resemblance to the
narrative of Antichrist's interactions with the plays' Converts and Martyrs. Both
boldly confront "the devil" in his various disguises. (Recall that Antichrist is repeatedly called tlacatecolotl, the word chosen for "devil.") In the account above "the
devil" takes the form of a flint blade-chewing priest of Ometochtli; in the plays he
appears as Antichrist or the six demon-*teteoh* who, like the priest, appear "wearing
the demon's attire." In Motolinía's account, the youths demonstrate their adoption of the friars' discourse of epistemic violence, correctly unmasking the priest of
Ometochtli as one who is "not a god, but the devil who is lying and deceiving you."
The martyrs cited above manifest the adoption of the same rhetorical strategy by
seeing through Antichrist's lies. When they are confronted by his claim to be God
they shoot back, "We will absolutely not believe in you, you were-owl!" (f. 161r). In
both accounts, model Nahua Christians are those who, like the friars, accept the
diabolization of native religion and condemn Indigenous priests and teteoh as devils and demons.

Other interactions between the priest of Ometochtli and the Nahua youths
sound strikingly similar to the plays' interactions between Antichrist and Converts
and Martyrs. In the passage above we hear the priest of Ometochtli threaten the
youths with death, stating "You are all going to die because you anger me." These
words are virtually identical to those uttered by Antichrist who, like the priest
of Ometochtli, represented forces resisting submission to the friars. Repeatedly,
Antichrist utters threats like "Right now I will spill your blood if you do not believe
in me" and "Do you want to die by my hand?" (ff. 156r, 159v). Referring to the
friars' systematic destruction of precontact temples, the priest of Ometochtli also
accuses the Christian youths of abandoning their former ways, saying, "[you] have

deserted my house, and have gone to the house of Holy Mary." Antichrist vents his
frustration in a similar manner, exclaiming, "Do not behave foolishly! Why did
you dismantle my home?" The play's six teteoh, who also "wear the demon's attire,"
offer an even closer parallel. One of these, Huitzilopochtli, echoes the priest of
Ometochtli when he laments to Hermit, "I am sad because my house was knocked
down, my image was destroyed. I am very sad because the cross of Jesus Christ
arrived" (f. 171v). Responding to the priest of Ometochtli, one of the older boys
in Motolinía's account declares, "You lie. We do not fear you, because you are not
God; you are the devil and a wicked deceiver." This bold statement is echoed by
Converts who, when asked by Antichrist, "Am I not Christ?" respond, "No indeed,
you are not Christ! You are just a were-owl [devil] . . . you are not a deity, you
are just a coyote! You want to devour us!" (f. 164r). Motolinía relates how a number of these zealous young Nahua converts paid the ultimate price for their faith
in the late 1520s. Most remembered of these were the "child martyrs" of Tlaxcala,
Cristobal, Antonio, and Juan, who were beatified by Pope John Paul II in 1990 and
canonized by Pope Francis in 2017. The fact that the Nahuatl Antichrist plays call
for multiple performances of acts of Nahua-Christian martyrdom strengthens
their connection to this early, violent period while also suggesting another link
between the plays and the *altepetl* of Tlaxcala.

The character Hermit offers another direct refutation of the "native as perpetual
neophyte" trope. It is unclear whether this character was adapted from the hypothesized source text or was the author's innovation. Hermits did occasionally appear
as the characters in miracle narratives and morality plays. It is also possible that
the author of the Nahuatl Antichrist plays found inspiration for Hermit among
the many hundreds of *exempla* in circulation at the time, such as those contained
in the *Golden Legend* or the *Flos sanctorum*. What is certainly attributable to the
author of the plays is Hermit's expanded role involving the interrogation of twenty-
five demons and condemned souls as well as the thoroughly Indigenous nature of
these characters' identities and actions. Another decision clearly attributable to the
author was conceiving of Hermit as an Indigenous person. I view this decision as
a direct challenge to the dominant tropes characterizing Nahuas and Nahua spirituality. The plays' Hermit is a charismatic, tough-talking, and energetic figure. He
speaks with unwavering conviction and with authority. Although the author does
not state it directly, I think it possible that he conceived of Hermit as a friar. For one,
he delivers admonitory speeches similar to sermons, addressing his "flock" using the
markers of homiletic discourse. At the end of *Antichrist and the Hermit* he declares,
"O my children (*nopilvanhe*)! Now (*yn axcan*) you have heard (*ovāquimocatique*)"
(f. 186v). Furthermore, he commands demons, and they obey him, cowering as
Hermit brandishes symbols of priestly authority. One of these confrontations is

especially suggestive of the priestly nature of Hermit's work. In this scene, he has been trying to get a demon to tell him his name, but the demon has repeatedly refused, exclaiming *Cah amo niceya*, "I don't want to!" (f. 166r). Exasperated with the demon's recalcitrance, Hermit proclaims:

Woe to you! You refuse to obey me! I recognize you, you are a were-owl! I just don't know your name. So be it. I will make [the sign of] the cross on you so that you will reveal your name to me! *Then Hermit will say, he will say to another person,* O my child, bring the blessed water here, the water of God. I will spread this on the were-owl so that he will suffer, so that he will reveal what his name is.

Then when he is about to spread the blessed water on him he will say, O were-owl! Reveal your name! For if you do not, I will pronounce God's words and God's prayers on you, and also I will spread the blessed water, God's water on you, so that you will suffer burning pain! Please tell me your name! (f. 166r–v)

With this the demon relents, saying, "Alas! How unfortunate I am! Now you have really shamed me. Even though I don't want to, you will now know my name because you made the [sign of the] cross on me" (f. 166v). Hermit takes a similarly hard-nosed approach with all the demons and condemned souls he questions. To Tezcatlipoca he barks, "Ah! You wicked one! What's become of you?" (f. 169v) and to Quetzalcoatl "Please go, you wicked one!" (f. 172r). He commands the audience to spit on various sinners and to avoid imitating their vile sins. He singles out nobles in particular, stating, "Now [you] noblemen, don't be lazy!" (f. 173r). None of this constitutes incontrovertible evidence that the author imagined Hermit as a friar. However, what is clear is that Hermit is a powerful spiritual authority. He speaks on behalf of God, commands demons, excoriates sinners, and urges the audience to fidelity. The author's characterization is a direct challenge to the spiritual colonizer's trope of Indigenous Christians as weak, prone to backsliding, lazy, and spiritually immature. This Nahua playwright brings his character to life on the page, but even more profoundly, he brings him to life on the stage. There, standing before the assembled community, Hermit would be embodied by a living Indigenous actor who struts, shouts, issues commands, and boldly displays a spiritual ideal that the ecclesiastical authorities deemed unachievable by Indigenous Christians. As such, the author of the plays presents a powerful counter-narrative to the one repeated time and again in sermons, catechisms, and official conciliar edicts.

In the preceding chapter I argued that the Aztec Antichrist can be interpreted as embodying the anti-mendicant voices of tlahtohqueh and *nanahualtin* (ritual specialists) who actively opposed submitting to the friars and renouncing their traditional rights and privileges. However, those were not the only two voices of the

1530s embodied by this complex and ambivalent character. In addition to giving Antichrist the voice of a *tlahtoani* and a *nahualli*, a closer look reveals the author's highly unorthodox decision to give Antichrist the voice of a friar as well.

Antichrist's speeches to Converts and Martyrs, which were aimed at convincing them to reject Christian faith and return to the ways of their ancestors, echo the sermons delivered by the friars, not so much in terms of content but due to the fact that they are delivered in the doctrinal register. In fact, Antichrist begins to entreat Martyrs to believe in him with the precise words found in the confessional manuals of Molina, the sermons of Sahagún, and many of the various catechisms of the day. Antichrist calls out to the *macehualtin* saying, *yn axcan tla xicmocaquitican nopilvanhe*, "Today won't you listen, O my children!" (f. 161v). In keeping with the paternalism of the preaching friar, Antichrist addresses them using terms of fatherly affection, calling them *notlaçovan* (my beloved ones), *nopilvane* (O my children), and uttering statements like "I love you very much!" (157v). Sprinkling his speech with doctrinal phrases and expression, the author of the plays further embeds Antichrist's discourse in the doctrinal register. In his opening speech, Antichrist declares, *ca nevatl yn amoteovh yn amotlatocavh*, "I am your deity, your ruler" (f. 157r), appropriating the ubiquitous Nahuatl-Christian couplet that the early friars and Nahuas devised to elevate and indigenize the "Only Deity." Later he tells Martyrs, *ca niteotl, ca nicristo*, "I am the deity, I am Christ!" (f. 157v), framing his statement as a couplet and therefore also locating it in the Nahuatl-Christian doctrinal register. However, this construction was much less common in the doctrinal literature where the name of Christ (or Jesucristo) was typically paired with and preceded by *totecuiyo*, "our Lord." Antichrist is not only parroting the friars' discourse but innovating within the doctrinal register as well.

In the hands of this Nahua writer, this Aztec Antichrist also co-opts the rhetorical strategies of the friars. He deploys a form of didactic terror, threatening the Christian macehualtin time and again with violence. This is a common utterance in the plays: "Do you want to die by my hand? Right now I will spill your blood if you do not believe in me!" (f. 156r). He even turns the friars' tactic of epistemic violence against them. Referring directly to the friars and their preaching, Antichrist tells the macehualtin, "I really, really pity you because of all those who went around teaching you, those who went around deceiving you [i.e., the friars]. Do not believe what they said to you!" (f. 157v). These are the very arguments that the friars devised to undermine Indigenous knowledge, to negate the wisdom of the Nahua elders, and to sway Nahuas to accept Christianity's exclusive message. To hear Antichrist turn this rhetorical tool back on Christians, and to have it uttered in the context of a religious drama that, ostensibly, sought to *further* the work of the friars, leaves us with a tangle of discourses not easily sorted out. In the character of Antichrist, we have an example of discourse on the loose, "in the wild" as it were, operating outside the bounds of the church's (fantasy of) control.

The author's appropriation of the doctrinal register for the character of Antichrist is an attempt to appropriate its authority, if not its content. The register itself is authoritative; any Nahua educated by the friars would have internalized this fact. What's fascinating is that the author gives this authoritative voice to a figure so opposed to the Christian message that his very name is *Anti*-Christ. My sense is that the author who adapted the Antichrist plays may not have been entirely clear about the nature of this figure whose name was uttered so rarely by the friars. As previously mentioned, the Antichrist barely ever appears in the sermons, catechisms, or devotional materials of the day. In fact, he was absent in all but a handful of texts, and even then he is only briefly mentioned. The author of the plays knew that the Antichrist was a devil or a demon, and also *cenca tlaveliloc iztlacatini*, "very wicked, a liar" (f. 160v) who would deceive many into following him as Christ. As such, the Antichrist had to have been a master rhetorician. For a Franciscan-trained Nahua living in the mid-sixteenth century, one logical model for the master rhetorician was a friar who wielded a bicultural, hybrid linguistic discourse based on elite Indigenous speech and drew upon a Nahuatl-Christian lexicon.

The irony is that by endowing the Antichrist with this kind of spiritual authority he may have unwittingly elevated that figure in the minds of his audience. Nahuas were accustomed to thinking of their teteoh in terms of pairs, such as Mictlantecuhtli (Mictlan-Lord) and Mictlancihuatl (Mictlan-Lady), or Ometecuhtli (Dual-Lord) and Omecihuatl (Dual-Lady), each an expression of the divine progenitor Ometeotl (Dual-deity). Such duality was fundamental to Mesoamerican religious thought, every force in nature requiring its balancing complement (as shown in the front and back covers of this volume). This form of Indigenous dualism is part of the reason why it was so difficult for Nahuas to embrace Christianity's good vs. evil dualism. Might the "Anti-Christ" have appeared to Nahuas at this very early stage in their confrontation with Christianity as a logical complement of the "Christ" spoken of so often by the friars? The Antichrist's association with the supernaturally gifted were-owl was cemented in both plays. An even closer association between Antichrist and the teteoh is made by Elijah who, at one point, declares, *tiquetzalcovatl*, "You [are] Quetzalcoatl!" (141v). Although it appears that Elijah levels this epithet at Antichrist as an insult in the vein of diabolism, it can also be read as an authoritative identification of this mysterious figure as one of the most revered deities in Mesoamerican religion. Instead of damnation, it might just have read as equation.

Thus the author consistently and repeatedly locates the Aztec Antichrist in the realm of the sacred power of teotl, whose essence was always ambivalent and whose being expressed itself in both creation and destruction, order and chaos. In light of this, we have to consider that Antichrist may actually have emerged from his stage debut with some esteem among Nahua audiences. Instead of being understood as a being of pure evil exiled to the Christian hell, it may have been possible for audiences to imagine "Anti-Christ" as a necessary, if terrifying, compliment to the equally powerful and terrifying "Christ" spoken of by the friars. This conjecture, and that's exactly what it is, is the closest I've come to explaining the mystery of why the Antichrist was sidelined from the friars' preaching and teaching in New Spain. Concerns about the inclination to pair Christ and Anti-Christ made it simply too risky to speak of him widely in their sermons and official doctrinal writing.

The question of the plays' reception among Nahua audiences necessitates a return to its engagement with the ethnographic research and writing of the friars. As previously discussed, the friars' ethnographic work was rooted in their growing realization that "idolatrous" practices persisted among the macehualtin and were encouraged by certain members of the Indigenous nobility. Only by understanding these "idolatrous superstitions," so the logic went, could they be effectively destroyed. But of course, while their research did produce detailed knowledge of Indigenous culture, it did not succeed in eliminating idolatry. Waging an "invisible war" against idolatry meant not only identifying and prosecuting offending individuals, but also forbidding writing about such practices, since writing granted a kind of immortality that threatened to enable them to endure. The scripting of roles for characters representing Tlaloc and Quetzalcoatl, as well as for others like Day Keeper and Healer who provide detailed information about their ritual practices violated the orders of church and Crown and thus rendered the plays illicit works of literature. It is in this sense that the plays engaged with the ethnographic work of the friars in such a way that ran counter to their ideologies and the goals of their mission. Like his appropriation of their doctrinal discourse, the appropriation also took his work in an alternative, Indigenous direction.

The author of the plays imagined performances of ethnography that, from the friars' perspective, risked facilitating the persistence of idolatry. This raises the question of how Nahuas might have received such performances. A closer look at one scene in particular will help approach an answer. During his Inquisition, Hermit calls on stage a character named Healer (Ticitl), a practitioner of traditional medicine. In the wake of the dismantling of the Mexica high priesthood after the conquest, the *titicih* (pl. of *ticitl*), like the tonalpouhqueh, came to occupy a central role in the spiritual lives of Nahua communities. The ticitl was a repository of traditional knowledge about local medicinal plants, illnesses, and the cures that had been relied on by Nahuas for centuries. Colonial Nahuas valued having recourse to their services when Christian methods were deemed ineffective or unsatisfying. In the early seventeenth century, rural priest Hernando Ruiz de Alarcón uncovered evidence of a flourishing local industry of Indigenous healers, and he recorded the incantations they uttered as remedies for a wide variety of ailments and problems.[31]

That so many titicih continued to thrive and offer their services to Nahua communities a full century following the so-called "spiritual conquest" is a testament to the durability of precontact practices. But it is also a reminder of the flexible way Nahuas approached Christianity. As Lockhart has noted, "Whenever Christianity left a niche unfilled . . . preconquest beliefs and practices tended to persist in their original form."[32] Keeping this in mind, consider this exchange between Hermit and Healer (Ticitl):

> *Then Hermit will say,* I ask you, who are you?
> *Then [Healer] will say,* It is I, Antonio. I am a healer.
> *[Hermit:]* And why did you go to Mictlan?
> *Then [Healer] will say,* Because I really devoted myself to healing and so deceived many because of it. My job was this: I scattered shelled maize grains before people; I used to count them. And those who I hated, I treated in such a way that they would die. Even though I heard the sacred words many times, I absolutely didn't want to confess, I absolutely didn't want to abandon my wickedness. And now because of this God has cast me down to Mictlan. Now I will always go along carrying on my back everything with which I divined. Because of this I am suffering greatly and those who I considered deities are whipping me; they're just the were-owls I called upon when I was divining.
> [. . .]
> *Then Hermit will say,* Alas, you liar! Don't you know what God taught while you were still living on earth? *Then he will say,* So be it! Please go, you wicked one! (f. 182r–183r)

On the surface, this scene aligns with the friars' dominant ideology of diabolism. Not only does Hermit condemn Healer and send him to hell, Healer offers his own public self-condemnation before the assembled audience. He confesses that he "deceived many" with his curing, and he admits that he rejected the word of God, lamenting, "Now I will always go along carrying on my back everything with which I divined." This is probably a reference to props he is carrying, props that symbolize his sinful ritual practices. These props might have been the maize kernels he used in his divination rituals or other unspecified ritual objects. (We are told that Day Keeper, for example, carries *yn imamo[x] yn teteoh*, the "book of the teteoh," i.e., his divinatory codex.) In this portrayal it would seem that there is no room for reading anything other than a clear demonization of Indigenous people and culture. However, returning the question posed above, we should consider the possibility that the public performance of Healer on the Nahuatl stage may have encoded alternate readings that would have been perceptible to Indigenous people alone. These readings constitute hidden transcripts embedded within and between the lines of script.

First, recall that Indigenous understandings of role-playing and performance differed in important ways from those of Europeans. It's true that all performances—Indigenous or otherwise—engage two different realities simultaneously, the one an imagined reality of angels and saints, and the other the "real" reality of the everyday life of actor and audience.[33] In the European tradition, the audience and the actors mostly remained cognizant of which reality was which. Allowing for certain exceptional performances, actors were conscious of being an actor performing a role; audience members made the same distinction. However, in the Mesoamerican tradition religious performances, particularly the high rituals of the Mexica state, regularly blurred the lines between actor/role, imagined/real. In fact, these categories are themselves thoroughly Western in nature and may have lacked clear distinction to Nahuas. In the course of certain rituals, the *teixiptlahuan* (deity impersonators) donned the garb and ritual paraphernalia of a particular teotl and performed the role of that deity as a part of the ritual. However, in the act of dressing the impersonator, the assembling of constituent parts mentioned in the introduction to this study, a transformation was understood to take place, one that far surpassed the "method acting" of the Western tradition. Inga Clendinnen offers an evocative description of this transformation:

> Flowers and incense, sweat and paint and the flat sweet smell of blood mingled in
> the distinctive scent of the sacred, which was signaled by the brush of feathers on
> skin, the sudden darkening and narrowing of vision as the masks slid down over the
> face, precise, repetitive movements as the lines of dancers interwoven and the drums,
> dance and voices intertwined.... And only then, as the self evaporated and the
> choreographed excitements multiplied and the sensations came flooding in, did the
> god draw near.[34]

These actions and sensory stimuli initiated a surging of the sacred power of teotl in its human receptacle such that the teixiptlahuan ceased to be mere representations of the deity and were transformed into that deity, even if for only a short time. So utter were transformations like these that often the performance was ended with the razor-sharp blade of a priest's obsidian knife.

There is further evidence supporting the blurring of lines between the Indigenous view of performed reality and "real" reality. In his fascinating account of mid-seventeenth century Mexico, English traveler Thomas Gage related that Native performers in religious theater often went to confession prior to performing the roles of saints, "saying that they must be holy and pure like the saint."[35] Similarly, after performing roles of evil characters like Herod or Herodias, they "would afterwards come to confess of that sin." Gage attributed this to mere "superstition," but a better way to read these actions is as evidence of the kind of transformation that Native peoples associated with performing roles.

In light of this, we must reconsider Healer's performance above, as well as the performances of Day Keeper, Merchant, and others whose speeches contain ethnographic material. On one level, they can be interpreted as performances of the dominant ideology condemning Indigenous religious practices as diabolical. This is obviously the dominant performance, the "public transcript," to use James C. Scott's parlance.[36] However, on another level, what the Nahua author has done is create a space, a very public space, where important members of Indigenous society are made present to the community as living embodiments of roles whose existence has been threatened by the spiritual colonizer. The speeches uttered by the likes of Healer cited above, also contain important cultural knowledge whose existence was under threat. This recording of Indigenous roles and Indigenous knowledge in scripts intended for performance, in the words of Klor de Alva, "helped to keep before the Nahua listeners a list of cultural and sociopolitical options that differed from or directly opposed Spanish polity and Christian ideology."[37] Such appropriations happened everywhere Nahuas like Aquino took up the pen and retold the stories of the Other in their own *nahuatlahtolli*, "Nahuatl speech."

CONCLUSION: ETC.

Consider one final, evocative datum that suggests these plays existed even farther outside of the friars' control than has already been proposed. It is a tiny, three-letter abbreviation: etc. In the sermon genre, etc. appeared at certain points in the text where the preacher was encouraged to extemporize on a theme.[38] In many of the sermons Sahagún edited, for example, we find statements such as this one, from a sermon for the fourth Sunday of Advent: *xicochpanili yn manima yn moteouh yn motlatocauh; ma ximoyolmelava ma ximonemilizcuepa, ma xitlamaceva etc.*, "Sweep out your soul [for] your deity, your ruler! Confess! Convert! Do penance, etc."[39] The etc. here signals to the preacher an appropriate place to offer additional words of exhortation in accordance with the friar's inspiration and his facility with Nahuatl expression. In the Nahuatl Antichrist plays, there are at least half a dozen instances where the author either inserts an etc. or gives instructions to the performers that invite them to elaborate on a particular topic. For example, in *Hermit*, at the end of a monologue by Enoch that reads like a sermon in condensed form, the author added etc. after the final scripted line. According to Louise Burkhart, the Antichrist plays' use of etc. is not found in any of the other surviving colonial neixcuitilli.[40] It's

presence here is highly suggestive of the author's familiarity with the writing practices of the friars as well as with Nahuatl sermons like Sahagún's.

Friars, of course, had the authority to do extemporize from the pulpit. However,
what are we to make of the following exchange between Hermit and Day Keeper?

> DAY KEEPER: I bear the book of the *teteoh*. I used to read the book in order
> to deceive people . . .
> HERMIT: Please tell me, when you used to do readings, what would you say
> to them?
> *Then he will say how he used to divine, etc. (177v)*

The italicized words at the end of this excerpt are stage directions. They are not followed by any text. The etc. sits there, blinking like a cursor at the end of a line, waiting for someone to proceed and fill in the blank. The full import of this decision
emerges upon recalling precisely what that etc. invites: an impromptu performance
of a tonalpouhqui's divination. The "someone" who the author intended to fill out
that blank was not a friar, not an official mouthpiece of the church, not a European,
but an Indigenous actor. Moreover, what he is being invited to do is utter the specialized formulae of the tonalpouhqui's incantations, a highly Indigenous form of
teotlahtolli, "sacred words," that had been branded diabolical and forbidden. The
fact that no script has been given leaves us to assume that the performer would
know what to say, which in turn suggests that the author may have been so bold
as to envision casting an actual tonalpouhqui for this role. Considered in this light
and against the church's efforts to suppress this sort of speech, the use of etc. must
be seen as calling for an illicit performance.

And this wasn't the only instance when such performances were called for.
Another is found in the scene cited above. After Hermit goads Healer, saying,
"Come now! How did you divine and so deceive the people? Please, divine it!" the
stage directions state, "Then here the diviner will make his prognostication." There
is no etc., but what is being called for is clear without it. Elsewhere, in *Antichrist and
the Final Judgment*, in the midst of Elijah and Enoch's verbal duel with Antichrist,
we find this instruction: "Then at this point Elijah or Enoch will speak, will teach"
(141r). Again, no text follows, presumably just the actors' improvisation. And in
Hermit, after Antichrist has performed a false miracle by raising Martyr's mother
and father from the dead, he asks: *ma xiquintlahtlanican quenamican yn opa
mi[c]tlan etc.*, "Ask them what sort of place Mictlan is, etc." (158v). Since they had
just been raised from the dead, Antichrist offers them the opportunity to recount its
terrors to their son. In the sermons genre, *quenamihcan*, "What sort of place?" was
sometimes used as a rhetorical device that, like etc., invited elaboration. Are we to

understand that the author was inviting the actors portraying Martyr's mother and father to expound on this theme? Again we find ourselves caught up in a thicket of conflicting discourses and their implications, where the Anti-Christ appropriates the words, the rhetorical tactics, and therefore the authority of those who are the defenders of Christ.

Each of these instances, the *etceteras* and *quenamihcans*, were invitations soliciting the performance of unofficial discourses by Nahuas on stages both physical and dialogical that were largely beyond the friars' control. In these heretofore unknown works of Indigenous literature, we witness the materialization of the friars' fears about Indigenous literacy: "Nahuas on Stage, Live and Uncensored!" This is what was referred to at the end of the last chapter as a double-edged sword. The Antichrist plays that Fabián de Aquino copied into his notebook condemn elements of Indigenous culture and so align themselves and their author with the ideologies of the friars. This was neither an act of betrayal nor a ruse intended to dissemble. These views of Indigenous Christianity, the tropes of cultural traitor and its opposite, the resister, are distractions that belie the richly complex and contradictory reality of Indigenous engagements with the religion of the colonizer. Hopefully this chapter has shown that these performances simultaneously bore the potential to preserve Indigenous knowledge while also offering narratives that countered the racist and paternalizing judgments of church and Crown. All of this serves to underscore the ambivalent nature of writing by colonial Nahuas, and indeed of colonial Nahuas themselves. In the hands of an Indigenous writer, etc. was a powerful rhetorical tool, its invitation to improvise spawning a multitude of unique and unofficial performances of Indigenous Christianities.[41]

CONCLUSION

APOCALYPSE AND TRAUMA

WHETHER OR NOT he was the Nahua who composed the Antichrist plays you are about to read, we can say with certainty that Fabián de Aquino was captivated by the subject matter. Perhaps this is unsurprising, since the plays he recorded have all the necessary elements to enthrall an audience: they involve conflict and violence, dramatic tension and its release, vivid characters, and scandalous acts, many of which involve sexual transgression. However, these factors alone do not explain Aquino's interest in the legend of the Antichrist. As already noted, the inclusion of texts in his notebook like the tract on the Four Last Things and his familiarity with the sermons of the "Angel of the Apocalypse," St. Vincent Ferrer, point to a broader fascination with the End of Days and allow us to identify Aquino as a Nahua apocalypticist.

As such, Aquino was part of the phenomenon of Indigenous apocalypticism that emerged out of the initial trauma of contact and had a long history of expression throughout the colonial period in numerous Indigenous prophets, rebellions, and traditionalist movements. Understanding Aquino as a Nahua apocalypticist adds yet another layer to our understanding of this difficult-to-pin-down historical figure, whose identity we have been chasing throughout this book. If the roots of his Antichrist plays lie in the dramatic events of early postcontact Mexico, together they can be considered as a sort of "foundational text" of Nahua apocalypticism. As a last effort to make sense of this enigmatic person, I will offer two final thoughts on why it may have been that Aquino and other Nahuas were drawn to these Last Things. The theme of the End seems like a fitting way to bring these chapters to conclusion.

The first final thought has to do with Aquino's position vis-à-vis Christianity and the work of the friars. Throughout the preceding chapters I've taken my time detailing the close nature of Aquino's relationship with the Franciscans and with their mission of combating idolatry at a pivotal early moment in the life of the Mexican church. Although I've avoided writing of it this way, it's possible that the reader has formed the impression of Aquino as a willing participant in the friars' missionary work, one who was wholly aligned with their goals and shared their values to the detriment of his own Indigenous heritage. This impression would not be entirely wrong, but as I stated at the end of the previous chapter, I see the "Indigenous collaborator" trope as distracting from a fuller understanding. It also wouldn't capture the fullest picture of Aquino either, as I hope chapter 3 made clear with its discussion of Indigenous counter-narratives embedded in the texts.

In the historiography of the colonial Americas, it is common to see Nahuas like Aquino identified as "converts" to Christianity. (The author of the plays used this very term to name characters playing Indigenous Christian neophytes.) However, in this book I've resisted using the terms "convert" and "conversion" because of what these words imply. For one, the way these terms are used presumes a rapid and wholesale change from one pattern of belief to another. Conversion implies a strict delineation between "before" and "after," where the convert utterly rejects former beliefs and embraces the newly revealed Truth. One reason this doesn't sit well with me is that it engages the same kind of epistemic violence the friars meted out in their sermons. Christianity in particular, with its exclusive claims on truth, requires the convert not just to reject former knowledge but to deny its very existence. I hope that by now I have made a strong enough case that the reader recognizes that this was not how early colonial Nahuas responded to the friars' teachings about *icel teotl dios*, "Only Deity, God." We need another way to talk about Indigenous responses to Christianity.

One way to get there is by looking at the other reason why conversion fails to capture early colonial Nahuas' ways of being Christian. I'm speaking of conversion's emphasis on belief. Despite the richness and depth of the documentary corpus, we know next to nothing for certain about what individual Nahuas like Aquino *believed*, since colonial Nahuas tended not to write reflexively about their private thoughts and experiences. Complicating the matter is the fact that, prior to the arrival of the friars, there existed no words in the Nahuatl lexicon that encompassed the Western notions of "belief" or "faith." In consultation with their Nahua assistants, the early friars fashioned new words to name these foreign concepts: *neltoca*, "to follow something as true" for the verb *creer* (to believe), and its derivative, *tlaneltoquiliztli*, "the action of following something as true" for *fé* (faith). Each of these neologisms betrays a semantic shift from the Western notion of "belief" as an intellectual assent to a creed to an Indigenous meaning that suggests a more embodied form of engagement in which the physical act of following is implied.

If a quest for Nahua belief falls short, when we search the sixteenth-century sources for evidence of things Nahuas *did* as part of their "following of" (*toca*) Christianity, we have much more material to work with. We find Nahuas decorating altars, adapting precontact dances to Christian themes, building churches, processing on feast days, venerating saints, erecting flower arches, making offerings, and composing and singing Nahuatl songs with Christian lyrics. As far as Fabián de Aquino is concerned, what his notebook permits us to conclude regarding his way of following Christianity is this: he invested an enormous amount of time and energy reading and absorbing religious literature, and copying, translating, and composing texts of his own into his notebook, two of which may earn him the title of playwright in addition to apocalypticist. In searching for new approaches to talking about Indigenous ways of being Christian in this early period, I see in Aquino a kind of active engagement with the ideas, stories, and even the affective and aesthetic aspects of the Christian religion in such a way that none of his Indigenous identity or social position is lost, but rather is enhanced. We might see his apocalypticism as one of the ways he did this.

Aquino, like so many other colonial Indigenous intellectuals from Cambridge, Massachusetts, to Cuzco, made a strategic decision to engage with the religion of the colonizer, and to affiliate himself with those who wielded power within that dominant system. In Aquino's case, this meant the Franciscans. In keeping with the actions-oriented view of Indigenous engagement with Christianity, we can assume that Aquino affiliated himself with the Franciscans because it *did something* for him personally, for his *altepetl*, or both. I read his act of collecting the Antichrist plays in his notebook—whether merely by copying them or actually composing them himself—as signaling some degree of participation in the Franciscans' campaign against idolatry. As I've already indicated, I also see this as indicative of his adoption of their apocalyptic outlook on the fraught moment of the 1530s and 1540s and the "antichrists" who were the targets of the Franciscans' legal and rhetorical campaigns. However, in stating that Aquino participated in these campaigns I am not saying that he did it for precisely the same reasons as the friars. Nor in stating that he adopted their apocalypticism am I stating that his apocalyptic thought was identical to theirs. Rather, Aquino's participation in both the friars' extirpation campaigns and their apocalyptic thought was decidedly Indigenous in motivation and hue, and it served Indigenous purposes.

The Franciscans' interpretation of idolatry as an existential threat requires little explanation. We do not excuse their ethnocentrism and narrow-mindedness, but we register it as a reality of the time period in which they lived and the product of the exclusive claims of Roman Catholic Christianity. It is less clear why idolatry may have posed a threat to a Nahua like Fabián de Aquino. Given the dynamics of power, Spain's Indigenous subjects had little choice but to desist in the more public expressions of their traditional religious practices. But there's a significant difference between passively desisting and actively participating in the rooting out of idolatry, which, at least on one level, is how Aquino's copying or composing of the Antichrist plays can be read. In order to understand why Aquino may have decided to participate in this way we must look beyond what he may or may not have believed to the real-world dynamics of Indigenous society in the middle years of the sixteenth century. The social field in which Aquino existed was a landscape whose contours the historical sources make vastly more familiar than the contours of belief, and it is to them that we turn for an explanation for his affiliation with the Franciscans and their apocalypticism.

In the aftermath of the Spanish invasion of their ancestral lands, Nahua *tlahtohqueh* and *pipiltin* stood to lose everything: territory, tribute, wealth, sustenance, not to mention power and prestige. The mendicants' "crusade against polygamy" and other privileges of the noble class added insult to injury.[1] As a result, some members of the Indigenous nobility openly resisted the Spanish and rose up in rebellion in the decades of the 1520s–1540s. However, this was not the tactic adopted by most who, correctly sensing the inevitability of Spanish rule, made different calculations for how to retain as much of their traditional privileges as possible through varying degrees of accommodation of the new rulers. One of the more common of these calculations was what Patricia Lopes Don calls the "arbitration of avoidance," a term that encompasses a wide range of tactics employed by tlahtohqueh including "concession, redefinition, toleration, threat, and deflection."[2] This approach allowed rulers to navigate between twin threats to their power: on the one hand, the friars with their persistent attacks on noble privilege, and on the other, members of the lower nobility and the *macehualtin* on whom their legitimacy depended. Some rulers, like Don Carlos Ometochtzin of Tetzcoco, ran afoul of ecclesiastical authorities because they became too bold in their denunciations of the friars and their defense of noble prerogatives. Others successfully threaded the needle and were able to secure their positions in the new social order. A principal means of doing so was affiliating with Christianity and its powerful barefoot representatives.

Of course, the degree to which each Nahua associated with friars and their mission varied widely across the sixteenth century. Some practiced the arbitration of avoidance, but others chose to more actively align themselves with their work. The author of the Antichrist plays was one such as this. Although he disagreed with their negative assessment of Indigenous Christians and their ability to "follow something as true," and even though his inclusion of detailed information about "idolatrous" practices ran contrary to their directives, his bold compositions indicate an embrace their anti-idolatry campaign. Aquino's decision to include these texts in his notebook suggests that, even if he were not their original author, on some level he, too, aligned himself with this campaign. After all, campaigns of extirpation continued throughout the late-sixteenth century, when I argue the plays were copied into Aquino's notebook.[3] This decision represented a strategic calculation aimed at securing the author's position in the hierarchy New Spanish society. For idolatry threatened not only the Franciscans' mission and their political privileges, but those of members of the Indigenous nobility who had staked their futures with that of the friars. If idolatry were allowed to persist, the friars would fail and the nobility's new and fragile foundation for legitimacy would collapse along with it.

A fascinating document has recently been published that sheds light on these very dynamics. Both in terms of content and what says about Indigenous engagement with idolatry extirpation render it a kindred of the Nahuatl Antichrist plays. Its editors claim that it is the earliest known Nahuatl document bearing a precise date, 1543, a datum that also links it to the exact historical period I have argued was the inspiration for the plays.[4] Issued by the Indigenous governor of Tlaxcala, don Valeriano de Castañeda, it is a directive which orders altepetl officials to identify and stop specific practices that are labeled sinful and idolatrous. Those listed in the document bear a striking resemblance to the sins dramatized in *Antichrist and the Hermit*. The document orders officials to arrest and punish anyone in the community found to be guilty of

> committing an adultery, stealing, beating people up, getting drunk, gambling; those
> of us men who bathe themselves together with women, those who bathe themselves in
> public. And perhaps others have been practicing the old idolatry, the eating of earth,
> the laying down of straw, rain divination; and those who divine with water, cast lots,
> or induce abortions; those who do not attend mass on Sundays and feast days and do
> not listen to the sermon, those who do not perform their [religious] duties; those who
> eat meat on Fridays and Saturdays and also during the Cuatro Témporas; and those
> who do other things that clearly appear to be sins. You are to arrest them peacefully. If
> they resist, then you will tie their hands. You will take them before the *alcaldes* so that
> they will judge them.[5]

The overlapping catalog of sins here and in *Hermit* establishes a kind of intertextuality between the two documents. The author of the plays and the 1543 order, both of whom were Nahuas and members of the nobility, seem to have adopted the same stance toward actions that non-Indigenous Others, namely the friars, have labelled illicit. Olko and Brylak's incisive analysis of the Tlaxcala document makes a strong argument why such a stance was adopted by tlahtoani don Valeriano. Responding to Lopes Don's theory of "the arbitration of avoidance," they assert that Valeriano's strategy "was not so much evasion but rather a carefully implemented act of long-term agency, in which the covert intent of keeping Spaniards and friars from invading indigenous autonomy underpinned apparent forms of collaboration."[6] In this reading, Nahuas who participated in the campaigns against idolatry were doing so less out of alignment with the friars' religious motivations but rather as a careful political calculation designed to keep the Spaniards and friars out of their business by handling these matters internally, at home.

I believe a similar reading can be made of the Antichrist plays, which in this light can be understood as expressions of agency directed toward the goal of facilitating the internal management of local affairs in an attempt to keep intrusive forces at bay. As Olko and Brylak point out, this strategy effectively "deprived the Franciscans of opportunities for targeting Indigenous elites and invading their traditional jurisdiction over their subjects."[7] The author of the plays, who was not likely the governor of his altepetl, nevertheless used the power he possessed by virtue of his education and his literacy to compose texts intended for local audiences and not Spanish ears. Targeting the very practices (or "sins") that he knew would attract the attention of the friars—attention that, during the 1530s anyway, could result in violent and even deadly shows of force—the author acted to defend the autonomy of his altepetl and his own elevated rank within it. His Hermit character is an especially vivid embodiment of this stance. Like don Valeriano, Hermit is an Indigenous voice that commands authority, demanding that his people cease with the activities that imperil Indigenous autonomy just as they imperil their souls. Together with the Tlaxcala 1543 document, the Antichrist plays Aquino added to his notebook offer further evidence of the "intertwining" of Indigenous "political activity and the processes of Christianization."[8]

Regardless of whether Aquino lived during the plays' original composition or years after, I have argued that his notebook suggests that he, too, was closely affiliated with the friars. Did this affiliation in the later years of the sixteenth century have the same pragmatic goals as don Valeriano's in the 1540s? Was he also striving to carve out spaces of Indigenous autonomy in the spiritual affairs of his altepetl? I cannot say for certain, but it seems like a viable theory. The historical record shows that the Mexican church's idolatry problem was by no means resolved during Aquino's time. Nor had the need diminished for Indigenous communities to establish boundaries of autonomy between their *altepemeh* and Spanish zones of influence. Far from it.

* * *

My second final thought has to do with Aquino's apocalypticism and its relationship to memories of the violent early period of Christianization. Can this too, like his affiliation with Christianity, be read as having a more pragmatic, this-worldly explanation that distinguishes it from its Franciscan apocalypticism? Here again Olko and Brylak's interpretation of the Tlaxcala document may shed some light. In their article, they argue that the violent initial wave of Christianization in the 1520s–1540s inflicted cultural trauma on the Nahuas. This assertion seems to be corroborated by Tlaxcallan historian don Juan Buenaventura Zapata y Mendoza, another Nahua intellectual who lived a generation after Aquino.[9] Looking back on the initiation of the Franciscan campaign against the idolatry in the late 1520s, he wrote, *oncan peuhqui ye nemauhtiloc*, "It was then that the terror began."[10] Olko and Brylak argue that don Valeriano's order in 1543 to participate in the Franciscans' crusade against idolatry makes most sense as an Indigenous response to the terrifying impacts of this early period of spiritual colonization, impacts they label as cultural trauma.

There is a large body of literature on trauma and its historical and generational legacy.[11] Studies of the impacts of historical trauma on Indigenous American communities are particularly relevant today, and they are an important part of white (North) America's ongoing process of coming to grips with the devastating legacy of slavery, oppression, and genocide against the Black and Indigenous peoples of the Americas.[12] Historical trauma theory has played a significant role in developing treatment strategies targeting communities of Native American and Alaska Native peoples who, like Indigenous peoples in Mesoamerica and South America, have some of the lowest indicators of health and social well-being of any group.[13] This is not the place to attempt a summary of this important research, but I do believe it represents an underutilized theoretical framework for understanding the experiences of Nahuas and other Indigenous peoples of early colonial Mexico. For the purposes of understanding Aquino, a less-studied but more-relevant offshoot of trauma studies looks at the connection between trauma and apocalyptic thought. This perspective views "apocalyptic sentiments" as "the expressions of traumatized people" and seeks to apply trauma theory as a hermeneutic for understanding apocalypticism in its varied manifestations.[14] This approach is ably summarized by Dereck Daschke, whose treatment I follow here.

Although apocalypticism is most often associated with dire predictions about impending doom, Daschke states that this phenomenon is less about the future and much more about the present and "remaking a world shattered by unexpected, unexplained pain and disillusionment [i.e., trauma]."[15] He cites Judith Herman who writes that traumatic events "shatter the construction of self . . . undermine the belief systems that give meaning to human existence . . . violate the victim's faith in a natural or divine order and cast the victim into a state of existential crisis."[16] Scholars of trauma have noted that the same impacts can be experienced by entire communities, which has led to the development of the concept of collective or cultural trauma. So damaging can large-scale traumatic events or conditions be that their effects can long outlast the generation that experienced them, which results in trauma of the historical or intergenerational type.

The violent conquest and systematic oppression of Indigenous America inflicted collective trauma on Indigenous communities in sixteenth-century Mexico, as it did all across the Americas. Daschke points out that the deepest damage done by traumatic events is to the worldview of the victim, or in the collective, the entire culture or people group. Others have made a similar argument. Nancy Farriss, in her study *Maya Society Under Colonial Rule*, argued that Christianization caused a spiritual crisis for Indigenous Mesoamericans, a crisis that constituted trauma. She argues that on some levels Christianization was even more disruptive than the wars of conquest, since unlike the military campaigns of the conquistadors, the crisis of religion demanded that Indigenous people "deny the existence of their entire religious cosmology,"[17] a reality which resulted from the missionaries' strategy of epistemic violence.

The shock to Indigenous cosmologies inflicted by the first wave of Christianization required Indigenous people to restructure their reality in its wake so that they could reestablish a stable place in the world.[18] Broadly speaking, this was the work of Indigenous cultural intermediaries, intellectuals like Aquino who reframed Christian teachings in such a way that permitted this restructuring and reestablishing to take place. One aspect of Christianity that seems to have been deemed useful in this effort was Christian apocalypticism. In their treatment of the so-called "Maya Apocalypse" of 2012, Restall and Solari identify Indigenous attraction to Christian apocalypticism as a response to the effects of epistemic violence. They write, "Apocalyptic narratives and their associated millennial theology were an ideal avenue through which converted Maya could make sense of the violence and cultural upheavals of the Spanish conquest and its chaotic aftermath."[19] Daschke argues that it is this process of "making sense" that lies at the heart of apocalyptic thought. Through visions, dreams, and prophecies, apocalypticists offer narratives that promise to "make the world make sense again."[20] They do this by explaining the inexplicable (i.e., the trauma) in terms of its relation to a larger historical narrative. Some scholars refer to this as the "apocalyptic cure," since it is a mechanism that facilitates the construction of a new worldview in which the trauma is integrated and is given meaning.[21] This strategy of explaining past events in terms of the present was widely practiced by colonial Indigenous writers and has been well-documented by many scholars. It is the strategy illuminated by Stephanie Wood in her work on the genre known as "primordial titles," Louise Burkhart in her treatment of the *Three Kings* Nahuatl drama, and Lori Diel in her analysis of the early colonial pictorial known as the Codex Mexicanus, among others.[22]

However, what has not been well-explored is the phenomenon of Indigenous apocalypticism as part of this strategy of historical reframing by Indigenous writers.

Mark Christensen's recent book, *Aztec and Maya Apocalypses: Old-World Tales of Doom in a New-World Setting*, does an excellent job of tracing the phenomenon of Indigenous apocalypticism through the colonial sources, offering invaluable insights through the comparison of Nahuatl and Yucatec Mayan texts. The explanation he gives for why Nahuas and Mayas were drawn to the Christian apocalyptic is one that is based largely on the existence of parallels between Mesoamerican and Christian cosmologies. Indigenous Mesoamerican understandings of the cyclical nature of time and the belief that destructive events brought major eras to an end is understood as facilitating the integration of Christianity's view of the consummation of history in the violent events of the Second Coming, the Final Judgment, and the end of the world. Like Restall and Solari, Christensen cites the adoption of apocalypticism as one of the many documented ways Indigenous Christians negotiated a form of continuity with their past by creatively adapting the dogmas of the colonial present.

As important as these insights are, what I am proposing is that apocalypticism among Nahuas and Mayas may also be considered a specific strategy of Indigenous historical, or perhaps cosmological, revisionism aimed at responding to the trauma of conquest and colonization. The apocalyptic narrative allows victims of trauma to reframe their suffering in the context of a divinely ordained timeline. The meaning of the cataclysm is revealed by seers like the plays' Sibyl. In her opening monologue in *Antichrist and the Final Judgment*, Sibyl addresses the audience of macehualtin and frames the ensuing performance by saying, "Look here! Come to your senses, you neophyte! See the *neixcuitilli* so that you will know when God's heart will determine to end the world" (f. 133r–v). The Christian *macehualtin* in the play model the correct understanding of these events, declaring, "when our Lord ascended to the heavens he told us that one would be born whose name would be Antichrist," an understanding that equips them to confront Antichrist and defiantly resist him with the words, "I want to live suffering for the true God!" (f. 158r). Even though Antichrist slays them for their faith, Christ later rewards them at the Judgment, saying, "because you are good Christians, come to be with me! Please rejoice! . . . enter now into my home!" (f. 145v). In spite of reality-shattering trials and tribulations, the apocalyptic narrative promises that ultimately redemption and salvation in paradise awaits those remain faithful to the end.

I want to be clear that I am making no claim that Aquino was suffering from the effects of trauma, such as PTSD or, what Evans-Campbell proposes to call CTR, "Colonial Trauma Response."[23] The diagnosis of individuals at a distance of over four centuries is a dangerous undertaking, as I have learned personally through past errors. However, I believe the links between apocalyptic thought and cultural trauma are so compelling that they should be considered as one possible reason why a Nahua like Aquino—and the Indigenous audiences he wrote for—may have found in the legend of the Antichrist a narrative that both explained the painful present (or the recent past) and offered a reimagined future that promised an end to all suffering. Whether by those directly experiencing the early traumas or by later generations for whom it lingered as a painful, historical memory, apocalypticism's relation to trauma remains to be more carefully examined by scholars. A book's conclusion is not the place to do so, but I hope others will find in the phenomenon of Indigenous apocalypticism a useful hermeneutic for a deeper understanding of Indigenous engagement with Christianity in the Colonial period.

As I write this I'm acutely aware of the irony, or as some might charge, the audacity of suggesting that Christianity, the religion wielded as a weapon of domination in wars of conquest and genocide, might have been a "cure" for the victims of trauma. Let me state emphatically that I'm not, at least not in the manner in which this statement smacks of Eurocentric "saviorism." What I have endeavored to show throughout this book is that Nahua intellectuals like Fabián de Aquino took part in a multigenerational project whereby the sword of Christianity was forged into something quite different and new. Nahua intellectuals, wielding the pen, helped construct a new narrative, one that held onto important elements of Indigenous culture while integrating those aspects of the foreign that aligned and resonated with them and rejecting those that did not. This new narrative emerged through decades of creative appropriation and continues to manifest itself today in the dizzying variety of expressions that mark Indigenous engagements with Christianity.

The two plays presented in this volume are part of this narrative, what I've referred to as both Indigenous performances of Christianity and performances of Indigenous Christianity (or, "Christianities"). Whether or not Fabián de Aquino himself experienced the tumultuous period of the 1530s and penned them in response or lived their painful legacy during the latter half of the century has been, and will have to remain, one of a number of unanswered questions. I have tried to be honest about my ability to answer them and accepting of the fact that it will probably be others who ultimately fill in the blanks. With this, I bring my "unbundling" of Aquino's Nahuatl Antichrist plays to an end and invite you to reach deeply into this textual *toptli, petlacalli,* "deep basket, chest of reeds," to savor these magnificent early works of Indigenous American literature.

PRESENTATION
OF THE PLAYS

NORMS OF TRANSCRIPTION
AND TRANSLATION

MY TRANSCRIPTION of Aquino's writing strives to precisely reproduce his orthography so that the reader of Nahuatl may have as direct an access to the original as possible. When my transcription diverges from the original, it is always with an eye to facilitate the intelligibility of the Nahuatl text. One exception to my claim of fidelity to the original is in the case of the spacing of words and lines. Sixteenth-century writers tended not to approach spacing (or capitalization, punctuation, etc.) with the same concern for rules and standardization as modern writers. Spacing within and between words was very fluid and could change from line to line. This was compounded when the writer was a Nahua, since Indigenous writers tended to write as they spoke, allowing words to flow together as they do in natural speech, and they shared little of their European counterparts' concern with grammatical rules. Therefore, I have taken the liberty of inserting spaces between words and removing spaces within so that the Nahuatl is more readily comprehended.

The reader of Nahuatl will quickly notice a number of idiosyncrasies in Aquino's writing. In order to keep footnotes to a minimum, I will summarize the most common of these here so as to avoid having to mention each one individually in the notes.

- Aquino tended to insert an *h* (a glottal stop) between words that ended in a vowel and began with the same vowel. For example, he wrote *cahamo* for *ca amo*. I have not omitted the *h* but inserted a space between the two words, as in *cah amo*.

https://doi.org/10.5876/9781646423002.c004

- The inconsistency with which Aquino wrote Nahuatl's ubiquitous /ts/ phoneme may be evidence of an early date of composition, since this became standardized as *tz* as early as the middle of the sixteenth century.[1] Throughout the text he writes this as *tz, z, ʦ, ç,* and a unique barred letter *z*.

- Elision is common in Aquino's writing. One of the most common instances is when Nahuatl's subordinating particle *in* (written *yn* by Aquino) is immediately followed by a word beginning with *n*. In this case, Aquino always combined both words and dropped one of the *n*'s. Common examples include *çaniman* for *çan niman* and *ynelli* for *yn nelli*. In these cases, I have separated the particle from the word but not added the missing *n*, hence *ça niman* and *y nelli*.

- Like other sixteenth-century writers trained in the schools of mendicant friars, Aquino employed certain standard abbreviations. These include *q̓* for *-qui, q̄* for *-que, ā* for *-am/-an, ē* for *-en/-em, ȳ* for *yn* [*in*], *t̄p̄c̄* for *tlalticpac, x̄p̄o* for *Cristo,* and *ilhᶜ* for *ilhuicac*. I have left all abbreviations as they appear in the text, saving clarification for notes when necessary. Also in the notes are mentions of instances when Aquino fashioned nonstandard abbreviations, one small but stark indicator of Indigenous scribal ingenuity.

Throughout the chapters in this book and the English translations of the two plays, the reader will notice that I have left certain words untranslated. These include terms like Mictlan (one of the Mesoamerican otherworlds of the dead, a translation of the Spanish *infierno*, "hell") and *teotl* (the Indigenous central Mexican concept of divinity, adopted as an equivalent for the Spanish *Dios*, "God"). I have made an exception in the case of *tlacatecolotl* and *tlatlacatecoloh* (adopted as a translation for the Spanish *diablo*, "devil"), opting instead for "were-owl," in order to spare the non-Nahuatl speaking reader from repeatedly grappling with this mouthful. The presence of untranslated words (like teotl) or words that aren't commonly associated with their intended meanings (such as "were-owl" for "demon") results in a degree of discomfort for the reader. This is intentional. It exists to remind us of the semantic gulf that existed between many religious concepts imported from Europe and those of Nahuatl-speaking peoples. If you feel this discomfort, you might imagine that it is akin to the discomfort Nahuas may have experienced when first hearing words like *Dios, ánima,* or *sacramento*.

Linguist Geoff Nunberg has said, "a great translation should allow us to hear a stubbornly alien language rustling in the background."[2] Though my translation may at times feel stilted, I have allowed it to retain some of this "background rustling" out of deference to the uniqueness and beauty of the Nahuatl language. As I work and rework my translations (a never-ending, iterative process) I always try to walk a line between an honest recognition of the original and a desire to produce a translation that is at least readable and at best enjoyable. Fabián de Aquino's Nahuatl prose contains little of the flowery quality of certain forms of more elegant Nahuatl writing. While he does incorporate the occasional *difrasismo* and some rudimentary forms of parallelism, his was a more work-a-day Nahuatl, less inclined to the flourishes common in the writing of some of his contemporaries. Rather, the rhetorical force of his work resided in his use of what has been called "didactic terror," a strategy commonly employed by mendicant friars and Nahua writers in doctrinal literature.[3] The apocalyptic tenor of his Antichrist plays coupled with the repeated mentions of the horrors of hell, bore the brunt of the didactic and admonitory intent of the plays. Despite the chasm created by the centuries, language, and orthography of Fabián de Aquino, his Converts, Martyrs, Antichrist, and Hermit characters will, I have no doubt, startle and delight modern readers today.

ANTICHRIST
AND THE
FINAL JUDGMENT

(MS NS 3/1, ff. 131r–150r)

NAHUATL PALEOGRAPHY

[131r]

⸿Nican peva yn itoca Detlayehyecalvilliztli¹ ynic tlayehyecalvilloz yn quenin ontlamiz cemanavac yn q̄nin yn iquac tetlatzonteq̇lliquivh .d.² ynic nenemilizcueppalloz yn oc nemova tp̄c³ ynic vel tlayehyecalvillo yevatl yn itoca avto monequi ontecpātli Onmatlactli Once yn tlaca yevantin yni[n]⁴ mochintin ȳtla q̇tozque no yvā monequi yn cequintin quinpalevizque yevatl yn yacachto [m]oneq̇ ytoca tetlanextilliani yteq̇vh yez q̇tenezcayotilliz yn ixq̇ch mochivaz ynic vel cacoz ynic vel onCuivaz

⸿Niman valquiçaz ce tlacatl ytoca S[i]bila [131v] pphetisa q̇valvicazque omētin yn āgellome nimā valquiçaz yn itoca antexp̄o⁵ quivalvicazque .r̄c.⁶ miyequintin q̇nmictiz yn aᵒ⁷ q̇neltocazque yevantin yn intoca martiles chiCuacemintin yezque nimā valquiçazque Omentin yn intoca Eliyas yvā y Enoc .d. ypillovan temachtiquivi yvicpa yn tlaveliloc Auh ca çan ipalt̥inco .d. ymac miq̇zque nimā ya⁸ ce tlacatl yn ayocmo q̇moCuiti .d. Occeppa q̇moCuitiz yvā ceq̇ntin yn iycnivā yevātin yn intoca : Conversos nimā q̇nvalmivalliz yn toteᵒ.⁹ xp̄o [132r] ce angel yn itoca .S. miguel yn q̇mictiq̇vh yn ātexp̄o nimā valquiçaz̄q̄ yn mictlan yn tlahtlacateᵒ.¹⁰ chicomētin Canaq̇vi yn ātexp̄o. Ce ytoca loçiber ynic ii tlaloc ynic .iii. tezcatlipoca ynic iiii viçilopochtli ynic .v. q̇tzalcovatl ynic vi Otontecvh[c]tli ynic chi.¹¹ vii. civacovatl q̇valvicazque chiCuaCemintin yn pahpavaq̄ nimā q̇nvalvicazque yn aomoq̇neltocaque¹² .d. chiCuacemintin yezque niman q̇nvaltocatiyazque yn oq̇chivhtiyaq̄ yn tlavellilocayotl Ce tlatovani tonalpovhq̇ pochte[c]atl [132v] motolliniyani telpochtli

https://doi.org/10.5876/9781646423002.c005a

ENGLISH TRANSLATION

[131r]

Here begins what is called "a representation"[1] *in which it will be represented how the world will end, how when God comes to judge there will be many lives turned around while there is still living on earth. In order for what is called "a play" to be well represented, fifty-one people are needed. If all of these are to speak, then some others will need to help them. The first one who is needed is called "the revealer"*[2] *whose job will be to make known all that will happen so that [the play] can be understood, so that it can be comprehended.*

Then a person named Sibyl, [131v] *a prophetess,*[3] *will enter. Two angels will bring her out. Then the one named Antichrist will enter;*[4] *they will bring him out. He will slay many who do not believe in him. They are called martyrs [and] there will be six of them. Then two will enter whose names are Elijah and Enoch, God's noblemen. They will come to preach against wickedness and by the grace of God they will die by [Antichrist's] hand. Then, a person who no longer accepts God will once again accept him along with some of his friends, those who are called converts.*[5] *Then our Lord Jesus Christ will send* [132r] *an angel named St. Michael who will come to kill Antichrist. Then the were-owls will enter from Mictlan.*[6] *Seven will come to take Antichrist. The first is named Lucifer, the second Tlaloc, the third Tezcatlipoca, the fourth Huitzilopochtli, the fifth Quetzalcoatl, the sixth Otontecuhtli, the seventh Cihuacoatl. [Next] they will bring out six priests.*[7] *Then they will bring out those who do not believe in God; there will be six of them. Then following these will be those who have committed wicked acts: a*

https://doi.org/10.5876/9781646423002.c005b

aviyani Tetlanochilliyani ticitl ychtaca tetlaxīqui : motlahtlaxilliani moteçacatilliani Detenanavatilliani[13] ychtequini yn oq̇tecac yn ivayorq̄[14] mopatlachviani Cuilloni nimā ce tlacatl valquiçaz yn itoca Ermitano ynpan quichivaz yn Cruz + ytēcopa yn .d. q̇nnavatiz ynic q̇nextizque yn intlavellilocayo ynic quilvizq̄ yn tleyn ypāhpa tonevativi Nimā yevatl yn tote°. yn yesuxp̄o. valmonestitiyaz[15] tetlatzonteq̇liquivh ytlan valmātiyazque mieyeq̇ntin ynā[133r]gellome yvā yn itlaçonāt̄in yn .s. mā.[16] yvā yn apostollome Auin[17] iq̄c tlapitzalloz niman mozcalizque yn ixq̇chtin yn mimique avh yn ᵃqualtin ynic yazq̇ue mictlan etc. Auh yn qualtin ynic pahpactiyazque yn ihlᶜ.[18] ytlan .d. cemi[c]ac motlamachtitivi Omentin yn āgellome quitozque Detlatzonteq̇lliq̇vh[19] .d. yn iquac tlamiz Cemanavac

SIBILA QUITOZ

¶yz tonoc yn tiCuitlapilli yaq̇ne[20] yn tatlapalli Sivallachiya yaquine ximozcalli y[n] te[133v]vatl titlazcaltilli tiq̇ttaz y neyxCuitilli ynic vel ticmatiz yn iCuac .d. yyolo tlamatiz yn q̇ntlamiz cemanavac

¶Ma vel xistlamaticā tleyca Çanē anenemi mah amechmavhti yn ipaltinemi ma xicnotlamatican ma xiquimacaçican yn itleyo yn [i]maviçavhca Ca yevatl .d. ytlaço motlecaviz yn ilhᶜ.

¶Sibila nevatl notoca onechvalmivalli .d. : ma tlahtlacolcavallo yxcavilloz yn inotzaloca yesoxp̄o ytenevaloca ma novian tlacamachoz Ca yevatl yximachoz yCuac tlamiz Cemanavac

¶[S]pū.S.to yCualticat̄in [134r] yesuxp̄o monacayotico ynacayot̄in q̇Cuico yn ihitect̄inco yn .s. māçin yn yevatli .y. totlatocat̄in ynic oquichtli ytech Cruz .+. Omomiquilli neltocoz Çā topanpa .tp̄c.

¶Eylhuitica yn mozcalli ypillovan qui°nextilito[21] no yvā quinyollalito Onpovallilvitica O[m]otlecavi ylhᶜ. Otechmocencavilli Occeppa amechtlatzontequilliq̇vh : yyxpāt̄inco anquitlalitivi yn ovanquichivhque .tp̄c. :

¶Mah anmochintin xiçacā ca yvhqui yn ācochtinemi yn Cualli ancovicayztinemi av in tlahtlacolli ye anquiyecmati Auh ynin namechilvia yn tlahtlacolli : xictlaçacan ycel .d. sicneltocacan yehic[a] a° [134v] amechtlaçaz mictlan yc a° onpa tlahtlaz yn a°yollia Cemicac

¶Ma vel amitec motlali yn tleyn quito .S. juā Ca yvayolqui yezq̇ya yn ātexp̄o. Cenca aqualli yn q̇moteotiz yvhqui yn qualli yc vel teca mocacayavaz Cenca vell ic mochicavaz yn iztlacatilliztli Cemanavac

¶Ynic vel tetlaneltoq̇ltiz. xp̄o q̇motocayotiz. miyeq̇ntin q̇nyollitiz Ca yn omicca quinyolliti[z] teyxp̄ā yn tenā quinextiz Ca çā tlacatecolotl yvhq̇ynma ocelotl miyec anaz tp̄c.

ruler, a day keeper, a merchant, [132v] *a poor person, a young man, one who indulges in pleasure,*[8] *a procuress, a healer, a secret adulterer, one who induces her own abortion, one who sterilizes herself, a hypocrite, a thief, one who slept with his relative, a* patlach-huiani,[9] *[and] a* cuiloni.[10] *Then a person will enter who is called Hermit. He will make the [sign of the] cross on them. By God's command he will order them to reveal their wickedness, so that they will say to him the reason they are suffering. Then our Lord Jesus Christ will reveal himself, he will come judging people. Arrayed with him will be many angels* [133r] *along with his beloved mother Saint Mary and the apostles. And when there is blowing [of wind instruments] then all the dead will return to life. Then the bad ones will go to Mictlan, etc. The good ones will each go happily to the heavens*[11] *with God [where] forever they will rejoice. The two angels will say, "God will come to judge when the world ends!"*

SIBYL WILL SAY,

Here you are at last, you tail, you wing![12] Look here! Come to your senses, you [133v] neophyte![13] See the *neixcuitilli* so that you will know when God's heart will determine to end the world. Be very prudent![14] Why do you loiter about in vain? May The One by Whom We Live[15] frighten you! May you be saddened, may you fear his fame, his glory.[16] For it is the beloved of God who will ascend to the heavens. Sibyl is my name. God sent me. Let there be abandoning of sin, let there be attending to the counsel of Jesus Christ, let his exposition be obeyed everywhere.[17] Indeed, it shall be known when the world will end. Through the Holy Spirit's goodness, [134r] Jesus Christ came to take on flesh. He came to assume his body inside of Saint Mary. It shall be believed that Jesus, our ruler, died on the cross as a man on behalf of us on earth. On the third day he returned to life. He went to show himself to his noblemen and also to console them. Forty days later he ascended to the heavens. He prepared us [for when] he will come again to judge you [and] you will present to him what you did on earth. Awake, all of you! It is as if you are sleeping. You consider what is good to be difficult [and] you consider sin to be a virtue. And this I say to you regarding sin: cast it away! Believe in Only God[18] so that he will not [134v] cast you into Mictlan, so that your souls won't burn there forever.

May it be placed firmly within you what Saint John said, that one of his relatives would be the Antichrist.[19] Those who will worship him are very bad. Likewise the good will be thoroughly deceived. As a result, lying will be greatly strengthened in the world. In order to cause people to believe, he will call himself Christ. He will bring many back to life, he will give life to those who had died, he will cause someone's mother to appear before him.[20] [However,] he is just a were-owl.[21] Like a jaguar he will snatch many on earth.

¶Yevatl tlaveliloc yta yez Cenca veventin av[i]n inan cenca ylama[135r]ţin no yvhqui yez yn tlalloc ytech quitlamiz yn mochivhtoc ynic vel teyztlacaviz yn quinequi ayac motlecaviz yn itlan .d. yn ilhᶜ.

¶Yevatl yn iayaqualneɫmilliz yn çan amechmchtiquivh²² yvā amechititiq̇vh yn iyaqualtemachtilliz : macayac yztlacatilliztli ytech momachiy[o]ti macamo : canapa yylloti²³ yn teotlatolli tp̄c.

¶Yquivic²⁴ quinetoltiz yn motollinia teoCuitlatl Oc cequintin tilma matlatl yevātin quintlamaviçoltiz Ca çan ic noviyan yllotiz .d. ytlatolţin tlachiyaloni ynic caviz neltoconi ynic tonevaloz cemicac

¶Yn aᵒ qualtin xp̄ānome yn tleyn q̇nma[—]caz²⁵ [135v] quiCuizque vel quitlaca-matizque yn yevantin yn aviyanime Çan ivhqui yn teCuanime qualtin ypā quima-tizque ynic q̇nmahamavhtizque Cequin miquizque yn imac

¶Aqualtin quintlaçotlaz ynic yvicpa yztiyazque av in amo q̇neltocazque q̇ntlavel-lilocatocaz yn aqualtin quinmacaz yevatl yn itlatocayo yehica yn itlavelilocayo Oq̇chivhque .tp̄c.

¶Yn ivh caçiz yn michin yn aquin tlahtlamatinemiz Çano yvhqui quinmicti-tinemiz yn pihpiltotontin Auh yn chichi ca vel no yvhqui yvā ȳ mizton yn çā qui-michtacah ana ȳ quimichime Auh ca çano yvhqui yn tl[a]cateᵒ. ca çan q̇michtaca an[a]z yn vel monemitia [136r] tp̄c.

¶Ytlacaţintiayā yn .d. yn opa valazque eliyas enoc yvicpa yn tlavelliloc quitoquivi yn aqualli Cavaloz Auh yn qualli chivalloz ma novian teytec motlalli yn teotlatolli Cenca qualli ynic yaovaz yn ilhᶜ.

¶Ynic vel tlaneltocoz çan oc mocnonemitiquivh : Çan motollinitinemiquivh ynic ynemilliztocoz ynic atle ypan ytoz y nican .tp̄c.cayotl Can ilvicac tlatocayotl Cen machoz yn .tp̄c.

¶Auh occeppa tlaneltocazque yn ayomo²⁶ quimoCuiti ca .d. yn iteotlatolţin neɫ-tocoz Auh yn aᵒ qualnemilliztli quicavazque nimā yc q̇nmictizque²⁷ niman ayac quintocaz t̶o̶ ynin omentin vevetq̇ .d. ypillovā yehica yn oq̇Cuepq̇ ynteyaqualnemi-lliz . t[p̄c]. [136v]

¶Auh nimā vehveztozque yeilvitica yn inacayoţin ytencopaţinco yn toteᵒyoţin Auh yeylvitica nimā valyollizq̇ nimā ȳlvicac q̇nvalmanilizque yn āgellome ynic cemicac ahaviyazque yn ōpa yn niman aq̇n mochivazque q̇npahpaq̇ltiz .d. Cemicac

¶Auh yn iquac yn iycpalpā motlalliz yn yevatl yn tlavelliloc niman Ce an[g]el .d. ypillo yn opa q̇nvalmivalliz nimā yxq̇ch q̇tlaxilliz yn inacayo yaq̇ne ynic q̇tlaçaz tletitlan ynic onpa tlahtlaz yn intlan aqualtin Cemicac

¶Yn axcan namechititiya Ca quimotemaq̇lliz .d. Onpovalilvitl ynic chipavaloz yevatl yn teyollitiya yehica .d. q̇moneq̇ltia mah amechocti²⁸ yn aᵒtlahtlacol yehica yn aᵒ tlaca[t]eᵒ. yn amechanaq̇vh .tp̄c. [137r]

The wicked one's father will be very old. And his mother [will be] a very old woman. [135r] Moreover, he will be like Tlaloc to whom is attributed everything that was made so that people will be thoroughly deceived.[22] He desires that no one ascend to be with God in the heavens. He will come to teach you his bad way of life and he will come to show you his bad teaching. Let no one be marked by lying. May the sacred words[23] not diminish anywhere on earth. In this way, he will promise gold to the poor person, cloaks and nets to still other people. He will cause them to marvel. As a result, God's word, the seeing device[24] will diminish everywhere. The articles of the faith will be abandoned, and there will be eternal suffering. The bad Christians will take [135v] what [the Antichrist] gives them. The pleasure-seekers[25] will readily obey him. They are just like wild beasts that really frighten the good ones; some will die by their hand. [The Antichrist] will love the bad ones and they will be drawn to him. And he will consider wicked those who will not believe in him. He will give the bad ones his kingdom because they did his wicked deeds on earth. He will snatch up like a fish the one who lives presumptuously.[26] In the same way he will go about killing small children. It is just the same with dogs and cats who secretly snatch up mice. In the same way, the were-owl will secretly snatch up those who live virtuously [136r] on earth.

From the founding place of God's lineage will come Elijah [and] Enoch.[27] They will come to speak against wickedness; that which is bad will be abandoned, that which is good will be done. May the very good sacred words be placed inside of people everywhere so that people will go to the heavens. So that there will be believing, they will come living humbly, they will come living as poor ones. Therefore, their example will be imitated, earthly things here will be disparaged, [and] the kingdom in the heavens will be fully known on the earth. Those who no longer accept him will believe once more. Indeed, the sacred words of God will be believed. They will abandon the bad way of life. Then for this reason [the Antichrist] will kill them. Absolutely no one will bury these two old men,[28] God's noblemen, because they turned people from their bad way of living on earth. [136v] Then at our Lord's command their bodies will lie fallen for three days. But they will come back to life on the third day. Then the angels will take them to the heavens so that they will rejoice there forever. Absolutely nothing will happen to them; God will cause them to rejoice forever. And when the wicked one sits on his throne, then an angel, God's nobleman, he will send for them.[29] He will cast down everything. At last he will throw [the Antichrist's] body into the flames so that it will burn there forever with the bad ones.

Today I will show you how God will grant people forty days in order that the soul may be purified because God desires that you weep for your sins [and] so that the were-owl won't come to snatch you on earth.[30] [137r]

¶Auh çatepā a° vecavh noviyan Cenca tlachinaviz yn ixq̇ch yn oc atley ça niman caviz Auh quimoneq̇ltiz yn totlatocavh yn totemaq̇sticavh nimā mochi neltiz yn itlatolţin yn oq̇to yn iquac yn iyeçoţin yn onoq̇vico .tp̄c̄.

¶Auh çatepā amo vecavh tetlatlatzonteq̇lliquivh .d. mah axcanpa ylnamicoz tleyn q̇teylviz : totlatzonteccavh quenin amechilviz toteyocoxcavh yn iquac valanextiti-yaz yn aqualtin q̇nvallaveliztiyaz Ca çā valtemoz ylhᶜ.

¶Yn ixquichtin yn āgelome ytlan .d. valmātiyazque ynic tlacapehpenazque ya nelli qualtin xpīāno²⁹ no yevātin yn apostollome ytlanţinco tote°. yezque quintlavel-littaz yn aq̇q̇ vel nemizquiya .tp̄c̄. [137v]

¶Yn iquac tlapitzalloz yn vell omicca mozcallizque : mochi tlacatl vel yollizque yxpā tote°. tlapovalloz ynic ōpa nenemilliznextiloz Onpa cacoz yn canpa yaovaz ynic onpa nelli xelliovaz Auh catlyevatl yn otli tocoz yn iCuac

¶Auh quitlapovillizque .d. yvā quimitlanilliz yn .d. mochintin yn tlatoq̇ no yxq̇chtin yn onoque quenin yn omonemitique quinmotlahtlanilliz .d. av in ixq̇chtin yn qualtin quinmocnelliliz yn macevaltin vel quintlatoltiz no yevātin [y]n tlavellilo-que vel tlahtlativi Cemicac

¶Auh mictlan temozque yn pipiltin yn ōcate yn inmecavā yn cenca miyeq̇ yn inçovavan³⁰ no onpa temozque yn telpohpochtin yehica yn mieyeq̇ yn ichpo-pochtin yn oq̇nxapotlatinen[138r]que yn oq̇ncentecpavitinēque yn imecavā .tp̄c̄.

¶Au inin Onpa chocazque mochintin yn amo q̇ximatizneq̇ : y nelli .d. Ceq̇ntin Onpa CueCuechcazque miyequintin yehica yn amo moquahatequizneq̇ yehica yn a° q̇Cueppaznequi yn imaqualnemilliz .tp̄c̄. finis Nican tlatoz yn ātēx̄

¶Niman valquiçaz yn itoca antexp̄ō. nimā q̇toz Ca nevatl yxquich novelli niman ayac nivhqui yn .tp̄c̄. Onicchivhqui yn cemanavac Ca çan noçelţin yn onamechic-neli yn a° ma çan nicpiqui Ca ya nelli yn axcā namechmachtico

¶Auh yn axcan q̇lmach Ovanquineltocaque yn jesoxp̄ō mamacovhticac³¹ ynin cah amo Ca çan ic ovanechelcavhque yn āceq̇ntin .tp̄c̄. av in axcan macayac q̇[—]olo³² [138v] y notlatolţin yn aq̇n quipoloz niman nicnoquiz yn iyezço nomac miquiz .tp̄c̄.

¶Auh yntlah anechtlacamatizque niman āquittativi yn amonemac nochanţinco : ynic cemicac notlan anmonemitizq̇ nimā Onpa Octli : amechitizque yn yevātin y nomacevalvā yvā Onpa yezque yn amoçivavā ynic cēca anvellamatizque

¶Yvā namechmac[—]az³³ tlaxcalţintli ynic a° āteocivizque ynic vell onpa āmocevizque yvā āconizque necvhţintli yn onpa cenca q̇alli yn mochiva chilţintli y [n]ochanţinco yvā yn onpa Oc yovaţico qualli anquizque atolţintli

¶Au in axcā namechmacaznequi Cenca miyec : teoCuitlatl yzcatqui yn tlaço til[m]atli yntlah anechtlacama[139r]tiznequi yntlaca° anmiquiznequi nimā anech-vicazque yn āmochintin yntlah annechneltocazque Auh yn ceq̇ntin yehica yn a° miquizneq̇

Not long afterward everywhere will be burned, absolutely nothing will be left. Our ruler will desire this. All the words that he said when he came to spill his blood on earth will then come true. Not long afterward God will come judging people. From that time forward, let it be remembered what our judge will accuse people of, in what manner our creator will speak to you when he comes in radiance. He will go raging at the bad ones as he descends from the heavens. All the angels will go advancing with God for the purpose of selecting those who are true, good Christians. The apostles will also be with our Lord. He will look with hatred at those who should have lived honestly on earth. [137v] When [wind instruments] are blown those who have died will return to life; every person will truly live again. There will be an accounting made before our Lord, and a revealing of each and every life. It will be heard where one will go; in this way there will be a dividing up [of people] there. And which road will be taken then?[31] And all the rulers and everyone who is there will give an account to God. God will ask them how they lived, God will question them. He will favor all the good ones, he will really intercede for the common people, [but] those wicked ones will really burn forever.[32] The nobles will descend to Mictlan [where] their mistresses and a great many of their women are. Lots of young men will also go down there because they went around deflowering many young women, [138r] they went around despoiling their mistresses on earth. Furthermore, all those who did not want to acknowledge the true God will weep. Many others will quake because they did not want to get baptized, because they did not want to turn around their bad way of living on earth.

Finis.

Here Antichrist will speak.

Then he who is called Antichrist will enter, then he will say,

I am all powerful! There is absolutely no one like me on earth! I made the world! I alone have favored you—I'm not just making this up![33] In truth, today I have come to teach you. And now they say that you have believed that Jesus Christ was cruci- fied. This is not so! Because of this some of you on earth have forgotten me. Today let no one disregard [138v] what I have to say. I will spill the blood of whoever does! He will die by my hand on earth. But if you will obey me then you will receive your reward in my home, you will live with me forever. There my subjects will give you pulque to drink,[34] your women will also be there so that you will be really content. Also, I will give you some nice tortillas[35] so that you won't be hungry, so that you can rest yourselves there. And you will drink nice honey! There are very good chili peppers growing in my home, and you will drink good *atolli* there in the morning. Right now I want to give to you a whole lot of gold! Here is a fine cloak! If you wish to obey me, [139r] if you do not want to die, then come with me all of you, if you will believe in me. But you others are about to die!

¶Ynin vel nican tlatoz temachtiz av in iquac yn ceq̇ntin tiᴛ yn oq̇Cuique yn tlatquitl yn oq̇neltocaque Cenca quintlaçotlaz Auh yn a° q̇neltocazneq̇ nimā q̇mavaz quinmictiz Auh nim[ā] motlalitivh yn iycpalpan

Auh niman valquiçazque eliyas Enoc.

ELIAS

¶Auh nimā quitozque yn yevātin yn vehuetq̇ yn axcan otivallaque tomentin yn ōpa yn otivalevaq̇ yn itlacaʈintiayan .d. ynic otechvalmivalli yehica yn amo neltocoz yn tleyn axcan yn ovāquicaq̇ yn ovamitec q̇tlallitiaq̇ yn tlavelliloque nimā : axcan yn ovamechmaca[q]ue yn imaxca ynic ovame[c]hiztla[139v]cavitiyaque

ENOC

¶Auh nimā . q̇.tozque yn eliyas enoc yn tevantī ca otamechqualnemillizmachtico yvā otamechititico yn nelli .d. yn iyximachoca Auh ma yxcavillo yn inotzaloca ynic amo mictlan vilovaz novian moneq̇ vnCuivaz yn icel teotl yn itenevalocaʈin

/ELIAS /

¶Nican nimā q̇neltocazque yn aomo[34] quimoCuitique .d. yn intoca Conversos

¶Nimā .q̇.[35] yn vevetq̇ Ça ce .d. yn oquiyox yn ixq̇ch mochivhtoc niman atley Çan omochivh yn onoc yvā topāpa yn otlayocox yn iyolloʈin ynic oq̇chtli yn itech Cruz + yn omomiquilli .tp̄c. ynic tlecovaz yn ilh°. yn itlatolʈin neltocoz

(ENOC)

¶Auh nimā quitozque yn eliya[s] Enoc maca xicnel[140r]tocacan yn ovamechilvi tlavelliloc Ca niman atley yn iyasca yn ixq̇ch yn mochivhtoc maca° xictlaçotlacā maca° ytlan ximovican Ca yn opa yevatl yn amechititiz yn toneviztli yn chichinaquiztli : maca° xictlacamatican

This will be spoken, will be preached here. And then he will really love those who took the goods[36] *[and] believed in him. And he will scold, he will kill those who do not want to believe in him. And then he will settle himself on his throne.*[37]
Next Elijah [and] Enoch will enter.

ELIJAH

Then the old men will say,
Today we two have come. We have come from the founding place of God's lineage. For this he sent us, so that what you have heard today, what the wicked ones have placed within you, will not be believed.[38] Today they have given you their goods and with that [139v] they have deceived you.

ENOCH

And then Elijah and Enoch will say,
We came to teach you the good way of living and we came to show you the knowledge of the true God. May his counsel be heeded so that no one will go to Mictlan. It is necessary that Only Deity's proclamations are understood everywhere.

ELIJAH

Here those who no longer acknowledged God will [again] believe. They are called Converts.
Then the old men will say,
There is only one God who created everything that was made. There is nothing that was made that he did not make. Because of us his heart grieved. He died on the cross as a man [while] on earth so that there will be ascending to the heavens [and so that] his words will be believed.

ENOCH

Then Elijah and Enoch will say,
Do not believe [140r] what the wicked one said to you! He isn't the creator of anything.[39] Do not love him, do not go with him, for there [in his home] he will show you pain, affliction. Do not obey him!

ELIAS

¶Nimā quitoz elias ma vell amitec motlalli yn itlatolt̤ī yn icelt̤in nelli .[d]. yn jesuxpō. ma ycelt̤in tlacamacho ma°chi³⁶ tlacatl mozcalli X³⁷ ma yevatl teytec quitlalli yn iqualtica ynicacoz³⁸ yn itlatolt̤in ynic neltocoz ca çan icel cēca qualli

/ENOC /

¶Nimā quitoz enoc ma xitlamacevacan ẏn a°chintin .tp̄c̄. yc āyazque yn ilvicac ma ximoyormellavacan³⁹ ma xinētlamaticā ypanpa yn a°tlahtlacol [y]nic a° [140v] tlacate°. yn amechvicaz yn opa yn ichā yn mictlā

¶Auh niman q̇tozq̇ yn cōvelsox Ca ya neli yn axcā Otechiztlacavica yn tlavelliloque yn teca mocacayavani yn itzel teotl Ca ya oticyollitlacoque avin axcā ma ticyorcevican ma tictonemilliztican yn itlatolt̤in ȳ jesuxpō ma tlacava yn a°yollot̤in ma to[p]āhpa xicmotlahtlavhtillican yn totat̤in

Nimā q̇ncētlalizq̇ yn oq̇Cuiq̇ ȳ tlatquitl

ELIAS

¶Nimā q̇tozq̇ yn itlaçopilvā .d. ma xim[o]tlanquaqueçacā yn iyxpāt̤inco yn ipalnemovani Ca cēca tetlayocolliani ma yyxpāt̤inco xichocacā ma xitlayocoyacan ma niman amechocti⁴⁰ yn a°tlahtlacol : ma n[i]mā xicchichacā yn tlac[a]te°. ma çan icel .d. [141r] xictlacamatican yvā xictlatlavhtican

¶Auh yn elias yn enoc yn imomextin nimā q̇tozque yevatl yn itoca Oraçion.

¶Diose ma xiquintlayocolli ynin tlahtlacovanipohpol : ca oq̇miztlacavi yn tlacate° ma °palt̤inco⁴¹ xiquinpohpolvilli ma no yvā xiq̇nmochicavilli ynic amo CueCuetlaxivizque ynic mopalt̤in[c]o vel miquizque ma ymitec xictlalli yn moqualticat̤in

¶Nimā nicā tlatoz temachtiz yn elliyas yn anoço Enoc ynic nechicavalloz Auh nimā Occeppa ypā acizquivh yn ātexp̄ō. nimā cēca quimavaz yvā q̇nmimictiz ypāhpa yn tlaneltoq̇lliztli

ANTEXP̄Ō

¶Nimā q̇toz yn ātexp[ō] q̇[n]ī yn ovāq̇ntlapololtique y no[141v]tlaçovā yn ovāq̇nmachtico : yvan yn ovelanquimiztlacavico Ca çan ic ovāquinyolpoloq̇ vel amonezca yn ātlaveliloq̇ yn axcā vel miquiz yn a°nacayo ypāhpa yn a°tlavellilocayo yntlaca° ylloti yn ovāquitoque

ELIJAH

Then Elijah will say,
Firmly place the words of the one true God, Jesus Christ, within you. May he alone be obeyed. May all people be raised to life by Christ. May his goodness be placed within people so that his words will be understood, so that it will be believed. For he alone is very good.

ENOCH

Then Enoch will say,
Do penance, all you on earth, so that you will go to the heavens! Confess! Grieve for your sins so that the were-owl won't [140v] bring you there to his home, Mictlan.

Then the Converts will say,
It is true that today the wicked ones have fooled us. We have offended Only Deity. And now may we appease him, may we live by the words of Jesus Christ. Please grant this, please pray to our father on our behalf!
Then they will gather up, they will take [Antichrist's] goods.[40]

ELIJAH

Then God's beloved noblemen will say,
Kneel down before The One by Whom There is Living. He is very merciful. Weep before him! Mourn! May your sins cause you to weep. Spit on the were-owl![41] Obey Only God [141r] and pray to him!

Elijah and Enoch both will then say what is called a "prayer."
O God, have mercy on these wretched sinners! The were-owl has deceived them. Pardon them through your grace and also strengthen them so that they will not faint, so that they will die for you. Place your goodness inside of them.
Then at this point Elijah or Enoch will speak, will teach in order to strengthen people.[42] *And then again they will approach Antichrist. He will vehemently scold them, and he will kill them because of the faith.*

ANTICHRIST

Then Antichrist will say,
How did you confuse my beloved [141v] ones? You came to teach them and you came to deceive them, and as a result you have just disturbed them. This is proof that you are wicked ones![43] Today your bodies will perish because of your wickedness unless you take back what you have said.

ELIAS

¶Nimā . q̇toz. yn eliyas yyoyavhe yn tiquetzalcovatl ca vel monezc[a] yn titlaveliloc
motech ticmotlamillia ȳ mochi Onoc .tp̄c̄. Ca niman atley yn maxca yntlanel ça ce
yn ovatl niman a° maxca av inin aço ticon[e]vh ȳ civacovatl ypāhpa Ca timoteotoca-
tinemi ma nimā : mizmicti yn ipalnemovani Ca ovel yca ticmocacayavh yn imacev-
altin .d.

ENOC

¶Nimā quitoz enoc yn axcan ayc moCue[142r]ppaz .d. ytlatolt̨in Auh yn axcan Ca
çan ipalt̨inco timiquizque ynic ytlant̨inco titocevizque ca çan topāpa yn onoquivico
yn itlaçoyezçot̨in ma techmoviquiq̇li ȳ tote°.yot̨in niman axcā yn ilhᶜ. ma noviyā
Cemanavac Onchicava yn teyollot̨in

¶Nimā nican q̇nmictiz yn antexp̄o yn elliyas Enoc Auh nimā q̇mavaz ynic ceq̇ntin
q̇ne[lt]ocazque yvā cequintin q̇nmictiz yn oq̇ntlaneltoquiltique yn vevetque yn
oquimoneltoquiltique ȳ jesuxp̄o. Ca çā yevātin ȳ vel mochicavazq̇ yn amo q̇maca-
çizque Ca çan nimā yyxco q̇tlaçazque yn itlatq̇ yn oquinmacaca etc. nimā motlalitivh yn iycpalpā Auh nimā q̇valmivalliz ce āgel .d. Ca yevatl yn itoca .s. miguel ynic
quimictiq̇vh yn ātexp̄o Auh yn .d. nimā q̇noça[z] q̇lviz [f.142v] .s. miguel Auh yn
yevatl yn .s. miguel nimā motlāCuaqueçaz

¶q̇lviz micayeltze xicmocaq̇ti niman icivhca xiquechcotonati yn vey tlacate°. Ca
yevatl yvhqui yn ma[42] pitzotl maçivi yn omic yolliti tleypāpa yn oquintlapollolti
yn yevātin yn otlachivalvan Auh ma nima[n] ⁱcivhca : Axcā xitemo yniquicivhca[43]
ticmictiz

¶Auh yn oq̇mit[al]villi yn tote°. : niman icivhca valmovicaz yn .s. miguel av in
iquac yn ovacico nimā q̇lviz yn ātexp̄o

¶Axcā ycivhca ximoteca yn titlacate°. Ca vel iten[c]opat̨inco yn icel teotl yn .d.
nixpā vel ximopechteca niman içivhca nimiztlaçaz yn ayeccan yehica yn otimote-
otocac vel cemicac mictlā titonevaz yn opa Cenca ceva yvā tona yvā yeheca

.S. MIGUEL.

¶[N]imā . q̇. yn .s. miguel ye[143r]hica yn tlahtlatinemi Cenca miyeq̇ntin mopāhpa
yn mictlan axcan mizmotlaxilliz yn ya nelli yn ipaltinemi Auh yn mochintin

ELIJAH

Then Elijah will say,

Alas, you Quetzalcoatl!⁴⁴ That you take credit for everything on earth is proof that you are wicked! You have nothing to your name, not even have a single green maize shoot! Furthermore, perhaps you are the offspring of Cihuacoatl since you go around following her as a deity.⁴⁵ May The One by Whom There is Living kill you now! You really have mocked God's subjects.

ENOCH

Then Enoch will say,

Now the words of God [142r] will never return.⁴⁶ Now we will die for him so that we will rest with him. For it was on our behalf that he came to pour out his precious blood. May our Lord now bring us to the heavens. May people's hearts be strengthened all over the world.

Here Antichrist will kill Elijah and Enoch. And then he will scold them⁴⁷ so that some will believe in him and others he will kill. Those who the old men caused to believe, those who believed in Jesus Christ, they will be strong, they will not fear him. Before him they will cast his goods, those which he gave them, etc.⁴⁸ Then [Antichrist] will go sitting on his throne. And then God will send an angel named Saint Michael to come and kill Antichrist. God will summon him, he will speak to Saint Michael. [142v] And then Saint Michael will kneel down.

[God] will say to him,

O Michael! Listen up! Swiftly cut off the head of the great were-owl! He is like a pig! Even though he died, he returned to life.⁴⁹ Why did he confuse those who are my creations? May you now swiftly descend and kill him!

When our Lord has said this to him, then Saint Michael will come down quickly.

Upon arriving he will then say to Antichrist,

Now lie right down, you were-owl! By the command of Only Deity, God, bow down before me! Then I will swiftly cast you to a bad place because you considered yourself a *teotl*! You shall truly suffer forever in Mictlan, for it is very cold, and hot, and windy down there.⁵⁰

ST. MICHAEL

Then Saint Michael will say, [143r]

Because there are so many burning in Mictlan on your account, he who is true, the

miztlavelilocatocazque yn iz nemi yvā tetonevhcā miznamoyazque : yn yeȳatin yn
otiquintlayecoltitinenca

¶Auh nimā niCan valq̇çazque yn tlahtlacate°. yvā ceq̇ntī yn itlan cate ynic quivi-
cazq̄ mictlan yn ātexpō yn iquac yn oquimicti yn āgel nimā q̇taquivi Cuicaq̇vi
yn inCuic Cenca tetlayocolti yezqui q̄vazq̄ yn to[n]oq̄ nicā ma tichocanca[44] ma
tichocacan

   ¶Ma tichocacan yn axcā timochintin ma nimā Ceq̇ntī tlayocoyacan
   ¶xitlaçoçonacā maca xitlatzivican ma nimā xonelçiçivican ma tiq̇çacan
   ¶ximotecpanacā tict[a]ni[143v]litivi yevatl yn tocnivh xinenemicā
   ¶xitotoyocacan ticmaviztillizque tictoviq̇llizque yn opa tletitlan

   ¶Auh nimā nicā valq̇çaz ce tlacatl ynitoca ~~ante~~ ermitano nimā q̇ntlahtlaniz yn
tlahtlacate°. ynic q̇tozque yn cāpa vi ynic q̇nextizque yvā q̇ntlahtlaniz yn tle ynezca
yn [i]xq̇ch yn quitq̇tivi

ERMITANOS[45]

¶Auh nimā q̇toz yn ermitano ma xinechilvican Canpa yn ayavi yn a°chintin tle ynic
toneva yn mochintin maca° xictlatican ma çā xinechititicā yn tleyn yn a°tlatq̇ yetivh
av aquin axcan ancanativi ma nimā xicnextican

¶Auh yn yevātin niman amo quinextizneq̇zque Auh niman ytēcopa yn .d. nimā
q̇nav[a]tiz Cenca vecavh mononoçazque yehica yn °.[144r]chintin[46] yn ovalquizque
mictlan Auh nimā quilvizque yn tleyn ynic tonevativi Auh yn iquac q̇navatiz ynic
yazque nimā yazq̄ Auh yn iquac ya canaznequi yn antexpō nimā Occeppa q̄vazque
yn inCuic yn iquac ya yyxpā cate niq̇mā q̄vazque q̇tozq̄

¶Ca çaⁿ ⁱᶜ tichoca yn otimizpoloque yn axcan yn ixq̇chtin yn ovallaq̄ m[a]
mizmoviquilicā

¶Niman quitozq̄ ma xicnapalocan yn inacayoṭin yvā yn iyezçoṭin tla xocōCuican
tla xoconololocan

True One, The One by Whom We Live will now cast you down. All those who will wickedly follow you while living here, those who you used to serve, will take you away to the place of suffering.

At this point the were-owls will enter along with some others who are with them in order to bring Antichrist to Mictlan when the angel kills him. They will come to see him, they will come singing. Their song will be very sad, they will raise it up:

May we who are here weep, may we weep,
Let us now weep all of us. Let some others now be sad.
Beat the drums! Be not lazy! Now sigh! Come out!
Line up! Let's go get [143v] our friend. Get moving!
Run along! Let us honor him, let us carry him there among the flames.
Here at this point a person named Hermit will enter. He will ask the were-owls to tell him where they come from so that they will reveal it to him, and he will ask them what everything they are carrying with them means.[51]

HERMIT

Then Hermit will say,

Tell me where all of you are going! Why are all of them suffering?[52] Do not hide it, just show me what you are carrying. Who is it that you are taking away? Show him to me now!

But they will not want to show him. Then by God's command he will order them. All those [144r] who came out of Mictlan will confer among themselves for a very long time. Then they will tell him what it is that causes them to suffer.[53] *And when he orders them to go, then they go. And when they are about to take up Antichrist['s body] they will again raise their voices in song. When they are before him they will raise up their song saying,*

It is because of this that we weep:
we lost you!
Today all who have come
may they carry you off!

Then they will say,

Bear up his dear body in your arms,
and his dear blood!
Grasp him!
Wrap him up![54]

¶A[u]h nimā Occeppa q̃pevaltiya yn inCuic ynic q̃vicativi mictlan yn ātex av in oq̃vicaq̃ mictlā yn antexp̄o Ca nimā yçivhca navhcanpa tlachinaviz ynic neçiz yn q̃nin Centlapanaviya ynic tlahtlaz yn ō[p]a [144v] mictlan

¶Auh nimā yçivhca valmonextiz yn .s. miguel quinmonochiliz yniq̃chtin⁴⁷ yn omomiq̃lli ca ynic niman mozcallizq̃

.S. MIGUEL

¶Nimā q̃toz yn .s. migel mimiq̃he ximoqueçacan ma nimā yçivhca xitlapovaq̃ yyxpāṭinco ȳ .d. nimā xicnextiq[u]i yn ixq̃ch yn aᵒcatzavaca niman icivhca xivallacan yn omacevalloc ya oncelliloz ynicā yyxpāṭinco ȳ .d. tla yc ximozcallican

¶Auh nimā tlapitzaloz yevatl niman ic valmonextiya yn ixq̃chtin mimicq̃ yyxpāṭinco yn jesuxp̄o nimā motlancuaq̃tzazque Auh nimā valquiçazque yn tlaht-lacateᵒ. ynic q̃nvicazque yn aᵒqualtin yn opa mictlan av [i]n iyxpanṭinco toteᵒ. mochi [145r] tlacatl viviyocazque niman quimonavatilliz yn toteᵒ. yn āgellome ynic q̃npehpenazque yn ixquichtin yn amoqualtin ynic quintlallizque yn iyopochcopa avh yn qualtin ynic q̃ntlalizque yn imayeccanpa Auh niman motlanquaqueçazque yn āgellome yyxpāṭinco yn jesuxp̄o

.XP̄O.

¶Auh nimā quitoz yn totemaquixticaṭin yn jesuxp̄o. yn amevātin yn amāgelotin tla xicmocaq̃tican ma xiq̃nmopehpenillicā yn qualtin xp̄īanotin ma niman xiq̃ntlaliti yn yectin yn omayavhcāpa Auh yn aᵒ qualtin nopochcopa xiquimiquaniti

¶Auh nimā tlatzotzonalloz yn iquac quimiquanizque : yn qualtin xp̄īanome y[n] yevātin yn angelome ynic [t]eyquanizq̃ [145v]

¶Auh nimā ˣᵖ̄ᵒ quitoz yn totemaquixticaṭin yn jesuxp̄o⁴⁸ tla xicmocaq̃tican yn axcā : nopilvanhe yehica yn āqualtin yn āxp̄īanome ma notlāṭinco xivalmovicacā tla ximotlamachtican Ca ypāhpa yn ovanechtlayecoltitinenq̃ yehica y notlatolṭin yn ovāquipixque ma nimā nochāṭinco xicalaq̃can

¶nimā q̃toz y[n] toteᵒyoṭin yn iquac .tp̄c. ninonemitiaya yn aᵒchanṭinco ovanechcellitinēque yvā ovanechtlayocollitinēque yn iquac niteocivhtinēca Auh nimā ovāquinmacaque yn aᵒnenca yn motorinia Ca ça nopalṭinco yn iquac nicatca Cuavhcalṭinco Cenca ovanechmoCuitlavitinēque

Again they will begin their song as they go bringing Antichrist to Mictlan. And once they have brought Antichrist to Mictlan then quickly the four directions are burned to show how surpassing the fire will be there in [144v] Mictlan.[55] *Then quickly Saint Michael will appear. He will call out to all who have died and they will then return to life.*

SAINT MICHAEL

Then Saint Michael will say,

O dead! Get up! Come at once to be counted before God! Come reveal all of your filth. Come swiftly! The one who is deserving will be received here before God. Therefore, please arise!

And then [wind instruments] will be blown. Thereupon all the dead will appear before Jesus Christ. Then they will kneel down. And then the were-owls will enter bringing out the bad ones from Mictlan. And in the presence of our Lord, all [145r] people will tremble. Then our Lord will command the angels to gather all the bad ones and place them at his left hand. And the good ones he will place at his right hand. And then the angels will kneel down before Jesus Christ.

CHRIST

Then our savior Jesus Christ will say,

You, my angels, please listen! Gather the good Christians, place the virtuous ones at my right hand. But get rid of the bad ones at my left hand![56]

And then there will be beating of drums when the angels move the good Christians to the side so that they can get rid of [the bad Christians] [145v].

Then our savior Jesus Christ will say,

Now please listen, O my children. Because you are good Christians, come to be with me! Please rejoice! Because you lived serving me, because you kept my words, enter now into my home!

Then our Lord will say,

When I lived on earth you always received me into your homes, and you always had mercy on me when I was hungry. And when you gave your sustenance to the poor it was on my behalf. When I was in jail you took very good care of me.

¶Niman ꝗtozque yn intoca .b̄t̄s̄

B̄T̄S̄

¶[to]te°.he Ca niman ayc otimiztlaqualtiꝗ ynic noviã [146r] cemanavac niman ayc nicã tp̄c̄. Otimiçatlitique ayc timiztlaqualtique yn timotlachivalvan yn ivh tic-mitalvia ynic vel otimizmoCuitlaviꝗ cah a°

.X P̄O.

¶Auh nimã ꝗtoz yn tote°hyoꞩin Cuix a° yvh y nevatl yn ovanechtlayocolitineꝗ[49] yn aꝗque motoliniya yn ovãquintlayocollitineꝗ Ca vel nevatl yn ovanechmomaꝗllique av in iquac yn ovãquimottillique yn aꝗꝗ Cuavhcalꞩinco cate yn ovãꝗnmotlapalvique Ca vell ic ovanechmotlayecoltilliꝗ

¶Auh nimã ꝗmilviz yn aqualtin

¶yn amevantin yn ovãtlavellilocatique Ça nimã ãꝗniçacvhctiyazꝗ[50] yn mictlã yehica yn amaxca yn ovãꝗmixcavillique yehica yn a° ovantetlayocollique yn manel anmoCuiltonovaya amo vãꝗntlayocolliaya yn motoll[i]nia [146v] a° anꝗntlaqualtiaya

¶Au in amevãtin tla xivalachiyacan yn ovanechmamaçovaltiꝗ yzcatꝗ yn ovãquicocoyoniꝗ y nomaꞩin t°[51] xiquallittacã yvã yn nocxiꞩin xiꝗtacan yn itech cruz + yn ovanechichinazque Ca nelli axcã mictlan anyazꝗ antlachiyativi yn onpa aqualcan

¶Auh yn iquac yn ovamechmachtiaya y nopilvã yn ya vecavh ca nevatl namotla-tocavh yn a° anꝗneltocaya yn çan anꝗntlavellittaya yn çan ãnmiquiztemachitinenca no yvã anquichicoytotinẽca nopãhpa anꝗnmictiaya

¶yn iquac yn amoCuiltonovaya yvhqui yn atley ypã yn aquimittaya[52] yn aꝗꝗ vel motolliniaya Ca çan ic cẽca amatlamatinẽca av in aꝗꝗ yn omopetlaviltitinẽca yn amo [a]nꝗnꝗntiznecꝗ çan illiviz [147r] ynic ovanteoyevacatiꝗ yn a° anteycnoyztinenque[53]

¶Çan ovãquinixcavitinẽque miyequintin yn amocivavan cenca miyeꝗ yn amomeca-van yn ovãquinmoCuitlavitinẽca yn iquac yn ovãtetlaxintinenca Ca çan ic pachiviya yn amoyollo Auh yn axcã yvh nicnonequiltiya ma nimã mictlã xiquittati yn a°nemac

¶Yvã yn ixquichtin yn motolliniya a[y]c nopalꞩinco : ovanꝗntlayocollique Ovãꝗntlaqualtique Çan ovãꝗnCuallancayttaꝗ yn iquac Calaquiya yn a°chanꞩinco a° vãꝗntlayocollique av ꟼx namevãtin[54] nimã anvalmevaya yn a°chanꞩinco yn iquac yovaꞩinco nimã tlaqualli Çan ãquixcaviaya yvã ãmonepãCuaya ynin yevatl yc amo anyazque nochã[ꞩ]inco [147v]

¶Au in iquac nimotlalliaya Cuavhcalco niman a° anechittato amoma ytla anechmacato macivi yn a°Cuiltonovaya vel anquintlaqualtiaya yn tozneneme yn a°cochovã Auh yn yevãtin yn motollinia y notlaçovã Çan ovãquimapizmictiaya

Then those who are called "the blessed" will say,

THE BLESSED

O our Lord! Never in the whole world did we feed you, [146r] never here on earth did we give you drink, never did we your creations feed you and thus really care for you like you said—no, indeed!

CHRIST

And then our Lord will say,

Were you not having mercy on me [when] you had mercy on the poor? It really was to me that you gave. And when you went to see those who were in jail and you helped them, in this way you were really serving me.

Then he will say to the bad ones,

Those of you who were wicked, you will be locked up in Mictlan because you were preoccupied with your own possessions, because you did not show mercy to people. Even though you were rich you did not show mercy to those who suffer; [146v] you did not feed them.

And you all, won't you look here? You have crucified me! Behold, you made holes in my hands! [—]57 Come look at my feet as well! Look! You made me suffer on the cross. In truth, today you will go to Mictlan where you will behold a bad place.

And when my children taught you long ago that I am your ruler, you did not believe them, you just hated them, you just wished for their death and also you spoke ill of them. You killed them because of me.

When you were rich you considered those who were very poor to be worthless. How very arrogant you were! You did not want to cover up those who went around naked, you were inconsiderate [147r] in how greedy you were, you did not take pity on people.

You just lived devoting yourselves to your many women, your very many mistresses, those who you lived caring for. You were merely satisfying yourselves when you committed adultery. And now I desire that you should see your reward in Mictlan.

And all those who are poor, never did you have mercy on them on my behalf, never did you feed them. You just glared at them angrily. When they came into your home, you did not have compassion on them. In the morning you would rise up in your homes and you would just devote yourself to food and you would eat among yourselves. It is because of this that you will not go to my house. [147v]

And when I was sitting in jail you did not go to see me, you did not go to give me anything even though you were rich. You used to feed your yellow parrots and your white parrots well, but those who are poor, my beloved ones, you left them to starve.

¶Auh nimā nican tlatoz yn itoca Danā Dos[55]

¶Niman q̇toz yntla timiztotiliani niman timiztotlaq̇tillizquiya yvā ytla timiz-tomaquillizquiya ypanpa Ca vel mopalnemovani yntla xitechmonextilliani nimā timiztotlavtillizqui[56] yvā timiztotlaqualtillizquiya timiztatlitillizquiya ypāhpa Ca çan mocel titeyocoyani

(.JESUXP̄O.)

¶Auh niman q̇toz yn totlatocaҭin Ovamotlaveliltic xiccaq̇cā yehica yn motolliniya yn aᵒ anq̇ntlayocollitinēq̇ yn iC[u]ac moteocivititinēca [148r] av in amevātin Ca cenca anmoCuiltonovaya Ca ça q̇ntlatzivhcayttaya[57] ma nimā yc mictlan xicallaq̇can ma nimā xitonevati ypāhpa cah atley nopalҭinco anq̇chivaya

¶Ca nimā tlatoz yntoteᵒ. q̇milviz yn qualtin tleypāhpa q̇moviquillia yn ilhᶜ. av in aqualtin quimilviz tleypāhpa quinmotlaxillia mictlan .d. nimā q̇nvicazque yn tlaht-lacatecollo : yn aqualtin yn ōpa mictlan Ceq̇ntin q̇nmamazq̇ Cenq̇ntin quinapal-lozque mochintin : Cen[c]a chocazque q̇totiyazque yn intoca Dana Dos

¶yyoyave maca tiyeni yyoyave Otovitique

¶Ma nimā titochocacan ma titlayocoyacan ma mictlan ticalaquican ma mochi tlacatl quito yyoyave [148v]

¶Ma yca titlatelchivacan : yn otechivaco nican xiquintlatzivhcayttacan yaq̇ne yyovahe

¶Macayac techivani ᵐᵃcahamo[58] yevatl techyollitiyani y yevatl ypalnemovani yye[59] yc tiq̇yovitivi yyovavhe

¶Ca ya nelli titlahtlativi : mictlan titonevativi Ca onpa titoyolcocotivi yc tiqui-tova axcā y[yo]yavhe

¶Auh yn tiquintlatzilviaya yn iquac motolliniaya yn axcan ya ytlan .d. motle-caviya av ī tevantin ya mictlan tivi yyovavhe

¶Auh yn iquac yn ocalaq̇ mictlā niman q̇mitalviz yn .s. mā : yyxpāҭinco yn toteᵒ.

¶Noconeҭin Ca vell otiquintlatzonteq̇lli yn amo qualtin Auh ihūxᵒeᵒ[60] yn qualtin Cenca otiqu[i]nmocnellili ma ᵒpalҭin[149r]coᵒ[61] xiquinmotlecavilli yn motlaçovā yn ilhᶜ. ma nimā onpa quitati yn inemac Cenca : yectli Cenca qualli

Here the one called "condemned" will speak. Then he will say,

If only we had seen you then we would have fed you and we would have given you something because you really are The One by Whom There Is Living! O if only you had revealed yourself to us! Then we would have prayed to you and we would have fed you, we would have given you something to drink because you are the only Creator!

JESUS CHRIST

Then our ruler will say,

Woe to you! Listen! Because you did not have mercy on the poor when they were hungry [148r] and you all really enriched yourselves [and] just looked at them with laziness, because of this may you enter Mictlan! Now you must suffer because you did nothing in my name!

Then our Lord will speak, telling the good ones why he brings them to the heavens. And he will say to the bad ones why God casts them into Mictlan. Then the were-owls will bring the bad ones to Mictlan. Some they will carry on their backs, others they will carry in their arms.[58] All of them will weep a great deal; those called the condemned will go saying,[59]

Alas! If only we were never born! Alas! We were in danger!

Let us now weep, let us be sad, let us enter Mictlan! Let all people say, Alas! [148v]

With this let us be despised! Look lazily upon those who came to send us away from here! Alas!

O do not let anyone send us away! If only The One by Whom There is Living hadn't given us life! It is because of this that we go suffering! Alas!

In truth, we will go burning in Mictlan, we will go suffering. Indeed, we go there sadly because of what you said just now. Alas!

We were repulsed by them when they suffered. Now they have now ascended to be with God, and we are now going to Mictlan. Alas!

And when they have entered Mictlan, saint Mary will say in the presence of our Lord,

My child, you have judged the bad ones properly and the good ones you have favored, O Jesus Christ. [149r] By your grace, raise your beloved ones up to the heavens. There may they see their very right, very good reward.

APOSTOLES .S. PE°.[62]

¶Nimā quitozque yn apostolome ma moyecteneva yn motocaçin Ca çan mopalçīco yn titonemitiya Ca çan ic vel titomaquixtia yehica yn oticcellique yn maçin Ca çan mocel titotlatocaçin : yn axcan vel otitetlatzontequilli yn motlaçovā otiquīmocnellili Otiquinmomaq̇xtilli yn iyolliyaçin.

.X P̄O.

¶Nimā q̇toz yn ᵗᵒtlaçotlatocaçin ma xivalmovicacan nopilvanhe y notlaçinco ma namechnoviquillitivh yn nochāçinco mah anmochintin xivallecovan[63] ma yc xipahpaq̇cā [149v] Ca cemicac anmotlamachtizque yn a°tlatocayo anq̇mottillizque yn ovāquimacevhtinēque nicā .tp̄c.

¶Niman nican quimoyectenevillizque ʸⁿ ᵗᵒᵗᵉᵒ.[64] yn qualtī xp̄iānome yn iquac ya motlecavia nimā Cuicatiyazque q̇vazque quināq̇llizq̇ yn āgellome . q̇tozq̇.

¶Ma moyecteneva ȳ tote°. yn totlatocavh yn totemaq̇sticavh

¶yyo tote°he .d.he[65] q̇nin cemanavac Otitechmopepenilli Otitechmocnellili nicā .tp̄c. ynic ya titechmoviquilliya yn ilhᶜ. yn titoteyo[co]xcavh titotemaq̇sticavh

¶Auh yn tote°. Ca çā cemicac tictlaçomatizque tiq̇cnellilmatizque ynic amochi toyolliçin Auh yn yevaçin otlacavhqui yn iyolloçin yn ᵗotepixcaçin[66] yn toteyocox-cavh [150r]

¶Auh yn .d. ynotzaloca yn iyectenevalloca ma tiquitoti ma ticmaviçoti yn iyecte-nevaloca yn iyximachoca yn toteyocoxcavh totlatocavh

¶Nimā q̇tozque yn ixq̇chtin ma vel ticcemittani yn .d. tp̄c. macamo nel ylvicacay-otl yc ticmacevani ma çan tiquixcaviyani yn toteyocoxcavh Ca totepixcaçin

¶Nimā q̇toz[q̇]. yn ti.s.māçin Cenca timitzicnellilmati yvan timitztlaçomati Ca titotepātlatocaçin yn iy̆xpāçinco yn totepixcaçin Ca totlatocaçin totecemitocavh

nimā q̇vhtiyazque yn yevatl yn imavizyectenevalocatin[67] yn iᵗoca Te Deū laudam[us] te d[omi]n[um].[68]

THE APOSTLES [AND] ST. PETER

Then the apostles will say,

May your name be praised. It is only by your grace that we live. By it are we saved because we received your water.[60] Indeed, you alone are our ruler! Today you have judged your beloved ones well. You favored them, you saved their souls.

CHRIST

Then our beloved ruler will say,

Come here beside me, O my children. Let me bring you to my home. Come up, all of you.[61] Rejoice! [149v] You will be content forever. You will see your kingdom, that which you merited while here on earth.

Here the good Christians will praise our Lord when they have ascended. Then they will go singing, raising their voices in song. They will answer the angels saying,[62]

May our Lord, our savior be praised!

Ah! O our Lord, O our God! How is it that in all the world you chose us? You favored us here on earth and because of this you our creator, our savior has brought us to the heavens!

And we will forever thank our Lord and be grateful to him with all our hearts. He is the one who has granted this, our guardian,[63] our creator. [150r]

And let us go saying God's counsel, his song of praise, let us go marveling at his song of praise,[64] the knowledge of our creator, our ruler.

Then everyone will say,

Let us fix our gaze upon God [while] on earth. Truly we do not merit the things of the heavens. Let us just devote ourselves to our creator, for he is our guardian.[65]

Then they will say,

We are very grateful to you, Saint Mary, and we thank you, you who are our advocate before our guardian, our ruler, our promised one.

Then they will go raising up his honored song of praise called the Te deum.[66]

ANTICHRIST
AND
THE HERMIT

(MS NS 3/1, ff. 155r–187r)

NAHUATL PALEOGRAPHY

[155r]

❡Nican onpeva yn itoca Auto Çan tlatori[1] mitoz yacachto quitoz yevatl ytoca Sibila

. SIBILA .

❡Nopilvanhe tla xivallachiyacan aço ovanꝗmocaquitique yn onamechmolvillico yn axcan ma vel namechtlaCuepcayotilli anꝗmatizque Ca yn icel teotl .d. Onechvalmivalli ytēcopaṭinco y nam[ec]hilvico Ca ontlamiz yn cemanavac noviyan micovaz noviyā atle caviz ca ça noviyan tlachinaviz Auh yn a° ontlami[2] cemanavac achtopa vallaz tlacatiz ce tlacatl tlavelliloc ytoca yez ātexp̄o av in ic vell amechiztlacaviz xp̄o. quimotocayotiz ca çan nelli yevatl tlacatecolotl amechmacaꝗvh yn teoCui[tl]atl [155v] yvā tilmatli .ets. yniꝗtlā[3] anyazꝗ amechilviz nevatl nixp̄o ca çan ic amechiztlacaviz ꝗntlamaviçoltiz yn aꝗꝗ quitlacamatizque ca çan icelṭin[4] yn aꝗltin ꝗntlaneltoꝗltiz Auh yn yevātin yn qualtin xp̄ānome çan ipalṭinco : .d. miꝗzꝗ ynic yazꝗ yn ilvicac Auh yn axcā nopilvanhe ma ximoyollapaltillican maca° niman itla anꝗcellizque yn amechmacaz yehica amo ytlan antonevativi mictlan cemicac tla ximovepavacan[5] ynic çan ipalṭinco .d. anmiquizque maca° xicuecuetlaxivican maca° ximoçoçotlavacan ma yntech xi[m]ixCuitican yn .s.tome [156r] ca çan ipalṭinco yn .d. temac omomiꝗllique yc oꝗmotlecavilli yn ichanṭinco tla vel xicnelto[ca]can yn icel

https://doi.org/10.5876/9781646423002.c006a

ENGLISH TRANSLATION

[155r]

Here begins what is called "a play"; it is to be said with words only.¹ First, she who is called Sibyl will say,

SIBYL

O my children, please look here! Perhaps you have heard what I have come to tell you. Today I will repay you well.² You will know that by his command Only Deity, God, has sent me to tell you that the whole world will end. There will be dying everywhere, nothing will be left behind for it will all be burned. But before the world ends, first a wicked person will come, will be born whose name will be Antichrist. But in order to thoroughly deceive you he will call himself Christ. [However,] he is really just a were-owl.³ He will come to give you gold [155v] and cloaks, etc. So that you will go with him, he will say to you, "I am Christ," and with this he will deceive you. He will cause those who obey him to marvel. The bad ones will believe in him alone,⁴ and the good Christians will die for God in order to go to the heavens. Today, O my children, take strength! Do not accept anything he gives you so that you will not go suffering forever with him in Mictlan. Strengthen yourselves so that you will die for God. Do not lose heart! Do not become faint! Follow the example of the saints, [156r] for they died by the hands of others for God, [and] because of this they ascended to his home. O please won't you believe in Only God,

.d. yn jexp̄o.[6] ximoCuahateq̇can ximoyolmellavacan ma ximoyorchicavacā maca°
amechyorpollo yn ovamechmachtico yn itlatenq̇xticavā .d. mah amechmomaq̇lli .d.
yn iqualtica ma yevatl amech[m]opiyalli ma namechmotlalcavilli

. QUTOZ . ANTEXP̄O [7]

¶Ma ximeviltitiyecā nopilv[a]nhe ma xivalmovicacan yn amochintin tleyn amaya
cuix nomac anmiq̇zneq̇ nimān axcan nicnoq̇z yn ameço yntlacamo xinechneltocacan Cuix a° anq̇mitta ceq̇ntin y notlāṭinco nemi yn motlamachtiya Cuix
a° Onamechnolvilli ca ça nocel yxquich novelli [o]nic[156v]chivh[8] yn ixquich
mochivhtoc macamo ximoyolpollocan tleyca yn ovanq̇xixitique[9] y yevatl y nochan-
çinco ca yn ya vevcavh vell oanechtlayecoltitineq̇ ca yn iaquac yn aquimeltequiya
yn a°malvan av in iquac yn amiçoya av in amevātin tlatoq̄he tleyca yn yah anqui°°tona
yn amonemilliz. tleyca yn yah anq̇ncava yn amoçivavan yn miyeq̇ntin ocatca yn
amomecavan Auh yn axcan ma xiquimixcavican yn ixquichtin çiva yn q̄xq̇chime yn
āquineq̇zque ca vell ic pachiviz y noyollo

¶No yvā yn amevatin[10] çiva ye vel namechnomaviçalviya ya yn a°xavaya yn amo-
potoniyaya[11] av in axcan tleyn oa°pan mochivh aquin oamechtlapololti ma xiquix-
cavican yn ixq̇ch yn ovāquixcavitinenca nopilvane cuix a° anquimaviçova [157r] y
notlatolṭin ca nevatl y namoteovh y namotlatocavh Ca nevatl nixp̄o. tla xivalmovicacan ca cenca namechCuiltonoz nochāṭinco vell anmotlamachtitivi ōpa vell
anmocevitivi āquiçativi yn a°nemac tleyca yn am° anechneltocaznequi yn a° anech-
moviquilliznequi tla xiq̇mitacan yn tlavelliloque niquinmictiz.

¶Nican quimotemaq̇lliz

¶Ac tevatl ca nevatl [ni]xp̄o nimā q̇llvizque can tivalleva nimā q̇toz onpā nochāṭinco
yn ilh[c] nimā q̇lvizque canin mochan q̇toz onpa yn ilh[c]. yn axcan ca namechmomaquix-
tillico namechmachtico namechititico yn mellavac yn otli ynic tocoz ynic villovaz

Jesus Christ! Be baptized, confess, take courage! Don't let [Antichrist] fool you into thinking that he came to teach you God's pronouncements. May God give you his goodness, may he guard you. Now I take my leave of you.

ANTICHRIST WILL SAY,

Do stay seated, O my children.[5] Come, all of you. What are you doing? Do you want to die by my hand? Right now I will spill your blood if you do not believe in me. Have you not seen that those living with me are rich? Did I not say to you that I alone am all powerful, that I made [156v] all that lies growing? Do not behave foolishly! Why did you dismantle my home?[6] In times past you served me well when you slashed open the chests of your captives and when you bled yourselves. And you, O rulers, why do you diminish your way of living? Why do you abandon your women? You used to have many mistresses! Now, devote yourselves to all the women, however many you want. This will really satisfy me. And also you women, I really wonder at you. You do not paint your faces anymore, you do not cover yourselves with feathers.[7] And now, what has happened to you? Who has confused you? Devote yourselves to everything that you used to devote yourselves to!

O my children, didn't you used to honor [157r] my words? I am your deity, your ruler![8] I am Christ! Please come, for I will make you rich! You will greatly rejoice and rest yourselves there at my home, you will go reaping your reward.[9] Why don't you want to believe in me? Don't you want to come with me? Look at those wicked ones! I will kill them!

Here he will give it to someone.[10]
[Martyrs will say]
Who are you?

[Antichrist will say]
It is I, Christ.

Then they will say to him,
Where do you come from?

Then he will say,
From up there, my home in the heavens.[11]

Then they will say to him,
Where is your home?

He will say,
Up there, in the heavens! Today I have come to save you, I have come to teach you, to show you the straight road that is to be followed in order for people to go to my

y nochanţinco yn opa necevilloz ca yn axcā namechCuiltonoco cah amoniceya yn amollinitinemizque ca [c]en[157v]ca namechnotlaço'tilliya¹² cah ānopilvan cenca cenca namechicnoytta yehica yn ixquichtī yn ovamechmachtitinenca yn ovamechiztlavitinēca¹³ maca° xiquineltocacan yn tleyn yn ovamechilvique av intlacamo annechtlacamatizque niman nomac anmiquizque av inī yntlaca° nomāg¹⁴ anmiḋzneḋ ca cenca namechCuiltonoz ca niteotl ca nix[p]ō Auh nimā quilvizque yn yevātin martilles Auh catli ya monezca ynic ᵗⁱx͞pō cah atley yn cruz yn itech Otimicḋ yehica amo tley oticCualitquic ca [y]evatl yc tineci tiztlacati Ca yn iv¹⁵ iCuillivhtica yn iquac yn motenestilliquivh yn yevatl yn ya nelli jex͞o͞p͞ō. yn iquac yn tetlatzontequilliquivh Ca ḋvallitquiz yn icruz ynic vell iximachoz y Auh yvan yv iCuillivhtica ca ce tlacatl tlacatiz [158r] yn t͞p͞c. moteotocatinemiz : yc miyeḋntin quimiztlacaviz : ca çan yehica amo neltocoz ca vel yevaţin Otechmolvilitiya yn tote°. yn iquac yn omotlecavi yn ilhᶜ. Ca tlacatiz ytoca yez antex͞p͞ō. Auh inin ca monezca yn tevatl ypāhpa amo titechmachtiya yn tleyn Otechmomachtillitiya yn jex͞p͞ō. nelli .d. ypāhpa yn amo nimizneltocaznequi ca titechiztlacaviznequi niman amo nicneḋ yn motlatqui Ca nimotollinitinemizneḋ ypalţinco y nelli .d. ynic nechmotlayocolliliz ynic nicmacevaz yn ilhᶜ. pahpaḋlliztli Ca yvh quimitalvitiya yn .d. chocovaz tlayocoyalloz tlahtlacolcavalloz tlalticpac netollinilloz ynic nemaḋstilloz ynic villovaz yn ilhᶜ. Au in tevatl tiqui[t]ova [158v] ma noviyā pahpacova netlamachtillo neCuiltonollo yc neçi cah amo nelli tix͞p͞ō Auh nimā quitoz yn antex͞p͞ō tleyca yn amo nevatl tla xicmocaḋti Cuix yaḋn iquac tinechneltocaz yntla niquimizcalli yn monanţin ȳ motaţin nimā quitoz yn martilles ca tiztlacati nimā ḋtoz ȳ antex͞p͞ō yn amevantin tla nimā ximozcallican tla nimā xivallauh yn tināţin yn titaţin Auh nimā mozcallizque cah amo nelli ca tlacatecolotl Auh nimā ḋtoz yn ātex͞p͞ō Cuix a° yzcatqui yn monā yn mota Cuix a° tiquiximati ca yn axcan Ca onpa Ovalaque yn mictlan onpa Otemoḋ ypanpa amo nechiximattiaḋ ma xiquintlahtlanican quenamican yn opa mi[c]tlan .etc.

home. There will be resting there. Today I have come to make you rich. I don't want you to be troubled. I love you [157v] very much, for you are my children. I really, really pity you because of all those who went around teaching you, those who went around deceiving you. Do not believe what they said to you! If you do not obey me, then I will slay you with my own hands. However, if you don't want to die by my hand, then I will make you very rich, for I am the deity, I am Christ.

And then Martyrs[12] will say to him,
What is the proof that you are Christ? The cross on which you died is meaningless because what you're carrying there is meaningless. Therefore, you seem to be lying. It is written that when the true Jesus Christ comes appearing, when he comes judging people, he will come bearing his cross so that he will be clearly recognized.[13] And furthermore it is written that a person will be born [158r] on earth who will be followed like a deity; because of this he will deceive many, because of this people won't believe. Indeed, when our Lord ascended to the heavens he told us that one would be born whose name would be Antichrist.[14] Moreover, this proves that it is you, because you don't teach us what Jesus Christ the true God taught us. Therefore, I don't want to believe in you, for you want to deceive us! I absolutely do not want your bribes![15] I want to live suffering for the true God so that he will have mercy on me, so that I will merit the joy of the heavens. God says in order for there to be saving of people and going to the heavens, there must be weeping, there must be sadness, there must be abandoning of sin on earth, there must be suffering. But you say, [158v] "Let there be happiness, enjoyment, riches everywhere!" This confirms that you are not the true Christ.

Then Antichrist will say,
Why am I not? O won't you please listen! Will you at last believe in me if I return your mother and your father to life?[16]

Then Martyr will say,
You're lying!

Then Antichrist will say,
You his mother, you his father, please return to life immediately, please come immediately!
And then they will return to life. (This is not true, for he is a were-owl.)[17]
Then Antichrist will say,
Are these not your mother and your father? Do you not recognize them? Today they have come from Mictlan where they descended because they didn't acknowledge me. Ask them what sort of place Mictlan is etc.!

niman q̇toz [159r] yn martilles ma niquiximati y notaṭin cah açomo[16] yevatl yntla
nelli yevatl yCuitlapā niquiximatiz Ca yn iquac oc nenca . tp̄c̄. yCuitlapā q̇quezca[17]
yn tlaloc ychicavaz xoxoctic Auh nimā q̇toz yn ātexpō tla xoconittillican ca oncan
onicac nimā q̇toz yn martilles Ca nelli Oncan achi nichicotl[a]mati ca tinechizt-
lacaviya Auh nimā q̇toz yn antexpō Cuix aº Otoconitilli yn imachiyo nimā
q̇toz yn martilles ca quemaca aço tlacatecolotl ca ya yvhq̇ Omonexti yn ivhqui
notaṭin ca çano ca timocacayava : ca ya tevatl yn tantexpō : yn otechtenevillico
yn yevatl civatl yn itoca ppetisa[18] ca otechilvico ca ce tlacatl [159v] vallaz teca
mocacayavhtinemiquivh quimotemaq̇lliq̇v teoCuitlatl yn ixq̇ch tlatq̇tl etc. yc
miyequintin q̇miztlacaviz Au inin vel monez[—]ca yn tevatl ca yvh tinemi cenca
nichicotlamati ca titlacatecolotl tantexpō : Auh nimā q̇toz yn atexpō aço nomac
timiquizneq̇ nimā quitoz y̶n̶ ̶ā̶t̶[e]x̶ yn martilles ma ypalṭinco yn .d. nimomiq̇lli
niman q̇toz yn ātexpō. tla xiq̇ximati yn yevatl yn monanṭin ynic tinech^neltocaz ca
yxquich novelli nimā q̇toz yn martilles yntla yevatl yn nonāṭin tleyca yn ayocmo
tlane ca yn iquac Omicq̇ tlanetiya nimā q̇toz yn antexpō ca ça n̄a ic ovezque[19] yn
itlavan[20] ypāhpa yn opa mictlan Cenca ceva cenca vi[160r]viyoca ynic aº. onpa
tiyaz : ma xinechneltoca ya mixpan Onicchivhqui yn tlamaviçolli ynic oniquin-
monextilli: yn monā yn mota ypanpa ca yc neçi Ca niteotl yntla xinechneltoca
nimizCuiltonoz nimiznoviquilliz y nochāṭinco yn ilhᶜ. ynic onpa tipahpaq̇z Ca
yn onpa Cenca pahpacova tlaCuallo Auh nimā quit[oz] yn martilles : Auh yntla
onpa pahpacova tlaquallo yn mochāṭinco aq̇ cenca axixtitlan Cuitlatitlan aq̇
cenca amo qualcan amo yeccan Auh ca niman aºh onpa niyaznequi

Then Martyr [159r] will say,
I recognize my father, [but] perhaps it is not him. If it is truly him I will recognize his back. When he still lived on earth he bore Tlaloc's green rattle stick on his back.[18]

And then Antichrist will say,
Go look for it.[19] It's right there.

Then Martyr will say,
It truly is there! [But] I am a little suspicious that you are deceiving me . . .

And then Antichrist will say,
Did you not see his mark?

Then Martyr will say,
Yes, perhaps in this way the were-owl made it seem like my father. You are just mocking. You are the Antichrist. That woman called "prophetess"[20] came to declare to us, came to tell us that a person [159v] would come to deceive people, he would come to give people gold and all sorts of goods, etc. He will deceive many because of this. Moreover, this proves it is you, for you live just like this! I really am suspicious that you are a were-owl, you are the Antichrist.

Then Antichrist will say,
Do you want to die by my hand?

Then Martyr will say,
I will die for God!

Then Antichrist will say,
Recognize your mother and believe in me! I am all powerful!

Then Martyr will say,
If she is my mother, why does she no longer have teeth? When she died she had teeth.

Then Antichrist will say,
Her teeth just fell out because down there in Mictlan it is very cold and she shivered [160r] a lot.[21] Believe in me so that you won't go there! I already performed a miracle right in front of you when I revealed your mother and your father. This confirms that I am the deity. If you believe in me I will make you rich, I will bring you to my home in the heavens so that you will be happy. There is great happiness and feasting up there!

Then Martyr will say,
If there is happiness and feasting at your home, one enters Urine Place, Excrement Place, one enters a very bad place, an unjust place.[22] I absolutely do not want to go

Ca çan opa niyaznequi yn ichaţinco[21] yn .d. Ca yn ōpa niman aº tlaqualli Ca çan ixcaȟvillo y netlamachtillo yxcavillo yn tto[22] yn q̄nin Cenca qualli yn icel teotl Ca çan ic pachiviz yn toyollo Auh y[n] ax[160v]can cenca nichicotlamati : cah aº nelli yevatl y nonāţin .y.[23] Ca çan tlacatecolotl no yvā ī tevatl cenca titlavelliloc tiztlacatini macivi yn tineçaçayanaz[24] ypāhpa amo niyaznequi yn mochan yn ixq̇ch yniquivic[25] yn tinechnetoltiya ca çan tlalticpacayotl Auh yn ya nelli .d. yniquivic nechnetoltia ca ylv[i]cacayotl yn ayc polliviz yn ayc tlamiz yn aq̄n mochivaz Auh nimā q̇toz tȟa yn ātexp̄o niman icivhca xiquīmictican notechivhcav[a]nhe

⁋nimā nican miquizque yn martilleme motlanquaq̄çazque q̇mocnellilmatizque ȳ .d. yehica çan ipalţinco yn miquizq̄ q̇tozque toteº.he. d.he jexp̄ohe ma xitechmocellili yn mochanţinco ma xiquinmotlay[oc]ollili xiq̇npohpolvi yn in[1611]tlahtlacol.

OCEQ́NTIN MARTILESME

⁋Nimā q̇toz yn ātexp̄o tla xinechneltocacā yntlacaº yn ānechneltocazneq̇ nimā nicnoq̇z yn ameço av inin : xinechneltocacan Cenca namechCuiltonoz yntla xinechmoviquillizneq̇can avh nimā q̇tozque yn martillesme ca niman aº timizneltocazque Ca titlacatecollotl Ca niman atley Oticchivh ȳ mochivhtoc Ca çan icel .d. Oquichivh yn ipaltinemi av in axcan Ca çan ipalţinco timiq̇zque ynic momaq̇stiz yn toyolliya Cah amo [—][26] onpa tiyaznequi yn mochā yn ōpa neaxixallo Auh nimā motlāCuaqueçazq̄ yn martillesme ynic quinmictiz yn ātexp̄o. Auh nimā quitoz yn ā[—]te[161v]xp̄o. yn axcā tla xicmocaq̇tican nopilvanhe ca ya vel ovāquimittaq̄ yn oniquinmicti yn tlavelliloque ca çano yvhqui yn aºpā mochivaz ma yc pachivi yn amoyollo xicneltocacan y namechnolvillia ca ya niyavh ma namechnotlalcavilli Occeppa nivallaz niq̇nmictiquivh yn amo nechneltocazque

NINCAN TLA[27] ENOC

⁋Nopilvanhe tla xicmocaq̇tican Ca çan aºpāhpa Otechvalmivalli yn .d. yn ōpa yn itlacaţintiayan yn opa yn oq̇nmochivilli yn achto tonā yn achto tota there! I only want to go to God's home. There is no food there but only devotion to teaching, devotion to our Lord. How very good Only Deity is! It is only because of him that we are satisfied. And now [160v] I am really suspicious. It is not true that she is my mother, it's just a were-owl. Also, you are very wicked, you are a liar! Even though you will cut me up into pieces, because of this I don't want to go to your home. Everything you promise me is just worldliness.[23] That which the true God promises me is heavenliness. It will never be destroyed, it will never end, nothing will happen to it.

And then Antichrist will say,
Now swiftly kill them, O my forefathers![24]

Here the martyrs will die. They will kneel down, they will give thanks to God because it is for him that they will die. They will say,
O our Lord! O God! O Jesus Christ! Receive us into your home. Have mercy on them, forgive them of [161r] their sins.

SOME OTHER MARTYRS

Then Antichrist will say,
Please believe in me! If you do not want to believe in me, then I will spill your blood! Furthermore, believe in me [and] I will make you very rich! O if only you desired to come with me!

Then the martyrs will say,
We will absolutely not believe in you, you were-owl! There is nothing that lies growing that you have made. For it is Only God, The One by Whom We Live, who made it. And now we will die for him so that our souls will be saved. We don't want to go to your home, there where there is urinating on people.
Then the martyrs will kneel down in order for Antichrist to kill them.
Then Antichrist [161v] will say,
Today won't you listen, O my children![25] You have seen how I killed those wicked ones. The same will be done to you! I hope you're satisfied with this! Believe what I say to you! Now I go, I take my leave of you. I will come again! I will come to kill those who will not believe in me!

HERE ENOCH WILL SPEAK.

O my children, won't you please listen! God has sent us on your behalf from the founding place of his lineage, there where our first father and our first mother were

Ca ya vecavh yn opa techmotlallili yn .d. ayc otimicque Ca çan oticchixticatca ~~yn.d.~~
yn yevatl tlav[el]liloc yn axcan ~~Catlal~~ [162r] Ca çan yevatl tlalticpacayotl yc ovamech-
tlapololtico ynic ovamechtlaxtlavico Auh yn axcan Ca yvicpa titemachtico ytencopa yn .d. tamechnemachtico tamechtolvillico ma çã yevatl xicchivacan yn amechmachtitinemi yn itemachticavan yn .d. yn padreme ca nelli yevatl yn itlatolţin yn ayc
caviz yn ayc polliviz yn amechtitinemi[28] [t]la xicneltocacã . yn icel .d. jesxp̄o. maca°
xicneltocacan yn aq̇li yn ayectli tlatoli yn ovamechilvico yn yevatl tlavelliloc ca mi[y]
equintin yn oquimiztlavi yn nican cate yn yevantī yn oquintlaneltoquilti ynic cemicac tonevativi mictlan yntlaca° q̇cotonacã yn imaqualnemilliz yntlacamo quinchocti
yn intlahtlacol Au yn amochintin ma nimã xic[162v]tlaçacan yn aqualli yn amitec
yn oquitlallitiya ma ximoyollapaltillican ynic amo ãquiyollitlacozq̄ yn .d. ma totech
ximixCuitican Ca nican techmictiquivh yn tlavelliloc nimã axcan Çan ipalţinco yn .d.
timiquizque yniquitlãţinco[29] titocevitivi cemicac yn ilhᶜ. Ca ynic onpa yaovaz moneq̇
. tp̄c. neltocoz y nelli .d. nequahateq̇lloz yn ica yn iyaţin yvã piyalloz yn itenavatilţin
yvã tlamacevalloz techoctiz[30] yn totlahtlacol yxcavilloz yn tlayecoltilloz yn icel .d. ynic
nemaquixtilloz ynic netlecavilloz yn ilhᶜ, mah amechmomaq̇lli .d. yn iqualtica ynic
ãquicot[o]nazque yn amaqualnemiliz ynic amo anyazque mictl[a]n ximoyolmellavacan [163r] niman nican tlaneltocazque yn aomo[31] quiCuitique dios etc.

YN ENOC NIMÃ Q̇NMOLVILLIZ
YN CONPERSOS[32]

¶Yn axcan nopilvane ovamechmotlayocollili .d. maca° Occeppa xictlahtlacalviz-
neq̇can ma çan ipalţinco ximiquicã Ca yevatl yn tlavelliloc techmictiquivh yn axcan
yn timochintin tla ximovapavacan maca° xiCueCuetlaxivicã ma chicava yn amoyollo
ma çan ipalţinco .d. ximiq̇can etc.

NIMÃ Q̇TOZ YN ĀTEXP̄O

¶Tla xiquimittacan yn yevantin yn tlavelliloque tla niman icivhca xiquinoquil-
lican yn imeço Cuix å p[i]nava yn ixpã tlatova : tleyca yn oquintlaneltoq̇lti[163v]
que y notlaçovã ma nimã miquican nimã nican quinmictiz yn ātexp̄o nimã quimilviz yn amevãtin tleyca yn ovanechmecavillique tleyca yn ovãquineltocaq̇ ynic ova-
mechtlapololtique yn tlavelliloque ca çan ic oniquinmicti yn amixpã Onoquivh
yn imezço Auh no yvh namechivaz[33] yn tlaca° notlan ximovicazneq̇c[a]n yntlaca°
xinechtlacamaticã tleyca yn ovanechcavhque Ca ya onamechcuiltono.

made. Long ago God placed us there. We never died, we were just waiting for the wicked one. Today [162r] he has come to confuse you with worldly things in order to bribe you. Today, by the order of God, we have come to preach against him. We have come to teach you, we have come to say to you, 'Do what God's teachers, the priests, go around teaching you!'²⁶ Truly, his words will go on instructing you forever and ever. Please believe in Only God, Jesus Christ! Don't believe in the bad, improper words that wicked one said to you. He has deceived many that are here. Those who he caused to believe in him will suffer forever in Mictlan if they do not desist from their bad way of life, if they do not weep over their sins.

And you, now cast off [162v] the badness he caused to be placed within you. Fortify your hearts so that you won't offend God. Follow our example! The wicked one is coming here to kill us. Therefore, we will die for God so that we may rest forever with him in the heavens. In order for people to go there it is necessary that there is believing in the true God here on earth, that there is baptism with his water and the keeping of his commands and the doing of penance, weeping for our sins, the serving of Only God so that there will be salvation, so that there will be ascending to the heavens. May God give you his goodness so that you will desist from your disordered way of life. Confess so that you don't go to Mictlan! [163r]

Then at this point those who no longer acknowledged God will believe, etc.

THEN ENOCH WILL SAY
TO THE CONVERTS

Today, O my children, God has had mercy on you! Desire not to offend him again! Just die for him. The wicked one is coming to kill you. Now strengthen yourselves, all of you, do not become faint. May your hearts be strengthened. Die for God, etc.!

THEN ANTICHRIST WILL SAY

Look at those wicked ones! Please won't you quickly go spill their blood!²⁷ Is it not shameful what has been said in their presence? Why did my beloved ones [163v] believe them? Let them die right now!

Here Antichrist will kill them.

Then he will say to them,

Why did you all trap me? Why did you believe the wicked ones so that they confused you? It is because of this I killed them, I spilled their blood right in front of you. And I will do the same to you unless you're willing to come with me, unless you obey me. Why did you abandon me? I have already made you rich!

NIMAN QUITOZQ̄ Ȳ CŌVELSOS

❡Yzcatqui yn moteocuitl[34] ȳ motilma amoma ticnequi Ca yn iquac ticcuizque yc cēca ticyollitlacozque yn .d. Auh nimā q̇toz yn ātexpō yc neci Ca ya ovamechixpohpoyotillique yn yevātin yn omētī [164r] yn vevetque Cuix a° ya nevatl nixp̄o. nimā quitozque yn convelsos cah a° tevatl yn tixp̄o Ca çan titlacatecolotl Ca cenca Otitechiztlacavi Ca yevātin yn itlaçovan y nelli .d. yn otechmolvillico yn Cualli tlatolli yaq̇ne çan ipalṭinco yn omomiquillique yn tispā yniq̇ntech[35] titixcuitizque Ca yn tevatl amoma titeotl çan ticoyotl titechquaznequi Ca çan ic titechcuitlaviltiya yn aqualli nimā q̇toz yn ātexp̄o tleyca yn amiztlacati : Cuix [a]mo cenca namechpaq̇ltia Cuix a° namechnolvillia yn opa nochanṭinco Cenca papacova Cenca tlacualo Ōpa Cate miyeq̇ntin çiva : Cenca chipavaque ynic pachiviz yn amoyollo nimā quitoz[36] yn convelsos Cuix amo [164v] ticcaq̇ cah a° onpa tiyazneq̇ yntlanel onpa tiyaznequi tleyca yn tlaCuallo Cuix a° yvā neaxixallo Ca çan nimā amo qualcan yn opa mochā yn ya neli yn ichā .d. niman a° tlacuallo Ca çan ixcavillo y netlamachtillo Ca y no yvan tiquitova yn opa mochan Onpa cate çiva Cenca chipavaq̇ ynic pachiviz ȳ toyollo Ca çan ic tineci yn titetlaxinqui yn titlavelliloc yn iquac yn ōtzōquiçaz yn nemillizçotl yn onpa yavi yn teyolliya Auh Cuix nimā[n] ōpa : tetlaximalloz Ca yn onpa mictlan Ca çan ixcavillo yn tonevallo Au in ilvicac yxcavillo yn ahaviyallo yn yaquine yevatl .d. Cenca q̇tlayllitta yn tetlaximalliztli Auh yn tevatl tictlaçotla [165r] Ca yc tineci yn ticaçavac yehica yn titechCuitlaviltiya yn aqualli yn manel titechmictiz niman a° motlan tiyazq̄ niman nican quinmictiz yvā quimavaz nimā motlallitivh yn ycpalpan Auh .S. Miguel nimā quimilviz ᵞⁿ ᵐᵒᶜʰⁱⁿᵗⁱⁿ yn iquac yn oquinmicti yn ātexp̄o

❡Dla xicmocaq̇tican yn yevatl yn itzel .d. Onechvalmivali ynic nicmictico yn yevatl yn tlavelliloc yehico[37] yn ovamechiztlacavitinemico yn omoteotocatinemico Ca çan tlacatecolotl miyequintin yn ipahpa ya toneva mictlan Çan iquipanpa[38] niman axcan ya quinamoyaquivi yn diabrome : ynⁱᶜ q̇vicazque mictlan Ca niman onpa yaz yn iyolliya : Ca çano yvā tleco monequi yn inacayo ypāpa yn itla[165v] vellilocayo niman axcā anquimatizque yn q̇nin Onpa tonevallo mictlan yn iquac quinapalloquivi yn tlahtlacatecolo Auh tla nimā xiccotonacan yn amonemiliz ynic amo Onpa anyazque mictlan

THEN THE CONVERTS WILL SAY

Here is your gold, your cloaks. We don't want them anymore! Were we to take them we would deeply offend God.

And then Antichrist will say,
This confirms that those two old men [164r] have blinded you! Am I not Christ?

Then the converts will say,
No indeed, you are not Christ! You are just a were-owl! You have seriously deceived us. The true God's beloved ones came to tell us the good words. They finally died for him right in front of us. We will follow their example. You are not a deity, you are just a coyote! You want to devour us! You only want to incite us to do wrong.

Then Antichrist will say,
Why are you lying? Have I not made you very happy? Have I not told you that up there in my home there is great happiness, there is great feasting, there are many beautiful women with whom to satisfy yourselves?

Then the converts will say,
Didn't [164v] you hear? We do not want to go there! Even if we wanted to go there, why is there feasting? Isn't there also urinating? Your home is not a good place. In truth, in God's home there is no feasting, there is only devotion [and] rejoicing. And you also say that in your home there are very beautiful women with which to satisfy ourselves. This proves that you are an adulterer, you wicked one! When history comes to an end, it is there the soul goes. And will there be adultery there in Mictlan? There is only devotion to suffering. And in the heavens there is only devotion to rejoicing. Furthermore, God greatly despises adultery, but you love it! [165r] This just confirms that you are filthy because you incite us to what is wrong. Even though you will kill us we absolutely will not go with you.

Then here [Antichrist] will scold them and kill them. Then he will sit on his throne. St. Michael will then say to everyone when Antichrist kills them,[28]
Please won't you listen! Only God sent me to come slay the wicked one because he came to deceive you. He was considered a deity [but] he is just a were-owl. Many are already suffering in Mictlan because of him. It's just because of him that right now the devils[29] will come to steal away with him and bring him to Mictlan. Then his soul will go down there. Also, cast his body into the fire because of his wickedness.[30] [165v] Then today you will now know that there is suffering there in Mictlan when the were-owls come to bear him away in their arms. And now, desist from your [bad] way of living so that you will not go to Mictlan.[31]

NIMAN Q̇TOZ YN ERMITANO

¶Dlahtlacatecolloye xinechilvican Canpa anyavi ac amevantin yn mochi tlacatl nimā q̇tozque yyxpan timovica Auh yn tevatl tle motoca Auh nimā quitoz
yn lociper ac tevatl yn tinechtlahtlaniya tle motoca Auh nimā q̇toz yn elmitano
Ca nevatl yn itetlayecolticavh .d. notoca niyermitano Auh nimā q̇toz yn ermitano Auh yn tevatl xinechilvi tleyn motoca nimā q̇toz yn loci[166r]per Cah
a° niceya nimā q̇toz yn ermitano tleyca yn amo ticeya niman q̇toz yn lociper
yehica amo nicneq̇ Auh nimā quitoz yn ermitano yyoyave yn titlavelliloc amo
tinechtlacamatiznequi vel nimiziximati Ca titlacatecolotl Ca çan amo nicmati
yn motoca ma yvi ma °pā³⁹ nicchiva yn cruz ynic ticnextiz ȳ motoca Auh nimā
quitoz y[n] yevatl yn ermitano quilviz yn occe tlacatl : yn tevatl nopilṭinhe
xicualcui yn tlateochichivallatl yn iyaṭin .d. ynin ypā nictecaz yn yevatl tlaca-
te°. ynic tonevaz ynic quinextiz yn tlēyn⁴⁰ yn itoca nimā ypā q̇tecaz^nequiz yn tla-
teochivatlatl niman quilviz tlacate°tle tla xicnexti yn motoca yehica a° mopan
niquitoz yn itlatolṭin [166v] yn itlahtlavhtillocaṭin .d. yvā amo mopan nictecaz yn tlateochivalatl yn iyaṭin .d. ynic cenca tichichinacaz tla xinechilvi yn
motoca Auh nimā quitoz yn loçiper ca amo niceya Auh nimā q̇toz yn ermitano

THEN HERMIT WILL SAY [32]

O were-owls! Tell me, where are you going? Who are you?
Then in his presence each person will say,
We come.[33]

And [Hermit will say],
You, what is your name?

And then Lucifer will say,
Who are you who asks me, 'What is your name'?

Then Hermit will say,
I am the servant of God. My name is Hermit.

Then Hermit will say,
And you, tell me, what is your name?

Then Lucifer [166r] will say,
I don't want to.[34]

Then Hermit will say,
Why don't you want to?

Then Lucifer will say,
Because I don't want to!

And then Hermit will say,
Woe to you! You refuse to obey me! I recognize you, you are a were-owl! I just don't know your name. So be it. I will make [the sign of] the cross on you so that you will reveal your name to me!

Then Hermit will say, he will say to another person,
O my child, bring the blessed water here, the water of God. I will spread this on the were-owl so that he will suffer, so that he will reveal what his name is.

Then when he is about to spread the blessed water on him he will say,
O were-owl! Reveal your name! For if you do not, I will pronounce God's words [166v] and God's prayers on you, and also I will spread the blessed water, God's water on you, so that you will suffer burning pain! Please tell me your name!

And Lucifer will say,
I don't want to!

Then Hermit will say,

yyoyave tlacatecolotle ytencopa yn jexp̄ō nelli .d. yvā ypāpa yn iCruz yn mopā
nicchiva yvā ypāhpa yn iyaʇin yn movicpa nicteca ma nimā xicnexti yn motoca
yvan yxquich ticnextiz y nimiztlahtlaniz Auh niman quitoz yn lociper Ayioyave
Onotlaveliltic yn axcan Cenca Otinechpinavhti : macivi yn a° niceya niman axcan
ticmatiz yn notoca yehica nopā Oticchivh ȳ Cruz .etc. Ca yc cenca Oti[167r]
nechtollini Otinechtonevh ma xicmati Ca nevatl notoca nilociper ya vecavh
Onechmochivilli .d. yn ilvicatl yhytec Ca cenca nitlaço nicatca .d. ynic nich-
ipavac niquinpanaviaya yn ixɋchtin yn itlachivalvan .d. Auh yehica yn onpa
Oninopovh OniCuecuenotic niman ic cēca Onicyollitlaco .d. yvā ceɋntin y
nocnivā Oɋyollitlacoque yc nimā Otechmotlaxilli yn .d. yn ōpa yn mictlā Auh
ypahpa yn totlahtlacol : titotlilotinemi yn tixɋchtin yn iztivi Auh canpa ayavi
niman quitoz yn lociper yn axcā Ca çan nican tivallaɋ ynic ticanaco yn ce tlacatl ȳ tocnivh yn otechtlayecoltitinēca yn nican tp̄c̄. Ca cenca miyequintin yn
oquintlaneltoɋlti yn otemoɋ mictlan yc tiquilvichivilliya Ca çan ic [167v] tichocativi yehica yn omomiquilli yntlaca° momiquilliani miyequintin Onpa yazquiya
tochan av inin Ca çan ic titlayocoxtivi Auh nimā quitoz yn ermitano Auh ȳtlah
antlayocoxtivi tleyca yn āCuicativi Nimā ɋtoz yn lociper Cuix mo tiCuica-
tivi Ca çan tichocativi Auh nimā ɋtoz yn ermitano ma yvi tla niman icivhca
xinech[il]vi tleyn ipā mitova yn Cuicatl maca° xiɋto yn tlatolli ma çā xicCuicayeva
ynic ɋcaquizque yn mochītin etc. Auh yn iquac yn omevhqui yn iCruz nimā quil-
vizɋ cah a°. tiCuica Ca çan tichoca Auh nimā ɋtoz yn ermitano : ɋlviz yn lociper
xinechivi[41] Cuix çan amoceʇin y nican yn a°vica yn āvalvezɋ yn ilhᶜ. Auh nimā
ɋtoz yn lociper [168r] Cuix mo çan to[c]elʇin Cenca timiyeɋntin Auh niman
quitoz yn ermitano tla xicnexti tle ynez[42] yn yevatl yn apilloli yn amomac ycativh

Alas, O were-owl! By the command of Jesus Christ the true God and by [the sign of] his cross which I make on you and because of his water that I spread on you, reveal your name and reveal everything that I will ask of you!

And then Lucifer will say,
Alas! How unfortunate I am! Now you have really shamed me. Even though I don't want to, you will now know my name because you made the [sign of the] cross on me, etc. With it [167r] you caused me pain, you afflicted me. Know that my name is Lucifer. A long time ago God created me in the heavens. I was God's very beloved one, I was the most pure of all God's creations. But because I was proud, I was haughty, I gravely offended God. Along with some of my friends who had grieved him, God cast us down to Mictlan. All of us who come here live blackened by our sins.

And [Hermit will say,]
Where are you going?

Then Lucifer will say,
We came here today to take a person, one of our friends, one who lived serving us here on earth.[35] Indeed a great many of those he caused to believe in him have descended to Mictlan. We celebrate a festival for him because of this.[36] [167v] We do nothing but weep because he died. If only he hadn't died, many of them would have gone there to our home. Because of this we live in sorrow.

And then Hermit will say,
If you are so sad, why are you singing?[37]

Then Lucifer will say,
We are not singing. We are just weeping.

Then Hermit will say,
Very well! Tell me quickly what is spoken of in the song. Do not say the words, just hum the tune so that everyone hears it, etc.[38]

And upon raising his cross they will say,
We are not singing! We are just weeping!

Then Hermit will say, he will say to Lucifer,
Tell me, was it only you who came here [when] you fell from the heavens?

Then Lucifer will say,
[168r] It was not just us alone; there were a great many of us.

Then Hermit will say,
Please won't you reveal what that water jar in your hands means![39]

nimā q̇toz yn lociper Ca yca toquitqui yn atl yvhqui yn patli ynic titeyahaltiya ynic
yollitlacollo dios ynic a° netlecavilloz yn ilvicac Ca yeica yn onpa tivalvezq̄ yc cenca
titoxicova yn iquac tiquimitta Cequintin yn onpa motlecaviya Auh niman q̇toz
yn ermitano tla xiquito quenami yn yevatl yn atl yn momac ycativh tleyn ic tic-
chiva tleyn [y]nezca nima q̇toz yn lociper Ca ynezca yn nepovaliztli Ca yehica yn
oninopovh cēca nicnequi ma noviyan nepovallo ynic temolloz mictlan Ca çan ic
pachivhiz yn noyollo : macivi Cenca nitlahtlatinemi Ca yevatl y notequivh y[168v]
nic nitenepovallizcuititinemi yn ica tlamachoz Ca yn ixquich yn amo qualli yn
ayectli nevatl Onicç̇inti Auh yn ixq̇chtin yni mictlan temova notech mixCuitiya
Nimā q̇toz yn ermitano Omotlaveliltic Ca cenca titlavelliloc ya miziximati yn
macevaltin av inic amo motech mixCuitizq̄ tla xiyavh

DLALOC

¶Nimā q̇toz yn ermitano q̇lvihz yn tlaloc ac tevatl tle motoca q̇.[43] Ca nevatl nitlaloc
Ayjoyavhe yn titlavelliloc tla xiquimilvi yn macevaltin quen ticmati Catlyevatl yn
motoca yn monezca ynic tł titeotl Nimā quitoz Cuix mo niteotl Ca çan itlachival
ȳ. d. Ca onpa O[169r]nivalvez yn ilvicac yehica yn oninopouh Auh çan no quiqui-
miztlacavitinenca yn macevaltin ynic nechteotocaya ynic notech quitlamiyaya yn
q̇yavitl ynin Ca çan ninca[44] ninocacayavaya Cenca nechilvichivilliaya etc. Au ni[45]
nimā . q̇. yn ermitano tle ynezca yn apillolli yn °.mac[46] ycativh tleyn itec catqui

Then Lucifer will say,

With it we carry water that is like a potion with which we bathe people so that God would be offended, so that there wouldn't be any ascending to the heavens. For because we fell down from there, we are very jealous when we see some others going up there.

Then Hermit will say,

Please say what the water you carry in your hands is like. What are you doing with it? What is its meaning?

Then Lucifer will say,

Its meaning is pride.[40] Because I was proud I yearned for there to be pride everywhere so that there would be descending to Mictlan. I will content myself with this even though I am really burning. That is my job [168v], making people proud. In this way all the bad and wicked things that I started will be known. All who seek Mictlan follow my example.

Then Hermit will say,

O how unfortunate you are! You are very wicked! The common people now recognize you! And so that they will not follow your example, please go![41]

TLALOC[42]

Then Hermit will say, he will say to Tlaloc,

Who are you? What is your name?

He will say,

It is I, Tlaloc.

[Hermit:]

Ah, you wicked one! Tell the common people how we know which of your names and your signs means you are a deity.[43]

Then he will say,

I am not a deity. I am just God's creation. Indeed, I [169r] fell down here from the heavens because I was proud. Likewise I just went around deceiving the common people so that they followed me as a deity, so that they attributed the rain to me. In this I vainly made a fool of myself. They used to enthusiastically celebrate feasts for me, etc.

Then Hermit will say,

What is the meaning of that water jar that you have in your hands? What is in there?

Niman . q̇. yn tlalloc Ca patlia ytoca tecocolliliztli[47] yc niquimahaltiya Ceq̇ntin yn
imitec nictlalliya ynic mococollizque ynic quiyollitlacozque .d. ynic temozque mictlan Nimā . q̇. ma yvi [169v] tla xiyvh[48]

DEZCATLIPOCA

¶Nimā q̇ yn ermitano nimiztlahtlaniya ac tevatl Nimā .q̇. Ca nitezcatlipoca
Ayioyavhe yn titlavelliloc quen timochiva Nimā .q̇. Ca nitlahtlatinemi Auh Cuix a°
cenca mizmaviztilliya yn macevaltin ynic motech quitlamiya yn mochivhtoc etc. ma
xin[e]chilvi quezq̇ntin yn mopāhpa Otemoque mictlan Nimā. q̇ . ȳ te̅z.[49] ca cenca
miyeq̇ntin vel q̇zquintin Cuix vel tiqui[n]povaz yn çiçitlaltin Ca vel no yvhqui
niman avel tiquinpovazque yn nopāhpa tlahtla mictlan Ca yevantin yn momatiya
: Ca oniquinchivhqui Auh cah atley Onicchivhqui Ca ça nitlachival yn .d . ypāhpa
[170r] y notlahtlacol nitlahtlatinemi ynic onpa Onivalvez yn ilhᶜ. Ca niquimiztlacav-
itinenca yn imacevā[50] . d . Auh nimā . q̇ . yn ermitano ya nimitziximati Cenca titlaveliloc Auh ma xinechilvi tleyn momac ycativh Nimā .qui.[51] Ca niquitqui yn atl yn itoca
tetlaximaliztli yvan tecuilontilliztli yc niquihimahaltiya yn cequintin yvā cequintin

Then Tlaloc will say,
It is a potion called "envy" with which I bathe them. I place it within some of them so that they will hate each other,[44] so that they will offend God and as a result will descend to Mictlan.

Then [Hermit] will say,
So be it! [169v] Please go!

TEZCATLIPOCA[45]

Then Hermit will say,
I ask you, who are you?

He will say,
I am Tezcatlipoca.

[Hermit:]
Ah, you wicked one! What's become of you?

Then he will say,
I am continually burning.

[Hermit:]
Don't the common people earnestly venerate you and credit you for what is made, etc.? Tell me, how many have descended to Mictlan because of you?

Then Tezcatlipoca will say,
Very many, indeed.

[Hermit:]
How many?

[Tezcatlipoca:]
Are you able to count the stars? It's just like that. It is not possible for us to count those who are burning in Mictlan because of me. Indeed, they think I made them, but there is nothing I have made. I am merely God's creation. Because of [170r] my sins I am continually burning. For this reason I fell from the heavens: I used to go around deceiving God's subjects.

And then Hermit will say,
I recognize you! You are very wicked! Now tell me, what do you have in your hands?

Then [Tezcatlipoca] will say,
I carry the water called "adultery" and *tecuilontiliztli*.[46] With it I bathe some, and

niquimititya ynic tetlaximazque ynic tecuilontizque ynic quitlahtlacalvizque .d. yn
ic ꝙnmotlaxiliz mictlan miyeꝙntin nechtlacamati yehica Cenca ꝙvelmati yn tetlaximalliztli çan ic cemicac tonevazque : O ca ça yevatl y notequivh Niman ꝙlviz tla
xiyavh ȳ titlaveliloc Ca ya mitziximati yn macevaltin Ca ti[170v]tlate°.

VITZILOPOCHTLI

¶Nimā quitoz yn ermitano Tla xinechilvi yn tevatl. tleyn motoca .ꝙ. Ca nevatl
nivitzilopochtli niꝙmiztlacavitinenca macevaltin nechteotocaya Ca çan itlachival ȳ
.d. Ca ypanpa notlahtlacol Onechvalmotlaxilli mictlan nitlahtlatinemi Cenca nechil-
vichiviliaya yn macevaltin yn iꝙac nolvivh quitzaya etc. yn axcā ca ca[52] nictlayocoya
noyollo yehica yn ovamopā[53] acico yn xp̄ānome Ca cēca yc nichoca yehica yn ovamechmachtico yn padretin yntla çan inceltʒin ȳ xp̄ānome yn vallani aço vel niqui-
miztlacavizquia aço vel yn ca ni[171r]nocacayavazquia aco[54] ceꝙntintin niquinvica-
zquiya mictlan ypanpa yn intlahtlacol Ca çā yevātin yn padretin nechtlacavaltiya yn
iquac ꝙnmachtitinemi ynic nenemillizcotonalloz Ca çan ic neyolmellavallo yc tlahtlacolcavallo Auh yn yevantin yn padretin : Oc°enca tlapanaviya chicavac yn iyollo[55]
ynic motlahtlacolcavaltia micivi[56] cenca miyepa[57] yn imitec nictlallia yn a[q]ualli yn
ayectli niman amo nechtlacamati Auh yntlah aca padre quichiva nimā moyolmellava ynic quimochipavilliya yn iyolliya[58] yn cenca tlamaceva nimā yc ꝙmoyolcevillia .d.
ynic avel niquinvica mictlan Auh ceꝙntin yn xp̄āme[59] yn aqualtin yn ꝙxcavitinemi
yn tlahtlacolli macivi yn moyolmellava cecexivhtica niman ypā quichiva yn tlahtlacolli Ca çan ic pachivi yn iyollo yn iquac Cequintin ypā miq[u]i [171v] yn temicti-
yani tlahtlacolli yc niquinvica mictlan Auh ca çan ic nitlayocoya yehica Oxitin yn
nocal yn opolliuh y nixiptla Cenca yc nitlayocoya yehica yn a°pan Ovacico yn iCruz
yn jexp̄ō Ca cenca niquimacaci yn iquac ce tlacatl yyollocopa ytech ꝙꝙtza yn niman
avel niquiztlacaviz Auh nimā quitoz yn ermitano Ayyoyavhe : tla xiyavh yn titlavelliloc Ca ya mitziximati yn macevaltin Auh ma oc xinechivi tleyn moma ycatiuh

to some others I give it to drink so that they will commit adultery, so that they will commit *tecuilontiliztli*, [and] so that they will offend God. Because of this he will cast many who obey me into Mictlan because they have found adultery to their liking. They will suffer forever as a result. This was my job.

Then [Hermit] will say to him,
Please go, you wicked one! The common people have now recognized you! [170v] You are a were-owl!

HUITZILOPOCHTLI[47]

Then Hermit will say,
Tell me, you. What is your name?

[Huitzilopochtli] will say,
It is I, Huitzilopochtli. I went around deceiving the common people. They used to consider me a deity, [but] I'm only God's creation. Because of my sins he cast me into Mictlan where I am continually burning. The common people used to celebrate a feast in my honor when it was my feast day, etc. Now my heart is sad because the Christians have arrived. I have been weeping greatly because the priests came to teach you. If only it had been just the Christians[48] who had come, perhaps I would have been able to deceive them, perhaps [171r] I would have been able to fool them, perhaps I would have brought some others to Mictlan because of their sins. Those priests just hold me back when they go around teaching them, and as a result there is life-changing,[49] there is confessing, there is abandoning of sins. The hearts of those priests are exceedingly strong and thus they cause [people] to abandon their sins. Even though many times I place bad, improper things within them, they don't obey me at all. If some priest does it[50] then they confess and cleanse their souls, earnestly doing penance. With this God is placated so that it is impossible for me to bring them to Mictlan. But the other Christians, the bad ones, they live devoted to sin. Even though they confess every year, they're doing it in [a state of] sin. I am satisfied when some die in [171v] mortal sin because I bring them to Mictlan. But I am sad because my house was knocked down,[51] my image was destroyed.[52] I am very sad because the cross of Jesus Christ arrived. I am really afraid when a person willingly raises it up,[53] then it is not possible for me to deceive him.

Then Hermit will say,
Alas! Please go, you wicked one! The common people have now recognized you. And furthermore tell me, what is in your hands?

[Huitzilopochtli:]

ma xicmati Ca yevatl patli ytoca qualanillizpatli yc niquimahaltiya yvā cequintin
yn itec nictlalliya yn qualanilliztli ynic mavazque ynic moqualanizque ynic momic-
tizque ynic moquazque ynic a° yazque yn ichāṭinco .d. Ca çan ic notlan cemicac
tlahtlazque Oca çan yevatl yn cemicac notequivh Auh nimā ḍtoz yn ermitano Ca
ꝗmaca yntla ya nelli titeotl Cah a° ticneḍzḍa y[ni]c nequalloz Au inin yc tine[172r]ci
yn ⁱⁱtlavelliloc tla xiyavh

QUETZALCOVATL

¶Niman .ḍ. yn ermitano : nimiztlahtlaniya ac tevatl nimā .ḍ. Ca nevatl niqueçal-
covatl Onechtlayecoltitinenca yn macevaltin nixpā Omiçoya etc. Auh nimiztlahtlaniya tleyn momac ycativh Nimā .ḍ. ca niquitḍ yn patli yevatl yn itoca xixicuiyotl yc
niquimahaltiya yvā cequintin ymitec nictlaliya. ynic moxv[i]tizque ynic tlavanazque
ynic miçotlazque ynic amo tlecozque yn ilhᶜ yn aḍn tlavātinemi niman avel quichivaz yn qualli .t̄p̄c̄. Ca çā yevatl y [n]oteḍvh .N.⁶⁰ ma yvi tla xiyavh yn titlavelliloc

OTONTECVHTLI

¶Nimā quitoz yn ermitano Nimiztlahtlaniya ac tevatl Ca nevatl notontecvhctli nech-
teotocaya yn macevaltin nechilvichivilliyaya nixpā ḍqu[e]çaya [172v] yn quavitl yn
itoca xoxocoquavitl. nimā nixpā mitotiaya yn telpohpochtin yvā yn çiva etc. Au in omo-
cavhque niman quinamoyaya yc quitemovaya yaoyotl yn momatiya yn macevaltin Ca
tepal tlamazque Auh ca çan ic niquimiztlacaviaya Ca çan a° niteotl Ca çan itlachival yn
.d. ypāhpa y notlacol.⁶¹ Onechvalmotlaxilli mictlan ynic onpa Cemicac nitlahtlatinemi

Know that this potion is called "anger-potion." With it I bathe them and I place anger inside others so that they scold each other, so that they become angry with each other, so that they kill each other, so that they devour each other, so that they will not go to God's home. They will burn forever with me. This is my job forever.

And then Hermit will say,
Yes, indeed. If you were truly the deity you wouldn't want there to be devouring of people. This confirms that [172r] you are wicked! Please go!

QUETZALCOATL[54]

Then Hermit will say,
I ask you, who are you?

Then [Quetzalcoatl] will say,
It is I, Quetzalcoatl. The common people used to serve me, they used to bleed themselves before me, etc.[55]

[Hermit:]
And I ask you, what do you have in your hands?

Then [Quetzalcoatl] will say,
I carry a potion that is called "gluttony." I bathe them with it and I place it within others so that they overeat, so that they get drunk, so that they bleed themselves, so that they will not ascend to the heavens. It is impossible for the one who goes around drunk to do good on earth. This alone is my job.

Then [Hermit will say],
So be it! Please go, you wicked one!

OTONTECUHTLI[56]

Then Hermit will say,
I ask you, who are you?

[Then Otontecuhtli will say,]
It is I, Otontecuhtli. The common people used to take me for a deity, they used to celebrate a feast in my honor. They used to raise [172v] a tree called the guava tree before me.[57] Then the young men and women danced before me, etc. And when they stopped, they stole it. War descended because of this. The common people thought with help they would take captives.[58] With this I deceived them. I am not a deity, I am merely God's creation. Because of my sins he cast me down to Mictlan where I live eternally burning.

Auh ma xinechilvi tleyn momac ycativh nimā .q̇. Ca niquitqui yn patli yevatl yn itoca tlatzivizpatli yc [—]⁶² niquimahaltiya yn tlatoq̄ yn pihpiltin no yevātin yn atlei yn inteq̇vh yn çanē nenemi Ça niquixcavitinemi yn imitec nictlalliya yn pipiltin tlatziviçotl ynic çan tlatzivhtinemizque ynic çā quimixcavizque [173r] yn quinte-mozque yn ichpohpochtin anoço yn tecivavan yniquintech⁶³ açizque Caca can ic⁶⁴ pachiviz yn inyollo Auh cenca miyequintin nechtlacamati yn telpohpochtin yehica yn atley yn intequivh atlei yn axtinemi Ça mochipa tlatziviçotl yntequivh Ca çā quixcavitinemi yn tlahtlacolli yc q̇tlahtlacalvitinemi yn .d. yc q̇ntlaçaz ȳ mictlan O ca ça yevatl y noteq̇vh ma yvi tla xiyavh yn titlavelliloc Au in axcan pihpil[tin] ma ca° xitlatzivican .etc.

CIVACOVATL

¶Nimā .q̇. yn ermitano Nimiztlahtlaniya ac tevatl .q̇. ca nev[a]tl nicivacovatl Oniq̇miztlacavitinenca yn macevaltin yn oninocuepqui yvhqui y nelli nicivatl nech-teotocaya ca nitlacate°. vel nechtlayecoltiaya : miyequintin nechmacaya yn niquīcuaya Auh a° niquincuaya yn ca[n]a tlaca ca niyavh yn tlaxcalteca yn vexoṭinca yvā yno[173v] tlamacazcavan yn imezço .ets. : Auh nimā quitoz yn ermitano : xinechilvi yn tevatl yn tiçiva tlavelliloc yn tleyn momac ycativh nimā .q̇. ca niquitqui yn patli ytoca teoyeva-catillizpatli ynic niquimahaltia yn macevaltin yn tlatoq̄ yn pipiltin ynic miquimitec⁶⁵ nictlallia yn teotevacatilliztli yn °cᶜē ca⁶⁶ teoyevacatizque ynic amo q̇ntlayocollizque ynic quimaxcatizque yn iyaxca yn .d. ynpāpa ca mochi yyaxcaṭin ca çano yc q̇ncuiltono ynic tetlayocollizque Auh yn iquac yn a° quintlayocollia yn tlayocolliloni Ca quimax-catia yc pachivi yn inyollo Auh Ca [y]c temozque mictlan O ca yevatl y notequivh

And [Hermit will say],
Tell me, what do you have in your hands?

Then [Otontecuhtli] will say,
I am carrying a potion that is called "laziness-potion" with which I bathe the rulers, the nobles, and also those who have no work, those who just walk around aimlessly. All I do is go around placing laziness within the nobles so that they will live slothfully, so that they will just do nothing but [173r] look for young women or perhaps some people's wives to have sex with. This really satisfies them. A great many of the youth obey me because they do nothing, they go around doing nothing. Laziness is their full-time work. They live giving themselves to sin and thus they live offending God. Because of this, he will cast them to Mictlan. This alone was my job.

[Hermit:]
So be it! Please go, you wicked one!

[To the audience:]
Now [you] noblemen, don't be lazy, etc.![59]

CIHUACOATL[60]

Then Hermit will say,
I ask you, who are you?

[Cihuacoatl] will say,
It is I, Cihuacoatl. I used to go around deceiving the common people by making myself look like a real woman.[61] They used to follow me as a deity, [but] I am a were-owl. They served me well. They used to give many [sacrificial victims] to me, [and] I used to eat them. But I didn't eat people from anywhere, I went to the Tlaxcalans, the Huexotzincans[62] and the blood of [173v] my priests, etc.

Then Hermit will say,
Tell me, you wicked woman, what is it you have in your hands?

Then [Cihuacoatl] will say,
I am carrying a potion whose name is "greed-potion" with which I bathe the common people, the rulers, the nobles, and thus place greed within them. They will be so exceedingly greedy that they will not show mercy, they will even take God's own property for themselves. He enriched them with his goods so that they would have mercy on people. And then they do not have mercy on those who deserve mercy, they seize their goods in order to satisfy themselves.[63] Because of this they will just go down to Mictlan. This was my job.

nimā .q̇. ma yvi tla xiyavh tlacatecolotlhe yn axcan Ca yah amechiximati yn macevaltin Ca cenca antlavelliloq̄ yvā Cenca amechtlavellilocatocazque yvā [174r] amechtlatzilvizque tleco mochi quitlaçazque yn amixiptlavā yn axcan Ca ya quimati ynic anquimiztlacavitinemi : y nicā moteotocatinemi Ca çan ātlahtlacatecollo Au in axcā yvhqui yn atle ypā amechittazque Occenca tlapanaviya amechichazque[67] Au in amevantin nimā xiquinchichacā yn amochintin yn āquitovaya toteovā Catca

HERMITANO

¶Auh nimā q̇toz yn ermitano xiccaq̇can tlahtlacatecollohe Ca ya ytencopa yn .d. yn ā[t]echilviya yn ixquich yn a°tlachival avh ma nimā xictlapanacā yn amapilol yn a°mac ycativh ma nimā xictlaçacan Auh tla nimā ycivhca ximotlatlallican Ca oc niquintlahtlaniz yn ixquich yn amicāpa yavi [174v] tle ynezca yn q̇mahmativi ynic quinextizque

XP̄ŌAQUE[—][68]

¶Nimā quitoz yn ermitano Au in amevātin xinechilvicā tleyn amotoca .q̇. xp̄. Ca tevātin yn tichicuacemintin tintlenamacahcavā yn tlahtlacate°. yn tixpā mātivi yn tiquinteotocaya Cah amo nelli teteo macivi yn cenca Otiquintlayecoltique Auh yn axcā Ca çan intlan titoneva mictlan yehica amo tiquiximattiyaq̄ yn nelli .d. yn axcan ya ticnelto[69] Auh macivi yn ticneltoca Ca çan a° yc titomaquixtizque Otovitique Ca yn axcā ya tiquitta yn tixpohpoyonemilliz ynic tixpohpoyotitinēca .tp̄c. niman ayc titoceviya çan mochipa titlahtla yn ōpa mictlan Ca cenca teçaçaya[175r]na yn otiquintlayecoltitinenca .tp̄c. yn ōpa Ceppa topā q̇teca yn coppalatl nimaya[70] no cuel ye ceppa yevatl yn tepoçatl ynic cenca tichichinaca Auh nimā .q̇. yn ermitano xinechilvi ~~no~~ yn tevatl tle ynezca yn āquimama

Then [Hermit] will say,
So be it! Please go, O were-owl!

[Addressing the seven demons:]
Today the common people have recognized you all. You are very wicked and wicked they will consider you to be, [174r] they will hate you, they will cast all your images into the fire. They now know that you deceive those here who follow them as deities, for you are just were-owls. Today they will despise you, they will exceedingly spit on you.

[To the audience:]
And now, all of you who used to say that they were our *teteoh*, spit on them![64]

HERMIT

And then Hermit will say,
Listen, O were-owls! By the command of God you have told us of all of your deeds. And now, break the water jars that you have in your hands! Throw them down! Let them quickly be scattered! I still have to question all those that follow you [174v] regarding the meaning of what they go bearing on their backs so that they will reveal it.[65]

YEAR KEEPERS[66]

Then Hermit will say,
And you all, tell me, what are your names?

The Year Keepers will say,
We six are the were-owls' fire priests. Before us [people] laid out offerings. Those who we used to follow as deities are not true deities, even though we earnestly served them. And now we suffer with them in Mictlan because we didn't acknowledge the true God. Now we believe in him. But even though we believe in him, we will not save ourselves with this. We placed ourselves in danger. Now we see our blind way of life by which we blindly lived on earth. Now we never rest, we just go along burning down there in Mictlan. Those that we used to serve on earth are all broken [175r] to pieces.[67] First they spread copal-water on us, then that metal-water. Because of it we are suffering great pain.[68]

Then Hermit will say,
Tell me, you, what is the meaning of what you all are carrying on your backs?

.x̄p̄. Ca ynezca yn imixpã yn toteovã ynic titehertequiya[71] yn tecpatl ynic otitemictique
Auh in onpa mictlan mochi[pa] ticmamatinemi yc cenca titoneva Auh no yevatl yn
ticmamatinemi yn tecciztli ynic titlapiçaya ynic tiquinechicovaya yn macevaltin y[n]
ic miçozque yn imixpã toteovã ynic tiquimiztlacavitinẽca yn macevaltin Ca yn ōpa
yn inchã toteovã çan tiquixcavitinẽca yn tlavellilocayotl ca çan ichtlaca yn intech
taciya yn inpilvã catca Onpa tlachpanavaya titecuillontiaya yc tiquim[i]z[175v]tlaca-
via y yn tlatoq̄ yvã yn mochi tlatl[72] ca yn momatiya ca vel tinemiya yn ichã toteovã
Auh nimiztlahtlaniya Cuix ça niyavh yn amotonevalliz[73] yn otinechilvi .x̄p̄. q̄ Cah a°
Ca cenca miyec yn totonevalliz Ca yn ōpa mictlan yn yevãtin yn toteovã yn tlahtlacatecolo ca çã quixcavia yn techitiya yn imeço ynmamaltin yn otiq̄meltecque nicã t̄p̄c̄
Ca cenca totōqui yn techitiya yvã techmecaviteq̄ Auh xinechilvi anq̄zq̄ntin yn onpa
ancate yn amo anquiximattiyaq̄ y nelli .d. jesux̄p̄ō nimã .q̄. Cah a[v]el titopovazq̄
Auh yn tevatl cuix vel tiquinpovaz yn xalli yn noviyan cemanavac Cah avelli amo cã[74]
tlapovalli .x̄p̄. Auh no yvhqui cah avel titechpovaz ca timiyeq̄ntin yvan timochintin
Onpa Cenca [176r] titlahtlatinemi Cenca titepanaviya Nimã .q̄. yn ermitano ma yvi
Ca ya ovamovitiq̄ xix tla xiviyan Ca yah amechiximati yn macevaltin

ATLANELTOCANI

Yn aq̄que Oquicaq̄ yn itlatoltzin .d. Ca çan a° Oquineltocaq̄

¶Niman quitoz yn ermitano yn amevãtin yn amomextin tleyn a°toca q̄tozque Ca
nevatl nitlacatecvhctli yevatl nocniuh yn itoca viznavatl

Year Keeper:

It represents how we used to cut open people's chests with flint knives and kill people in front of our *teteoh*. There in Mictlan we always go along carrying it on our backs and because of it we suffer greatly. We also go along carrying on our backs the conch shell that we used to blow to gather the common people to bleed themselves before our *teteoh*. In this way we went along deceiving the common people. There in the home of our *teteoh* we only devoted ourselves to wickedness. We used to secretly have sex with their children who used to sweep there. We committed *tecuilontiliz-tli*.[69] With this we deceived [175v] the rulers and all people who thought we lived [virtuously] in the home of our *teteoh*.

And [Hermit will say],

I ask you, did you say to me that you don't usually have a great deal of pain?[70]

Year Keeper will say,

Oh no, we have many pains there in Mictlan! Those who are our *teteoh*, the were-owls, do nothing but make us drink the blood of their captives, those whose chests we cut open here on earth. What they make us drink is very hot, and they whip us.

[Hermit:]

Tell me, how many of you are there that didn't acknowledge the true God Jesus Christ?

Then they will say,

We cannot count. And you? Can you count all the sand in the world? Indeed, it is not possible because it is infinite in number. *Year Keeper [will say],* Likewise it is impossible for you to count us because we are many, and all of us [176r] are continually burning in a way that surpasses comprehension.

Then Hermit will say,

So be it! You placed yourselves in danger. Please go! The common people have recognized you!

UNBELIEVER[71]

Those who heard the words of God but just didn't believe in him.

Then Hermit will say,

You two, what are your names?

They will say,

I am Tlacateuctli. My friend's name is Huitznahuatl.[72]

Auh tle ynezca yn āquimama tleyn ipanpa yn ātoneva . q̇. Ca yn ticmama [Ca] ynezca yn tonevalliztli ynic titoneva mictlan yehica ca topā Ovacico yn itlatoltzin .d. Çanē Oticneltocaq̇ çan ipā Oticamanaltique Ca çan ivhqui yn atle ypā Oticq̇taq̇ Auh [y] ehica yn a° techmictizque yn xpīanome nimā yc tic[x]i[176v]tiniyaya yn incal yn toteovā Auh cah a° toyollocoppa Ca çan ivhqui yn titec tiquinquechilliaya yn incal yvā vel tiquinpiyaya yn imixiptlavā yn toteovā ynic a° quitlatizque yn xpīanome av ītla ticnextiani ynic pachivizquia yn inyollo yn xpīanome Ca çan yevatl ticnextiaya yn ivhqui atle ypā tiquittaya Ca yevātin yn vel toteovā Cenca vel tiquinpiaya no yvā Çan ic otitoCuahatequique ynic pachiviz yn inyolo yn padretin amo ma toyol-locopa Ca çan tlapictli Auh [y]ehica yc titoneva yn a° ticneltocaq̇ yn ⁿelli jesuxp̄o. yn otechiximachtico yn padretin Ca can⁷⁵ ichtaca yn otiquintlayecoltitinēque yn toteovā Auh ca çan ic axcā yntlan titonevā yvā yntlan t[i]tlahtla yn itlenamacacavā [177r] yn toteovā Ca tiquineltocaya yn techilviaya macivi yc techiztlacaviaya Ca çan a° ticneltocaya ynCualli tlatolli yn otechilvico yn padretin Auh yn axcā ya tiquinpanaviya yn tonavā⁷⁶ yn totavā ynic titlahtla Cenca techtoneva yni⁷⁷ yevatl yn covatl yn ticteotocaya yn iyxpā titiçoya⁷⁸ yn iyxpā tamaxotlaya yn iyxpā titlenama-caya ynic cenca techtoneva yni yevatl Covatl yvā Cenca techichinaça⁷⁹ yn tlahtlaca-te°. Auh nimā . q̇. yn ermitano yyoyave Ovamotlavelliltic yn a° anquineltocatiyaq̇ y nelli .d. Auh anquezquintin . q̇. niman avel titopovazque Ca cenca timiyeq̇ntin a° çan titlapovaltin nimā .. yn ermitano ma yvi tla xivian yn ātlavelliloq̇

DONALPOVHQUI

¶Nimā .q̇. yn ermitano ac te⁸⁰ [177v]

[Hermit:]
And what is the meaning of what you are carrying on your backs? Why are you suffering under it?

They will say,
What we are carrying stands for the suffering by which we are tormented in Mictlan because the words of God reached us but we didn't take believing seriously, we just made fun of it, we just looked down on it. So that the Christians[73] wouldn't kill us, [176v] we broke down the houses of our *teteoh*. But we didn't do it willingly. It was as if we erected their houses within us and carefully protected the images of our *teteoh* so that the Christians wouldn't burn them. But if in order to placate the Christians we did reveal them, the ones that we revealed were those that we didn't care about. Those that really are our *teteoh* we kept carefully hidden. What is more, we got baptized to satisfy the priests. We didn't do it voluntarily, we did it dishonestly. And as a result we are suffering because we didn't believe in the true Jesus Christ, he whom the priests came to make known to us. We just served our *teteoh* in secret. It is because of this that we are now suffering and burning with the fire priests of [177r] our *teteoh*.[74] We believed what they used to say to us, even though in this way they deceived us. We didn't believe in the good words that the priests came to say to us. Now we are burning even more than our mothers and fathers are. The serpent that we used to follow as a deity,[75] he before whom we bled ourselves and before whom we burned papers and before whom we offered incense, he is greatly tormenting us. This serpent causes us to suffer greatly and the were-owls afflict us terribly.

Then Hermit will say,
Alas, how unfortunate you are, you who didn't believe in the true God! How many of you are there?

They will say,
It is utterly impossible for us to count ourselves. There are a great many of us; we just can't count!

Then Hermit will say,
So be it! Please go, you wicked ones!

DAY KEEPER

Then Hermit will say,
Who are you? [177v]

[Day Keeper:]

ca nitonalpovhqui Auh nima q̇toz ayyoyavhe tle ynezca yn ticmama nimā .q̇. Ca nic-
mama yn imamos yn teteo yn yevatl nicpovaya yn amostli ynic niteyztlacaviaya yn
iquac yn aca tlacatiya nimā nixpā quivalvicaya yn ināṭin yn itaṭin ynic niq̇milviz yn
catleyvatl tonalli yn ipa [—]n[81] otlacatqui yn iconevh ynic niq̇uimilviz yn tleyn ipā
mochivaz yn iconevh. t̄p̄c̄. ynic [n]iteyztlacaviaya Cah amo tley ȳ nicmatia Cuix ma
niteotl ca çan icel teotl quimomachitiya yn tleyn tepā mochivaz nimā .q̇. yn ermitano tla xinechilvi yn icuac titlapovaya tleyn toquitovaya[82] nimā .q̇. ynic tlapovaya
ets. nimā Occeppa quitoz Auh in axcan ytencoppa yn .d. nechmecavitectinemi
yn yevātī yn omētin yn tlahtlacate°. yehica yn cenca nivey nitlavelliloc miyeq̇ntin
Oniquimiztlacaviaya nimā .q̇. ma yvi tla xiyavh [178r]

DLATOVANI YTLATQUI

¶Niman .q̇. yn ermitano nimiztlatlaniya ac tevatl nimā .q̇. ca nevatl nitontiyeyo
nitlatovani Auh tleyca yn omizmotlaxilli .d. yn mictlan .q̇. Ca yehica yn onechmotlaxilli .d. yn avell onicpix yn itenavatilṭin Çan yehica y ninocuiltonovaya çan ic
ninopovhtinēca çan ivhqui yn atley ypā niquimittaya y nomacevalvā ça niq̇ntolliniaya
Cenca [n]iquintequitiaya mieyecpa niq̇mitlanilliaya yn intlatqui yvā nechmilchiv-
illiaya atley niquintlaxtlaviaya miyecpa nopāhpa monamacaya yn tlejn mach niqui-
mitlanilliaya macivi yn miyec nechmomaq̇lliaya ca çan amo yc noyollo pachivia Au
in axcā Ca vel yevatl yn mictlā ynic onitemoc yehica yn amo niquinmotlaxtlaviliaya

I am a day keeper.[76]

Then [Hermit] will say,
Alas! What is the meaning of what you are carrying on your back?

Then he will say,
I bear the book of the *teteoh*.[77] I used to read the book in order to deceive people. When someone was born the mother and father would bring him [or her] before me so that I would tell them under which day sign their child had been born, so that I would tell them what will happen to their child here on earth. In this manner I used to deceive them. What I used to know is nothing. Am I a deity? It is Only Deity who teaches people what will happen to them.

Hermit will then say,
Please tell me, when you used to do readings, what would you say to them?
Then he will say how he used to divine, etc.[78]
Then again [Day Keeper] will say,
And now at God's command two were-owls go whipping me because I am a very great wicked one, I have deceived many!

Then [Hermit] will say,
So be it! Please go! [178r]

RULER'S GOODS

Then Hermit will say,
I ask you, who are you?

Then [Ruler] will say,
It is I, Tontiyeyo,[79] I am a ruler.

[Hermit:]
Why has God cast you into Mictlan?

He will say,
God cast me down because it was impossible for me to keep his commands, because I enriched myself, [and] as a result I just lived haughtily. Likewise, I despised my subjects,[80] causing them to suffer, imposing much work on them. Many times I demanded their belongings from them. They cultivated fields for me [and] I paid them nothing for it. Often, even what I demanded of them was sold to benefit me. Even though they had given me much, I wasn't satisfied with it. And now, it is for this reason I have descended to Mictlan because I did not pay them, I made them

Oniquinmot[o]llinilli ypāpa Cemicac nitlahtlatinemi yehica ya̅ yn [a]° [178v] niquintlayxiptlacayotilli[83] y nomacevalvā çano yvā Onicmaxcati yn tleyn yvhqui Oqtlecotlaçato y nixpā yn icnopiltique a° niquinxelvi yvā niquinmaxcatiaya yn incivavh niquinmomecatiaya av in novayolque yn iquac momiquilliaya yvā notencopa yn tiyanqznepātla çan qtlayevillitinenca yn teteyamiqa[84] ets. Auh yc cen[c]a Onicyollitlaco yn .d. Auh yehica a° nimoyolmellavh yyxpāṭinco yc onechmotlaxilli mictlan nimā .q̇. yn ermitano ma yvi tla xiyavh yn titlavelliloc av inin yc ximozcallicā tlatoq̇he

POCHTECATL

¶Niman q̇toz yn ermitano nimiztlahtlaniya ac tevatl nimā .q̇. Ca nitoribio nipochtecatl ca noteqvh catca yn teca [ni]nocacayavhtinenca yn iq̅c [179r] yn tetech nitlayxtlapanaya yvā niquimichtectinemiya yn pihpilṭiṭintin : yn iquac y noztomecatiya niq̇michtacanamacaya yvā [—][85] nitetlacuicuillitinenca yvā nitetlanamaq̇ltitinenca yn icuac nicteylviaya yntlacamo ycuac yn onitlahtla ynic nechmacaz nimā motzonevaz : momimilloz Auh Cuix mo yvhqui quimonequiltia .d. yvā nicnaxcatiaya yn tp̅ccayotl amo niquintlayocolliaya yn motollinia yehica ninocuiltonovaya Ca ça niquixcaviaya yn tetlaximalliztli macivi ninomecavitequiya ca niman a° yc niquincavhqui y nomecavā niman amo yc nigotonaya[86] yn aqualnemilliz niman a° ninoyormellavh yc onechmotlaxilli .d. mictlan yevātin y nechmecavitectinemi ynezca y nomecavā nimā .q̇. cuix çan mocel yn ōpa tica nimā .q̇. yn pochtecatl Cah amo ça nocel ca miyeq̇ntin yn pochteca yn ōpa cate mictlan nimā .q̇. tla xiyavh yn titlavelliloc suffer. For this reason I live eternally burning [178v] because I didn't provide my subjects with any compensation. Also, I took for myself what they went to toss in the fire. In my presence they became impoverished; I just didn't give them a break.[81] Also, I took their women as my property, I made them my mistresses. And when my relatives died, at my command [their kin] just went along begging in the middle of the marketplace, selling goods, etc. In this way I greatly offended God. And because I didn't confess before him he cast me into Mictlan.

Then Hermit will say,
So be it! Please go, you wicked one!

[To the audience:]
In light of this, come to your senses, O rulers!

MERCHANT

Then Hermit will say,
I ask you, who are you?

Then [Merchant] will say,
I am Toribio, I am a merchant.[82] My job was mocking people: when [179r] I charged people excessive interest and went around stealing from the nobles; when I worked as an undercover merchant, secretly selling and swiping things from people and selling them to others.

Then I would denounce people [to the authorities], or otherwise burn that which they give me, then [the interest, profits] overflow, spill over.[83] Does God desire this? And also I made earthly things my property.[84] I didn't have mercy on the poor because I was enriching myself. I just completely devoted myself to adultery. Even though I would whip myself I would absolutely not abandon my mistresses, I wouldn't desist from my bad way of living, I wouldn't confess. Because of this God cast me into Mictlan. Those who represent my mistresses continually go whipping me.

Then [Hermit] will say,
Are you there alone?

Then Merchant will say,
I am not alone. There are many merchants who are down there in Mictlan.

Then [Hermit] will say,
Please go, you wicked one!

(MOTORINIANI)

¶Nimā .q̇. yn ermitano nimiztla[179v]tlaniya ac tevatl Ca nevatl niyūā. ninotoriniya nimā . q̇. tleyca yn otiya mictlan nimā tenāq̇lliz .q̇. yehica y niquallaniya ninoxicovaya yehica yn atley yn notlatq̇ amo ma yc pachivia y noyollo ca ça nitlaçivhtinenca .t͞p͞c. amo nellimiq̇a niman atley nayya[87] ynic neçizquiya y nocochca y nonehevhoa.[88] Ca çan niquixcaviaya y nitlacivhtinēca ynic nichtectinēca Ca ça nicochtinenca yehica yn aº ninoyolmellavh Onitemoc mictlan Auh cenca miyeq̇ntin yn ōpa nemi yn tlaçivini yc nechtoneva yn cocova yehica ninoxicotinenca yn atley notlatqui nimā .q̇. māvi[89] tla xiyavh

DELPOCHTLI

¶Nimā .q̇. yn ermitano nimiztlahtlaniya ac tevatl Auh ca nevatl nitelpochtli notoca locas Auh tleyca yn otitemoc mictlan .q̇. yehica miyequintin çiva niq̇nnomecatitinenca yn ipā Oninoquahateq̇ macivi miyecpa Onechilvique yn itemachticavan yn .d. ynic niq̇ncavaz[q]uia Auh amo niq̇ncavh çan ivhqui y[180r] n atley ypā niquittac yn intlatol yvā Ceq̇ntin y nomecavan Oniquincentecpavi[90] Auh yc cenca Onicyollitlaco .d. yehica yn amo nechocti[91] y notlahtlacol amo ninoyol-mellavh yc onechmotlaxilli : mictlan Auh yntla niccueppani y naqualnemilliz yntla ninoyolmellavani Ca nechtlayocollizquia yn .d. Auh çan illiviz yc onitlavellilocatiti-nenca Au in axcā nechmecavitectivi y nomecavā : yehica nopāhpa Otemoq̇ mictlā ypāhpa vel nemizneq̇a avh çan avel Onēque

POOR ONE

Then Hermit will say,
I ask you, [179v] who are you?

[Poor One:]
It is I, Juan. I am poor.

Then [Hermit] will say,
Why did you go to Mictlan?

Then [Poor One] will answer saying,
Because I was angry, I was envious. I had no possessions and because of this I wasn't content, I just lived lazily on earth. I didn't work the fields, I didn't do anything at all to earn my dinner, my breakfast.[85] I only devoted myself to being lazy and for this reason I turned to stealing. I just slept all the time. Because I didn't confess, I descended to Mictlan. A great many lazy people live there. For this reason the serpents afflict me because I was envious and I had nothing to my name.

Then [Hermit] will say,
So be it! Please go!

YOUNG MAN

Then Hermit will say,
I ask you, who are you?

[Young Man:]
It is I, a young man. My name is Lucas.

[Hermit:]
And why did you go down to Mictlan?

[Youth] will say,
Because I took many women as mistresses. Upon being baptized, I did not leave them even though God's teachers told me many times to leave them, [180r] I just despised their words. I had sex with some of my mistresses a whole lot! Because of this I offended God terribly. Because my sins didn't cause me to weep, I didn't confess, he cast me into Mictlan. If only I had turned around my bad way of life, if only I had confessed, then God would have had mercy on me. But I just lived wickedly and without care. And now my mistresses go whipping me, for on account of me they too have gone down to Mictlan. They wanted to live, but it was not possible for

Ça nevatl Oniquintlacavalti ynic onechtlacamatq̄ ynic notlan tonevativi Ca cenca miyeq̇ntin yn telpohpochtin yn onpa Otiyaq̄ mictlan nima . q̇. yn ermitano ma yvi tla xiyavh yn titlavelliloc

DETLANOCHILLIYANI

¶Niman .q̇. yn ermitano nimiztlaniya[92] ac tevatl nimā .q̇. Ca nevatl niyuana nitetla-valnochilliani Auh tleyca [180v] yn otiya mictlā nimā .q̇. yehica ca noteq̇vh Catca y niquimiztlacavitinēca yn ichpohpochtin y niq̇noçaya ynic yntlan cochizque : yn telpohtochtin Ca çan ic nechtlaqualtiaya yn telpohpochtin Çano yevatl y noconevh tetlanochilliani Auh yn axcan mictlan Otemoque[93] mochipa nicmamatinemi yehica notech Oq̇cuic yn tetlanochilliliztli Auh ya yc cenca titoneva yn tomextin yehica yn aº ypā titoyolmelavhzque[94] Auh nimā .q̇. yn ermitano tla xivh[95] yn titlaveliloc

AVIYANI

¶Nimā quitoz yn ermitano nimiztlahtlania ac teva[tl] .q̇. ca nevatl naviani niCatharinā notoca nimā q̇lviz Auh tleyca Otia mictlan Ca yehica niquimixcavitinenca y niq̇noztinenca yn telpohpochtin ynic notlan Cochiya Auh miyeq̇ntin nopāhpa Otemoque mictlan Ca ça noteq̇vh Ocen cat[181r]ca y nitenehnepilvillitinenca y nitemapilvitinēca yn otlica nitevezquillitinēca nitemanoztinēca niteyxnoztinenca them to live. It was I who prevented them. Since they obeyed me, they go along suffering with me. Indeed, there are very many young men who went down to Mictlan.

Then Hermit will say,
So be it! Please go, you wicked one!

PROCURESS[86]

Then Hermit will say,
I ask you, who are you?

Then [Procuress] will say,
It is I, Juana. I am a procuress.

[Hermit:]
And why [180v] did you go to Mictlan?

Then she will say,
Because my job was going around deceiving the young women. I used to solicit them to sleep with the young men. In this way the young men kept me fed. My own child is also a procuress. And now we have descended to Mictlan. I will always go along bearing her on my back because she took to procuring on account of me. And now as a result we both suffer greatly because we will not confess.

And then Hermit will say,
Please go, you wicked one!

ONE WHO INDULGES IN PLEASURE[87]

Then Hermit will say,
I ask you, who are you?

She will say,
I am an *ahuiani*. My name is Catarina.

Then [Hermit] will say,
And why did you go to Mictlan?

[One Who Indulges in Pleasure:]
Because I went around devoting myself to propositioning the young men to sleep with me. Many of them descended to Mictlan because of me. This was just my job. [181r] I stuck out my tongue at people, I pointed my finger at people in the road, I laughed at people, I beckoned with my hand to people, I beckoned with my head

Çan techā nicacalactinenca ynic ōpa notlā cochiya yn oḋchtin Ca çan ic pachiviya y noyollo ynic nipactinenca yn iquac nitetlaxintinenca yehica yn oc .t̄p̄c̄. ninēca aº ninoyolmellavh niman aº niccotōqui y naqualnemilliz Auh yn axcan yc onechmotlaxilli .d. yn mictlā ypāhpa Ca miyecpa yn oniccaḋ yn teotlatolli Ca çā centlacnepal Ocallacḋ Oc no centlacnepal Oḋzḋ niman avel nitec Omotla[x]lli Auh yn axcan Cenca tlapanaviya ynic nechtoneva : yn tlahtlacateº. Auh nimā .ḋ. yn ermitano Auh Cuix miyeḋntin yn aviyanime yn opa cate yn mictlan nimā .ḋ. Ca cenca timiyequintin yn opa ticate : yn amo çā tlapovaltin yn opa [181v] titlahtlatinemi nimā .ḋ. r.⁹⁶ ma yvi tla xiyavh yn titlavelliloc

YCHPOCHTLI

¶Nimā .ḋ. yn ermitano nimiztlahtlaniya ac tevatl : nimā .ḋ. Ca nevatl nichpochtli nicencilliya Auh tleyca yn otiya mictlan nimā .ḋ. Ca yehica yn iquac nichpochnemiya Ca ça niḋxcavitinemizquiya ynic nictlayecoltitinemizḋa yn .d. ynic aº ninoḋchvatizquiya Auh ca çā ceppa Onechiztlacavi yn tlacatecolotl ce piltontli ychtaca onictzizqui O nopā nictecac Auh macivi yn avel yn o[n]echtlaxin Ca cenca yc onicyollitlaco .d. yehica yn ma ninoḋchvatiyani niman aº nechiztlacavizḋa yn tlacateº. miyecpa Auh miyecpa yn onimoyolmellavh av in cētetl tlahtlahcolli niman ayc onicnexti ayc nicmolvilli yn padre [182r] çan onictlati yehica cenca nechpinavhtiaya y notlahtlacol macivi cenca nitlamacevhtinenca yehica ypan onimicḋ yn tlahtlacolli : yc onechmotlaxili .d. mictla Au intla ninoyormellavani nechtlayocollizquia .d. Auh yn axcan : niman ayc ninomaquiztiz niman ayc nechtlayocoliz Çan mochipa nitonevaz çan mochipa nicmamatinemiz yehica piltontli yn onechtecac yvā nitlahtlatinemi Auh no yvhqui [c]eḋntin Onpa cate cenca miyec to people, I frequently went into people's homes so that men would sleep with me there. This way I satisfied myself, it made me happy when I was committing adultery. Because I didn't confess and I absolutely didn't desist from my bad way of life while I was still living on earth, because of this God has cast me into Mictlan. Many times I heard the sacred words but they just entered on one side and came out on the other.[88] They didn't sink in at all.[89] Now the were-owls cause me to suffer exceedingly.

Then Hermit will say,
Are there many pleasure seekers down there in Mictlan?

She will say,
Indeed, there are many of us down there. We who are continually burning are without number. [181v]

Then Hermit will say,
So be it! Please go, you wicked one!

YOUNG WOMAN

Then Hermit will say,
I ask you, who are you?

Then she will say,
I am a young woman. I am Cecilia.

[Hermit:]
Why did you go to Mictlan?

Then she will say,
Because when I was a young woman I would devote myself to serving God, to the point where I didn't want to live as a married woman.[90] But just one time the were-owl deceived me. I secretly grabbed this boy and laid him down on me. Even though it was not possible for him to commit adultery with me, I greatly offended God.[91] If only I had married! Then the were-owl would not have deceived me so many times. I confessed frequently, but this one single sin I never revealed, I never said it to the priest. [182r] I just hid it because my sins shamed me greatly. Even though I lived very penitently, because I died in sin God cast me into Mictlan. If only I had confessed, God would have had mercy on me. But now I will never be saved, he will never have mercy on me. I will always suffer, always go around carrying that boy on my back because he slept with me and with him I am continually burning. It is like this also for the many others who are there.

nimā .q̇. yn er[97] ma yvi tla xiyavh yn titlaveliloc

DICITL

¶Nimā quitoz yn ermitano nimiztlahtlaniya ac tevatl nimā .q̇. Ca nevatl niyantonio niçitl[98] Auh tleyca yn otiya mictlan nimā .q̇. yehica Cenca nicnocuitlavitinenca yn ticiyotl ȳc[99] ni[q]uimiztlacavitinenca miyequintin ypāhpa Ca noteq̇vh [182v] catca yni[100] nicchayavhtinēca yn teyxpa tlayolli niquintlapoviyaya Au in aq̇q̇ niquintlavelittaya niquinpatiaya ynic miq̇zque macivi miyecpa yn onicaq̇ yn teotlatolli niman a° ninoyolmellavazneq̇ niman a° niccavazneq̇ yn notlavellilocayo Auh yn axcan yc onechmotlaxilli .d. mictlan yn axcan mochipa nicmamatinemi yn isquich ynic nitlapovhtinēca yc cenca nitoneva yvā mochipa nechmecavite[q̇] yn yevātin y niquinoteotitinēca ca ça tlahtlacate° y niquinoztinēca yn iquac nitlapovhtinenca nimā .q̇. yn ermitano tla xivallavh q̇nin titlapovtineca ynic tiquimiztlacavitinēca yn macevaltin tla xitlapovhaqui nimā nicā tlapovaz yn tlapovhq̇ nimā .q̇. yn ermitano yyoyave ȳ titeyztlacaviani Cuix ticmati yn oc tinemi .t̄p̄c̄. yn tleyn q̇momachitiaya .d. nimā .q̇. ma yvi tla [183r] xiyavh yn ᵗⁱtlavelliloc Auh ynī titiciye ynin maca° xicchivacā nin[101] maca° xiquimiticā yn patli Çan niman a° qualli yn civa : y oztiticate ynic q̇tlaçazque yn iconevā[102] maca° xiquimitican yn aqualli patli ynic moteçacatillizque ynic a° anyazque mictlan

Then Hermit will say,
So be it! Please go, you wicked one!

HEALER[92]

Then Hermit will say,
I ask you, who are you?

Then [Healer] will say,
It is I, Antonio. I am a healer.

[Hermit:]
And why did you go to Mictlan?

Then [Healer] will say,
Because I really devoted myself to healing and so deceived many because of it. My job [182v] was this: I scattered shelled maize grains before people; I used to count them. And those who I hated, I treated in such a way that they would die. Even though I heard the sacred words many times, I absolutely didn't want to confess, I absolutely didn't want to abandon my wickedness. And now because of this God has cast me down to Mictlan. Now I will always go along carrying on my back everything with which I divined.[93] Because of this I am suffering greatly and those who I considered deities are whipping me; they're just the were-owls I called upon when I was divining.

Then Hermit will say,
Come now! How did you divine and so deceive the common people? Please, divine it!
Then here the diviner will make his prognostication.[94]
Then Hermit will say,
Alas, you liar! Don't you know what God taught while you were still living on earth?

Then he will say,
So be it! [183r] Please go, you wicked one!

[Addressing the audience:]
Moreover, O healers, don't do this! Don't make women drink potions.[95] It is absolutely not good that women who are pregnant abort their children. Don't make them drink bad potions in order to become sterilized, so that you will not go to Mictlan.

MOTLAHTLAXILLIANI

¶Nimā .q̃. yn ermitano nimiztlahtlania ac tevatl nimā quitoz. Ca ni[f]rācisca Auh tleyca yn otiya mictlā nimā .q̃. yehica yn iquac yn oztli nicatca niquintla-çaya y noconevā yn iquac yn oc ninēca t͞p͞c niman amo niquimizcaltizneq̃a amo niq̃nvapavazneq̃ya ca ça niquixcavitinemiya y nitetlaxintinemiya Auh yehica yn a°. ninoyolmellavh yc onechmotlaxilli .d. mictlā yn cenca nitoneva mochipa niq̃nmamatinemi y noconevā yn oniq̃n[183v]tlaz yc cenca Onicyollitlaco .d. yehica yn ayamo moquahateq̃tiyaq̃ Ca ça nopāhpa nimā .q̃. .r. ma yvi tla xiyavh yn titlavelliloc

MOTETZACATILLIANI

¶Niman .q̃. yn ermitano nimiztlahtlaniya ac tevatl ca nevatl nimotetzacatilliyani : Auh tleyca yn otiya mictlan nimā .q̃. ca yehica yn oniquitlanilli yn tiçitl yn tetzaca-patli ynic onimotetzacatilli ynic a° nitlacachivaznequiya n[o]ztizneq̃ya ca çan niquix-cavitinemiya yn tetlaximalliztli yc pachivia yc noyollo yc cenca onicyolitlaco yn icel teotl yc onechmotlaxilli mictlan yehica yⁿ amo ninoyolmellavh yntla ninoyolmel-lavani nimā nechtlayocollizquiya .d. av in axcā yc nitlahtlatinemi yc nechmecavitec-tinemi yn nomecavā y niq̃nvicatinēca .t͞p͞c. ca vel ye[184r]vatl ypāhpa yn notlahtlacol

ONE WHO INDUCES HER OWN ABORTION

Then Hermit will say,
I ask you, who are you?

Then she will say,
I am Francisca.

[Hermit:]
Why did you go to Mictlan?

Then she will say,
Because when I was pregnant I aborted my children. While I was still living on earth I absolutely didn't want to raise my children, I didn't want to care for them, I just single-mindedly devoted myself to adultery. Because I didn't confess, God cast me into Mictlan where I am suffering greatly, where I always go along bearing my children on my back, those who I aborted. [183v] With this I deeply offended God, because they had not yet been baptized. It is all because of me!

Then Hermit will say,
So be it! Please go, you wicked one!

ONE WHO STERILIZES HERSELF

Then Hermit will say,
I ask you, who are you?

[One Who Sterilizes Herself:]
It is I, I am one who sterilizes herself.

[Hermit:]
Why did you go to Mictlan?

Then she will say,
Because I asked the healer for a sterilizing potion and with it I sterilized myself because I didn't want to give birth, I didn't want to get pregnant. I just lived devoting myself to adultery in order to satisfy myself. As a result I greatly offended Only Deity. Therefore he cast me to Mictlan because I didn't confess. If only I had confessed! Then God would have had mercy on me. As a result, now I am continually burning while my lovers, those who I used to accompany while on earth, whip me. This is all [184r] because of my sins!

ma vi[103] tla xiyavh yn titlavelliloc ·

MOYECTOCANI DEDENANAVATILLIANI[104]

¶Nimā .q̇. yn ermitano nimiztlatlaniya ac tevatl nimā .q̇. ca nevatl nidomingo nimoyectocani Auh tleyca yn otiya mictlā nimā .q̇. ca ypāhpa y nomoyectocati-nenca[105] ca ça noteq̇vh catca : y nitetenanavatilitinēca : tetech nictlamitinēca yn tlahtlacolli Ca çan ic niteyztlacaviyaya yehica Ceppa Onicteylvi Ce çivatl Otetlaxin ca çan yehica nictlavellittaya ca nic[t]enanavatilliaya ya yvā yvā[106] Occe civatl ytech niqualaniya nicnotzazneq̇a Ca çan nicqualancayttaya yn iquac nicnamiquiya yehica otitonotzque yn amo titonepātlaçotlaque yc onechmotlaxilli .d. mictlan yehica yn aᵒ ninoyorme[184v]llavh Auh cenca miyequintin yn opa cate mictlan yn ivhq̇ y yn intlahtlacol Auh ynin ca çan ic nitoneva yn nonenepil ynic nechcuapachivillitinemi yn tlatlahcateᵒ nimā .q̇. r. ma yvi tla xiyavh yn titlavelliloc

YCHTEQUINI

¶Nimā .q̇. yn ermitano nimiztlania[107] ac tevatl nimā .q̇. ca nevatl niyantoniyo Auh tleyca yn otiya m[i]ctlan niman .q̇. yehica ça noteq̇vh catca y nichtectinemiz y nictecuiliz ȳ tetilma yn teyaxca yn tecococavh yehica aᵒ ninoyolmelavh. ynic

[Hermit:]
So be it! Please go, you wicked one!

TRAITOROUS HYPOCRITE

Then Hermit will say,
I ask you, who are you?

Then [Hypocrite] will say,
It is I, Domingo. I am a hypocrite.[96]

[Hermit:]
Why did you go to Mictlan?

Then [Hypocrite] will say,
Because I lived as a hypocrite. I just made it my job to go around betraying people, unjustly accusing them of sin. I used to deceive people with this. One time I accused a woman of committing adultery just because I hated her. I betrayed her along with another woman with whom I was angry; I wanted to solicit her.[97] I would look at her with anger when I would meet her because we solicited each other [but] we didn't love each other. For this reason God cast me into Mictlan because I didn't confess. [184v] There are very many down there in Mictlan whose sins are like this. Furthermore, for this reason my tongue is in pain because the were-owls go along gagging me.[98]

Then Hermit will say,
So be it! Please go, you wicked one!

THIEF

Then Hermit will say,
I ask you, who are you?

Then [Thief] will say,
It is I, Antonio.

[Hermit:]
Why did you go to Mictlan?

Then [Thief] will say,
Because I would steal like it was my job. I would take a person's cloak from him, a person's property, things that belonged to other people. Because I didn't confess,

onechmotlaxilli .d. mictlan yc nitoneva nicmamatinemi yn Cuavitl ynic nechtlallia yn tlahtlacate°. Auh ynī ca timiyeą́ntin nimā quitoz .r. ma yvi tla xiyavh yn titlavelliloc [185r]

YNIN YVAYORĄ́ [108] TECAC

¶Nimā .ą̇. yn ermitano nimiztlahtlaniya ac tevatl ni. ą̇. [109] ca nevatl nimartin Auh tleyca yn otiya mictlan yehica yn onictecac ce civatl novayolą̇ yc cenca onicyollitlaco .d. yc onechtlaz mictlan yehica a° Onimoyolmellavh Auh ca no yevatl y novayrą̇ ça nopāhpa oyaqui mictlan Auh macivi y nevatl OnicCui[t]lavilti Ca çan a° Oninoyormellavh tomentin titlatlatinemi Ca çano yevatl nechmecavitectinemi Ceą̇ntin yn opa cate cenca miyeą̇ntin yn oą̇ntecatiyaą̇ yn invayorque yevatlin yn cenca noveytlatlacol nimā .ą̇. ma vi tla xivh yn titlavelliloc Auh ynin macayac yvhqui ą̇chivaz

CUILLONI [185v]

¶Nimā .ą̇. yn ermitano nimiztlaniya [110] ac tevatl nimā .ą̇. ca nevatl nicontzalo Auh tleyca yn otiya mictlā

God cast me into Mictlan. Because of this I am suffering, bearing on my back the wood[99] that the were-owls place on me. And there are many of us [there].

Then Hermit will say,
So be it! Please go, you wicked one! [185r]

THIS ONE SLEPT WITH HIS RELATIVE

Then Hermit will say,
I ask you, who are you?

Then he will say,
It is I, Martín.

[Hermit:]
Why did you go to Mictlan?

[Martín:]
Because I slept with a woman who was my relative. As a result I deeply offended God, as a result he cast me into Mictlan because I did not confess. And my relative also went to Mictlan because of me. Even though I forced her, I just did not confess [and therefore] both of us are continually burning. Likewise, some others who are there go along whipping me. There are many [there] who had sex with their relatives. This is my very great sin.

Then [Hermit] will say,
So be it! Please go, you wicked one!

[Addressing the audience:]
Furthermore, don't anyone do this!

CUILONI [185v]

Then Hermit will say,
I ask you, who are you?

Then [Cuiloni] will say,
It is I, Gonzalo.

[Hermit:]
Why did you go to Mictlan?

Then [Cuiloni] will say,

nimā .ꝗ. ca yehica centetl vey tlahtlacoltemictiani Cenca temamavhti macaᵒ niq-
uito Ca cenca temamavhti cenca nechpinavhtiya Cenca nechtēçacua nimā .ꝗ.
ayyoyavhe ancamo mizpinavhti¹¹¹ yn iCuac Oticchivh av in axcan ya ꝗn mizpi-
navhtiya ytencopaꜩinco .d. nimitzilviya ma niman xiquito av in Cuiloni nimā ꝗtoz
: Onotlaveliltic axcan ticmatiz Ca niCuilloni Cenca yc pachivia yn noyollo yn iquac
nechCuillontiaya nevatl niquinCuitlaviᶦtiaya yn ceꝗntin y notlan cochiya yntlacaᵒ
noyollo tlamatini amo nechcuillontizquia yn yevatl yn tlahtlacolli Cenca quitlavel-
litta ȳ .d. çan ic ovapachiovac yn ya ve[186r]cavh yn noviayā cemanavac : mochintin
Ovatoᶜᵒque Ovatlan micque Ca ça chiCueyntin acaltica Omomaquixtique ytenco-
paçinco yn .d. yehica tecuillontitinēque Auh ce tlacatl : ytlaço .d. Omomaꝗsti ytoca
: lot yvā Omētin ypilvā yc ticmatiz Ca cenca ꝗcualancaytta ȳ .d. yn aꝗꝗ teCuilontiti-
tinemi¹¹² Auh yntla nicotonani y naqualnemilliz yntla nimoyormellavani ca nechtlayocollizquia ȳ .d. av inin ca çan amo nimoyormellavhtia yc cenca nitoneva nechmecavitectinemi y nechcuilontique Ca nopāhpa Onpa Otemoque yn mictlan Ca çan
yevatlin .y. notlahtlacol nimā ꝗ. yn ermitano ma yvi tla xiyavh yn titlavelliloc nimā .ꝗ.
ma nimā xiquinchichacan yn amochintin : Ca vel tleco moneꝗ yn Cuillonime

[186v] DEPATLACHVIYANI

❡Nimā .ꝗ. yn ermitano ac tevatl .ꝗ. Ca nevatl nitepatlachviyani Ca nitominco nimā
Oc ceppa .ꝗ. Auh tleyca yn otiya mictlan nimā .ꝗ. Ca tevantin Çā nepanol . titopat-
lachviaya Ca cenca temahmavhti tlahtlacolli Auh amoh otechocti¹¹³ yn totlahtlacol
yc otechmotlaxilli .d. mictlā etc. nimā .ꝗ. yn ermitano O tla xiꝗnchichacan

Because of one single, great mortal sin. It is very frightening, let me not utter it! It is really frightening, it really shames me, it really renders me mute!

Then [Hermit] will say,
Alas! It didn't shame you when you did it! And now afterward it shames you? By God's command I say to you, Declare it now!

Then Cuiloni will say,
Woe is me! Now you will know that I am a *cuiloni.* I satisfied myself greatly when they did *cuiloni* to me. It was I who provoked others to sleep with me. If only I hadn't been such a coward they would not have done *cuiloni* to me. God really despises that particular sin. This was the reason that long ago [186r] the flood spread over the world. Everyone was carried away by the water, they died by the water because they went around doing *cuiloni.* By God's command only eight were saved in the boat. And one person, God's beloved, was saved along with his two children. His name was Lot.[100] Because of this you will know that God greatly despises those who go along doing *cuiloni* to others. If only I had desisted from my bad way of life, if only I had confessed, God would have had mercy on me. But I didn't confess, and because of this I am suffering terribly. Those who did *cuiloni* to me go along whipping me. They descended to Mictlan because of me. This is my sin.

Then Hermit will say,
So be it! Please go, you wicked one!

Then he will say [to the audience],
Now spit on them, all of you! It is necessary that the *cuilonimeh* be [cast] into the fire.[101]

[186V] *TEPATLACHHUIANI*

Then Hermit will say,
Who are you?

He will say,
It is I, a *tepatlachhuiani.* I am Domingo.[102]

Then again [Hermit] will say,
Why did you go to Mictlan?

Then he will say,
It was just that we did *tepatlachhuiani* to each other. Indeed, it is a very frightening sin. It didn't make us weep for our sins, therefore God cast us to Mictlan, etc.

Then Hermit will say [to the audience],
O please won't you all spit on them!

ĄUH YN ERMITANO NIMĀ
QMILVIZ YN MOCHINTIN

Nopilvanhe yn axcan Ca ya ovāquimocaq̇tique yn ixq̇ch yn tlahtlacolli ypāhpa temollo mi[c]tlā yvā Ovāquicaq̇ yn q̇nin Onpa tonevallo mictlan Auh yn axcan tla xicotonacan yn amacualnemilliz yehica amoh onpa āyazque maca° ytech ximixCu-itican yn aqualtin ma vel amitec motlalli yn teotlatoli [187r] nemaquixtilloni xic-neltocacan yn icel teotl yn jesuxpō y nelli .d. ynic a°maquistizque[114] Auh yntlacamo xiyectiyacan ȳtlaca° xicCueppacan yn amonemilliz yah amevā anq̇mati yn nevatl ya ninomaq̇stia

¶Auh nimā . q̇. yn ermitano tlahtlacatecolloyc tla xiviyan tla xicanati yn tlaveliloc xicvicacan yn mictlā Ca vel onpa moneq̇ yn inacayo yehica miyentin Oq̇miztlacavi Auh nimā .q̇. yn ermitano ma namechnotlalcavilli nopilvanhe Auh ca ya Cuicativi yn tlahtlacatecolo ynic q̇Cuicatizque yn ātexp̄ō ets.

AND THEN HERMIT WILL
SAY TO EVERYONE,[103]

O my children! Today you have heard about all of the sins because of which there is descending into Mictlan. You have also heard how there is suffering there in Mictlan. And now, desist from your bad way of living so that you will not go there! Don't follow the example of the bad ones. Place within yourselves the divine word, [187r] the instrument of salvation. Believe in Only Deity, Jesus Christ, the true God, so that you will be saved. And if you don't purify yourselves, if you don't turn around your lives, now you know that as for me, I am saved.[104]

And then Hermit will say,
O were-owls! Please go! Go grab the wicked one! Bring him to Mictlan! His body is needed there because he deceived many.

And then Hermit will say,
O my children, I take my leave of you!
At that, the were-owls go off singing.[105] In this manner they will sing for the Antichrist, etc.

NOTES

PROLOGUE

1. This is a somewhat looser translation of this proverb than that of Dibble and Anderson, made with linguistic assistance from Joe Campbell. Bernardino de Sahagún, *Florentine Codex: General History of the Things of New Spain*, ed. and trans. Charles E. Dibble and Arthur J. O. Anderson (Salt Lake City and Santa Fe: University of Utah and School of American Research, 1950–1982), Book 6, 247.

2. There are, of course, a multitude of Mexicans and Mexican Americans who live and work in Manhattan, many of whom likely consider themselves proud descendants of the Aztecs of precontact Mesoamerica. I mean no disrespect to them here. Regarding the term "Aztecs," Historians today commonly point out that this is not what the ethnic group that dominated central Mexico in the late Postclassic called themselves. These people, who ruled a sprawling empire from their capital city of Tenochtitlan, knew themselves as the Mexica (meh-SHEE-cah). From here forward, when referring specifically to this group and their close allies, I will use the term Mexica in lieu of Aztecs. When referring to Nahuatl-speaking peoples more generally, including those who were never conquered by the Mexica, I will use the term Nahuas. When referring to all Nahuatl-speaking peoples following the Spanish invasion, I will use the term Nahuas as well, since this is the term they used and continue to use for themselves. The one exception is in the use of the phrase "Aztec Antichrist," which I have coined to identify the literary creation of the Indigenous writer of the two Nahuatl Antichrist plays that are the subject of this book.

3. Mark Christensen, who works with both colonial Nahuatl and colonial Yucatec Maya religious texts, titled his first book *Nahua and Maya Catholicisms*. His point in insisting on the plural form of Catholicism is that using the singular form implies a uniformity of religious practice among Indigenous peoples that simply didn't exist then (nor does it exist today). I will follow this practice and refer to "Christianities" when discussing the many diverse responses Nahuas had to the religion of the Spanish friars who were their first teachers. See Mark Z. Christensen, *Nahua and Maya Catholicisms: Texts and Religion in Colonial Central Mexico and Yucatan* (Stanford, CA: Stanford University Press, 2013).

4. The manuscript is cataloged as Hispanic Society of America MS NS 3/1.

5. The phrase "hidden transcripts" was coined by James C. Scott in *Domination and the Arts of Resistance: Hidden Transcripts* (New Haven: Yale University Press, 1990).

6. Louise M. Burkhart, *Aztecs on Stage: Religious Theater in Colonial Mexico* (Norman: University of Oklahoma Press, 2012), 4.

7. Barry D. Sell and Louise M. Burkhart, *Nahuatl Theater*, Vol. 4, *Nahua Christianity in Performance* (Norman: University of Oklahoma Press, 2009), 9–12.

INTRODUCTION: FABIÁN'S NOTEBOOK

1. The phrase "chipping away on earth" is Dibble and Anderson's. The rest of the proverb's translation is my own. Sahagún, *Florentine Codex*, Book 6, 220–221. Linguistic assistance from Joe Campbell.

2. An excellent resource on the sacred deity bundles of the Nahuas is Molly H. Bassett, *The Fate of Earthly Things: Aztec Gods and God-Bodies* (Austin: University of Texas Press, 2015), 162–191.

3. Jason D. Haugen, "Uto-Aztecan Languages," Oxford Bibliographies Online, accessed July 25, 2018, https://www.oxfordbibliographies.com/view/document/obo-9780199772810/obo-9780199772810-0094.xml.

4. In the summer of 2009, I attended one such program at the Instituto de Docencia e Investigación Etnológica de Zacatecas (IDIEZ) in Zacatecas, Mexico. Directed by the passionate and learned Dr. John Sullivan, this program brought together native speakers of Nahuatl as instructors and tutors with students who received training in both modern and colonial variants of Nahuatl. Many fine scholars who today work with Nahuatl-language sources and/or Nahuatl-speaking communities got their start in one of Sullivan's summer courses.

5. John F. Schwaller, "The Expansion of Nahuatl as a Lingua Franca among Priests in Sixteenth-Century Mexico," *Ethnohistory* 59, no. 4 (2012): 675–690.

6. David Carrasco, ed., *The Oxford Encyclopedia of Mesoamerican Cultures* (New York: Oxford University Press, 2001), 2:254.

7. William F. Hanks, *Converting Words: Maya in the Age of the Cross* (Berkeley: University of California Press, 2010), 7.

8. "Reducir," Diccionario de la lengua Española, Real Academia Española, http://dle.rae.es/?w=reducir.

9. Hanks, *Converting Words*, 2, citing Covarrubias.

10. Joaquín García Icazbalceta, ed., *Códice franciscano, siglo XVI* (Mexico: Editorial Chavez Hayhoe, 1941), 58–59.

11. García Icazbalceta, 59.

12. Viviana Díaz Balsera, *The Pyramid Under the Cross: Franciscan Discourses of Evangelization and the Nahua Christian Subject in Sixteenth-Century Mexico* (Tucson: University of Arizona Press, 2005) and Justyna Olko and Agnieszka Brylak, "Defending Local Autonomy and Facing Cultural Trauma: A Nahua Order Against Idolatry, Tlaxcala, 1543." *Hispanic American Historical Review* 98, no. 4 (2018): 573–604.

13. For a pathbreaking exploration of the Latin education of Santa Cruz's students, see Andrew Laird, *Aztec Latin: Renaissance Learning and Nahuatl Traditions in Sixteenth-Century Mexico* (forthcoming).

14. Juan Bautista Viseo, *Sermonario en lengua mexicana* (Mexico: Casa de Diego López Dávalos, 1606), Prologo.

15. Barry David Sell, "Friars, Nahuas, and Books: Language and Expression in Colonial Nahuatl Publications," (PhD diss., University of California Los Angeles, 1993), 117.

16. Sahagún, *Florentine Codex*, Introductory volume, 83–84. Dibble and Anderson trans.

17. For an excellent recent study, see Kelly S. McDonough, *The Learned Ones: Nahua Intellectuals in Postconquest Mexico* (Tucson: University of Arizona Press, 2014). McDonough is one of a new generation of scholars who expertly and sensitively mingles modern Nahuatl and Nahua culture with their colonial antecedents. Andrew Laird's previously mentioned book *Aztec Latin* also contains detailed discussions of Santa Cruz's Latinists.

18. Sell, "Friars," 4.

19. Sell, 4.

20. Christensen, *Nahua and Maya Catholicisms*.

21. McDonough, *Learned Ones*, 20.

22. Just a brief selection of recent contributions include Camilla Townsend, *Here in This Year: Seventeenth-Century Nahuatl Annals of the Tlaxcala-Puebla Valley* (Stanford: Stanford University Press, 2010) and *Fifth Sun: A New History of the Aztecs* (New York: Oxford University Press, 2019), Benjamin Johnson, *Pueblos Within Pueblos: Tlaxilacalli Communities in Acolhuacan, Mexico, ca. 1272–1692* (Boulder: University Press of Colorado, 2018), Lori Boornazian Diel, *The Codex Mexicanus: A Guide to Life in Late Sixteenth-Century New Spain* (Austin: University of Texas Press, 2018), Olko and Brylak, "Defending Local Autonomy."

23. For Zapotecs see David Tavárez, *The Invisible War: Indigenous Devotions, Discipline, and Dissent in Colonial Mexico* (Stanford, CA: Stanford University Press, 2011), for Mixtecs see Kevin Terraciano, *The Mixtecs of Colonial Oaxaca: Ñudzahui History, Sixteenth Through Eighteenth Centuries* (Stanford, CA: Stanford University Press, 2004), for Yucatec Maya see Mark Z. Christensen, *The Teabo Manuscript: Maya Christian Copybooks, Chilam Balams, and Native Text Production in Yucatán* (Austin: University of Texas Press, 2016), and for K'iche' Maya see Gary G. Sparks, *Rewriting Maya Religion: Domingo de Vico, K'iche' Maya Intellectuals, and the* Theologia Indorum (Louisville: University Press of Colorado, 2020).

24. Online Nahuatl Dictionary, s.v. "tequitl," accessed June 18, 2019, https://nahuatl.uoregon.edu/content/tequitl. Molina was assisted in this project by his Nahua colleague Hernando de Ribas, a gifted scholar whose linguistic help was essential to the Franciscans in a number of important projects. See David Tavárez, "Nahua Intellectuals, Franciscan Scholars, and the *Devotio Moderna* in Colonial Mexico," *The Americas* 70, no. 2 (2013): 209.

25. Online Nahuatl Dictionary, s.v. "tlachihualli," accessed June 18, 2019, https://nahuatl.uoregon.edu/content/tlachihualli.

26. Online Nahuatl Dictionary, s.v. "tlatequipanolli," accessed June 18, 2019, https://nahuatl.uoregon.edu/content/tlatequipanolli.

27. In a personal communication (December 2020) Mark Christensen pointed out that there are a few examples of Indigenous authors stating their identities in Yucatecan Maya texts like the Chilam Balam of Ixil and the Teabo manuscript. See Christensen, *The Teabo Manuscript*, 19–20.

28. Cited in Martin Austin Nesvig, *Ideology and Inquisition: The World of the Censors in Early Mexico* (New Haven, CT: Yale University Press, 2009), 118.

29. Francisco Antonio Lorenzana, *Primero, y segundo, celebrados en la muy noble, y muy leal Ciudad de México, presidiendo el Illmo. Y Rmo. Señor D. Fr. Alonso de Montúfar, En los años de 1555, y 1565* (Mexico: Imprenta del Superior Gobierno Hogal, 1769), 144.

30. Christensen, *Nahua and Maya Catholicisms*, 15.

31. While this was the case in central Mexico, Gary Sparks has argued that in Guatemala the Dominicans were much more lenient regarding potentially problematic issues of translation. See Gary G. Sparks, *Rewriting Maya Religion: Domingo de Vico, K'iche' Maya Intellectuals, and the Theologia Indorum* (Louisville: University Press of Colorado, 2020).

32. Tavárez, "Nahua Intellectuals," 203–235.

33. David Tavárez, "A Banned Sixteenth-Century Biblical Text in Nahuatl," *Ethnohistory* 60, no. 4 (2013): 759–762.

34. Tavárez, "A Banned Sixteenth-Century Biblical Text." The other copy is found in the manuscript known as the *Miscelánea sagrada*, MS 1477, Colección Archivos y Manuscritos, Biblioteca Nacional de México, ff. 1–72.

35. Bernardino de Sahagún, *Comiença un exercicio en lengua mexicana sacado del Sancto Evango. y distribuido por todos los días de la semana*, MS 1484, Ayer Collection, Newberry Library, Chicago, f. 43r.

36. The original reads: Tan varia y tan indigesta y confusa. Juan de la Anunciación, *Sermonario en lengua mexicana* (Mexico: Antonio Ricardo, 1577), f. 3r.

37. The Tlaxcaltecah spoke a variant of Nahuatl that differed from the Nahuatl spoken in Tenochtitlan and the Valley of Mexico in certain characteristic ways. A number of these characteristics are found in the writings of Aquino; the following is a brief summary for the linguists reading this book. The most notable piece of evidence that Aquino spoke an eastern variant of Nahuatl is the presence in his writing of Nahuatl's archaic preterite suffix, *-qui*. Scholars have carefully mapped out how the Nahuatl language underwent progressive changes from ancient times through the contact period and on to the present. These studies have shown that in distant times, Nahuatl verbs in the preterite tense bore the suffix *-qui*. For example, the verb *mochihua*, "to do, make," would have been *omochiuhqui* in this early period before contact. However, by the time of contact, central valley Nahuatl had dropped the *-qui* suffix (rendering *omochiuh*), while the archaic form lingered in the eastern variants. The presence of preterite verbs using *-qui* is ubiquitous—though not exclusive—in Aquino's writing. Other pieces of linguistic evidence linking Aquino to the eastern region include his use of the *-qui* suffix for certain future tense constructions (such as *yezqui*, "he/she/it will be"), the presence of *ya* instead of *ye* in items like *yaquine* (vs. central Nahuatl's *yequene*), and the use of *mo-* as the universal reflexive prefix (see Townsend, *Here in This Year*, 55–58). The best attested examples of colonial eastern Nahuatl come from Tlaxcala, although many of these features can be found in variants from other eastern regions as well (Julia Madajczak, personal communication, November 18, 2015, and Gordon Whittaker, personal communication, May 22, 2016). Linking Aquino specifically to Tlaxcala based on linguistic evidence alone is difficult. It is worth noting that he does retain one characteristically Tlaxcalan feature: his use of *çovatl* (*zohuatl*) in place of *cihuatl* (woman) (Lidia Gómez García, personal communication, July 2018). Additionally, there are only two *altepemeh* (pl. of *altepetl*) mentioned by name in Aquino's notebook; both appear in *Antichrist and the Hermit*, and one of these is Tlaxcala (see the speech of Cihuacoatl on f. 173r).

38. James Lockhart, *The Nahuas After the Conquest: A Social and Cultural History of the Indians of Central Mexico, Sixteenth Through Eighteenth Centuries* (Stanford, CA: Stanford University Press, 1992), chap. 7.

39. Lockhart, *The Nahuas*, 304–314.

40. Aquino incorporates a host of common Spanish loans for religious and nonreligious terms. Standard examples include *dios*, "God," *cruz*, "cross," and *santo*, "saint." Other loans include *mandamiento*, "commandment" (spelled *mantaiyento*), *sombrero*, "hat" (spelled *sonprelo*), *escuela*, "school" (spelled *ixcuela*), *candela*, "candle" (spelled *cantella*), and *sacerdote*, "priest" (spelled *saceltote*). Aquino also inflects many of these loans. Notable examples

include *mobonete*, "your cap," *tisantamariatzin*, "you are [revered] Saint Mary," and *ticristiano*, "you are a Christian." Another fascinating indicator of Stage Two Nahuatl is Aquino's peculiar spellings of many of the loanwords, some of which are noted above. When Nahuas first came into contact with and began to learn Spanish, it became evident that there were certain sounds in the Spanish repertoire that were not present in the Nahuatl. When speaking, they tended to substitute Nahuatl sounds for those Spanish sounds that were foreign to them (Lockhart, *The Nahuas*, 294). When Nahuas began writing, these substitutions were transferred to their spelling of Spanish loanwords. Common examples drawn from Aquino's notebook include *c* for *g* substitution (*mactalena* for "Magdalena"), *r* for *l* (*diabro* for "diablo"), *t* for *d* (*saceltote* for "sacerdote"), and *p* for *b* (*anprossio* for "Ambrosio"). In some cases Aquino makes multiple substitutions in a single word, as in *artal* (for "altar") where he substitutes *r* for *l* at the beginning of the word and *l* for *r* at the end. In his catalog description of the manuscript, Karl Hiersemann categorized Aquino's writing as "a barbaric Latin and no less-corrupt Spanish." However, the particular ways that Aquino records text in his second language is not corrupt but idiomatic; he spells precisely as Nahuas pronounced Spanish words during this particular phase of contact. These idiomatic or noncanonical spellings are one of the hallmarks of Nahuatl written *by Nahuas*. To investigators like me, they practically leap off of the manuscript page, an unmistakable tell of the Indigenous identity of the writer.

41. Aquino writes /w/ as -*v* as opposed to -*hu/-uh*. Barry Sell writes that "by the end of the sixteenth century, *hu* became the prevailing standard . . . especially in church-related texts" (Sell and Burkhart, *Nahuatl Theater*, Vol. 1, 9). Aquino writes the phoneme [tˢ] in a host of ways including -*tz*, -*ç*, -*t̢*, and a modified "*z*" with a small vertical shaft before it. Of these, the t-cedilla was comparatively rare in the sources and is probably an indicator of a date somewhat earlier in the sixteenth century. Karttunen and Lockhart write "as early as the mid-sixteenth century the convention of *tz* had become standard" (Karttunen and Lockhart, *Nahuatl in the Middle Years*, 66).

42. While it is reasonable to state that the texts in Aquino's notebook were redacted between c. 1560 and 1600, chapter 2 will argue that certain texts, such as the two Antichrist plays, may very well have been composed one to two decades prior.

43. Lockhart, *The Nahuas*, 126.

44. Lockhart, 126.

45. In a personal communication with me, William Taylor suggested that Aquino could have been a mestizo akin to Diego Muñoz Camargo or Diego de Valadés, who came from privileged backgrounds but never used the title "don" (email correspondence, February 23, 2018).

46. Sahagún, *Florentine Codex*, Book 3, 11.

47. Gordon Whittaker has recently shown, however, that the Nahuas had developed a hieroglyphic writing system by the time of the Spanish invasion. Texts such as those he analyzes recorded speech and could be read as in any other writing system. Gordon Whittaker,

Deciphering Aztec Hieroglyphs: A Guide to Nahuatl Writing (Berkeley: University of California Press, 2021).

48. Sahagún, *Florentine Codex*, Book 1, 5. Dibble and Anderson trans.

49. Sahagún, *Florentine Codex*, Book 3, 13, and 23. Dibble and Anderson trans. The words *tlacatecolotl* and its plural form *tlatlacatecoloh* are high-frequency words in Nahuatl Christian texts, a fact which reflects the ubiquity of devils and demons in the thinking, writing, and preaching of the friars. My general practice is to leave terms like these untranslated, since not doing so implicitly suggests an easy equivalence between Indigenous and Euro-Christian concepts. However, in the case of this word in particular I will make an exception, due to the possibility that the reader will find repeated use of *tlacatecolotl* and *tlatlacatecoloh* a stumbling block. Instead, I will opt for "were-owl," the term employed by Gordon Whittaker in *Deciphering Aztec Hieroglyphs*. It is hoped that the oddness of this term will encourage the reader to remember that the original term was not a straightforward translation of "demon."

50. Sahagún, *Florentine Codex*, Book 3, 11.

51. Bernardino de Sahagún, *Adiciones, apéndice a la postilla y ejercicio cotidiano*, ed. and trans. by Arthur J. O. Anderson (Mexico: UNAM, Instituto de Investigaciones Históricas, 1993), 180.

52. Alfredo López Austin, "Cosmovision," in *The Oxford Encyclopedia of Mesoamerican Cultures*, ed. Davíd Carrasco (New York: Oxford University Press, 2001), 268–274.

53. J. Jorge Klor de Alva, "Christianity and the Aztecs," *San Jose Studies* 5 (1979), 15.

54. Following Burkhart in her introduction to *Words and Worlds Turned Around: Indigenous Christianities in Colonial Latin America*, ed. David Tavárez (Boulder: University Press of Colorado, 2017), 7, where she cites numerous examples.

55. Burkhart's seminal study is *The Slippery Earth: Nahua-Christian Moral Dialogue in Sixteenth-Century Mexico* (Tucson: University of Arizona Press, 1989). All those who follow her, myself especially, are indebted to Burkhart's contributions in the field.

56. See for example Yanna Yannakakis, *The Art of Being In-Between: Native Intermediaries, Indian Identity, and Local Rule in Colonial Oaxaca* (Durham: Duke University Press, 2008) and McDonough, *The Learned Ones*.

57. Mary Louise Pratt, "Arts of the Contact Zone," *Profession* (1991): 36.

58. This is the perspective of Roxanne Dunbar-Ortiz in, for example, *An Indigenous Peoples' History of the United States* (Boston: Beacon Press, 2014).

59. In chapter 2 of my dissertation, I argue that another of the texts Aquino copied into his notebook was directly influenced by a sermon of St. Vincent's titled *De septem Luciferi capitaneis* (On the seven captains of Lucifer). Ben Leeming, "Aztec Antichrist: Christianity, Transculturation, and Apocalypse on Stage in Two Sixteenth-Century Nahuatl Dramas" (PhD diss., University at Albany, SUNY, 2017), 74.

60. Sell and Burkhart, *Nahuatl Theater*, Vol. 1, ix.

61. More often apocalypticism is used as a framework for understanding the Franciscans. In the historiography the emphasis has long been on these figures and less on their Indigenous colleagues and other Indigenous writers. A recent exception is Mark Christiansen, *Aztec and Maya Apocalypses: Old-World Tales of Doom in a New-World Setting* (Norman: University of Oklahoma Press, 2022).

CHAPTER 1: FIRST THEATER OF THE AMERICAS

1. This account is taken from Antonio de Ciudad Real, *Tratado curioso y docto de las grandezas de la Nueva España*, Vol. 2, ed. Josefina García Quintana y Víctor M. Castillo Farreas (Mexico: UNAM, 1993).

2. Ciudad Real, *Tratado curioso*, 101.

3. Ciudad Real, *Tratado curioso*, 102.

4. Barry D. Sell and Louise M. Burkhart, *Nahuatl Theater*, Vol. 1, *Death and Life in Colonial Nahua Mexico* (Norman: University of Oklahoma Press, 2004), 142–143. Burkhart trans.

5. Sell and Burkhart, *Nahuatl Theater*, Vol. 4, 47.

6. Hanks, *Converting Words*.

7. Sahagún, *Florentine Codex*, Book 8, 8.

8. Cited in Fernando Horcasitas, *El teatro Náhuatl: Épocas novohispana y moderna* (Mexico City: UNAM, 1974), 562.

9. In order these are from: Robert Ricard, *The Spiritual Conquest of Mexico* (Berkeley: University of California Press, 1966); Horcasitas, *El teatro náhuatl*; and Othón Arróniz, *Teatro de evangelización en Nueva España* (Mexico: UNAM, 1977).

10. Sell and Burkhart, *Nahuatl Theater*, Vol. 1, ix.

11. Cited in Agnieszka Brylak, "Los Espectáculos de los nahuas prehispánicos: entre antropología y teatro" (PhD diss., University of Warsaw, 2015), 209–210.

12. Brylak, "Espectáculos," 53.

13. Louise M. Burkhart, *Holy Wednesday: A Nahua Drama from Early Colonial Mexico* (Philadelphia: University of Pennsylvania Press, 1996), 43.

14. Lockhart, *Nahuas*, 243.

15. Burkhart, *Holy Wednesday*, 46; Karttunen defines this term as "example, model, pattern." Frances Karttunen, *Analytical Dictionary of Nahuatl* (Norman: University of Oklahoma Press, 1992), 163, https://nahuatl.uoregon.edu/content/neixcuitilli.

16. Aesop's Fables were translated into Nahuatl sometime in the middle years of the sixteenth century. For more information see Andrew Laird, "A Mirror for Mexican Princes: Reconsidering the Context and Latin Source for the Nahuatl Translation of Aesop's Fables," *Brief Forms in Medieval and Renaissance Hispanic Literature* (2017): 132–167.

17. G. R. Owst, cited in Edgar Schell, *Strangers and Pilgrims: From the Castle of Persever-ance to King Lear* (Chicago: University of Chicago Press, 1983), 11.

18. Cited in Ricard, *Spiritual Conquest*, 201.

19. Daniel Breining, *Dramatic and Theatrical Censorship of Sixteenth-Century New Spain* (Lewiston, NY: E. Mellen Press, 2002), 76–77.

20. In *Aztecs on Stage* Burkhart lists twenty-nine (220–224). Since publishing that list, Burkhart has identified three additional scripts—all of Passion plays—which brings the count to thirty-two (personal communication, July 8, 2019). Aquino's raises the tally to thirty-four. There are, undoubtedly, more that will come to light in time.

21. Barry Sell address the matter of dating the plays in his essay "Nahuatl Plays in Context," in *Nahuatl Theater*, Vol. 1.

22. Burkhart, *Holy Wednesday*, 52.

23. Sell and Burkhart, *Nahuatl Theater*, Vol. 4, xii.

24. Klaus Aichele, *Das Antichristdrama des Mittelalters der Reformation und Gegenrefor-mation* (The Hague: Martinus Nijhoff, 1974).

25. Richard Kenneth Emmerson, Keith Glaeske, and David F. Hult, eds., *Antichrist and Judgment Day: The Middle French Jour du Jugement* (Asheville: Pegasus Press, 1998).

26. See Emmerson, Glaeske, and Hult, *Antichrist and Judgment Day*.

27. David Mills, *The Chester Mystery Cycle: A New Edition with Modernised Spelling* (East Lansing, MI: Colleagues Press, 1992), f. 388.

28. See Ursula Schulze, ed., *Churre Weltgerichtsspiel* (Berlin: Erich Schmidt, 1993).

29. Léo Rouanet, ed., *Colección de autos, farsas, y coloquios del siglo XVI*, 4 vols. (Hildesheim and New York: Georg Olms, 1979).

30. Hilaire Kallendorf, e-mail message to author, January 14, 2016.

31. Richard K. Emmerson, e-mail message to author, February 10, 2015.

32. Miguel M. García-Bermejo Giner, *Catálogo del teatro español del siglo XVI. Índice de piezas conservadas, perdidas y representadas* (Salamanca: Ediciones Universidad de Salamanca, 1996), 252.

33. Even though these plays are referred to as "Aquino's" the question of authorship is a difficult one to answer definitively. As this chapter will argue, Aquino may not have been the original composer of the plays but merely the one who collected them, copying them into his devotional notebook.

34. The French *Mystère de l'Antéchrist et du jugement de Dieu* performed in Modane in 1580 is one, and the fourteenth-century Middle French *Jour du jugement* is another; Emmerson, Glaeske, and Hult, *Antichrist and Judgment Day*, xx.

35. The question of when the Antichrist *neixcuitilli* were intended to be performed is a difficult one to answer with certainty. Mystery plays were most commonly associated with Corpus Christi in the European tradition, which as a moveable feast would occur sometime

in May or June. However, the strong influence of the morality genre in *Hermit* and the repeated theme of confession suggests a Lenten performance, at least for that play. Finally, eschatological themes (especially including sibyls and the Antichrist) are strongly associated in the church calendar with Advent. Therefore, we must also consider this a possible season for the performance of one or both plays.

36. Sell and Burkhart, *Nahuatl Theater*, Vol. 1, 29.

37. Sell and Burkhart, *Nahuatl Theater*, Vol. 1, 191. Burkhart trans.

38. Recall that my use of "were-owl" serves as an easier-to-pronounce alternative to the Nahuatl word *tlacatecolotl* (pl. *tlatlacatecoloh*), the word used in colonial Nahuatl-Christian texts to name the devil and demons. See the introduction, note 49.

39. Schell, *Strangers and Pilgrims*, 11.

40. *Códice franciscano*, in Joaquín García Icazbalceta, ed., *Códice franciscano, siglo XVI* (Mexico: Editorial Chavez Hayhoe, 1941), 41.

41. *Códice franciscano*, 41.

42. Passages are all from Sell and Burkhart, *Nahuatl Theater*, Vol. 1, 213, 165, and 259. Translations by the authors.

43. Note that when referring to the malevolent being of medieval apocalypticism I will include the article "the," as in "the Antichrist will arrive at the end of time." However, when referring to the character in Aquino's Nahuatl dramas, the article will be dropped leaving us with "Antichrist will say," etc.

44. Passages are all from *Antichrist and the Hermit*, ff. 158r, 164r, 160v-161r.

45. Sell and Burkhart, *Nahuatl Theater*, Vol. 4, 321. Burkhart trans.

46. David J. Leigh, "The Doomsday Mystery Play: An Eschatological Morality," *Modern Philology* 67, no. 3 (1970): 214.

47. Leigh, 214.

48. Moshe Lazar, ed. and trans. *Le jugement dernier (Lo jutgamen general): Drame provencal du XVe siecle*. Paris: Klincksieck, 1971; Ursula Schulze, ed. *Churre weltgerichtsspiel*. Erich Schmidt Verlag, 1993; and Gustave Cohen, ed., *Nativités et moralités Liégeoises du Moyen-Age* (Bruxelles: Palais Des Académies, 1953).

49. Emmerson and Hult, *Antichrist and Judgment Day*, 73.

50. José Guadalajara Medina, "La venida del Anticristo: Terror y moralidad en la Edad Media hispánica." *Culturas populares* 4 (2007): 7. Viviana Díaz Balsera uses the term "discursive terror" to refer to virtually the same thing. See Viviana Díaz Balsera, *The Pyramid Under the Cross: Franciscan Discourses of Evangelization and the Nahua Christian Subject in Sixteenth-Century Mexico* (Tucson: University of Arizona Press, 2005), 41.

51. Sell and Burkhart, *Nahuatl Theater*, Vol. 4, 329. Burkhart trans.

52. Sell and Burkhart, *Nahuatl Theater*, Vol. 4, 331. Burkhart trans.

53. Steven E. Turley, *Franciscan Spirituality and Mission in New Spain, 1524–1599: Conflict Beneath the Sycamore Tree (Luke 19: 1–10)* (New York: Routledge, 2014).

54. Exemplars consulted for this study include Richard K Emmerson, "Antichrist as Anti-Saint: The Significance of Abbot Adso's *Libellus de Antichristo.*" *Benedictine Review* 30, no. 2 (1979): 175–190 and *Antichrist in the Middle Ages: A Study of Medieval Apocalypticism, Art and Literature* (Seattle: University of Washington Press, 1981); José Guadalajara Medina, *Las profecías del Anticristo en la Edad Media* (Barcelona: Editorial Gredos, 1996) and *El Anticristo en la España medieval* (Madrid: Ediciones del Laberinto, 2004); Bernard McGinn, *Visions of the End: Apocalyptic Traditions in the Middle Ages* (New York: Columbia University Press, 1998); Delno C. West, "Medieval Ideas of Apocalyptic Mission and the Early Franciscans in Mexico," *The Americas* 45, no. 3 (1989): 293–313; and Delno C. West and Sandra Zimdars-Swartz, *Joachim of Fiore: A Study in Spiritual Perception and History* (Bloomington, IN: Indiana University Press, 1983).

55. One of these is in a language other than Nahuatl. Fray Maturino Gilberti's 1559 publication *Diálogo de doctrina Cristiana en lengua de Michoacán* contains extensive discussions of Antichrist's coming in the Last Days as well as recommendations of how Indigenous Christians should prepare for and respond to his advent. See Moisés Mendoza "Maturino Gilberti, Traductor: Dialogo de la Doctrina Cristiana en lengua de Mechuacan." (PhD diss., Universidad Nacional Autónoma de Mexico, 2008).

56. David Tavárez writes that Bautista's *Libro de la miseria y breuedad de la vida del hombre* is actually an un-acknowledged translation of Fray Luis de Granada's 1554 *Libro de la oracion y meditación*; see Tavárez, "Nahua Intellectuals," 231.

57. Juan Bautista, *Libro de la miseria y breuedad de la vida del hombre* (Mexico: López Davalos, 1604), f. 81r.

58. These are from Sell and Burkhart, *Nahuatl Theater*, Vol. 1, 199, Vol. 4, 329, and Vol. 4, 381. Translations by the authors.

59. Francisco Fernández Del Castillo and Elías Trabulse, *Libros y libreros en el siglo XVI. 2a Ed.*, facsimile ed. (Mexico: Archivo General de la Nación [y] Fondo de Cultura Económica, 1982), 513.

60. Berenice Alcántara-Rojas counts just two or three instances in entire corpus of colonial doctrinal Nahuatl writing. Berenice Alcántara Rojas, "La 'mala nueva': La llegada del cristianismo en sermones en lengua náhuatl de la primera mitad del siglo xvi" *Iberoamericana* 19, no. 71 (2019), 88, n. 7. The three sources noted are the Dominican *Doctrina cristiana en lengua española y mexicana* (1548), the *Coloquios y doctrina christiana* (1564), and the Appendix to Book 1 of the Florentine Codex. I add one more: in the sermon for the fourteenth Sunday after Pentecost from the Nahuatl sermonary overseen by Sahagún (Ayer MS 1485, 1540–1563).

61. Codex Magliabechiano, 150 13.3 (B.R. 232), facsimile ed. Austria: Akademische Druck- u. Verlagsanstalt, 1970, Biblioteca nazionale centrale di Firenze, http://www.famsi .org/research/graz/magliabechiano/thumbs_0.html.

62. Since early colonial times, *cuiloni* has been translated "sodomite" and *cuilontia* as "sodomy." Since these terms are deeply laden with cultural baggage, I follow the practice

of leaving them untranslated. I follow Pete Sigal in using the phrase "do *cuiloni* to" in *The Flower and the Scorpion: Sexuality and Ritual in Early Nahua Culture* (Durham, NC: Duke University Press, 2011), 99–101.

63. Lockhart, *Nahuas*, 403.

CHAPTER 2: AMERICAN APOCALYPSE

1. "Proceso inquisitorial del cacique de Tetzcoco," in *Publicaciones del Archivo General de la Nación*. Vol. 1 (Mexico: Eusebio Gómez de la Puente, 1910), 84.

2. Robert Ricard, *The Spiritual Conquest of Mexico* (Berkeley: University of California Press, 1966), 255.

3. Dereck Daschke, "Apocalypse and Trauma," in *The Oxford Handbook of Apocalyptic Literature*, ed. John J. Collins (Oxford: Oxford University Press, 2014) 457–472.

4. Matthew 24, Mark 13, and Luke 21.

5. Fray Toribio de Benavente, *Motolinía's History of the Indians of New Spain*, trans. Francis Borgia Steck (Washington, DC: American Academy of Franciscan History, 1951), 232. All translations from Motolinía's *Historia* are by Francis Borgia Steck.

6. Benavente, *Motolinía's History*, 178.

7. Benavente, 180.

8. Benavente, 245.

9. Benavente, 182.

10. Benavente, 337.

11. Nesvig, *Ideology*, 105.

12. Benavente, *History of the Indians*, 186.

13. Kenneth R. Mills and William B. Taylor, eds., *Colonial Spanish America: A Documentary History* (Rowman & Littlefield Publishers, 2002), 61.

14. Benavente, *History of the Indians*, 53, cited in Patricia Lopes Don, *Bonfires of Culture: Franciscans, Indigenous Leaders, and the Inquisition in Early Mexico, 1524–1540* (Norman: University of Oklahoma Press, 2010), 38.

15. Lopes Don, *Bonfires*, 39.

16. Lopes Don, 39.

17. Benavente, *History of the Indians*, 100.

18. James Lockhart and Enrique Otte, eds., *Letters and People of the Spanish Indies: Sixteenth Century* (Cambridge: Cambridge University Press, 1976), 215.

19. Cited in Lopes Don, *Bonfires*, 42.

20. Michael Stogre, *That the World May Believe: The Development of Papal Social Thought on Aboriginal Rights* (Sherbrooke, QC: Canada: Editions Paulines, 1992), 87.

21. Lopes Don, *Bonfires*, 45.

22. Lopes Don, 45–51.

23. David Tavárez, citing Bishop Diego de Hevia y Valdés of Oaxaca in *The Invisible War: Indigenous Devotions, Discipline, and Dissent in Colonial Mexico* (Stanford: Stanford University Press, 2011), 3.

24. It should be noted that not *all* Indigenous rulers were allied against Christianity and the friars. As Lopes Don points out, the *tlahtohqueh* adopted a wide variety of strategies as they sought to negotiate positions of influence within the new colonial regime. See Lopes Don, introduction.

25. Nesvig, *Ideology*, 107.

26. Tavárez, *Invisible War*, 35; Nesvig, *Ideology*, 109; Lopes Don, *Bonfires*, 45.

27. Tavárez, *Invisible War*, 35.

28. Robert Haskett, *Indigenous Rulers: An Ethnohistory of Town Government in Colonial Cuernavaca* (Albuquerque: University of New Mexico Press, 1991), 10.

29. Lockhart, *Nahuas*, 102.

30. Lopes Don, *Bonfires*, 41.

31. J. Jorge Klor de Alva, "Martin Ocelotl: Clandestine Cult Leader," in *Struggle and Survival in Colonial America*, ed. David G. Sweet and Gary B. Nash (Berkeley: University of California Press, 1981), 130.

32. Richard E. Greenleaf, *Zumárraga and the Mexican Inquisition: 1536–1543* (Berkeley: Academy of American Franciscan History, 1961), 50–52; *Procesos de indios*, 1–16.

33. In the Gospel of Matthew 4:19. Greenleaf, *Zumárraga*, 54.

34. Greenleaf, *Zumárraga*, 55.

35. Lopes Don, *Bonfires*, 168–169.

36. Lopes Don, 72.

37. An anonymous reviewer of this book pointed out that in their testimony before the Inquisition the noblemen who were present at this meeting had nothing to say about Don Carlos's supposed idolatry, instead reporting only that people, perhaps *macehualtin*, were continuing to ascend Mt. Tlaloc to conduct precontact-style rituals. This somewhat undermines the dichotomy established in this chapter between "recalcitrant *tlahtohqueh*" and "impressionable *macehualtin*." Additionally, since these men were themselves powerful Indigenous lords and future *tlahtohqueh*, this also subtly undermines the dichotomy between "recalcitrant *tlahtohqueh*" and "mendicant friars." The argument put forth in this chapter risks over-generalizing the responses and positions of large swathes of the population, and so I am grateful for this correction and the opportunity to restate that not *all* members of either class, *tlahtohqueh* or *macehualtin*, behaved in the same fashion. The argument being made here is that certain elements of the Indigenous nobility presented a serious challenge to the friars' mission and were therefore identified as "Antichrists" by the composer of the two *neixcuitilli* under study here.

38. Klor de Alva, "Martin Ocelotl," 137, 139.

39. See Greenleaf, *Zumárraga*, 52.

40. Patrick Thomas Hajovsky, *On the Lips of Others: Moteuczoma's Fame in Aztec Monuments and Rituals* (Austin: University of Texas Press, 2015), 52.

41. John Bierhorst, *A Nahuatl-English Dictionary and Concordance to the Cantares Mexicanos* (Stanford, CA: Stanford University Press, 1985), 143.

42. Tavárez, *Invisible War*, 37.

43. Tavárez, 37.

44. Note I am not stating that it actually *was* copied out of the records of Zumárraga's Inquisition. The anonymous reviewer referenced above cautioned that this is what the argument seems to imply. To be clear, this is not what I am arguing, at least not in the sense that the playwright literally had access to the official records of the Inquisition. Rather, what I am hypothesizing is that the playwright was one of the Nahuas closely connected with the circle of friars to whom this information was available, regularly discussed, and for whom it was common knowledge.

45. *Procesos de indios*, 11.

46. *Procesos de indios*, 11.

47. There are notable examples of exceptions to this overly neat distinction. Bartolomé de las Casas, a Dominican, was famously opposed to the application of any physical coercion or punishment of the Indigenous population.

48. Joaquín García Icazbalceta, *Don fray Juan de Zumárraga: primer obispo y arzobispo de México* (Mexico: Andrade y Morales, 1881), 122.

49. The *Ordenanzas* are reproduced in Spanish in Mina Garcia Soormally, *Ideology and the Construction of the Spanish Empire* (Louisville: University Press of Colorado, 2019), 169–173.

50. Soormally, *Ideology*, 172.

51. *Procesos de indios*, 207; cited in Lopes Don, *Bonfires*, 6; Lopes Don translation.

52. Nesvig, *Ideology*, 107.

53. Nesvig, 110.

54. Sahagún, *Florentine Codex*, Introductory volume, 48. Dibble and Anderson trans.

55. Fernando Cervantes, *The Devil in the New World: The Impact of Diabolism in New Spain* (New Haven: Yale University Press, 1997), 8.

56. Jorge Cañizares-Esguerra, *Puritan Conquistadors: Iberianizing the Atlantic, 1550–1700* (Berkeley: Stanford University Press, 2006), 5.

57. Cervantes, *The Devil*, 8.

58. Lopes Don, *Bonfires*, 182–183.

59. Lopes Don, 185. This theory warrants a couple of qualifications. First of all, there was a long history of diabolism in Europe over the centuries preceding contact. Also, as Cervantes notes, the devil arrived as soon as Europeans set foot on Caribbean sand in the late fifteenth century. Although she may not mean to do so, Lopes Don gives the impression that this was a novel innovation of the 1540s. That was simply not the case. In fact, the Inquisition records from 1536 to 1540 are filled with references to the devil, the devil's association

with the *teteoh* and precontact religious practices, as well as with the "idolaters." Second, it's difficult to know precisely *when* the "theological linkage" between idolatry/idolaters and the devil occurred, since there wasn't a great deal of theology happening in New Spain in the first two decades after the invasion. Nor was there much writing and publishing. The first book published in the Americas was Zumárraga's 1539 *Breve y mas compendiosa doctrina cristiana* (Brief and most compendious Christian doctrine). The very earliest substantive Nahuatl writing that survives—civil or religious—dates to the early 1540s, with the first imprint in the language being either Alonso de Molina's or Pedro de Gante's Nahuatl catechisms, both around 1546 or 1547. (Justyna Olko and Agnieszka Brylak published what they claim to be the earliest surviving dated piece of Nahuatl writing, an order by the Indigenous governor of Tlaxcala seeking the arrest and punishment of people caught committing certain illicit activities. The document is dated 1543. Olko and Brylak, "Defending Local Autonomy.") However, regardless of precisely when the rhetorical strategy of diabolization emerged, it came to permeate the doctrinal writing produced under the friars' supervision starting in the 1540s and would have been one of the most often-heard messages by Indigenous people from then onward.

60. Fray Bernardino de Sahagún, *Siguense unos sermones de dominicas y de santos en lengua Mexicana*, MS 1485, 1540–1563, Ayer Collection, Newberry Library, Chicago, p. 5. The sermons were edited by Sahagún in 1563.

61. Mario Alberto Sánchez Aguilera translated MS 1485 as part of his dissertation. See Mario Alberto Sánchez Aguilera, "La Doctrina Desde el Púlpito: Los Sermones del Ciclo de Navidad de Fray Bernardino de Sahagún" (PhD diss., UNAM, 2019). In 2022, this was published as an edited edition, Bernardino de Sahagún, *Siguense unos sermones de dominicas y de sanctos en lengua mexicana, Ms. 1485, Ayer Collection, The Newberry Library* (Mexico City: Universidad Nacional Autónoma de Mexico). In 2021–2022, I will be working on the first English translation of Sahagún's sermonary in 2021–2022, thanks to funding from the National Endowment for the Humanities. As of the time of this book's publication, I am under advanced contract with University of Utah Press to publish this work.

62. Domincans, *Doctrina cristiana en lengua española y mexicana* (Madrid: Ediciones Cultura Hispánica, 1944 [1548]), ff. 39v–40r.

63. Fray Andrés de Olmos, *Tratado de hechicerías y sortilegios (1553)*, ed. and trans. Georges Baudot (Mexico: UNAM, 1990), 42–43. This is my retranslation of the Nahuatl text.

64. Georges Baudot, *Utopia and History in Mexico*, trans. Bernard R. and Thelma Ortiz de Montellano (Niwot: University Press of Colorado, 1995), 244.

65. Baudot, *Utopia*, 244.

66. Lockhart, *The Nahuas*, 102. Note that the classification *pipiltin* (sing. *pilli*, "noble") refers in a broad sense to all categories of elite Nahua society: the *huei tlahtoani* (emperor), the *tlahtohqueh* (rulers), and the *teteuctin* (lords) were all *pipiltin*.

67. *Procesos de indios idolátras y hechiceras*, 56–57.
68. Olmos, *Tratado de hechicerías*, 48–49.
69. Horcasitas, *El teatro náhuatl*, 50 and 563.
70. Mendieta, for example. Cited in Horcasitas, 562–563.
71. Horcasitas, 563.

CHAPTER 3: A NAHUA CHRISTIAN WRITES BACK

1. Mary Louise Pratt, "Arts of the Contact Zone," *Profession* (1991): 35.

2. Much of the following has been shaped by my work on a multi-year, international collaboration to translate a sixteenth-century collection of sermons held at the Biblioteca Nacional de México (MS 1482). The project is titled "Sermones en Mexicano" and is headed by Berenice Alcántara Rojas of the Instituto de Investigaciones Históricas at UNAM. For more information, see https://sermonesenmexicano.unam.mx/index.html.

3. Other examples of lexical derivation include *tlaneltoquiliztli* for "faith" (lit. "the act of following something as true"), *tlateotoca* for "to idolize" (lit. "to follow something as a *teotl* [deity]"), and *mamazouhtihcac* for "crucified" (lit. "stands with arms outstretched").

4. Louise Burkhart's study of *tlahtlacolli* remains the standard treatment of this process and the varied, rippling effects of its use on the Nahuatl-Christian moral dialogue. See Burkhart, *The Slippery Earth*, 29–31. Other examples of lexical derivation include *tlamacehualiztli* for the sacrament of penance (from *macehua*, "to merit, deserve something"), *nemaquixtiliztli* for the Christian notion of salvation (from *maquixtia*, "to redeem, liberate, salvage"), and *izcalia* for "to resurrect" (lit. "to revive, come to").

5. Jane H. Hill, "The Flower World of Old Uto-Aztecan." *Journal of Anthropological Research* 48 (1992):117–144.

6. William F. Hanks, *Language and Communicative Practices* (Boulder, CO: Westview Press, 1996); Jan Blommaert, *Discourse: A Critical Introduction* (Cambridge, UK: Cambridge University Press, 2005).

7. Hanks, *Converting Words*, introduction.

8. Díaz Balsera, *The Pyramid Under the Cross*, 24.

9. J. Jorge Klor de Alva, "The Aztec-Spanish Dialogues of 1524." *Alcheringa* 4, no. 2 (1980): 152; cited in Díaz Balsera, *The Pyramid Under the Cross*, 224, n. 11. Translation mine.

10. Guadalajara Medina, "La venida del Anticristo," 7.

11. Ben Leeming, "The Poetics of Terror: Depictions of Hell in Ecclesiastical Nahuatl Literature," (Unpublished paper, last modified May 30, 2012).

12. Sahagún, *Siguense unos sermones*, 122, and the anonymous *Sermones y santoral en mexicana*, M-M 464, early seventeenth century, f. 278r, Bancroft Library, University of California, Berkeley.

13. Hanks, *Converting Words*, chapter 8.

14. Christensen, *Nahua and Maya Catholicisms*.

15. Nancy Farriss, *Tongues of Fire: Language and Evangelization in Colonial Mexico* (New York: Oxford University Press, 2018), 286.

16. Fray Alonso de Molina, *Confessionario mayor en lengua mexicana* (Mexico: Antonio Espinoza, 1565), f. 19v and f. 79v.

17. Molina, *Confessionario mayor*, f. 2v.

18. Sahagún, *Siguense unos sermones*, 165.

19. Sahagún, *Florentine Codex*, Book 10, table of contents. Dibble and Anderson trans.

20. Victoria Ríos Castaño argues that Book 10's lists of virtues and vices, as well as the thesaurus-like listing of nouns, verbs, and adjectives describing people who exhibit them, are based on European sources such as confession manuals, treatises on virtues and vices, and the writings of Augustine. While this seems undeniable, she tends to downplay the equally important influence exerted by Indigenous rhetorical forms and the Indigenous colleagues of Sahagún. See Victoria Ríos Castaño, *Translation as Conquest: Sahagún and* Universal *History of the Things of New Spain* (Madrid: Iberoamericana, 2014), 138–149.

21. Sahagún, *Florentine Codex*, Book 10, 15. Dibble and Anderson trans. Note that the Nahua author of this passage practiced a form of "Indigenous diabolization," making reference to frightening beings from the Indigenous cosmos in lieu of European demons.

22. Sahagún, *Florentine Codex*, Book 10, 53. Dibble and Anderson trans.

23. "Prostitute" obviously reflects the moralizing judgments of the friars and those Indigenous Christians affiliated with them. However, in precontact times the *ahuiani* was not a prostitute per se, but a temple dancer and a participant in ritual performances. Lisa Sousa, "Flowers and Speech in Discourses on Deviance in Book 10," in *The Florentine Codex: An Encyclopedia of the Nahua World in Sixteenth-Century Mexico*, ed. Janette Favrot Peterson and Kevin Terraciano (Austin: University of Texas Press, 2019), 185, 189.

24. Stafford Poole, *Pedro Moya de Contreras: Catholic Reform and Royal Power in New Spain, 1571–1591* (Berkeley: University of California Press, 1987), 266, n. 13.

25. Sahagún, *Florentine Codex*, Introductions and Indices, 98.

26. *Rudes* (Lat. "crude"), *de menor capacidad* (Span. "of lesser ability"). Poole, *Pedro Moya de Contreras*, 153.

27. Fray Geronimo de Mendieta, *Historia eclesiástica indiana* (Ciudad de México: F. Díaz de León y Santiago White, 1870; Biblioteca Virtual Miguel de Cervantes, 1999), Book 4, chap. 23, http://www.cervantesvirtual.com/obra-visor/historia-eclesiastica-indiana--o/html/.

28. Mendieta, *Historia eclesiástica indiana*, Book 4, chap. 23; also cited in Osvaldo F. Pardo, *The Origins of Mexican Catholicism: Nahua Rituals and Christian Sacraments in Sixteenth-Century Mexico* (Ann Arbor: University of Michigan Press, 2006), 50.

29. Benavente, *History of the Indians*, 302.

30. Benavente, 302–303.

31. Hernando Ruiz de Alarcón, *Treatise on the Heathen Superstitions that Today Live Among the Indians Native to this New Spain, 1629*, ed. J. R. Andrews and Ross Hassig (Norman: University of Oklahoma Press, 1984).

32. Lockhart, *The Nahuas*, 258.

33. Burkhart, *Holy Wednesday*, 4.

34. Inga Clendinnen, *Aztecs: An Interpretation* (Cambridge: Cambridge University Press, 1991), 258, 259.

35. Cited in Horcasitas, 87.

36. James C. Scott, *Domination and the Arts of Resistance: Hidden Transcripts* (New Haven: Yale University Press, 1990).

37. Jorge Klor de Alva, "Nahua Colonial Discourse and the Appropriation of the (European) Other," *Archives de Sciences Sociales des Religions* (1992): 30.

38. Sánchez Aguilera, "La Doctrina," 134.

39. Sahagún, *Siguense unos sermones*, 18.

40. Louise Burkhart, personal communication.

41. A version of this chapter was published by the University Press of Colorado. Ben Leeming, "A Nahua Christian Talks Back: Fabián de Aquino's Antichrist Dramas as Autoethnography," in *Words and Worlds*, ed. David Tavárez, 172–192.

CONCLUSION: APOCALYPSE AND TRAUMA

1. Olko and Brylak, "Defending Local Autonomy," 591.

2. Lopes Don, *Bonfires*, 13.

3. Nesvig, *Ideology and Inquisition*; Tavárez, *Invisible War*.

4. In a note written in 1563, Bernardino de Sahagún writes at the beginning of the collection of sermons whose composition he oversaw (*Siguense unos sermones*) that the sermons were composed in 1540. However, the manuscript that survives is not the original of 1540 but is a copy dating to 1548.

5. Olko and Brylak, "Defending Local Autonomy," 575.

6. Olko and Brylak, 592.

7. Olko and Brylak, 599.

8. Olko and Brylak, 574.

9. McDonough discusses this important Indigenous intellectual in chapter 2 of *The Learned Ones*.

10. Cited in Olko and Brylak, "Defending Local Autonomy," 586. Translation by the authors.

11. See Judith Lewis Herman, *Trauma and Recovery: The Aftermath of Violence from Domestic Abuse to Political Terror* (New York: Basic Books, 1992); Cathy Caruth, *Unclaimed Experience: Trauma, Narrative and History* (Baltimore: Johns Hopkins University Press,

2010); Stef Craps, *Postcolonial Witnessing: Trauma Out of Bounds* (London: Palgrave Macmillan, 2012); Ogaga Ifowodo, *History, Trauma, and Healing in Postcolonial Narratives: Reconstructing Identities* (New York: Palgrave Macmillan, 2013); Hilary N. Weaver, *Trauma and Resilience in the Lives of Contemporary Native Americans: Reclaiming Our Balance, Restoring Our Wellbeing.* (New York: Routledge, 2019).

12. Lisa D. Butler, Filomena M. Critelli, and Janice Carello, eds., *Trauma and Human Rights: Integrating Approaches to Address Human Suffering* (Cham, Switzerland: Springer International Publishing, Imprint: Palgrave Macmillan, 2019).

13. Teresa Evans-Campbell, "Historical Trauma in American Indian/Native Alaska Communities: A Multilevel Framework for Exploring Impacts on Individuals, Families, and Communities," *Journal of Interpersonal Violence* 23, no. 3 (March 2008): 316–338.

14. Daschke, "Apocalypse and Trauma," 458.

15. Daschke, 458.

16. Judith Lewis Herman cited in Daschke, 459.

17. Nancy M. Farriss, *Maya Society Under Colonial Rule: The Collective Enterprise of Survival* (New Haven: Princeton University Press, 1984), 287.

18. Paraphrasing Arthur Neal in Daschke, "Apocalypse and Trauma," 459.

19. Amara Solari and Matthew Restall, *2012 and the End of the World: The Western Roots of the Maya Apocalypse* (New York: Rowman & Littlefield Publishers, 2011), 107.

20. Daschke, "Apocalypse and Trauma," 460.

21. Daschke, 460, 463.

22. Stephanie Wood, *Transcending Conquest: Nahua Views of Spanish Colonial Mexico* (Norman: University of Oklahoma Press, 2012); Louise M. Burkhart, "Meeting the Enemy: Moteuczoma and Cortés, Herod and the Magi," in *Invasion and Transformation: Interdisciplinary Perspectives on the Conquest of Mexico*, edited by Rebecca P. Brienen and Margaret A. Jackson (Boulder: University Press of Colorado, 2008), 11–23; and Lori Boornazian Diel, *The Codex Mexicanus: A Guide to Life in Late Sixteenth-Century New Spain* (Austin: University of Texas Press, 2018).

23. Teresa Evans-Campbell, "Historical Trauma in American Indian/Native Alaska Communities," *Journal of Interpersonal Violence* 23, no. 3 (2008): 316–338.

APPENDIX: PRESENTATION OF THE PLAYS

NORMS OF TRANSCRIPTION AND TRANSLATION

1. Frances Karttunen and James Lockhart, "The Art of the Nahuatl Speech. The Bancroft Dialogues in Nahuatl Studies Series Number 2," *UCLA Latin American Studies* 65 (1987): 66.

2. Geoff Nunberg interview, December 26, 2013, *Fresh Air*, WHYY.

3. Guadalajara Medina, "La venida del Anticristo."

ANTICHRIST AND THE FINAL JUDGMENT:
NAHUATL PALEOGRAPHY

1. Read *Tetlayehyecalvilliztli*. There are a number of instances where Aquino substitutes a *d* for *t*. Since Nahuatl doesn't contain the *d* sound value, *t* was frequently substituted. For example, he writes the word for priest, *sacerdote*, as *saceltote*. Using *d* for *t* probably reflects the Indigenous view that the *d* and *t* sounds were interchangeable.

2. Here and throughout read *dios*.

3. Here and throughout read *tlalticpac*.

4. MS NS 3/1 is riddled with holes. Where I have had to guess the identity of letters that have been partially or entirely consumed by some inconsiderate worm, I have included my conjecture in square brackets.

5. Here and throughout read *xp̄o* as *Cristo* and *ātexp̄o* as *Antecristo*. This abbreviation for Christ is ubiquitous in early colonial Nahuatl doctrinal texts and was borrowed from the medieval scribal tradition.

6. The abbreviation used here also comes from the medieval scribal tradition that Aquino would have been taught by his Franciscan instructors. Here and throughout it will be rendered *etc.*

7. Here and throughout read *amo* or *ahmo*. The abbreviation *aᵒ* was not borrowed from the medieval tradition but was the innovation of Indigenous writers of Nahuatl texts. See Justyna Olko, "Alphabetic Writing in the Hands of the Colonial Nahua Nobility," *Contributions in New World Archaeology* 7 (2014): 182.

8. This is a variant of *ye* that is used in these two texts. See Horacio Carochi and James Lockhart, *Grammar of the Mexican Language With an Explanation of Its Adverbs (1645)* (Stanford: Stanford University Press; UCLA Latin American Center Publications, 2001), 133–34 n. 4, 222 n. 1, 223 n. 3, 225 n. 4, 245 n. 6, and 515, https://nahuatl.uoregon.edu/content/ya.

9. Here and throughout read *totecuiyo*. This is another common abbreviation in early Nahuatl doctrinal texts.

10. Here and throughout read *tlatlacatecolo*.

11. It appears that Aquino began writing the word *chicome* (seven), but then returned to Roman numerals, writing *vii*.

12. Read *amo omoquineltocaque*.

13. Read *Tetenanavatilliani*.

14. Read *ivanyolque*.

15. Read *valmonextitiyaz*. This is one of many instances where Aquino uses *s* for *x* and is further evidence in support of an early date for the text.

16. Read *yn santa maria*. The use of a macron over the *a* of *Maria* is a novel extension of the macron's use as an abbreviation typically only applied to -*an* or -*am*.

17. Here and throughout read *avh in.*

18. Here and throughout read *ilhuicac.*

19. Read *Tetlatzontequilliquivh.*

20. *Yaquine* is another example of the author's regional variant of Nahuatl. In the standard form associated with the central valley of Mexico this is typically spelled *yequeneh.*

21. The placement of the "o" in superscript is strange. This should probably be read *oquinextilito.*

22. Read *amechmachtiquivh.*

23. Read *yloti,* "to turn back, go back, to return; to diminish; for a disease to become less severe, abate." Online Nahuatl Dictionary, s.v. "iloti," accessed May 31, 2021, https://nahuatl .uoregon.edu/content/iloti. Louise Burkhart sees the use of this word as something uncommon and perhaps one of Aquino's regional variant (personal communication).

24. Read *yc ivic.*

25. Tentatively read *quinmacaz.*

26. Here and throughout read *ayamo.*

27. Read *quinmictiz.*

28. Read *ma amechchocti.*

29. Read *xpiānome.*

30. This spelling of *cihuatl* (woman) is characteristics of Nahuatl from the region east of Central Mexico. According to Lidia E. Gómez García, it is especially typical of Tlaxcalan Nahuatl (personal communication, July 2018).

31. Read *mamaçovhticac.*

32. Worm damage; tentatively read *quipolo.*

33. Illegible; tentatively read *namechmacaz.*

34. Read *aocmo.*

35. This abbreviation can signify both *quitoz* and *quitozque*; here read *quitozque.*

36. Read *ma mochi.*

37. This *X* has a hooked right foot. I am assuming it's an abbreviation for *Cristo.*

38. Read *ynic cacoz.*

39. Read *ximoyolmellavacan.*

40. Read *amechchocti.*

41. Read *ma mopalţinco.*

42. Read *yuhquinma.*

43. Read *ynic icivhca.*

44. Read *ma tichocacan.* This phrase may be repeated for effect or because Aquino made a mistake on the first one and just didn't cross it out.

45. The use of the plural *Ermitanos* (Sp. *ermitaños,* "hermits") for "Hermit" suggests the author is unaware that the *-s* is the plural suffix in Spanish. See also his use of *martilles* (Sp. *mártires,* "martyrs") to name a single individual in *Antichrist and the Hermit.*

46. Read *mochintin*. This is an interesting application of the superscript ° in which Aquino adapts it for use outside of its usual association with *amo/ahmo*.

47. Read *yn ixq[ui]chtin*.

48. Aquino's correction adds a superfluous *xp̄ō* here.

49. Read *-tinenque* here and in the following.

50. Read *anquintzavctiyazque*.

51. Reading unclear, possibly *totecuiyo*.

52. Read *anquimittaya*.

53. Read *anteycnoitinenque*.

54. Read *avh in ameva[n]tin*.

55. "Dana[n] Dos" is *Condenados*, "the condemned." This highly idiosyncratic spelling approximates an Indigenous pronunciation of the Spanish term, roughly *[con]denados*, the *t* for *d* being the common substitution in Nahuatl speaking and writing of this period. Clearly the author isn't clear about the Spanish and whether it is one or two words, singular or plural.

56. Read *timitztotlavhtillizquiya*.

57. Read *çan anquintlatzivhcayttaya*.

58. Read *macamo*.

59. Read *yn yevatl*.

60. Read *jesucristoe*. The use of the vocative is irregular, since women typically didn't use the *e* ending.

61. Read *ma mopalţinco*.

62. It seems either "The Apostles [and] St. Peter" or "The Apostle St. Peter" is intended. If the latter, then this may be another instance where Aquino evinces confusion about the Spanish plural ending. The former reading is supported by the use of the plural *apostolomeh* in the next line.

63. This may be *hual+tlehco*, but ought to end with the appropriate optative ending, *-can*.

64. Read *in tote°* (*totecuiyo*).

65. Read *yyo totecuiyoe diose*.

66. Here and below this could also be *teopixcaţin*.

67. Read *imavizyectenevalocat[z]in*.

68. The liturgical song called the "Te Deum" begins with these words, *Te deum laudamus, te dominum confitemur* (we praise thee, we acknowledge thee to be Lord).

ANTICHRIST AND THE FINAL JUDGMENT:
ENGLISH TRANSLATION

1. Here the author uses the term *tetlayeyecalhuiliztli* ("representation," or "imitation") in place of the standard Nahuatl word for colonial didactic religious plays, *neixcuitilli* ("example"). This term does not appear in any of the other surviving colonial Nahuatl plays.

2. The Nahuatl word is *tetlanextiliani*, "he (or she) who customarily reveals things to people." The author may be innovating a term for "director," since this person has no speaking role in either of the plays.

3. The identity of this particular Sibyl is likely the Tiburtine Sibyl. Sibylline prophecies became a staple in the Antichrist tradition after Adso's *Libellus de Antichristo* (c. 954). See Richard K. Emmerson, *Antichrist in the Middle Ages: A Study of Medieval Apocalypticism, Art and Literature* (Seattle: University of Washington Press, 1981).

4. When the term it is used to refer to the deceiver of Christians from the medieval tradition in general, Antichrist will be preceded by "the," as in "the Antichrist." However, when used to name the plays' central character, it will appear without the definite article.

5. In the Antichrist legend, Elijah and Enoc reconvert those who were once Christian but were tricked into apostasy by the deceitful preaching of the Antichrist. In the context of these plays, these are presumably Indigenous people who had initially been converted by the friars, but due to the influence of certain Indigenous rulers and religious figures who opposed the friars, had abandoned the new religion.

6. "Were-owl(s)" is *tlacatecolotl* or *tlatlacatecoloh* (lit. "human horned owl[s]"). See introduction, n. 49.

7. These are Indigenous priests, not Roman Catholic. Here they are identified as *pahpahuaqueh*, but in *Antichrist and the Hermit* they are referred to as *tletlenamacaqueh* (fire priests).

8. "One who indulges in pleasure" is *ahuiani*. In precontact times, the *ahuiani* was a female temple assistant and dancer. The friars chose *ahuiani* to translate the Spanish *puta* (whore). As Lisa Sousa points out, this term is often translated "prostitute" in English, a decision with further perpetuates the friars' misunderstanding and negative value judgement; therefore, the word "prostitute" will be avoided. See Sousa, "Flowers and Speech," 189.

9. *Patlachhuiani* is a little-understood term. Molina defines it as "woman who does it with another woman; lesbian" (Joe Campbell, personal communication, August 10, 2018). Due to this uncertainty, here and below I have chosen to leave this term untranslated. This character's appearance in *Antichrist and the Hermit* reveals a startling new piece of information about this mysterious term. See f. 186v.

10. As stated in chapter 1, *cuiloni* has typically been translated as "sodomite" and *cuilontia* as "sodomy." According to Pete Sigal's analysis of this term, it derives from the passive form of the verb *cui*, "to take," (*cuilo*) and means "one who is taken." He argues for the translation of *cuiloni* as "one taken from behind," i.e., the "passive" homosexual act. See Sigal, *The Flower and the Scorpion*, 193. This term will remain untranslated so as to prevent the transfer of non-Indigenous attitudes toward this type of sexual act.

11. The term *ilhuicac* will be translated as "the heavens," which is slightly less evocative of the Christian concept than "heaven." *Ilhuicac* also can be translated as "the sky." In Indigenous cosmology, *ilhuicatl* (the absolutive form of *ilhuicac*) was the location of certain deities

and otherworlds, but it was not the destination of souls deemed morally pure in the sense understood by Christian theology.

12. The couplet "tail, wing" is a *difrasismo*, or semantic couplet, meaning *macehualli* (pl. *macehualtin*), "commoner or vassal." Its use here highlights that the intended audience for the plays was the Nahua *macehualtin* whose "hearts and minds" were the focus of the campaigns of persuasion of the Franciscan friars and certain traditionalist *tlahtohqueh* and *nanahualtin*, as chapter 2 argued. Note that the singular is used here.

13. The Nahuatl is *tlazcaltilli*, which can mean "well brought up" in a general sense or, more specifically, someone who is currently under tutelage, a pupil, or one in the process of being indoctrinated (Online Nahuatl Dictionary, s.v. "tlazcaltilli," accessed May 21, 2021, https://nahuatl.uoregon.edu/content/tlazcaltilli). The choice of "neophyte" reflects the argument made in chapter 2 that the plays were originally composed during a period when Christian indoctrination was not yet widespread. However, I acknowledge that the more general reading of "well brought up" is equally justified.

14. Here Sibyl shifts from the singular to the plural, perhaps addressing the audience or other characters on stage.

15. The phrase *ipal tinemih* is related to the more common form *ipalnemohuani* (The One by Whom There Is Living) which was one of a number of precontact deity epithets appropriated in early colonial times by friars and Nahuas to name the Christian God.

16. "His fame, his glory" (*itleyo imahuizyo*) is a common Nahuatl difrasismo used to refer to a person or being of great esteem.

17. "His counsel" and "his exposition" refer to the teachings of Jesus Christ and/or the doctrines of the Catholic Church.

18. "Only God" is *ycel dios*. When the author uses the Spanish loan *dios* I have translated it as "God," but each time he uses the Nahuatl *teotl* I have translated it as "deity." The reason for the distinction is that *teotl* and *dios* each represented very different ways of understanding the divine in their respective cultures. Henceforth, I will treat the phrase *icel teotl* as an neologized deity epithet ("Only Deity") along the lines of the repurposed Nahua epithet *ipalnemohuani*. The related phrase *icel dios*, Only God, will receive similar treatment.

19. It is unclear whose relative is being referred to, Jesus's or John's. Questions regarding the ancestry of the Antichrist were addressed by the medieval legend, which stated that, like Christ, the Antichrist would be a Jew. In medieval times this was used to justify acts of discrimination and violence against European Jews.

20. Bringing the dead back to life is one of the false miracles performed by the Antichrist in the medieval tradition. This may also be a reference to an exchange in *Antichrist and the Hermit* between Antichrist and the character named Martyr in which Antichrist raises Martyr's mother and father from the dead. See ff. 158v–159v.

21. This is either "*a* were-owl" (*tlacatecolotl*) or "*the* were-owl." It is unclear here whether the author means to say that Antichrist is merely *a* devil (i.e., a demon) or *the* devil himself.

22. Tlaloc was the ancient Mesoamerican deity of rain and lightning. The translation of this passage about the father and mother of the Antichrist is tentative.

23. "Sacred words" is *teotlahtolli* (lit. "*teotl*-words, speech"). "Word of God" (sacred scripture) was intended, but owing to the lack of equivalency between the Indigenous concept of *teotl* and the Christian God, I have opted for this more neutral phrase.

24. I am unsure how to translate *tlachialoni* ("seeing device"). In the precontact context a *tlachialoni* was used in divination rituals. This term's appearance in Nahuatl-Christian contexts is rare. Another example can be found in a collection of late-sixteenth century sermons paired with the word *temachtilli* ("doctrine, teaching"; *De contempu[s] omnium vanitatum huius mundi*, Codex Indianorum 23, John Carter Brown Library, Brown University, https://archive.org/details/decontemptuomniuoobern, f. 166r). This suggests *tlachialoni* was repurposed by the friars and their Nahua assistants and was used in association with divine teaching.

25. "Pleasure-seekers" is *ahuianimeh* (sing. *ahuiani*).

26. This may be a reference to Ecclesiastes 9:12 "Man knoweth not his own end: but as fishes are taken with the hook, and as birds are caught with the snare, so men are taken in the evil time, when it shall suddenly come upon them" (Douay-Rheims 1899 American Edition, accessed May 6, 2022, https://www.biblegateway.com/passage/?search=ecclesiastes+9%3A12&version=VULGATE,DRA). The Old Testament books of wisdom were the favored sources of Franciscan and Nahua writers.

27. According to the Antichrist legend, Elijah and Enoch were the "two witnesses" referenced by St. John in Revelation 11:3, chosen by God to come back to earth and preach against the Antichrist at the end of time. In some traditions, Enoch and Elijah wait in Earthly Paradise until the Antichrist's coming; this appears to be what is being referenced when they say they have come back from the "founding place of God's lineage" (i.e., Eden).

28. In the Antichrist tradition Enoch and Elijah are slain by the Antichrist and remain dead for three days before they are raised to life by Christ and brought to heaven.

29. "Them" is presumably Elijah and Enoch. The angel is St. Michael. In some versions of the Antichrist legend, it is Christ himself who slays the Antichrist.

30. This is a reference to a detail in the Antichrist legend stating that God will grant forty days of penance to the faithful between the death of the Antichrist and the Final Judgment. Some Antichrist traditions stipulate forty-five days. See Emmerson, *Antichrist in the Middle Ages*, 182 n. 15.

31. "It will be heard . . . taken then." Tentative translation.

32. "Common people" is *macehualtin*. The "wicked ones" are understood to be members of the noble class (*pipiltin*). Thus is established the strong pro-*macehualtin* anti-*pipiltin* bias of the two plays. See chapter 2.

33. In a sermon for the first Sunday of Advent, Sahagún's team writes of Nahua elders and ritual specialists, *çan amo nelli quitoa çan quipiqui*, "What they say is absolutely not true;

they are just making it up" (Sahagún, *Siguense unos sermones*, 8). Antichrist's words here bear the clear mark of the doctrinal discourses of the author's day, as discussed in chapter 3.

34. Pulque is a traditional Mesoamerican alcoholic beverage made from fermented maguey sap.

35. In the medieval legend, gifts are one of the three ways the Antichrist entices the faithful to believe in him (the other two are miracles/signs and by terrifying them). Here the gifts offered by Antichrist take on a decidedly Indigenous flavor: tortillas, chili peppers, atole, tilmas, etc.

36. That is, the things offered by Antichrist as bribes.

27. "On his throne" is *icpalpan*. The *icpalli* was an Indigenous-style seat. The word was often paired with *petlatl* (reed mat) to form a *difrasismo* meaning "authority."

38. Note that he is speaking of "the wicked ones" (*tlahuelliloqueh*) in the plural. This suggests Antichrist may be on stage with other characters, perhaps demons, who participate in bribing the *macehualtin* with gifts. Alternatively, this might be a general reference to anyone who opposed the teaching of the friars, such as the rulers and ritual specialists discussed in chapter 2.

39. More literally, "Out of everything that has been made absolutely nothing is his."

40. Presumably this instruction is referring to stage hands who are directed to remove the props representing Antichrist's bribes since the converts have now rejected them.

41. There are more commands to spit on people in the second play. This is the first reference to spitting, and while it is directed to the actors playing converts, it may be seen as applying to the audience as well. Spitting is also commanded in the *Coloquios*. Speaking to the Mexica priests and *tlamatinimeh* (wise men) in this reimagined early encounter, the friars declare, "It is very necessary . . . that you spit on those whom you used to follow as gods" (J. Jorge Klor de Alva, "The Aztec-Spanish Dialogues of 1524" *Alcheringa* 4, no. 2 [1980]:100).

42. This is one of a number of instances in the plays when actors are called on to give impromptu speeches to the audience. This underscores the didactic nature of this genre of religious theater as well as suggests a number of risks inherent in Indigenous appropriations of the colonial *neixcuitilli*, as discussed in chapter 3.

43. The Nahuatl is *huel amonezca in antlahueliloqueh*. This is a difficult phrase to translate. It literally reads, "It is really your symbol/sign/mark/omen/meaning that you are wicked ones." The phrase appears again just below in the words of Elijah. With this utterance, Antichrist seizes the rhetoric of the friars and levels it at the representatives of God.

44. Translated this way, the statement *tiquetzalcoatl* reads like an insult. It could also be translated, "You are Quetzalcoatl." In this case, Elijah may be contradicting Antichrist's previous claim to be God the creator by declaring him to be instead one of the precontact *teteoh* demonized by the friars' rhetoric of diabolism.

45. I translate the verb *teotoca* as "to follow something as a deity." However, as Molina makes clear, the dominant reading promoted by the friars was *ydolatrar* "to idolize" (Online

Nahuatl Dictionary, s.v. "teotoca," https://nahuatl.uoregon.edu/content/teotoca). Since the terms "idolatry" and "idolize" have carried a negative connotation throughout Western history, I choose to render *teotoca* more literally.

46. Or, "never be translated." The meaning of this is unclear. Perhaps they are declaring that God's prophecy will now come true, that the Two Witnesses will be slain by the Antichrist.

47. Presumably another group of *macehualtin* or those reconverted by Elijah and Enoch.

48. This seems to refer to the rejection of Antichrist's bribes by tossing them at his feet.

49. Some versions of the Antichrist legend state that the Antichrist will perform the false miracle of dying and coming back to life, an evil parody of Christ's own death and resurrection designed to deceive Christians.

50. Colonial ethnographic sources describe the Indigenous underworld, called Mictlan, as cold and windy; "hot" is the expected descriptor of the Christian hell.

51. During the interrogation of the twenty-five demons and condemned souls in *Antichrist and the Hermit* we learn that many of these characters are carrying props that symbolize the sins each one stands for.

52. "All of them" is probably referring to the eighteen condemned souls who accompany the seven demons.

53. In *Antichrist and the Hermit* we hear that each of the condemned souls is being tormented in hell by a person or thing related to their particular sin.

54. This image of the demons treating the body and blood of Antichrist with such reverence is evocative of the treatment of the consecrated Eucharist in Catholic rites and suggests that the author was aware of the parallels between Antichrist and Christ. Parallels like these were a staple in the Antichrist tradition, where Antichrist was imagined as having his own circumcision, presentation in the temple, death, resurrection, etc. However, in the context of the friars' indoctrination efforts among Indigenous Mesoamericans, these parallels must have been perceived as risky. As I argued in chapter 2, this may explain why the Antichrist and his legend were mostly left out of the friars' teaching and doctrinal writing. Relatedly, the image of the wrapping of objects associated with sacred beings recalls the Indigenous practice of creating sacred bundles (*tlaquimilolli*), pushing this text farther into the richly complex and hybrid space of early Nahuatl Christian writing.

55. This suggests that the stage will be made to look like it is burning. We know visual effects were common in colonial *neixcuitilli*, including the use of fireworks and even real flames to simulate a frightening hellscape.

56. The ensuing sequence, often referred to as "the separation of the sheep and the goats," is standard to most Final Judgment narratives and is based on Matthew 25:31–46.

57. In this space Aquino inserted an abbreviation (t^o), which has not been translated due to uncertainty about its meaning.

58. Actors playing the demons may very well have dragged their unwilling and terrified victims down through a trapdoor in the stage to a space representing hell. Vertical arrangements of heaven and hell in colonial Nahuatl set design are discussed in Horcasitas, *El teatro náhuatl*, 114–116.

59. Although singing is not directly referenced here, I think it's possible that what follows is another song text. The author has used pilcrows to denote specific stanzas just as he did for the songs previously sung by the demons. The repeated element *yyoyahue* (Alas!) reinforces this sense.

60. That is, baptism.

61. In all likelihood, the actor playing Christ has at this point ascended to a platform above the stage via a ladder and is beckoning for the Blessed to literally ascend the ladder to join him in heaven.

62. What follows may also be considered a song.

63. Also possibly "our priest."

64. This is referring to the liturgical song called the "Te Deum."

65. "Let us fix . . . our guardian." Tentative translation.

66. In medieval religious theater, productions often concluded with the singing of the "Te Deum." Its inclusion here may suggest a European source text for *Antichrist and the Final Judgment* or merely that the originator of the play was familiar with this tradition.

ANTICHRIST AND THE HERMIT: NAHUATL PALEOGRAPHY

1. Read *tlatoli*.

2. Read *Auh ayamo ontlami*.

3. Read *ynic itlan*.

4. Note that Nahuatl's reverential form is used here for Antichrist.

5. Tentatively read *ximovapavacan*.

6. Read *Jesucristo*. After using the reverential form *iceltzin* for Antichrist above, here the author uses just *icel*, referring to God without the reverential form. This adds to the oddity of the author's use (and omission) of reverential forms, a subject I have not pursued here but that begs for further investigation.

7. Read *quitoz antecristo*.

8. This word is difficult to read. Transcription tentative.

9. This is another difficult sequence to read. Transcription tentative.

10. Read *amevantin*.

11. This will be read as *yn anmoxavaya yn anmopotoniyaya*.

12. Read *namechnotlaçotilia*.

13. Read *oamechiztlacavitinenca*.

14. Read *nomac*.

15. Here and below read *iuh*.

16. Read *ca acazomo*.

17. Read *quiquetza*.

18. Read *profetisa*.

19. Read *ovetzque*.

20. Read *itlanhuan*.

21. Read *ichanţinco*.

22. Read *totecuiyo*.

23. Abbreviation unknown.

24. Read *tinechçaçayanaz*.

25. Here and below read *ynic ivic*.

26. Illegible mark.

27. Read *Nican tlatoz*.

28. Read *amechmachtitinemi*.

29. Read *ynic itlantzinco*.

30. Read *techchoctiz*.

31. Read *aocmo*.

32. Read *conversos*.

33. Read *namechchivaz*.

34. Read *teocuitlatl*.

35. Read *ynic intech*.

36. Read *quitozque*.

37. Read *yehica*.

38. Read *ic ipampa*.

39. Read *mopan*.

40. Read *tleyn*.

41. Read *xinechilvi*.

42. Read *inezca*.

43. Here and below read *quitoz*.

44. Read *ca çannen ca*.

45. Read *Auh in* or *Auh niman* (erroneous duplication of *ni-*).

46. Read *yn momac*.

47. Read *teyolcocoliztli*? Aquino wrote *te-* then reached the end of the line. When he picked up on the next line he may have skipped over *-yol* and finished the word *-cocoliztli*. However, in the next line, where there was no break interrupting his train of thought, he wrote *mococolizqueh*, "they will hate each other," which suggests he intended "hatred" for both. However, hatred is not one of the seven deadly sins.

48. Read *xiyavh*.

49. This is another novel application of mendicant scribal practices by an Indigenous writer working outside of the friars' sphere of influence. In religious texts we typically see abbreviations involving the overbar (macron) used to shorten names like Jesus Christ, Holy Spirit, etc. Its use here to abbreviate one of the Mexica *teteoh* is, to my knowledge, unique.

50. Read *imacevalvan*.

51. Read *quitoz*.

52. Read *ca çan*.

53. Read *in oamopan*. The first *o* is an "outrigger *o*," meaning it has been detached from its verb *acico*. See three lines down for another example.

54. Read *aço*.

55. Read *yn inyollo*.

56. Read *macivi*.

57. Read *miyecpa*.

58. Read *inyolliya*.

59. Read *xpīānome*.

60. Read *Niman*.

61. Read *yn notlatlacol*.

62. Illegible mark.

63. Read *ynic intech*.

64. Read *ca çan ic*.

65. Read *ynic imitec*.

66. Read *occenca*.

67. Read *amechchichazque*.

68. In the introduction to *Antichrist and the Final Judgment* the author refers to these priests as *pahpahuaqueh*. However, here they are called *tletlenamacaqueh* (fire priests). Neither of these appear to match this challenging abbreviation. Instead, I will tentatively read the above as *xiuhpohuaqueh*, "readers/diviners of the *xiuhpohualli*" (the Nahuas' 365-day solar calendar). The fact that this looks like the ubiquitous abbreviation for Christ is only a distraction, as the context will show. The author's use of it despite this potential for confusion is yet another example his independence and creativity. Thanks to the many *nahuatlahtos* who have broken their heads helping me try to decipher this difficult puzzle.

69. Read *ticneltoca*.

70. Read *niman ya*.

71. Read *titeheltequiya*.

72. Read *tlacatl*.

73. My translation of this difficult line relies on reading this as *yn ahmo amotonehualiz*. It is not difficult to find examples of apocopation in Aquino's writing.

74. Read *çan*.

75. Read *çan*.

76. Read *tonanvan*.

77. Here and below read *ynin*.

78. Read *titoeçoaya*.

79. Read *techchichinaça*.

80. Read *tevatl*.

81. Illegible mark; tentatively read *y*.

82. Read *otiquitvaya*.

83. Thanks to John Sullivan for working out the morphology and meaning of this verb (personal communication, November 25, 2015).

84. Read *tiamiquia*.

85. Text crossed out. Illegible.

86. Read *niccotonaya*.

87. Read *ni+ay+ya* (*ay*, "to do").

88. Read *noneuhca*.

89. Read *ma ivi*.

90. Read *oniquincentecpanvi*.

91. Read *nechchocti*.

92. Read *nimitztlahtlaniya*.

93. Read *otitemoque*.

94. Read *titoyolmelavazque*.

95. Read *xiyavh*.

96. Read *yn ermitano*.

97. Read *yn ermitano*.

98. Read *niticitl*.

99. Read *ynic*.

100. Read *ynin*.

101. Read *ynin*.

102. Read *inconevan*.

103. Here and below read *ivi* (*ihui*).

104. Read *Tetenanavatilliani*.

105. Read *nimoyectocatinenca*.

106. Aquino mistakenly wrote *yvan* twice.

107. Read *nimiztlahtlania*.

108. Read *yvanyolqui*.

109. Read *niman quitoz*.

110. Read *nimiztlahtlaniya*.

111. Read *ca amo anmizpinavhti*. It is very interesting to see the second person plural subject prefix *an-* behaving like an "outrigger" morpheme affixed to the negative *ahmo*.

112. Read *tecuilontitinemi*.

113. Read *otechchocti*.

114. Read *anmomaquixtizque*.

ANTICHRIST AND THE HERMIT: ENGLISH TRANSLATION

1. *Antichrist and the Final Judgment* contained a number of songs. However, the author of *Hermit* made the decision that this second play should not include singing. See Hermit's interaction with Lucifer on f. 167v regarding songs and singing. Ecclesiastical authorities fretted much about the Nahuas' singing of songs in religious settings and periodically made efforts to regulate the practice. Fray Bernardino de Sahagún and his Nahua assistants composed a lengthy collection of Nahuatl liturgical songs with Christian content (the *Psalmodia christiana*, composed from 1558–1560 and published in 1583) in an attempt to offer an alternative to songs that may have contained content deemed "idolatrous." The author's decision to limit singing in this play may be a reflection of the touchiness of this subject at the time of its composition.

2. Tentative translation. I believe the essence of this is, "You will profit from watching today's production."

3. As in *Antichrist and the Final Judgment*, the author's use of *tlacatecolotl* here is ambiguous, leaving us to wonder whether he considered the Antichrist a devil (i.e., a demon) or *the* devil.

4. "Him alone" is *ca çan iceltin*. Here the author takes a stock phrase from the Nahuatl-Christian lexicon typically used in reference to the Christian God and uses it to refer to Antichrist. Note that as in the previous play, here Antichrist is treated with the reverential form, *iceltzin*. This is a striking divergence from how the reverential form is used in the doctrinal discourses of the day, where it was typically only applied to beings deemed worthy of esteem or worship, such as God, Christ, Mary, the saints, etc.

5. According to Karttunen and Lockhart, the imperative *ximehuiltihtiecan* "do stay (remain) seated" is a polite greeting or welcome, similar to "hello," "good day," or "greetings" (*The Art of Nahuatl Speech*, 24). This is another example of Antichrist speaking in the formal register of an Indigenous nobleman or an otherwise respected authority.

6. "My home," i.e., precontact temple. Here we see the author associating Antichrist with Nahua *teteoh*. This was one of the universal rhetorical strategies employed by the friars in their efforts to persuade Nahuas to abandon their former gods.

7. In her notes to Durán's *History of the Indies* (524, n. 2) Doris Heyden writes about the adornment of young women whose cheeks were painted red and whose arms and legs were adorned with feather plumes when dancing in festivals for the gods. The writers of the Florentine Codex note in Book 2 that during the feast of Toxcatl "the women, the maidens painted their faces; they pasted themselves with red feathers" (Book 2, 74).

8. This expression is *amoteouh amotlatocauh*, another stock phrase from the Nahuatl-Christian lexicon devised by the early friars and their Nahua colleagues as an epithet of the Christian God. The author's use of it in a speech by Antichrist is a striking appropriation of doctrinal discourse, as was discussed in chapter 3.

9. "Reaping your reward." Tentative translation.

10. This is probably referring to the bribes that Antichrist is offering to entice the *macehualtin* to believe in him.

11. "Up" is not necessarily implied in *ompa* ("there" in the sense of "in the distance"). However, in the production of colonial *neixcuitilli*, heaven was sometimes located in an elevated space above the stage. It is likely that Antichrist would gesture upwards while uttering these lines. In a similar vein, the word "down" will occasionally be added to references to Mictlan (hell).

12. Although the author wrote *martilles* (for Spanish *martires*, "martyrs"), the following is spoken by a single individual.

13. Antichrist would seem to be carrying his own prop, a cross. This is likely a reference to the medieval tradition that stated that at the end of time a sign would appear in the heavens in the form of Christ's cross and the instruments of his Passion. This appears to be based on Matthew 24:30 in which Christ pronounces, "then will appear the sign of the Son of Man in heaven." This "eschatological cross" was also associated with the legend of the Antichrist in medieval times. See Jaime Lara, *City, Temple, Stage: Eschatological Architecture and Liturgical Theatrics in New Spain* (Notre Dame, IN: University of Notre Dame Press, 2004), 47.

14. Jesus doesn't mention the Antichrist in any of the ascension narratives. However, in Matthew 24:24 he declares, "false christs and false prophets will rise and show great signs and wonders to deceive, if possible, even the elect." (This also appears in Mark 13 and Luke 21.)

15. Literally, "your goods, possessions."

16. In the medieval tradition, the raising of people's mothers and fathers from the dead was one of the false miracles performed by the Antichrist and/or his followers. St. Vincent Ferrer, who wrote extensively about the Antichrist and with whose works Aquino was familiar, mentions this precise miracle in a sermon preached in July of 1411 in Toledo. See Pedro Cátedra García, *Sermón, Sociedad y Literatura en la Edad Media: San Vicente Ferrer en Castilla (1411–1412)* (Salamanca, Spain: Junta de Castilla y León/Consejería de Cultura y Turismo, 1994), 541, and in Ferrer's third sermon for the second Sunday of Advent from *Sermones Hyemales* (Leiden: Iacobi Junctae, 1558), 61–69.

17. "This is not true." I take this to be a warning spoken to the audience, or perhaps by the director to the players, urging them not to be fooled by Antichrist's apparent miracle. The implication is that there is a perceived risk that some might mistake the action portrayed on stage for the real thing. This is evocative of the liminality of Indigenous performances that was discussed in chapters 1 and 3.

18. This could refer to a distinguishing feature such as a birthmark or perhaps a prop Martyr's father is carrying.

19. Here Antichrist switches to the plural, perhaps suggesting that he is urging the audience to look as well.

20. That is, Sibyl.

21. This is a rare and delightful example of humor captured in a colonial Nahuatl Christian source. That it is a distinctly Indigenous form of humor makes it all the more precious. Note that the joke only works if one's understanding of the underworld holds that it is a place of freezing cold. There is another comedic exchange below in Hermit's interaction with Lucifer. For more on humor in colonial Nahuatl drama, see Louise M. Burkhart, "Humour in Baroque Nahuatl Drama," in *Power, Gender, and Ritual in Europe and the Americas: Essays in Memory of Richard C. Trexler*, ed. Peter J. Arnade Michael Rocke (Toronto: Center for Reformation and Renaissance Studies, 2008). Also, at the time of this book's publication, Agnieszka Brylak is finishing what is sure to be an important new contribution to studies of humor and laughter among the precontact Nahua.

22. "If there is happiness . . . an unjust place." Translation tentative. The phrase *in axixtli in cuitlatl* (urine, excrement) was a *difrasismo* denoting moral decay or evil. Assessing whether the phrase existed prior to contact is difficult. The majority of the attestations come from the works of Fray Andrés de Olmos (his *Arte* of 1547 and his *Tratado sobre los siete pecados mortales*) or those influenced by him (such as Fray Juan Bautista); see Mercedes Montes de Oca Vega, *Los difrasismos en el náhuatl del siglo XVI* (Mexico: UNAM, 2000), 458, 571.

23. "Worldliness" is *tlalticpaccayotl*. This can reference mundane things generally (as opposed to heavenly things, *ilhuicaccayotl*), but often it has the connotation of "carnal things," i.e., illicit sexual activities and pleasures.

24. "O my forefathers" is *notechiuhcahuane* (also "elders, ancestors," Joe Campbell, personal communication). This is a term of respect that illustrates how in polite Nahuatl speech roles are inverted to show respect. Here, Antichrist refers to his underlings, the demons, as his forefathers.

25. Addressing the audience.

26. The author uses the Spanish loan word *padre* with the Nahuatl nominal plural ending, *padremeh*. This is referring to the friars, most likely the Franciscans, since it was with members of this order that the author was closely affiliated.

27. This is an extremely polite way to call for the deaths of Elijah and Enoch. It underscores the formal register in which Antichrist speaks, a fact that would have lent him greater authority in the eyes of the Indigenous audience, and also associated him more closely with the *tlahtohqueh* and *pipiltin*.

28. This appears to be directed to the audience as well as the other players.

29. Here for the first and only time in both plays the author uses the Spanish loanword *diablo* (with the Nahuatl plural ending *-meh*) rather than the word *tlatlacatecoloh*.

30. The expression *tleco monequi yn inacayo* is more literally, "his body is needed/required in/at the fire." The same phrase shows up again in Hermit's directive to burn the *cuiloni* on f. 186r.

31. This whole speech of St. Michael's refers to the death of Antichrist and his being spirited away to hell by the demons (all of which is part of the Antichrist legend), but curiously there is no mention of St. Michael actually slaying him. We must presume that he is dead after this point.

32. Hermit enters here without any introduction. Perhaps the author felt it was unnecessary in light of the information contained in *Antichrist and the Final Judgment*. This highlights the intertextuality of the two plays.

33. Tentative translation. My sense is that the demons' statement "We come" is similar to a student's reply "present" when the teacher takes attendance.

34. This section of Hermit's exchange with Lucifer is another example of comedy spicing up the play's didacticism.

35. Referring to Antichrist.

36. This comment underscores the idea that the author considered the Antichrist to be one of the Nahua *teteoh* against whom the friars fought in their "invisible war" on idolatry. It is unclear which festival is being referred to here.

37. This is another example of the intertextuality of the two plays. Singing took place in *Antichrist and the Final Judgment*. However, at the beginning of this play we are told that it is supposed to be performed *zan tlahtolli*, with "words only" (i.e., no singing).

38. Hermit's instructions are confusing, and the translation is somewhat tentative. It seems as if Hermit wants to know what the song is about while keeping it from being performed. Here he is behaving like the friars who were very concerned that the songs Indigenous people sang during Christian worship may have held idolatrous content.

39. Beginning with Lucifer, each of the eight demons carries a water jar (*apilloli*) that represents one of the seven deadly sins. The author might have adapted this idea from the seven angels in Revelation who each pour out seven "bowls" (or "vials") of God's wrath upon the earth (see Revelation 16). Another possible interpretation was suggested by Nathaniel Tarn who asked, "Could the *apilloli* jars here conceivably be related to [those the] Rain Gods . . . would spill water from when fertilizing the earth?" (personal communication, March 20, 2018).

40. In this play Lucifer represents the deadly sin of pride (Nahuatl *nepohualiztli*), as he has throughout Christian history. It is likely that the source script adapted by the author as *Antichrist and the Final Judgment* also cast Lucifer as the demon of this capital sin.

41. "The common people" is *macehualtin*. Chapter 2 argues that both friars and resistant *tlahtohqueh* were striving for the allegiance of this group in the 1530s and 1540s. The statement "The common people (*macehualtin*) have recognized you," repeated frequently in this extended portion of the play, is one of a number of close parallels to the story referenced in Motolinía's *Historia* and discussed in chapter 3.

42. Tlaloc was the Nahua god of rain and lightning and was therefore considered a principal provider of sustenance. One of the two shrines atop the massive Templo Mayor in the Mexica capital of Tenochtitlan was dedicated to Tlaloc. Here he may represent the deadly sin of envy (*neyolcocoliztli*; see note below for caveat). The deadly sins assigned by the author to the six *teteoh* that follow don't appear to have any direct connection with known attributes of the deities.

43. I believe the sense of this is something like, "How do we know you're who you say you are?" Thanks to the attendees at 2015 meeting of the Association of Nahuatl Scholars for help with this.

44. It is unclear whether the sin the author attributes to Tlaloc is envy (*neyolcocoliztli*) or hatred (*tecocoliztli*). Note that hatred is not one of the canonical seven deadly sins. See note 47 of the Nahuatl transcription.

45. Tezcatlipoca, "Smoking Mirror," was one of the most important *teteoh* of the Nahuas who, along with Quetzalcoatl, was responsible for all creation. Here he is made to represent the deadly sin of lust (*tlaelpaquiliztli*). However, instead of using the word *tlaelpaquiliztli*, later in this exchange the author lists a number of acts deemed lustful by the friars.

46. This term has traditionally been translated "sodomy," however, as stated in note 10 of the translation of *Antichrist and the Final Judgment*, it will be left untranslated here in order to lessen the risk of mapping Euro-Christian concepts onto Indigenous ones.

47. Huitzilopochtli was the patron deity of the Mexicas, associated with the sun and fire. He was a warrior god who led the Mexica's ancestors from their place of origin to the site where their capital city of Tenochtitlan was founded. His shrine sat next to that of Tlaloc on top of the Great Temple. Here Huitzilopochtli represents the deadly sin of anger (*cualaniliztli*).

48. The author makes a distinction between "priests" (friars) and "Christians." It seems that the latter refers to Spaniards, who were infamous for being poor representatives of the faith. The friars tried to keep Spaniards away from Indigenous Christian communities because of their negative influence.

49. The expression *nenemillizcotonalloz* (there is cutting off/breaking of people's lives) is difficult to translate. It is also used on f. 165v and there it's more clear that the sense of it is "making a break with a former way of life," or more broadly "conversion." In an effort to avoid using that word, which would have made little sense to the audience, I opted for "life-changing."

50. It is unclear what the act implied here is. Perhaps it refers to preaching.

51. That is, the precontact temple dedicated to him was destroyed. Note that the destruction of temples in the central valley of Mexico happened quite early in the contact period. I take the plays' multiple references to the tearing down of temples as data anchoring their original composition in this early period or not long thereafter.

52. "My image" is *nixiptla*. An *-ixiptla* was either a physical image (a statue, for example) or a person specially chosen to represent one of the *teteoh* in important festivals (see Molly Bassett, *The Fate of Earthly Things*, chapter 4, for an excellent treatment). Here presumably the former is intended.

53. Perhaps "raising up the cross" is taken to be a sign of personal affiliation with Christianity and the rejection of traditional religious practices. In this way, Huitzilopochtli is aligned with Antichrist and the characters representing certain *tlahtohqueh* (rulers) who oppose the Christianization of the Nahua people and the work of the friars.

54. Quetzalcoatl, or "Feathered Serpent," was one of the most ancient of Mesoamerican *teteoh* with origins stretching back to the Formative Olmec. Here he is made to stand for the deadly sin of gluttony (*xixicuinyotl*).

55. This line ends with another *etcetera*, which may have invited the actor to give an unscripted elaboration in which the memory of ritual practices dedicated to the Feathered Serpent are revived and made present to the Nahua audience.

56. Otontecuhtli (Otomí Lord) was the patron deity of the Otomí and of the Mexicas' powerful neighbor, the Tepaneca. He was also the patron of the important Mexica festival of Xocotl Huetzi (The Fruit Falls). Here he represents the deadly sin of laziness (*tlatzihuiztli*).

57. This is a reference to the central ritual of the Xocotl huetzi festival, the erecting of a towering pole upon which fruit was ritually placed then caused to fall. Some accounts state that instead of fruit, sacrificial victims were cast down from the pole, symbolizing "living fruits" falling from the heavens. See Justyna Olko, *Insignia of Rank in the Nahua World: From the Fifteenth to the Seventeenth Century* (Boulder: University Press of Colorado, 2014), 91.

58. "And when they stopped . . . they would take captives." I am uncertain what is being referenced here. Tentative translation.

59. This is one of multiple references which suggests that the author of the plays viewed members of the Nahua nobility as threats to the success of the Franciscan mission. Here, again, the Nahuatl ends with an *etcetera*, suggesting that the speaker may have been intended to elaborate extemporaneously.

60. Cihuacoatl (Serpent Woman) was one of a number of Mexica mother goddesses worshipped at the time of contact. She is often depicted with attributes of war, since as the patroness of midwives, she assisted women in the "battle" of childbirth. Here she represents the deadly sin of greed (*teoyehuacatiliztli*).

61. The translation of this entire paragraph is tentative.

62. This could be a reference to the Mexica's frequent "flower wars," battles waged for the purpose of capturing enemy warriors for sacrifice during high state festivals. The *altepemeh* of Tlaxcala and Huexotzinco were the traditional enemies of the Mexica and targets of such campaigns.

63. Tentative translation.

64. With this, Hermit reveals his Indigenous identity and aligns himself with the *macehualtin* by acknowledging that the six preceding deities-cum-demons "were our *teteoh*."

65. The eighteen sinners that follow the seven demons each bear some kind of prop representing their sins.

66. "Year Keepers" is *xiuhpohuaqueh*, a tentative decipherment of the difficult abbreviation the author devised to name this group of Indigenous priests. See note 68 in the Nahuatl transcription.

67. "Those that we used to serve" refers to the *teteoh* and/or their images. This is another reference to the destruction of Indigenous sacred and ritual objects that marked the early decades of the missionization of New Spain.

68. As we saw in the exchange between Hermit and Lucifer, the application of holy water was understood to cause demons burning pain. Presumably, it is the fact that copal was burned as incense that gave *copalatl* this association. *Tepozatl* (metal-water) may have been associated with molten metal or lava.

69. As previously mentioned, this has traditionally been translated as "sodomy." Pedro de Gante wrote in a 1529 letter that some native priests "did not have wives, and in their stead they had boys, whom they abused" (cited in Tavárez, *The Invisible War*, 33, 297, n. 53).

70. Tentative translation. This is based on Molina's definition of *zan ic niyauh* "to have something as a custom; to do something often" (Online Nahuatl Dictionary, s.v. "zanic niyauh," accessed May 21, 2020, https://nahuatl.uoregon.edu/content/zanic-niyauh).

71. In the Nahuatl only the singular form (*atlaneltocani*) is given, but it seems clear that the plural was intended.

72. See chapter 2 for a discussion of these names. Both are understood to be *tlahtohqueh* (Indigenous rulers).

73. Here again the author is referring to Spaniards when he writes Christians. See note above.

74. "Fire priests" is *tlenamacaqueh*. These were a division of the institutional Mexica priesthood that offered incense during religious rituals.

75. The serpent (*coatl*) mentioned here may refer to the Feathered Serpent, Quetzalcoatl. It also may be a reference to the devil, often imagined as a serpent in the Christian tradition, and therefore could be seen as a transference from the teaching of the friars.

76. "Day keeper" is *tonalpouhqui* (reader of day signs). These ritual specialists played a central role in precontact Nahua religious life. Their primary function was conducting divination rituals, during which they would consult the richly painted divinatory codices called *tonalamameh* (sing. *tonalamatl*, "book of days"). See chapter 36 of Book 6 of the Florentine Codex for a detailed description a divination ritual at the birth of a child. This ritual is referenced in the speech that follows.

77. "Book of the *teteoh*" is *in imamox in teteoh* (i.e., divinatory codex). There is ample evidence that early colonial Indigenous communities secretly kept their sacred books from

the prying eyes of the friars and the bonfires that consumed so many cultural treasures in the years following first contact. It is possible that this statement indicates the actor is carrying a prop, which may have been an ordinary book or perhaps the community's own sacred *in imamox in teteoh*.

78. This is another invitation to an unscripted performance of Indigenous knowledge that would likely have transgressed the boundaries of what authorities deemed appropriate. See the conclusion of chapter 3.

79. Tentative translation. Could possibly be "Otontiyeyo." The original spelling is *nitontiyeyo*.

80. Here and below "subjects" is *macehualtin*.

81. "Also, I took for myself . . . didn't give them a break." Tentative translation.

82. An entire book of the Florentine Codex (Book 9) is devoted to the *pochtecatl* (merchant), signaling the importance of this class of Nahua society. Some merchants, known as *oztomecah*, performed important roles in service of Mexica rulers, serving essentially as secret agents and spies. A couple of lines down the merchant, Toribio, confesses to operating in this capacity.

83. "Then I . . . spill over." This is a very difficult passage to decipher. Highly tentative translation.

84. "Earthly things" (*tlalticpaccayotl*) can have a sexual connotation. In this sense, Merchant may be alluding to indulgence in illicit sexual activity, behavior he makes explicit in the following lines.

85. "My dinner, my breakfast" is *in nocochca in noneuhca*, a *difrasismo* meaning "my daily sustenance."

86. "Procuress" is *tetlanochiliani*. Book 10 of the Florentine Codex clearly shows the influence of Christian indoctrination when it states that the "procuress is verily a demon (*tlacatecolotl*)" (57). It continues, declaring, "the aforementioned one [is] a deceiver, a perverter, a provoker . . . [she is] flowery of speech, gentle of words, mellifluous of speech" (57). As with any topic involving sexuality, the colonial ethnographic sources must be understood as reflecting to varying degrees the influence of Christianity.

87. "One Who Indulges in Pleasure" is *ahuiani*. The use of "prostitute" has been avoided, even though that is most likely what was intended here. See *Antichrist and the Final Judgment*, English translation note 8 as well as the treatment of this exchange in chapter 3. Also see Florentine Codex, Book 10, 55–56.

88. Thanks to the Nahuatl listserv, especially Michael McCafferty, Michel Launey, and Magnus Pharao Hansen, for help with this (exchanges dated September 28, 2014).

89. Literally, "they didn't sink into my belly (*nihtic*)."

90. Even though she was utterly devoted to God, Young Woman's sin was refusing to get married. In the friars' teaching, this refusal threatened to lead a woman into sexual sin. Teaching on this subject was part of the friars' program targeting the sexual mores and

marriage practices of Nahuas. A case similar to Cecilia's can be found in the *neixcuitilli* titled *Final Judgment*, where a woman named Lucía suffers infernal torments due to her refusal to marry. See Sell and Burkhart, *Nahuatl Theater*, Vol. 1, 199.

91. Presumably this is because neither was married at the time, so technically their liaisons didn't constitute adultery. Alternatively, this may be suggesting that even though the two didn't have intercourse, just the act of lying together was deemed a sin.

92. "Healer" is *ticitl*, which identifies this person as a practitioner of Indigenous medicine and curing rituals. This was another category of Indigenous ritual specialist with which the friars were deeply concerned, both for their supposed collaboration with the devil and for the central importance they played in the lives of the *macehualtin*. Book 10 of the Florentine Codex describes the "bad physician" as one who "bewitches, is a sorcerer (*nahualli*, pl. *nanahualtin*), a soothsayer, a caster of lots, a diagnostician by means of knots. He kills with his medicines; he increases [sickness]; he seduces women; he bewitches them" (30).

93. This alludes to the props carried by Healer which probably included his ritual paraphernalia.

94. Presumably there follows here another impromptu performance of Indigenous knowledge.

95. "Potions" refers to an abortifacient. Apparently, the author's chief concern with traditional healers was their role in helping women have abortions or sterilize themselves. The use of abortifacients by *titicih* (pl. of *ticitl*) was cause for great alarm among the friars and was specifically called out in numerous writings, such as Molina's confession manuals, cited in chapter 3. The Nahua rulers of Tlaxcala were aware of this and specifically listed "inducing abortions" in the 1543 list of activities to be suppressed in their *altepetl* in order to avoid scrutiny by the church authorities (Olko and Brylak, "Defending Local Autonomy," 575).

96. A Nahuatl sermon for the Seventh Sunday after Pentecost targets hypocrites, mostly rulers (Sahagún, *Siguense unos sermones*, 152–153). This exchange here seems directed at anyone, especially sexual sinners.

97. Literally, "I wanted to summon her" (*nicnotzaznequia*). The intent here is to summon for sex, to solicit. In the *Confessionario breve*, Molina and his Nahua associates write the following questions regarding the sixth commandment ("Thou shalt not commit adultery"): "Did you desire a woman? Did you have relations with her? How many women did you have relations with? Was she your relative? How do you summon her (*ticnotza*)?" (f. 11r).

98. Domingo's hurting tongue and the mention of being "gagged" by demons echoes the apostle James's comparison of putting bits in the mouths of horses to "taming the tongue" in 3 James 3:2–8. In this passage, as in this play, it is the tongue that is blamed for leading a person into sin through what they say.

99. Antonio appears to be carrying a bundle of wood. This echoes another series of questions in Molina's *Confessionario breve*. Regarding the seventh commandment ("Thou shalt not steal"), Molina and his Nahua associates ask, "Did you cut down wood from someone

else's forest? Or did you take someone's wood?" (f. 14v). This is further evidence of the author's familiarity with the doctrinal discourses of the friars, as argued in chapter 3.

100. This is an example of the author conflating two different passages from scripture, in this case the story of Noah and the Great Flood and that of Lot and the destruction of Sodom and Gomorrah. I interpret this as more evidence that this play was written with little to no supervision by a friar, since it is difficult to imagine a friar seeing this confusion of scriptural passages and not correcting it. In a sermon for the first Sunday of Advent, Sahagún and his Nahua associates discuss the Flood and Sodom in such a closely connected way that one might confuse the two. See Sahagún, *Siguense unos sermones*, 7. This can also be seen in Sahagún's *Apéndice a la postilla*. See Bernardino de Sahagún, *Adiciones, apéndice a la postilla: y ejercicio cotidiano*, edited and translated by Arthur J. O. Anderson (Mexico City: Universidad Nacional Autónoma de México, Instituto de Investigaciones Históricas, 1993), 101.

101. Book 10 of the Florentine Codex states that the *cuiloni* "merits being committed to flames, burned, consumed by fire" (38).

102. Although the etymology of this word is uncertain, most commentators since Molina have assumed the *tepatlachhuiani* was a woman who engages in sexual acts with another woman. However, what we have here, to my knowledge, is the only colonial usage of the term that identifies the individual as a male thus suggesting we still lack an adequate understanding of Nahua sexual practices such as those encompassed by this term.

103. Here "them" refers to the Nahua "neophytes" who are the presumed audience of these plays. See Sibyl's opening monologue, *Antichrist and the Final Judgment*.

104. "And if you don't . . . I am saved." Tentative translation.

105. Here singing is called for, despite the injunction against it at the beginning of the play. The ending imagined by the author stands in stark contrast to that of the first play, which ends on a more optimistic note with the righteous singing the "Te Deum" with the saints in heaven. This ending shares the dour tone of medieval doomsday plays.

BIBLIOGRAPHY

Aichele, Klaus. *Das Antichristdrama des Mittelalters der Reformation und Gegenreformation*. The Hague: Martinus Nijhoff, 1974.

Alarcón, Hernando Ruiz de. *Treatise on the Heathen Superstitions that Today Live Among the Indians Native to this New Spain, 1629*. Edited by J. R. Andrews and Ross Hassig. Norman: University of Oklahoma Press, 1984.

Alcántara Rojas, Berenice. "La 'mala nueva': La llegada del cristianismo en sermones en lengua náhuatl de la primera mitad del siglo xvi." *Iberoamericana* 19, no. 71 (2019): 77–98.

Anunciación, Fray Juan de la. *Sermonario en lengua mexicana*. Mexico City: Antonio Ricardo, 1577. https://archive.org/details/sermonarioenlengoojuan.

Aquino, Fabián de. *Sermones y miscelánea de devoción y moral en lengua mexicana*. MS NS 3/1, ca. 1550–1600. Hispanic Society of America, New York.

Arróniz, Othón. *Teatro de evangelización en Nueva España*. Mexico City: Universidad Nacional Autónoma de México, 1977.

Díaz Balsera, Viviana. *The Pyramid Under the Cross: Franciscan Discourses of Evangelization and the Nahua Christian Subject in Sixteenth-Century Mexico*. Tucson: University of Arizona Press, 2005.

Bassett, Molly. *The Fate of Earthly Things: Aztec Gods and God-Bodies*. Austin: University of Texas Press, 2015.

Baudot, Georges. "Fray Andrés de Olmos y su *Tratado de los pecados mortales en lengua náhuatl*." *Estudios de Cultura Náhuatl* 12 (1976): 33–59.

Baudot, Georges. *Utopia and History in Mexico*. Translated by Bernard R. and Thelma Ortiz de Montellano. Niwot, CO: University Press of Colorado, 1995.

https://doi.org/10.5876/9781646423002.c007

Bautista, Fray Juan. *A Jesu Christo S.N. ofrece este sermonario en lengua mexicana*. Mexico City: Diego Lopez Davalos, 1606. https://archive.org/details/iesuchristosnofroojuan.

Bautista, Fray Juan. *Libro de la miseria y breuedad de la vida del hombre*. Mexico City: López Davalos, 1604.

Bierhorst, John. *A Nahuatl-English Dictionary and Concordance to the Cantares Mexicanos*. Stanford: Stanford University Press, 1985.

Blommaert, Jan. *Discourse: A Critical Introduction*. Cambridge, UK: Cambridge University Press, 2005.

Boone, Elizabeth Hill. *Stories in Red and Black: Pictorial Histories of the Aztecs and Mixtecs*. Austin: University of Texas Press, 2000.

Breining, Daniel. *Dramatic and Theatrical Censorship of Sixteenth-Century New Spain*. Lampeter, Wales: E. Mellen Press, 2002.

Brylak, Agnieszka. "Los Espectáculos de los nahuas prehispánicos: entre antropología y teatro." PhD diss., University of Warsaw, 2015.

Burkhart, Louise M. *Aztecs on Stage: Religious Theater in Colonial Mexico*. Norman, OK: University of Oklahoma Press, 2012.

Burkhart, Louise M. *Holy Wednesday: A Nahua Drama from Early Colonial Mexico*. Philadelphia: University of Pennsylvania Press, 1996.

Burkhart, Louise M. "Humour in Baroque Nahuatl Drama." In *Power, Gender, and Ritual in Europe and the Americas: Essays in Memory of Richard C. Trexler*, edited by Peter J. Arnade Michael Rocke, 257–272. Toronto: Center for Reformation and Renaissance Studies, 2008.

Burkhart, Louise M. "Meeting the Enemy: Moteuczoma and Cortés, Herod and the Magi." In *Invasion and Transformation: Interdisciplinary Perspectives on the Conquest of Mexico*, edited by Rebecca P. Brienen and Margaret A. Jackson, 11–23. Boulder: University Press of Colorado, 2008.

Burkhart, Louise M. *The Slippery Earth: Nahua-Christian Moral Dialogue in Sixteenth-Century Mexico*. Tucson: University of Arizona Press, 1989.

Burkhart, Louise M. *Staging Christ's Passion in Eighteenth-Century Nahua Mexico*. Louisville: University Press of Colorado. (In Press.)

Butler, Lisa D., Filomena M. Critelli, and Janice Carello, eds. *Trauma and Human Rights: Integrating Approaches to Address Human Suffering*. Cham, Switzerland: Springer International Publishing, Imprint: Palgrave Macmillan, 2019.

Cañizares-Esguerra, Jorge. *Puritan Conquistadors: Iberianizing the Atlantic, 1550–1700*. Stanford, CA: Stanford University Press, 2006.

Carochi, Horacio, and James Lockhart. *Grammar of the Mexican Language with an Explanation of Its Adverbs (1645)*. Stanford: Stanford University Press ; UCLA Latin American Center Publications, 2001.

Carrasco, Davíd. *City of Sacrifice: The Aztec Empire and the Role of Violence in Civilization*. Boston: Beacon Press, 1999.

Carrasco, Davíd, ed. *The Oxford Encyclopedia of Mesoamerican Cultures*. New York: Oxford University Press, 2001.

Carrasco, Davíd. *Religions of Mesoamerica*. Long Grove, IL: Waveland Press, 2014.

Caruth, Cathy. *Unclaimed Experience: Trauma, Narrative and History*. Baltimore: Johns Hopkins University Press, 2010.

Castillo, Bernal Diaz del. *The History of the Conquest of New Spain*. Edited by Davíd Carrasco. Albuquerque: University of New Mexico Press, 2008.

Cátedra García, Pedro. *Sermón, sociedad y literatura en la Edad Media: San Vicente Ferrer en Castilla (1411–1412)*. Salamanca, Spain: Junta de Castilla y León/Consejería de Cultura y Turismo, 1994.

Cervantes, Fernando. *The Devil in the New World: The Impact of Diabolism in New Spain*. New Haven: Yale University Press, 1997.

Chambers, Edmund Kerchever. *The Mediaeval Stage*. Mineola, New York: Dover Publications Inc., 1996.

Christensen, Mark Z. *Aztec and Maya Apocalypses: Old-World Tales of Doom in a New-World Setting*. Norman: University of Oklahoma Press, 2022.

Christensen, Mark Z. *Nahua and Maya Catholicisms: Texts and Religion in Colonial Central Mexico and Yucatan*. Stanford, CA: Stanford University Press, 2013.

Christensen, Mark Z. *The Teabo Manuscript: Maya Christian Copybooks, Chilam Balams, and Native Text Production in Yucatán*. Austin: University of Texas Press, 2016.

Ciudad Real, Antonio de. *Tratado curioso y docto de las grandezas de la Nueva España*. Vol. 2, edited by Josefina García Quintana and Víctor M. Castillo Farreas. Mexico City: Universidad Nacional Autónoma de México, 1993.

Clendinnen, Inga. *Aztecs: An Interpretation*. Cambridge, UK: Cambridge University Press, 1991.

Codex Magliabechiano. Facsimile edition. Austria: Akademische Druck- u. Verlagsanstalt, 1970. Biblioteca nazionale centrale di Firenze. http://www.famsi.org/research/graz/magliabechiano/thumbs_0.html.

Códice franciscano. In *Códice franciscano, siglo XVI*, edited by Joaquín García Icazbalceta. Mexico City: Editorial Chavez Hayhoe, 1941.

Cohen, Gustave, ed. *Nativités et moralités liégeoises du Moyen-Age*. Bruxelles: Palais Des Académies, 1953.

Collins, John J. *The Apocalyptic Imagination: An Introduction to Jewish Apocalyptic Literature*. Grand Rapids, MI: Eerdmans, 1998.

Craps, Stef. *Postcolonial Witnessing: Trauma Out of Bounds*. London: Palgrave Macmillan, 2012.

Daniel, E. Randolph. *The Franciscan Concept of Mission in the High Middle Ages*. Lexington, KY: University Press of Kentucky, 1975.

Daschke, Dereck. "Apocalypse and Trauma." In *The Oxford Handbook of Apocalyptic Literature*, edited by John J. Collins, 457–472. London: Oxford University Press, 2014.

De contempu[s] omnium vanitatum huius mundi. Codex Indianorum 23. John Carter Brown Library, Brown University. https://archive.org/details/decontemptuomniuoobern.

Díaz Balsera, Viviana. *The Pyramid Under the Cross: Franciscan Discourses of Evangelization and the Nahua Christian Subject in Sixteenth-Century Mexico.* Tucson: University of Arizona Press, 2005.

Dibble, Charles. "The Nahuatlization of Christianity." In *Sixteenth-Century Mexico: The World of Sahagún,* edited by Munro Edmonson, 225–233. Albuquerque: University of New Mexico Press, 1974.

Diel, Lori Boornazian. *The Codex Mexicanus: A Guide to Life in Late Sixteenth-Century New Spain.* Austin: University of Texas Press, 2018.

Dominicans. *Doctrina cristiana en lengua española y mexicana.* Madrid: Ediciones Cultura Hispánica, 1944. https://archive.org/details/doctrinacristianoodomi.

Dunbar-Ortiz, Roxanne. *An Indigenous Peoples' History of the United States.* Boston: Beacon Press, 2014.

Durán, Fray Diego. *The History of the Indies of New Spain.* Edited and translated by Doris Heyden. Norman: University of Oklahoma Press, 1994.

Eguiara y Eguren, Juan José de. *Historia de sabios novohispanos.* Mexico City: Universidad Nacional Autónoma de México, 1998.

Emmerson, Richard K. "Antichrist as Anti-Saint: The Significance of Abbot Adso's *Libellus de Antichristo.*" *Benedictine Review* 30, no. 2 (1979): 175–190.

Emmerson, Richard K. *Antichrist in the Middle Ages: A Study of Medieval Apocalypticism, Art and Literature.* Seattle: University of Washington Press, 1981.

Emmerson, Richard Kenneth, Keith Glaeske, and David F. Hult, eds. *Antichrist and Judgment Day: The Middle French Jour du Jugement.* Asheville, NC: Pegasus Press, 1998.

Emmerson, Richard Kenneth, and Bernard McGinn. *The Apocalypse in the Middle Ages.* Ithaca, NY: Cornell University Press, 1992.

Evans-Campbell, Teresa. "Historical Trauma in American Indian/Native Alaska Communities: A Multilevel Framework for Exploring Impacts on Individuals, Families, and Communities." *Journal of Interpersonal Violence* 23, no. 3 (March 2008): 316–338.

Farriss, Nancy M. *Maya Society Under Colonial Rule: The Collective Enterprise of Survival.* Princeton: Princeton University Press, 1984.

Farriss, Nancy. *Tongues of Fire: Language and Evangelization in Colonial Mexico.* New York: Oxford University Press, 2018.

Fernández del Castillo, Francisco, and Elías Trabulse. *Libros y libreros en el siglo XVI.* Facsimile edition. 1982. Archivo General de la Nación [y] Fondo de Cultura Económica, Mexico.

Ferrer, St. Vincent. *Sermones Hyemales Autoris vitam, indicemque locupletissimum in fronte libri praefiximus. Eisdem denuo summa cura per D. Damianum Diaz Lusitanum. Recognitis luculentae adnotationes in margines accesserunt.* Leiden: Iacobi Junctae, 1558.

Gante, Fray Pedro de. *Doctrina christiana en lengua mexicana.* Mexico City: Centro de Estudios Históricos Fray Bernardino de Sahagún, 1981.

García Icazbalceta, Joaquín. *Don fray Juan de Zumárraga: Primer obispo y arzobispo de México*. Mexico City: Andrade y Morales, 1881.

Garibay, Ángel María. *Historia de la literatura náhuatl*. Mexico City: Editorial Porrúa, 1953.

Gibson, Charles. *The Aztecs Under Spanish Rule*. Stanford, CA: Stanford University Press, 1964.

Gilberti, Fray Maturino de. *Diálogo de doctrina cristiana en lengua de Michoacan*. Mexico City: Juan Pablos Bressano, 1559. https://archive.org/details/dialogodedoctrinoogilb.

Giner, Miguel M. García-Bermejo. *Catálogo del teatro español del siglo XVI: Índice de piezas conservadas, perdidas y representadas*. Salamanca, Spain: Ediciones Universidad de Salamanca, 1996.

Greenleaf, Richard E. *Zumárraga and the Mexican Inquisition: 1536–1543*. Berkeley: Academy of American Franciscan History, 1961.

Gruzinski, Serge. *Man-Gods in the Mexican Highlands: Indian Power and Colonial Society, 1520–1800*. Redwood City, CA: Stanford University Press, 1989.

Guadalajara Medina, José. *El Anticristo en la España medieval*. Madrid: Ediciones del Laberinto, 2004.

Guadalajara Medina, José. *Las profecías del Anticristo en la Edad Media*. Barcelona: Editorial Gredos, 1996.

Guadalajara Medina, José. "La venida del Anticristo: Terror y moralidad en la Edad Media hispánica." *Culturas populares* 4 (2007): 1–20.

Hajovsky, Patrick Thomas. *On the Lips of Others: Moteuczoma's Fame in Aztec Monuments and Rituals*. Austin: University of Texas Press, 2015.

Hanks, William F. *Converting Words: Maya in the Age of the Cross*. Berkeley: University of California Press, 2010.

Hanks, William F. *Language and Communicative Practices*. Boulder, CO: Westview Press, 1996.

Haskett, Robert. *Indigenous Rulers: An Ethnohistory of Town Government in Colonial Cuernavaca*. Albuquerque: University of New Mexico Press, 1991.

Herman, Judith Lewis. *Trauma and Recovery: The Aftermath of Violence from Domestic Abuse to Political Terror*. New York: Basic Books, 1992.

Hill, Jane H. "The Flower World of Old Uto-Aztecan." *Journal of Anthropological Research* 48 (1992): 117–144.

Horcasitas, Fernando. *El teatro náhuatl: Épocas novohispana y moderna*. Mexico City: Universidad Nacional Autónoma de México, 1974.

Ifowodo, Ogaga. *History, Trauma, and Healing in Postcolonial Narratives: Re-constructing Identities*. New York: Palgrave Macmillan, 2013.

Johnson, Benjamin. *Pueblos Within Pueblos: Tlaxilacalli Communities in Acolhuacan, Mexico, ca. 1272–1692*. Boulder: University Press of Colorado, 2018.

Karttunen, Frances. *An Analytical Dictionary of Nahuatl*. Norman: University of Oklahoma Press, 1992.

Karttunen, Frances, and James Lockhart. "The Art of the Nahuatl Speech." *UCLA Latin American Studies* 65 (1987): 1–219.

Karttunen, Frances, and James Lockhart. *Nahuatl in the Middle Years.* Berkeley: University of California Press, 1976.

Klor de Alva, J. Jorge. "Christianity and the Aztecs." *San Jose Studies* 5 (1979), 6–22.

Klor de Alva, J. Jorge. "Martin Ocelotl: Clandestine Cult Leader." In *Struggle and Survival in Colonial America,* edited by David G. Sweet and Gary B. Nash, 129–141. Berkeley: University of California Press, 1981.

Klor de Alva, J. Jorge. "Nahua Colonial Discourse and the Appropriation of the (European) Other." *Archives de Sciences Sociales des Religions* (1992): 15–35.

Laird, Andrew. *Aztec Latin: Renaissance Learning and Nahuatl Traditions in Sixteenth-Century Mexico.* (Forthcoming.)

Laird, Andrew. "A Mirror for Mexican Princes: Reconsidering the Context and Latin Source for the Nahuatl Translation of Aesop's Fables." *Brief Forms in Medieval and Renaissance Hispanic Literature* (2017): 132–167.

Lara, Jaime. *City, Temple, Stage: Eschatological Architecture and Liturgical Theatrics in New Spain.* Notre Dame, IN: University of Notre Dame Press, 2004.

Lazar, Moshe, ed. and trans. *Le jugement dernier (Lo jutgamen general): Drame provencal du XVe siecle.* Paris: Klincksieck, 1971.

Leeming, Ben. "Aztec Antichrist: Christianity, Transculturation, and Apocalypse on Stage in Two Sixteenth-Century Nahuatl Dramas." PhD diss. University at Albany, SUNY, 2017.

Leeming, Ben. "A Nahua Christian Talks Back: Fabián de Aquino's Antichrist Dramas as Autoethnography." In *Words and Worlds Turned Around: Indigenous Christianities in Latin America,* edited by David Tavárez. Boulder: University Press of Colorado, 2017.

Leeming, Ben. "The Poetics of Terror: Depictions of Hell in Ecclesiastical Nahuatl Literature." Unpublished paper, last modified May 30, 2012.

Leigh, David J. "The Doomsday Mystery Play: An Eschatological Morality." *Modern Philology* 67, no. 3 (1970): 211–23.

Leonard, Irving Albert. *Books of the Brave: Being an Account of Books and of Men in the Spanish Conquest and Settlement of the Sixteenth-century New World.* Berkeley: University of California Press, 1949.

León-Portilla, Miguel. *Aztec Thought and Culture: A Study of the Ancient Nahuatl Mind.* Norman: University of Oklahoma Press, 1963.

León-Portilla, Miguel. *Bernardino de Sahagún: First Anthropologist.* Norman: University of Oklahoma Press, 2002.

León-Portilla, Miguel. *The Broken Spears: The Aztec Account of the Conquest of Mexico.* Boston: Beacon Press, 1992.

León-Portilla, Miguel. *Pre-Columbian Literatures of Mexico.* Norman: University of Oklahoma Press, 1986.

León-Portilla, Miguel. "Testimonios Nahuas Sobre la Conquista Espiritual." *Estudios de Cultura Náhuatl* 11 (1974): 11–36.

Lockhart, James. *The Nahuas After the Conquest: A Social and Cultural History of the Indians of Central Mexico, Sixteenth Through Eighteenth Centuries.* Stanford, CA: Stanford University Press, 1992.

Lockhart, James. *Nahuatl as Written: Lessons in Older Written Nahuatl, With Copious Examples and Texts.* Stanford, CA: Stanford University Press, 2001.

Lockhart, James, Frances Berdan, and Arthur J. O. Anderson. *The Tlaxcalan Actas: A Compendium of the Records of the Cabildo de Tlaxcala (1545–1627).* Salt Lake City: University of Utah Press, 1986.

Lockhart, James, and Enrique Otte, eds. *Letters and People of the Spanish Indies: Sixteenth Century.* Cambridge: Cambridge University Press, 1976.

Lopes Don, Patricia. *Bonfires of Culture: Franciscans, Indigenous Leaders, and the Inquisition in Early Mexico, 1524–1540.* Norman: University of Oklahoma Press, 2010.

López Austin, Alfredo. "Cosmovision." In *The Oxford Encyclopedia of Mesoamerican Cultures,* edited by David Carrasco, 268–274. New York: Oxford University Press, 2001.

López Austin, Alfredo. *The Human Body and Ideology.* Translated by Thelma Ortíz de Montellano and Bernard Ortíz de Montellano. Salt Lake City: University of Utah Press, 1988.

Lorenzana, Francisco Antonio. *Primero, y segundo, celebrados en la muy noble, y muy leal Ciudad de México, presidiendo el Illmo. Y Rmo. Señor D. Fr. Alonso de Montúfar, En los años de 1555, y 1565.* Mexico City: Imprenta del Superior Gobierno Hogal, 1769.

Mathes, W. Michael. *The America's [sic] First Academic Library: Santa Cruz de Tlatelolco.* Sacramento: California State Library Foundation, 1985.

McDonough, Kelly S. *The Learned Ones: Nahua Intellectuals in Postconquest Mexico.* Tucson: University of Arizona Press, 2014.

McGinn, Bernard. *Visions of the End: Apocalyptic Traditions in the Middle Ages.* New York: Columbia University Press, 1998.

Mendieta, Fray Geronimo de. *Historia eclesiástica indiana.* Mexico City: F. Díaz de León y Santiago White, 1870; Biblioteca Virtual Miguel de Cervantes, 1999. http://www.cervantesvirtual.com/obra-visor/historia-eclesiastica-indiana--o/html/.

Mendoza, Moisés Franco. "Maturino Gilberti, Traductor: Dialogo de la Doctrina Cristiana en lengua de Mechuacan." PhD diss., Universidad Nacional Autónoma de Mexico, 2008.

Mills, David. *The Chester Mystery Cycle: A New Edition with Modernised Spelling.* East Lansing, MI: Colleagues Press, 1992.

Miscelánea sagrada. MS 1477. Colección Archivos y Manuscritos. Biblioteca Nacional de México.

Molina, Fray Alonso de. *Confessionario breve en lengua mexicana.* Mexico City: Antonio Espinoza, 1565. https://archive.org/details/confessionariobroomoli.

Molina, Fray Alonso de. *Confessionario mayor en lengua mexicana y castellana*. Mexico City: Antonio Espinoza, 1565. https://archive.org/details/confessionariomao1moli.

Molina, Fray Alonso de. *Vocabulario en lengua castellana y mexicana y mexicana y castellana*. Mexico City: Antonio de Spinosa, 1571.

Montes de Oca Vega, Mercedes. *Los difrasismos en el náhuatl del siglo XVI*. Mexico City: Universidad Nacional Autónoma de México, 2000.

Motolinía, Fray Toribio de Benavente. *Motolinia's History of the Indians of New Spain*. Edited and translated by Francis Borgia Steck. Washington, DC: American Academy of Franciscan History, 1951.

Nesvig, Martin Austin. *Ideology and Inquisition: The World of the Censors in Early Mexico*. New Haven: Yale University Press, 2009.

Olko, Justyna. "Alphabetic Writing in the Hands of the Colonial Nahua Nobility." *Contributions in New World Archaeology* 7 (2014): 177–198.

Olko, Justyna. *Insignia of Rank in the Nahua World: From the Fifteenth to the Seventeenth Century*. Boulder: University Press of Colorado, 2014.

Olko, Justyna, and Agnieszka Brylak. "Defending Local Autonomy and Facing Cultural Trauma: A Nahua Order Against Idolatry, Tlaxcala, 1543." *Hispanic American Historical Review* 98, no. 4 (2018): 573–604.

Olmos, Fray Andrés de. *Arte de la lengua mexicana*. Edited by Ascensión H. de León-Portilla, and Miguel León Portilla. Mexico City: Universidad Nacional Autónoma de México, 2002.

Olmos, Fray Andrés de. *Tratado de hechicerías y sortilegios (1553)*. Edited and translated by Georges Baudot. Mexico City: Universidad Nacional Autónoma de México, 1990.

Olmos, Fray Andrés de. *Tratado sobre los siete pecados mortales*. Translated by Georges Baudot. Mexico City: Universidad Nacional Autónoma de México, 1996.

Online Nahuatl Dictionary. Wired Humanities Project. 2000–2020. University of Oregon. https://nahuatl.uoregon.edu.

Pardo, Osvaldo. F. *The Origins of Mexican Catholicism: Nahua Rituals and Christian Sacraments in Sixteenth-Century Mexico*. Ann Arbor: University of Michigan Press, 2006.

Phelan, John Leddy. *The Millennial Kingdom of the Franciscans in the New World*. Berkeley: University of California Press, 1970.

Poole, Stafford. *Pedro Moya de Contreras: Catholic Reform and Royal Power in New Spain, 1571–1591*. Berkeley: University of California Press, 1987.

Pratt, Mary Louise. "Arts of the Contact Zone." *Profession* (1991): 33–40.

Pratt, Mary Louise. *Imperial Eyes: Travel Writing and Transculturation*. New York: Routledge, 2007.

"Proceso inquisitorial del cacique de Tetzcoco." In *Publicaciones del Archivo General de la Nación*. Vol. 1. Mexico City: Eusebio Gómez de la Puente, 1910.

"Procesos de indios idolátras y hechiceras." In *Publicaciones del Archivo General de la Nación*. Vol. 3. Mexico City: Tipográfico Guerrero, 1912.

Ricard, Robert. *The Spiritual Conquest of Mexico*. Berkeley: University of California Press, 1966.

Ríos Castaño, Victoria. *Translation as Conquest: Sahagún and* Universal History of the Things of New Spain. Madrid: Iberoamericana, 2014.

Rouanet, Léo, ed. *Colección de autos, farsas, y coloquios del siglo XVI*. 4 vols. Hildesheim and New York: Georg Olms, 1979.

Sahagún, Bernardino de. *Adiciones, apéndice a la postilla: y ejercicio cotidiano*. Edited and translated by Arthur J. O. Anderson. Mexico City: Universidad Nacional Autónoma de México, Instituto de Investigaciones Históricas, 1993.

Sahagún, Bernardino de. "The Aztec-Spanish Dialogues of 1524." Translated by J. Jorge Klor de Alva. *Alcheringa* 4, no. 2 (1980): 52–193.

Sahagún, Bernardino de. *Coloquios y doctrina christiana*. Edited by Miguel León-Portilla. Mexico City: Universidad Nacional Autónoma de México, 1986.

Sahagún, Bernardino de. *Comiença un exercicio en lengua mexicana sacado del Sancto Evango y distribuido por todos los días de la semana*. Ayer MS 1484. 1574. Newberry Library, Chicago.

Sahagún, Bernardino de. *Florentine Codex, General History of the Things of New Spain*. Edited and translated by Charles E. Dibble and Arthur J. O. Anderson. Salt Lake City and Santa Fe: University of Utah and School of American Research, 1950–1982.

Sahagún, Bernardino de. *Psalmodia Christiana*. Translated by Arthur J. O. Anderson. Salt Lake City: University of Utah Press, 1993.

Sahagún, Bernardino de. *Siguense unos sermones de dominicas y de santos en lengua mexicana*. MS 1485. 1540–1563. Ayer Collection. Newberry Library, Chicago.

Sahagún, Bernardino de. *Siguense unos sermones de dominicas y de sanctos en lengua mexicana, Ms. 1485, Ayer Collection, The Newberry Library*. Edited by Mario Alberto Sánchez Aguilera. Mexico City: Universidad Nacional Autónoma de Mexico, 2022.

Sánchez Aguilera, Mario Alberto. "La doctrina desde el púlpito: Los sermones del ciclo de navidad de fray Bernardino de Sahagún." PhD diss., Universidad Nacional Autónoma de México, 2019.

Schell, Edgar. *Strangers and Pilgrims: From the Castle of Perseverance to King Lear*. Chicago: University of Chicago Press, 1983.

Schulze, Ursula, ed. *Churre Weltgerichtsspiel*. Berlin: Erich Schmidt, 1993.

Schwaller, John F. "The Expansion of Nahuatl as a Lingua Franca among Priests in Sixteenth-Century Mexico." *Ethnohistory* 59, no. 4 (2012): 675–690.

Scott, James C. *Domination and the Arts of Resistance: Hidden Transcripts*. New Haven: Yale University Press, 1990.

Sell, Barry David. "Friars, Nahuas, and Books: Language and Expression in Colonial Nahuatl Publications." PhD diss., University of California Los Angeles, 1993.

Sell, Barry D., and Louise M. Burkhart. *Nahuatl Theater*. Vol. 1, *Death and Life in Colonial Nahua Mexico*. Norman: University of Oklahoma Press, 2004.

Sell, Barry D., and Louise M. Burkhart. *Nahuatl Theater*. Vol. 4, *Nahua Christianity in Performance*. Norman: University of Oklahoma Press, 2009.

"Sermones en mexicano: Catalogación, estudio y traducción de sermones en lengua náhuatl del siglo XVI de la Biblioteca Nacional de México." UNAM-PAPIIT IN401018. Mexico City: Universidad Nacional Autónoma de México, 2017–Present. https://sermonesen mexicano.unam.mx/index.html.

Sermones y santoral en mexicano. M-M 464. Early seventeenth century. Bancroft Library, University of California, Berkeley.

Sigal, Pete. *The Flower and the Scorpion: Sexuality and Ritual in Early Nahua Culture*. Durham, NC: Duke University Press, 2011.

Solari, Amara, and Matthew Restall. *2012 and the End of the World: The Western Roots of the Maya Apocalypse*. New York: Rowman & Littlefield Publishers, 2011.

Soormally, Mina Garcia. *Ideology and the Construction of the Spanish Empire*. Louisville: University Press of Colorado, 2019.

Sousa, Lisa. "Flowers and Speech in Discourses on Deviance in Book 10." In *The Florentine Codex: An Encyclopedia of the Nahua World in Sixteenth-Century Mexico*, edited by Janette Favrot Peterson and Kevin Terraciano, 184–199. Austin: University of Texas Press, 2019.

Sparks, Gary G. *Rewriting Maya Religion: Domingo de Vico, K'iche' Maya Intellectuals, and the Theologia Indorum*. Louisville: University Press of Colorado, 2020.

Sten, María, ed. *El teatro franciscano en la Nueva España: Fuentes y ensayos para el estudio del teatro de evangelización en el siglo XVI*. Mexico City: Facultad de Filosofía y Letras, Universidad Nacional Autónoma de México, 2000.

Stern, Charlotte. *The Medieval Theater in Castile*. Binghamton, NY: Medieval & Renaissance Texts & Studies, 1996.

Stogre, Michael. *That the World May Believe: The Development of Papal Social Thought on Aboriginal Rights*. Sherbrooke, QC: Editions Paulines, 1992.

Tavárez, David. *The Invisible War: Indigenous Devotions, Discipline, and Dissent in Colonial Mexico*. Stanford, CA: Stanford University Press, 2011.

Tavárez, David. "Nahua Intellectuals, Franciscan Scholars, and the *Devotio Moderna* in Colonial Mexico." *The Americas* 70, no. 2 (2013), 203–235.

Tavárez, David, ed. *Words and Worlds Turned Around: Indigenous Christianities in Colonial Latin America*. United States: University Press of Colorado, 2017.

Terraciano, Kevin. *The Mixtecs of Colonial Oaxaca: Ñudzahui History, Sixteenth Through Eighteenth Centuries*. Stanford, CA: Stanford University Press, 2004.

Townsend, Camilla. *Fifth Sun: A New History of the Aztecs*. New York: Oxford University Press, 2019.

Townsend, Camilla. *Here in This Year: Seventeenth-Century Nahuatl Annals of the Tlaxcala-Puebla Valley*. Stanford: Stanford University Press, 2010.

Turley, Steven E. *Franciscan Spirituality and Mission in New Spain, 1524–1599: Conflict Beneath the Sycamore Tree (Luke 19: 1–10)*. New York: Routledge, 2014.

Valadés, Diego. *Rhetorica christiana ad concionandi et orandi vsvm accommodata*. Petrumia-cobum Petrutium. Perugia, 1579. https://archive.org/details/rhetoricachristioovala.

Weaver, Hilary N. *Trauma and Resilience in the Lives of Contemporary Native Americans: Reclaiming Our Balance, Restoring Our Wellbeing*. New York: Routledge, 2019.

West, Delno C. "Medieval Ideas of Apocalyptic Mission and the Early Franciscans in Mexico." *The Americas* 45, no. 03 (1989): 293–313.

West, Delno C., and Sandra Zimdars-Swartz. *Joachim of Fiore: A Study in Spiritual Perception and History*. Bloomington, IN: Indiana University Press, 1983.

Whittaker, Gordon. *Deciphering Aztec Hieroglyphs: A Guide to Nahuatl Writing*. Berkeley: University of California Press, 2021.

Wickham, Glynne. *The Medieval Theatre*. Cambridge, UK: Cambridge University Press, 1987.

Wood, Stephanie. *Transcending Conquest: Nahua Views of Spanish Colonial Mexico*. Norman: University of Oklahoma Press, 2012.

Yannakakis, Yanna. *The Art of Being In-Between: Native Intermediaries, Indian Identity, and Local Rule in Colonial Oaxaca*. Durham, NC: Duke University Press, 2008.

INDEX

Page numbers followed by *f* indicate figures.